CW00420009

CHILDHOOD

CHILDHOOD

A Collins Anthology

Edited by

Penelope Hughes-Hallett

COLLINS
8 Grafton Street London W1
1988

William Collins Sons & Co. Ltd
London · Glasgow · Sydney · Auckland
Toronto · Johannesburg

BRITISH LIBRARY CATALOGUING IN PUBLICATION DATA

Childhood: an anthology
1. Childhood
I. Hughes – Hollett
305.2'3

ISBN 0–00–217795–1

First published 1988
Copyright © Penelope Hughes-Hallett 1988

Photoset in Linotron Sabon by
Ace Filmsetting Ltd, Frome, Somerset
Printed and bound in Great Britain by
Butler & Tanner Ltd, Frome, Somerset

To my husband

. . . those first affections,
Those shadowy recollections,
Which, be they what they may,
Are yet the fountain-light of all our day,
Are yet a master-light of all our seeing . . .

William Wordsworth

. . . the children we still remain, in the most profound and passionate part of ourselves, are filled with desires as vast and mysterious as the world of childhood itself, and as bitter as our regret for a past beyond recall . . .

Alain-Fournier

CONTENTS

AUTHOR'S NOTE

In compiling this anthology my first thanks are to my son-in-law Dan Franklin. The book was his idea, and he has been most generous with advice and help. He and my daughter Lucy have made countless suggestions and have lent me enormous numbers of books, and I am truly grateful to them both.

I am keenly aware of my good fortune in having Ariane Goodman as my editor at Collins. Her patience and enthusiasm, and her sympathetic and skilful guidance have made work a pleasure, and she has my warmest thanks. I am also most grateful to Joy Law, whose masterly solution of bibliographical and copyright mazes borders on the miraculous.

I am particularly indebted to Ann Gold for her kind assistance and to Earl Cawdor for many fruitful ideas. I should also like to thank the following for helpful suggestions: Constantia Arnold; Rosemary Chaplin; Caroline Dawnay; Polly Devlin; Celia Goodman; Ruth Harris; Susan Heyworth; Mark Hichens; Elspeth Huxley; Simon King; Graeme Laing; Denise Pelczynski; Anne Platt; Lord Quinton; Mary Somerville, and Miranda Tennant.

Douglas Matthews, Librarian of the London Library, has provided me with an index and a wealth of ideas, for which I am most grateful, and I would like to thank him and his staff at the Library for their kindness and help.

The writings on childhood of Walter de la Mare, especially *Come Hither* and *Early One Morning*, have been a source of inspiration to me, as has the work of Iona and Peter Opie, and Edward Wagenknecht's *When I Was a Child*.

I am grateful to my son James for good ideas and constructive comments; and to my son Thomas and daughter-in-law Juliet for one especially central contribution. My chief debt of gratitude is to my husband for his constant encouragement and forbearance.

INTRODUCTION

A child has been given a crystal prism, taken from an aunt's lustre ornament. To own it seems to him a miracle. He lays it across the bridge of his nose and peers in:

> The world was not the tame world to which I had grown accustomed, but this new unbalanced moving place, where all its commonest objects were transfigured by edges of goodly colours; and yet it was the same old world.[1]

This quality of perception, of things being at once miraculous and everyday, is one of the salient differences between the child's world and that of the adult; and perhaps some of the recollections and poems in this book will move the reader, recapturing glimpses of such an earlier state, to exclaim, 'Yes, that is just how it was!'

Much has been written about changing attitudes to childhood: children as miniature adults, as Rousseauesque innocents, as Victorian little cherubs, and so on; but I have preferred to focus on the child as individual and unique. The field is as wide as the memories are varied, and the pages of this anthology are peopled with all kinds of children, from those characterized by Vaughan as 'bright shoots of everlastingness' to a number of ruthlessly tough and resourceful delinquents. But one linking thread is that visionary capacity peculiar to childhood, described by T. S. Eliot in 'Animula' as a consciousness that 'Confounds the actual and the fanciful'. Such an awareness is that of the eight-year-old Blake, who saw angels in the trees on Dulwich Hill and narrowly escaped a beating for telling lies when he recounted his experience at home. My three-year-old grandson, struggling, with his grandfather's help, to land a large trout, wondered if it might be a mermaid. By next summer his expectations may be less dramatic; but they belong to a kind of perception that is beautiful, and, because it is vulnerable and brittle (like Kendon's crystal prism),

[1] THE SMALL YEARS by Frank Kendon.

9

of great poignancy. Not many children are capable of the ecstatic intensity of the infant Traherne:

> The corn was orient and immortal wheat which never should be reaped nor was ever sown. I thought it had stood from everlasting to everlasting...

but James Kenward, loosed into a field of buttercups for the first time, and overcome with a madness of possession and destruction, knows a kindred explorer's delight.

With these qualities go expectations different from those of the adult world, stemming partly from limited experience. Moving house, for Kathleen Raine, heralds the disappearance of all familiar objects and, for all she knows, familiar people too. Romilly John takes it for granted that hell is situated in the bottomless bathroom cupboard: he can hear it hissing. Laurie Lee pushes a little girl, dressed as an angel with wings, off the mantelpiece and is outraged at her failure to fly. The kind guide who pins a live butterfly to young Agatha Christie's sun hat hopes to give her pleasure; but the child is overwhelmed with horror at wearing a hat on which a living creature is being tortured to death. This unequivocal viewpoint, which the adult cannot always hope to recognize, also manifests itself in a sharply black-and-white awareness of sin. Rosamond Lehmann's baby brother drinks the eau-de-Cologne she has given him to smell, and she knows herself to be a murderess.

Osbert Sitwell sees scale as one cause of the gulf between the child's and the adult's vision of the world. Children at play are so much closer to the ground that grass, in their landscape, becomes

> ... that enormous wood the blades of which point to heaven as if they were the spears and lances of a great army, and the green depths of which are full of crepitation and the whirring of wings, while through them move fearful monsters, comparable to those painted by Hieronymus Bosch, armoured beetles, spectral green grasshoppers chafing their legs, and caterpillars with vast protruding eyes. Above these writhing and terrifying creatures, far above them, tower the flaming forest trees, sorrel and flowering grass, and the huge

moons of the ox-eye daisies seem to them to hang down from the sky itself...

In 'The Sweet Shop Round the Corner' Robert Graves mistakes a stranger for his mother:

> And not for a long while did the child begin
> To feel a dread that something had gone wrong:
> Were Mother's legs so clean, or her shoes so long,
> Or her skirt patched, or her hair tousled and grey?

— a catalogue of horror, as his eyes move slowly upwards from his normal range of vision, the stranger's shoes and legs.

In R. S. Thomas's 'Children's Song' there is a specific warning against striving too officiously to share the child's view of things:

> We live in our own world,
> A world that is too small
> For you to stoop and enter
> Even on hands and knees,
> The adult subterfuge . . .

Peter Quennell's father, trying to play with him on the beach, fails to enter that world and only succeeds in causing his son acute embarrassment.

In assembling this anthology the criteria of choice have been excellence and variety, my aim being to create a patchwork of juxtaposed experiences differing in time, place and emotional response, that illuminates the intrinsic nature of childhood. Sometimes I have gone out of my way to avoid the obvious; at others the obvious has also been clearly the best. With a few exceptions the extracts are non-fictional, the great bulk being made up of the memories of children filtered through their later adult consciousness. This means of course that, as with the refraction of light through water, there is an inevitable distortion of the child's original experience. And yet, though the episode of Lord Berners throwing his mother's spaniel out of the window may have been embellished and made elegant by an adult humour, the selection of anecdote itself does capture the essence of the child he once was.

The sorrows of the much-parodied Sensitive Little Boy, or of course Girl, are to the fore, partly because these unfortunates so often grow up to become excellent memoirists. Stephen Spender suffers agonies at school; Lytton Strachey is desolate at the loss of a poppy, a totemic and precious object; Elizabeth Bowen is humiliated by failure at the dancing class; and André Gide longs to be like other people. Others have a more robust and confident view of life: Bertrand Russell is passionate, whether over the revelatory nature of Euclid or the absence of a sponge cake.

I have taken childhood as ending somewhere around the age of twelve, although I have occasionally bent this rule to admit special favourites, such as the fourteen-year-old Jane Austen's violently partisan account of the kings and queens of England. Juvenilia (notably from the pens of those incomparable authoresses Marjory Fleming and Daisy Ashford), nursery rhymes and of course poems all help to elucidate the perspectives of the child's vision. Edward Lear's 'The Vestments' is an example of that wayward illogicality children accept with relish. There is a certain amount of autobiography thinly disguised as fiction, without which the anthology would have been the poorer. In Stendhal's *The Life of Henri Brulard* the young protagonist refuses to kiss an over-rouged elder cousin: '"Kiss me, Henri", she said to me. I refused, she got annoyed, I bit her hard. . .'. I can think of no excuse for including an extract from Maurice Baring's *The Diary of Smith Minor*.

When double figures are reached the earlier singleness of vision dims and blurs a little as adult values begin to impinge. A two-way tug sets in, as the child looks forward, if a little apprehensively, to the unexplored regions of adolescence and lingeringly back at familiar territory about to be left behind. In the anthology's final section the young Nigerian Camara Laye, returning home after the ritual of circumcision, feels something of this new disjointedness; and Robert Frost's lines about transience hauntingly articulate a sense of loss.

What has been lost? With the passing of childhood there is some dissipation of that fine intuitive quality of the imagination, that openness of expectation expressed by Wordsworth in his image of a child with a sea shell pressed to his ear:

> To which, in silence hushed, his very soul
> Listened intensely; and his countenance soon
> Brightened with joy; for from within were heard
> Murmurings . . .

However full the years ahead may prove, these murmurings become muted, sometimes silenced. My hope is that their echoes may be reawakened by the voices in this anthology.

1

FIRST MEMORIES

Out of the darkness of my infancy there comes only one flash of memory. I am seated alone, in my baby-chair, at a dinner-table set for several people. Somebody brings in a leg of mutton, puts it down close to me, and goes out. I am again alone, gazing at two low windows, wide open upon a garden. Suddenly, noiselessly, a large, long animal (obviously a greyhound) appears at one window-sill, slips into the room, seizes the leg of mutton and slips out again. When this happened I could not yet talk. The accomplishment of speech came to me very late, doubtless because I never heard young voices. Many years later, when I mentioned this recollection, there was a shout of laughter and surprise: 'That, then, was what became of the mutton! It was not you, who, as your Uncle A. pretended, ate it up, in the twinkling of an eye, bone and all!'   FATHER AND SON *by Edmund Gosse (1849–1928)*

I was set down from the carrier's cart at the age of three; and there with a sense of bewilderment and terror my life in the village began.

The June grass, amongst which I stood, was taller than I was, and I wept. I had never been so close to grass before. It towered above me and all around me, each blade tattooed with tiger-skins of sunlight. It was knife-edged, dark, and a wicked green, thick as a forest and alive with grasshoppers that chirped and chattered and leapt through the air like monkeys.

I was lost and didn't know where to move. A tropic heat oozed up from the ground, rank with sharp odours of roots and nettles. Snow-clouds of elder-blossom banked in the sky, showering upon me the fumes and flakes of their sweet and giddy suffocation. High overhead ran frenzied larks, screaming, as though the sky were tearing apart.

For the first time in my life I was out of the sight of humans. For the first time in my life I was alone in a world whose behaviour I could neither predict nor fathom: a world of birds that squealed, of plants that stank, of insects that sprang about without warning. I was lost and I did not expect to be found again. I put back my head and howled, and the sun hit me smartly on the face, like a bully.

From this daylight nightmare I was awakened, as from many another, by the appearance of my sisters. They came scrambling and calling up the steep rough bank, and parting the long grass found me. Faces of rose, familiar, living; huge shining faces hung up like shields between me and the sky; faces with grins and white teeth (some broken) to be conjured up like genii with a howl, brushing off terror with their broad scoldings and affection. They leaned over me – one, two, three – their mouths smeared with red currants and their hands dripping with juice.

'There, there, it's all right, don't you wail any more. Come down 'ome and we'll stuff you with currants.'

And Marjorie, the eldest, lifted me into her long brown hair, and ran me jogging down the path and through the steep rose-filled garden, and set me down on the cottage doorstep, which was our home, though I couldn't believe it.

CIDER WITH ROSIE *by Laurie Lee (1914–   )*

Happy those early days, when I
Shined in my angel-infancy!
Before I understood this place
Appointed for my second race,
Or taught my soul to fancy aught
But a white celestial thought;
When yet I had not walked above
A mile or two from my first love,
And looking back, at that short space,
Could see a glimpse of his bright face;
When on some gilded cloud, or flower,
My gazing soul would dwell an hour,

And in those weaker glories spy
Some shadows of eternity;
Before I taught my tongue to wound
My conscience with a sinful sound,
Or had the black art to dispense
A several sin to every sense,
But felt through all this fleshly dress
Bright shoots of everlastingness.

from 'The Retreat' by Henry Vaughan (1621–95)

William Hutton survived an early life of poverty and harshness – he was working in a silk mill by the age of seven – to become the respected county historian of Derby. The following gives a taste of his idiosyncratic view of life and of his racy tone; it describes an incident that took place when he was three.

Every class of the animal world associates with its like. An old couple, Moses Simpson and his wife, who lived at the next door, took great notice of me, but I shunned them with horror; had they been young, I should probably have sought *them*, but I was fully persuaded they would kill me. I stood at the top of a flight of stairs, and this woman at the bottom, coaxing me to come to her. She might as well have intreated the moon. I instantly tumbled to the bottom. She took me in her arms, endeavoured to pacify me, dandled me on the knee, and I was surprized that I escaped with life.

THE HISTORY OF THE LIFE OF WILLIAM HUTTON *(1723–1815) by Himself*

The very earliest recollection of my life is bound up with an Oxford and Cambridge Boat Race. I was walking with my nurse along the Broad Walk in Kensington Gardens, and she stopped to talk to some other nurse, with whom, I suppose, she was acquainted. I remember that my nurse said, 'What are *you*?' and that the other nurse answered, 'I am Cambridge.' 'Oh,' rejoined my nurse, 'I am Oxford.' Not having yet seen more than three summers, I was too young to understand this elliptical mode of speech, and long after, whenever Oxford and Cambridge were mentioned in my presence, I thought that Oxford was my nurse,

and Cambridge the other one. So deeply do things root themselves
in the brain of a little child that even now, after the lapse of so
many years, the names of the two great Universities do still
vaguely suggest to me the image of these two nurses. And I
attribute my early preference of Oxford to the notion I had that
Oxford was *my* nurse. When the time came for me to choose the
venue of my adolescence, how could I hesitate? Oxford received
its sacred trust. Oxford moulded me. How petty, devious and
remote are the details that inform a world's destiny!

THE BOAT RACE *by Max Beerbohm (1872–1956)*

Infant Sorrow

My mother groan'd! my father wept.
Into the dangerous world I leapt:
Helpless, naked, piping loud:
Like a fiend hid in a cloud.

Struggling in my father's hands,
Striving against my swadling bands,
Bound and weary I thought best
To sulk upon my mother's breast.

SONGS OF EXPERIENCE *by William Blake (1757–1827)*

My earliest recollections are connected with Kensington Palace,
where I can remember crawling on a yellow carpet spread out for
that purpose – and being told that if I cried and was naughty my
'Uncle Sussex' would hear me and punish me, for which reason I
always screamed when I saw him! I had a great horror of bishops
on account of their wigs and aprons, but recollect this being
partially got over in the case of the then Bishop of Salisbury by his
kneeling down and letting me play with his badge of Chancellor of
the Order of the Garter. With another bishop, however, the
persuasion of showing him my 'pretty shoes' was of no use.
Claremont remains as the brightest epoch of my otherwise rather
melancholy childhood ... I used to ride a donkey given me by my

Uncle, the Duke of York, who was very kind to me. I remember him well – tall, rather large, very kind but extremely shy. He always gave me beautiful presents.

MEMOIRS OF QUEEN VICTORIA'S EARLY YEARS *by Herself (1819–1901)*

Wadham had some famous and fascinating old members, whom I met in my first years. The most astonishing was Frederick Harrison. He was ninety-two, and his first question to me was, 'When did you come up to Oxford?' I told him, 'In 1919,' and he answered, 'I came up in 1848.' So indeed he had. What is more, he had toured parts of Europe in that year of revolutions and had vivid memories of Paris after the fall of Louis Philippe. He remembered the accession of Queen Victoria when he was seven years old. He was playing with his bricks when his father came in and told him that the king was dead. He asked who the new king was going to be, and his father said, '"We are not going to have a king, Frederick; we are going to have a queen" . . . I said, "It's come to that, has it?" and went on playing with my bricks.'

MEMORIES 1898–1939 *by Maurice Bowra (1898–1971)*

It is here at Sandy-Knowe, in the residence of my paternal grandfather, already mentioned, that I have the first consciousness of existence; and I recollect distinctly that my situation and appearance were a little whimsical. Among the odd remedies recurred to to aid my lameness, some one had recommended that so often as a sheep was killed for the use of the family, I should be stripped, and swathed up in the skin, warm as it was flayed from the carcase of the animal. In this Tartar-like habiliment I well remember lying upon the floor of the little parlour in the farmhouse, while my grandfather, a venerable old man with white hair, used every excitement to make me try to crawl. I also distinctly remember the late Sir George MacDougal of Makerstoun joining in this kindly attempt. . . . I still recollect him in his old-fashioned military habit (he had been colonel of the Greys), with a small cocked hat, deeply laced, an embroidered scarlet waistcoat, and a light-coloured coat, with milk-white locks tied in a military fashion, kneeling on the ground before me, and dragging his watch along the carpet to induce me to follow it. The benevolent old soldier and the infant wrapped in his sheepskin would have afforded an odd group to uninterested spectators. This must have happened about my third year.   AUTOBIOGRAPHY *of Sir Walter Scott (1771–1832)*

The first thing I can remember is biting the cheek or forehead of my cousin Mme Pison du Galland, wife of that witty fellow who was a deputy in the Constituent Assembly. I can see her now, a plump woman of twenty-five wearing a great deal of rouge; it must have been this rouge that offended me. As she sat in the middle of the field that was known as the Slope of the Porte de Bonne, her cheek was exactly at my level.

'Kiss me, Henri,' she said to me. I refused, she got annoyed, I bit her hard. I can still see the scene, but that's probably because I was immediately given such a dressing-down, and never heard the end of it.   THE LIFE OF HENRI BRULARD *by Stendhal (1788–1842)*

My first recollection is of seeing the devil! As soon as I was three or four years old, I was allowed to go to church every Sunday, and I used to look forward to this the whole week through. I can still feel on my lips our servant-girl's cotton glove, which she used to hold over my mouth when I yawned or sang too loud. And now every Sunday I noticed in a bright frame by the side of the organ a shaggy face which was continually turning about and looking down into the church. So long as the organ was playing and the singing going on it was visible, but as soon as my father was praying at the altar it disappeared. When the playing and singing began again it reappeared, but as soon as my father began his sermon it was again lost to sight, to show itself once more for the closing hymn and voluntary. 'This is the devil that is looking down into the church,' I said to myself, 'but as soon as father begins with God's Word, he has to make himself scarce!' This weekly dose of visible theology gave quite a distinctive tone to my childish piety. It was only much later, when I had been at school a fairly long time, that I understood that the face which came and disappeared so strangely was that of Daddy Iltis, the organist, and was created by the mirror which was fastened up near the organ so as to let the player see when my father was at the altar and when he went up into the pulpit.

MEMOIRS OF CHILDHOOD AND YOUTH *by Albert Schweitzer (1875–1965)*

A Terrible Infant

I recollect a nurse called Ann,
    Who carried me about the grass,
And one fine day a fair young man
    Came up and kissed the pretty lass:
She did not make the least objection!
    Thinks I, *Aha!*
When I can talk I'll tell Mamma!
– And that's my earliest recollection.

Frederick Locker-Lampson (1821–95)

My first visual memory is of a camera obscura on the pier at Weston-super-Mare. On that day, I have been told, I suffered an absurd and nearly fatal accident. I was biting a hard-boiled egg when the yolk suddenly shot from its white case and lodged entire in my throat, threatening me with asphyxiation. Apoplectic of face I was thumped and shaken by the heels. It was a close-run thing whether that hard ball came up, went down or stuck there to throttle me. It went down. Others, rather often, reminded me of the alarm I caused. My only recollection of that picnic is of the luminous, circular table-top in the dark hut, over which there mysteriously moved the reflections of passing holiday-makers.

A LITTLE LEARNING *by Evelyn Waugh (1903–66)*

I begin: the first memory.

This was of red and purple flowers on a black ground – my mother's dress; and she was sitting either in a train or in an omnibus, and I was on her lap. I therefore saw the flowers she was wearing very close; and can still see purple and red and blue, I think, against the black; they must have been anemones, I suppose. Perhaps we were going to St Ives; more probably, for from the light it must have been evening, we were coming back to London. But it is more convenient artistically to suppose that we were going to St Ives, for that will lead to my other memory, which also seems to be my first memory, and in fact it is the most important of all my memories. If life has a base that it stands upon, if it is a bowl that one fills and fills and fills – then my bowl without a doubt stands upon this memory. It is of lying half asleep, half awake, in bed in the nursery at St Ives. It is of hearing the waves breaking, one, two, one, two, and sending a splash of water over the beach; and then breaking, one, two, one, two, behind a yellow blind. It is of hearing the blind draw its little acorn across the floor as the wind blew the blind out. It is of lying and hearing this splash and seeing this light, and feeling, it is almost impossible that I should be here; of feeling the purest ecstasy I can conceive. . . . When I think of the early morning in bed I also hear the caw of rooks falling from a great height. The sound seems to fall through an elastic, gummy air; which holds it up; which prevents it from being sharp and distinct. . . .

The next memory – all these colour-and-sound memories hang together at St Ives – was much more robust; it was highly sensual. It was later. It still makes me feel warm; as if everything were ripe; humming; sunny; smelling so many smells at once; and all making a whole that even now makes me stop – as I stopped then going down to the beach; I stopped at the top to look down at the gardens. They were sunk beneath the road. The apples were on a level with one's head. The gardens gave off a murmur of bees; the apples were red and gold; there were also pink flowers; and grey and silver leaves. The buzz, the croon, the smell, all seemed to press voluptuously against some membrane; not to burst it; but to hum round one such a complete rapture of pleasure that I stopped, smelt; looked.

A SKETCH OF THE PAST *by Virginia Woolf (1882–1941)*

The 'two flamboyant fathers' of the title of Nicolette Devas's memoirs are Robert Macnamara, hero of this episode, and her stepfather Augustus John.

The time was late May, 1914.

The place, Ennistymon House, County Clare.

In this memory I am three years old and standing at the top of the stairs in a white winceyette nightgown. The stairs lead down to the hall in a wide curve of shallow steps. From below, a shadowy journey away it seemed to me, my father is shouting for me to come down. He is long-legged, giant-sized and his voice reverberates against the panelling. The prospect appals me, I ought to be in bed, and I peep through the banisters. The next moment I am snatched up into my father's arms, kidnapped, nursery rules broken, and as we leap down the stairs I feel the draught in my hair from the open front door. We jump the stone steps in front of the house, rush across the lawn, and I am dropped with my bare feet on the damp grass. The lawn, with a copper beech at the edge standing like a sentinel, is a platform high above the river. My father flings himself down on his hands and knees in front of a clump of pampas grass and half disappears inside it. The cold sound of the waterfall drifts up through the mist in the valley. It is dusk, the rooks in the rookery are silent, the hooded crows are already roosting in the copper beech above my head. My father backs out of the pampas grass with a short-eared owl in his arms. The owl's astonished speckled head swivels around and I see its yellow eyes. In my arms it is quiet and feathery and I cannot find a piece of solid to hold and hug it tight. My father dives into the pampas grass again and brings out a fledgeling owl, immense staring eyes in a ball of fluff.

I seem to remember a fuss. If I don't, I remember another fuss of the same kind. For the pattern of this owl episode was to be repeated many times. My mother or Sophy the nurse protesting because the rules had been broken. 'The child over excited ... a cold ... bare feet on the wet grass ...' My father roared, his arms flaying the air, 'What was a cold or a restless night?' An owl to hug was more important, a miracle I would remember for the rest of

my life. My father was always to set the world topsy-turvy for a
touch of magic, for a grand gesture.

Two Flamboyant Fathers *by Nicolette Devas (1911–87)*

As a proof of my readiness to accept autobiographical convention, let me at once record my two earliest memories. The first is
being loyally held up at a window to watch a procession of
decorated carriages and waggons for Queen Victoria's Diamond
Jubilee in 1897 (this was at Wimbledon, where I had been born on
July 24th, 1895). The second is gazing upwards with a sort of
despondent terror at a cupboard in the nursery, which stood
accidentally open, filled to the ceiling with octavo volumes of
Shakespeare. My father had organized a Shakespeare reading
circle. I did not know until long afterwards that this was the
Shakespeare cupboard but, apparently, I already had a strong
instinct against drawing-room activities. And when distinguished
visitors came to the house, such as Sir Sidney Lee with his Shakes-
pearean scholarship, or Lord Ashbourne, not yet a peer, with his
loud talk of 'Ireland for the Irish', and his saffron kilt, or Mr
Eustace Miles the English real-tennis champion and vegetarian
with his samples of exotic nuts, I knew all about them in my way.

Nor had I any illusions about Algernon Charles Swinburne,
who often used to stop my perambulator when he met it on
Nurses' Walk, at the edge of Wimbledon Common, and pat me on
the head and kiss me: he was an inveterate pram-stopper and
patter and kisser. Nurses' Walk lay between 'The Pines', Putney
(where he lived with Watts-Dunton), and the Rose and Crown
public house, where he went for his daily pint of beer; Watts-
Dunton allowed him twopence for it and no more. I did not know
that Swinburne was a poet, but I knew that he was a public
menace.   Goodbye to All That *by Robert Graves (1895–1985)*

The Bards

My aged friend, Miss Wilkinson,
  Whose mother was a Lambe,
Saw Wordsworth once, and Coleridge, too
  One morning in her 'pram'.[1]

Birdlike the bards stooped over her
  Like fledgling in a nest;
And Wordsworth said, 'Thou harmless babe!'
  And Coleridge was impressed.

The pretty thing gazed up and smiled,
  And softly murmured, 'Coo!'
William was then aged sixty-four
  And Samuel sixty-two.

[1] This was a three-wheeled vehicle
  Of iron and of wood;
It had a leather apron,
  But it hadn't any hood.

COLLECTED RHYMES AND VERSES *by Walter de la Mare (1873–1956)*

2

THE NURSERY

Reflection on Babies

A bit of talcum
Is always walcum.

Ogden Nash (1902–70)

For sheer pleasure few methods of progression, one comes gradually to realize, can compare with the perambulator. The motion is agreeable, the range of vision extensive and one has always before one's eyes the rewarding spectacle of a grown-up maintaining prolonged physical exertion. Moreover, the sensation of pasha-like power which all this induces is not illusory for, by the simple device of repeatedly jettisoning a teddy-bear or a rattle, any display of independence on the part of the mahout can successfully be countered, and should she, maddened beyond endurance, be provoked to reprisals a piteous howling will soon attract the friendly interest of sympathetic passers-by and expose her to public, if unjustified, rebuke.

ALL DONE FROM MEMORY *by Osbert Lancaster (1908–86)*

Childhood and Interruption

Now it is time to go for a walk
Perhaps we shall go for a walk in the park
And then it will be time to play until dark
Not quite, when the shadows fall it is time to go home
It is always time to do something I am never torn
With a hesitation of my own

For always everything is arranged punctually
I am guarded entirely from the tension of anxiety
Walk tea-supper bath bed I am a very happy child really
And underneath the pram cover lies my brother Jake
He is not old enough yet to be properly awake
He is alone in his sleep; no arrangement they make
For him can touch him at all, he is alone,
For a little while yet, it is as if he had not been born
Rest in infancy, brother Jake; childhood and interruption come
    swiftly on.

Stevie Smith (1902–71)

The following extract is taken from a conversational manual by Peter Erondell published in 1605.

LADY: Good morrow nurse.
NURSE: God give you good morrow, Madame.
LADY: How now, how doth the childe?
NURSE: He is fayre and plumpe, and doth very wel thanks be to God, saving that he hath been somewhat waiward the last night.
LADY: Hath he so? What shold ail him? It may be he hath some tooth a growing, is he in his cradle? See if he sleepeth.
NURSE: He is full awaken, Madame.
LADY: He is not yet made readie is he?
NURSE: No, Madame, I have let him sleepe all this morning.
LADY: Unswaddle him, undoe his swaddling bands, give him his brekefast while I am heere, make his pappe, take away that fier-brand that smoketh for it will taste of the smoke, where is his little spoone? Wash him before me, have you cleane water? O my little hart! God blesse thee. Rub the crowne of his head.... 'What hath he upon his eyelid? Me thinks his eyes are somewhat watrish, make them cleane; how quick is his eyebal, hath he not a pimple upon his nose? His little cheeks are wet, I believe you did leave him alone to crye and weepe; picke his nostrils, wipe his mouth and his lips. How many teethe hath he? His gummes be sore. Showe me his tongue, let me see the pallet of his mouth, he hathe a prettie chin. What a fair necke he hath! Pull off his shirt, thou art prety

and fat my little darling, wash his arme-pits; what ayleth his
elboe? O what an arme he hath! His hand wrist is very small; open
his right hand; the palme of his left hand is all on water, did he
sweat? How he spreadeth his small fingers. . . .

'You have not washed the insides nor the soles of his feete;
forget not to make cleane his toes, the great toe and all, now
swaddle him againe, but first put on his biggin, and his little band
with an edge, where is his little petticoat? give him his coate of
changeable taffeta, and his sattin sleeves; where is his bibbe? Let
him have his gathered aprone with stringes, and hang a muckin-
der to it; you need not yet to give him his corall with the small
golden chayne, for I beleeve it is better to let him sleepe till the
afternoone. Give him some sucke. . . .

'Set on the coverlet, now put him in his cradle and rocke him till
he sleepe but bring him to me first that I may kisse him; God send
thee good rest my little boykin. I pray you Nurse have a care of
him.'

Our family had only one faithful Nan, who came to us after the
birth of my eldest brother Horace in 1888 and stayed until old age
and infirmity took her to a 'home'. Lizzie Croucher was her
extraordinary name. I was the youngest of our well-spaced-out
family of six, so there was no one to supplant me in the honour
and pleasure of sharing her bedroom. In the mornings I lay snug
and warm in bed, watching the fascinating ritual of her getting
dressed. There was never a flash of nudity, but like a skilled
conjuror she inserted herself into bodice and stays and long frilled
drawers, and then put over them two flannel petticoats, one red
and one royal blue. After that she brushed out her long, straight,
mouse-coloured hair, plaited it tightly and fastened it in a small
knot behind her head. (It was so fine and silky that she once made
substitute paintbrushes out of it when nursery supplies had run
out.) What reassurance her whole appearance gave me! She was
tiny, and therefore seemed halfway between a child and an adult;
her face was pale and her small round head was like the top of a
ninepin. Spiritually she was a natural object, a tree in the garden,
something taken for granted and always relied upon to be *there*,

sitting in the nursery mending stockings – someone who had a purely instinctive but effective manner of dealing with bawls, bangs or knots in crochet. She was aware of our failings but accepted them as we accepted her, so that there was no danger of disappointing her and letting her down, as there was with our parents. I wish I could remember all her runic sayings, like 'If you want your hair to curl you must eat fried bread behind the door'. (I did and it did.) And when later on I shared a bedroom with Eleanor, she used to call us with the mysterious formula: 'Look at the moon! And the *stars*! And Eleanor's NOSE and Frances's WHISKERS!', pouncing on us with the last two, so as to rouse us thoroughly and send us into fits of giggles. She led a rich religious life centring round the picture of Gentle Jesus knocking on the door by Holman Hunt in her bedroom, and I am sure he was more real to her than any friend. 'I dreamed of JE-sus last night,' she told us once in the high sing-song voice she reserved for other-worldly things. 'He came to me carrying a beautiful blue vase, and he said, "Nan", he said, "please clean this for HEAven."'

MEMORIES *by Frances Partridge (1900–   )*

Jemima

There was a little girl, and she wore a little curl
   Right down the middle of her forehead
When she was good, she was very, very, good,
   But when she was bad, she was horrid!

One day she went upstairs, while her parents, unawares,
   In the kitchen down below were occupied with meals,
And she stood upon her head, on her little truckle bed,
   And she then began hurraying with her heels.

Her mother heard the noise, and thought it was the boys
   A-playing at a combat in the attic,
But when she climbed the stair and saw Jemima there,
   She took and she did whip her most emphatic.

Anon

At the time of her mother's death, Elizabeth was at Hunsdon under the charge of Lady Bryan, who had been Lady Mistress, or Governess, to Mary when a baby. It was a household of troubles; or so Lady Bryan thought as she poured them out in a letter to Thomas Cromwell. Elizabeth, she wrote, was put from her rank of princess and she had no notion, except from hearsay, of her charge's new rank, or how she should order her, or order herself and the women and grooms under her authority. The child, too, was lamentably short of clothes; she had neither gown, nor kirtle, nor petticoat, nor any manner of linen for smocks, nor several other necessaries. It was impossible to make shift any longer. Moreover, the male head of the household, Mr Shelton, had been lording it over Lady Bryan, interfering with her charge and insisting on my Lady Elizabeth dining and supping in state, publicly. 'Alas! my Lord,' wrote the harassed lady, 'it is not meet for a child of her age to keep such rule yet. I promise you, my Lord, I dare not take it upon me to keep her Grace in health, and she keep that rule; for there she shall see divers meats and fruits and wine, which would be hard for me to refrain her Grace from. Ye know, my Lord, there is no place of correction there. And she is yet too young to correct greatly. I know well, and she be there, I shall neither bring her up to the King's Grace's honour, nor hers; nor to her health, nor my poor honesty.' 'God knoweth,' she went on, 'my Lady hath great pain with her great teeth, and they come very slowly forth, and causeth me to suffer her Grace to have her will more than I would. I trust to God, and her teeth were well grafted, to have her Grace after another fashion than she is yet; so as I trust the King's Grace shall have great comfort in her Grace. For she is as toward a child, and as gentle of conditions, as ever I knew any in my life. Jesu preserve her Grace!'

QUEEN ELIZABETH *(1533–1603) by J. E. Neale*

Lytton Strachey was born at Stowey House, Clapham Common, on 1 March 1880, the eleventh of thirteen children, three of whom died in infancy. He was christened Giles Lytton. . . . As a young child he was high-spirited and loquacious – for the only time in his life. 'Giles is the most ridiculous boy I ever saw,' Lady Strachey wrote to her daughter Dorothy shortly after his third birthday: 'he said to me, "Yesterday in the streets I saw a cow eating the birds!" He then enacted a drama of which the punishment of the unnatural cow was the motive; as a policeman he flung himself on one knee and upraised his arms at the cow with a most fine dramatic gesture of Command; a terrific combat then ensued in which he wielded the peacock broom with might, and finally cried sternly, "Go to be dead!" and laid his broom on the floor saying, "Now the cow is dead." He never ceases talking for a single minute.' LYTTON STRACHEY *(1880–1932) by Michael Holroyd*

Was I a pleasant child? During her pregnancy, my mother said, she would often indulge in agreeable daydreams of the kind of son that she awaited. She had already decided that I was to be a son; and she pictured me merry, red-headed, talkative, constantly 'running around and making new friends'. A false dream, as she herself admitted. I was 'always a *difficult* child', she sighed, though, of course, she loved me dearly; and at an early stage she began to suspect that I was showing signs of undue 'cleverness', which did not exactly accord with her dream-picture of the gay, mercurial, red-headed imp. Once more I refer to an early photograph; and a curious photograph it is, taken, I imagine, when I was three or four years old. Seated on an upturned basket, I am looking sideways at the photographer, giving him or her a slightly mistrustful, perhaps a faintly hostile glance. My eyebrows are tilted; the line of my mouth droops; and, beneath the blond fringe that partly covers it, the shadow of an infantile frown seems to be gathering across my brow. Maybe I was squinting against the sun; possibly my six-buttoned black boots had been causing me discomfort. I am surprised, indeed, that my mother or my nanny should have expected me to wear them; for otherwise I am dressed in a decidedly picturesque style – in a smock-frock copied from the sturdy uniform, made of substantial unbleached linen, still worn by old-fashioned country labourers at the conclusion of the nineteenth century.

It is not, I think, a particularly childish face; and some of my early sayings that were afterwards repeated to me suggest a rather doubtful, even a mildly cynical attitude towards the world in which I found myself. Thus a friend described how she had seen me grasping the bars of my nursery play-pen – evidently I was then too young to be allowed the unhampered freedom of the floor – and heard me intoning for my visitor's benefit a refrain that touched her sentimental heart. 'What we *want*,' I repeated, 'and what we *get* are *two different things*!' This, I assume, was one of my nanny's wise old saws, brought out if I made some unreasonable demand; but I put into the words such a poignant strength of feeling that they appeared to represent my own convictions. I was also regarded as an oddly self-centred child, never fond of sharing with other children any toy I really valued. A little girl cousin, for example, whom I was obliged to entertain in my nursery, once spilt a favourite pot of paint. Besides wasting my paint, she had spoiled her new dress. My aunt betrayed some agitation. Whereat I approached her in a manner that I meant to be both courteous and diplomatic, assuring her that it was 'not my *best* paint', and was astonished to hear my civil remark dismissed as a piece of deliberate impertinence.

Until my fifth year, I had no companion in my pleasant, roomy nursery, with its raftered roof and dormer-windows; nor, when an infant sister appeared, did I welcome her arrival. I enjoyed my comparative solitude; I was not a gregarious child. ... Meetings with unknown children ... at crowded children's parties often ended in humiliation. I would stand and sulk; my silver-buckled patent-leather shoes seemed to have developed leaden soles. 'Won't you dance with my little boy?' demanded my anxious mother, leading me up towards a little girl; and 'No, I *won't*!' the little girl would reply, turning her back and waywardly mincing off.   THE MARBLE FOOT *by Peter Quennell (1905–   )*

'Aunt Monie' of this extract is E. M. Forster's great-aunt Marianne Thornton (1797–1887).

The truth is that [my mother] and I had fallen in love with our Hertfordshire home and did not want to leave it. It certainly was a lovable little house, and still is, though it now stands just outside a twentieth-century hub and almost within sound of a twentieth-century hum. The garden, the overhanging wych-elm, the sloping meadow, the great view to the west, the cliff of fir trees to the north, the adjacent farm through the high tangled hedge of wild roses were all utilized by me in *Howards End*, and the interior is in the novel too. The actual inmates were my mother, myself, two maids, two or more cats, an occasional dog; outside were a pony and trap with a garden boy to look after them. From the time I entered the house at the age of four and nearly fell from its top to its bottom through a hole ascribed to the mice, I took it to my heart....

Aunt Monie had urged my mother to take the house (provided it was on gravel), so she had no grounds for complaint, and it had seemed to her quite proper that a beautiful young widow should bury herself in the wilds for the sake of a supposedly delicate son. All the same, there was this nagging desire to see us – me particularly. Her thirst for youth had become cannibalistic. My mother's letters fall into three classes – those in which she undertook to go to Clapham, those in which she excused herself from going, and those in which she fed the old lady with amusing bits of news about the Important One, in the hope of keeping her quiet. ...

Out of the endless trifles she now dished up I will select a few on the subject of Pink-Faced Emma. ... Pink-Faced Emma was our housemaid, and she was so called to distinguish her from Aunt Monie's White-Faced Emma.

Emma arrives:

> Morgan got much excited on Thursday at the thought of the new maids, he would watch for Emma at 4, she not being expected till 5.30. When time drew near he picked a huge yellow pansy to make himself smart. He asked her her name the moment she arrived and took her up to her room. At tea he said 'She calls me *Sir*, mamma, it is really very awkward. She doesn't know my name and now will she ever. She might ask me.' I think she must think he is mad, for he said to her 'Have you heard one of my long stories about things that

have never happened except inside my head – I'll tell you one, it is called "Excited maids under the Clothes line".'

Emma under instruction:

M. invited the maids to tea with him yesterday, and he said he must give them some amusement, so he armed himself with astronomical diagrams and said they had better do a little learning. He explained all and they giggled like a pair of noodles. He then proposed Hide & Seek. He then took them both into the hall and instructed them in moves at chess. He flew all over the hall carpet saying 'Now I go like a knight, now like a castle &ct. He is chalking a map of South America, and implored me to help him before I went out yesterday 'for I know Emma won't think it matters a bit whether I put Patagonia in the place of Ecuador'.

Emma under examination:

Did I tell you of the conversation I overheard (I was supposed to be asleep) between Emma & Morgan.

E. You know a good deal about stars, don't you Master Morgan?

M. (humbly) No not very much. Do you?

E. Oh no.

M. *What* do you know about? (What indeed!!! Long pause.)

E. Oh only what you have taught me.

M. Botany?

E. Yes, about the Great Bear & Little Bear.

M. – scornfully – That's not Botany, that's Astronomy. Botany is about flowers and *Cology* about shells. I don't know very much of both those.

E. Oh I think you know a great deal, Master Morgan.

M. – very self-satisfied tone – Oh, do you.

Emma leaves. My cleverness and rudeness were more than she could stand. The break came gathering primroses. I sneered at her for picking them with short stalks, she jeered at me for picking so few. I hit at her basket and upset it, she hit at mine. I hit her, she hit me and tore my little coat. 'But I had to hit Master Morgan, ma'am, he hit me,' she explained mildly. I was sorry when she left and rather ashamed, for I knew it was my fault. She was such a suitable companion, and our chant of

> Oh the corns and bunians how they do grow,
> They hurt me so oh oh oh oh oh oh

still sometimes rings in my ears.

MARIANNE THORNTON by E. M. Forster (1879–1970)

The Changeling

> When larks gin sing
> Away we fling,
> And babes new-born steal as we go;
> An elf instead
> We leave in bed,
> And wind out, laughing, Ho, Ho, Ho!

Anon

Priscilla Napier is growing up in Egypt, where her father is in the colonial administration.

Early childhood holds aching stretches of boredom, as well as its griping eternities of grief and fear, its spell-binding hours of delight. Its strength lies in its forgetfulness. Sometimes those Nanny-and-May walks seemed endless, day after day, along the glittering Nile in its afternoon breeze-ruffled greenness. Little gusts of dustiness teased one's eyes, ruffled the fringe of the pram canopy. A mile south along the river bank was the bridge to Giza, interestingly called the Pongly-Zongly: it was many years before these words revealed themselves to me as Pont des Anglais. Half-way there, by the race-course entrance, lived the Goschen family. ... One of the younger ones had a glass eye, and their Nanny made such immense capital out of this fact that an aura of pride and specialness came to envelop the whole family, for of all the weapons in the Nanny-armoury an incurable disability in one of her charges is the most powerful (short of having one of them a royal bridesmaid)....

We never seemed to get anywhere on our walks. The Pongly-Zongly might at least have had some traffic or camels or something diverting on it. We would simply turn round and go back by the same way. 'It's cooler by the river. Lay hold of the pram handle, dear, while we cross the road.' This was an unnecessary precaution; the roads were empty. Nothing came along but an occasional rattling arabiyeh, a rare carriage, or Colonel Blunt in his dog-cart, a smart syce up behind. The Nile island of Gezira was still pastoral and not yet suburban. Fields held thin tethered donkeys, occasionally accompanied by an enchanting baby donkey covered in milk-white curls. Enormous water buffaloes rolled slowly along the dusty un-macadamized roads and into the snake-grass surrounded fields. Little Egyptian girls, with long pink cotton dresses and gold ear-rings in their small milk-chocolate coloured ears, tended the buffaloes and in loud trenchant tones directed their desultory progress across the waste spaces of the island. Gathering up the buffalo dung as soon as it fell, to be dried and used as fuel, the little girls piled it into baskets with their bare hands and swayed gracefully on, carrying the baskets on their heads.

'Fancy! In their bare hands!' Ena said shockedly to Nanny, unaware that Herodotus too in his day had commented upon this Egyptian peculiarity. 'To think of human people doing that! You'd think they'd learn to make themselves spades.'

Nanny, now in her third winter in Egypt, decided to play this down.

'I'll thank you, William, not to walk just in front of the pram.'

'It's grievous,' Ena said, and I drew down a disapproving upper lip in sympathy. We hurried across the Boulac Road and never under any pretext went down it. Nanny-and-May, or Nanny-and-Ena, once they had got over being shocked, preferred not to notice what went on. The Boulac Road was a place where people cursed and shouted and incessantly called upon God to witness their wrongs; when not spitting out chewed sugar-cane they spat out spit, they wiped their noses unashamedly on the back of their hands or held their noses and blew them into the dust and shook their heads free, they greeted one another across great distances in tones of untrammelled pleasure or dislike, they passed or squatted as need arose in wide open spaces, they begged unceasingly in high whining desperate voices which they switched off without difficulty when greeting an acquaintance in the same line of business.

'Why can they do it, Nanny, and not us?'

'They're heathens.'

'Father says they aren't heathens,' William pointed out.

'Well then, don't ask me, dear. We must suppose they know no better.'

It was a moment of relief when the iron gates of the Sirdaria clanged tight. Even inside this stone-walled haven which lay along the Boulac Road one did not feel too secure. The harsh incessant shouting floated over, the braying of donkeys rising to fever pitch, the rattle of the flat carts, their drivers shouting comments, yelling Oh-ah! Oh-ah! Oh-ah riglac! and people on foot complaining passionately at being hustled off the road. The gardens themselves were large and empty of people and full of possibilities. There were groves of poinsettias with their strange thick red flowers that were the same shape as their leaves, and of orange trees, heavy with ripe fruit, and blossom, and small hard green oranges, all at the same time. In a corner under the high wall, away from Nanny and the pram, there was a fine hidden place in which to be secret, in which to enter a world unorganized by grown-ups. We retired into a domestic bliss of mud-cakes and leaf plates and piles of berries for fruit. Here, uninterrupted, William and I could make and be busy, thickening out the hibiscus walls with palm beaches and eucalyptus boughs, at peace and very muddy in a dim, green, shuttered world. The lizards and the grasshoppers and the large burnt-sienna butterflies and the hornets were all shut out.

Suddenly from behind the stone wall came the unmistakable loud blood-curdling roar of a lion. Starting low and growlingly, it rose to a throbbing rage, sank again, gave to our thudding hearts the hope that the peril had passed. We had heard lions often enough in the Giza Zoo before feeding time. Sounding still nearer, the roar rose again to a crescendo of fury. Any minute now the lion would leap over the wall and devour us. We faced each other, panic-stricken amongst the poinsettias. For a full moment we stood with our mouths open in a suffocating fear, before we found courage even for flight. We fled past the orange trees and the little channels that watered the petunia beds, over the grass and under the date palms to where Nanny was knitting in inexplicable calm beside the pram, and cast ourselves into the shelter of that starched and lifebuoy-soaped embrace.

'There,' Nanny said, 'to think of you both being so silly, and you a great boy nearly seven, William!'

'Not till August,' William gulped, factual in the teeth of woe.

'Fancying it was a lion! The very idea. It's only a camel you heard, roaring in the Boulac Road. Whatever made you take such a thing in your head? Surely to goodness you know what an angry camel sounds like by now?'

Sobered, we walked home shufflingly to tea.

A LATE BEGINNER *by Priscilla Napier (1909–)*

This is winter. Well never mind it. We will sit by the fire, and read and tell stories, and look at pictures.

Take care, little boy, you stand too near the fire. You will burn your shoes.

Do not spit on the floor. Spit in the corner. It is dark. Light the candle. Shut the window-blinds. Bring in some wood.

The sun is gone to bed. The chickens are gone to bed; and little boys and girls must go to bed.

Poor little boy is sleepy. He must be carried upstairs.

Pull off his shoes. Pull off his frock and petticoat. Put on his nightcap.

Lay his head upon the pillow. Cover him up. Good night.

THE CHILD'S SPELLING-BOOK: Calculated to Render Reading Completely Easy to Little Children, *Massachusetts, 1798*

3

MOTHERS

Marjory Fleming (1803–11), whose delightful and witty writings earned her a place in the Dictionary of National Biography, *wrote the following letter in the year she died, at the age of eight.*

My Dear Mother,

You will think that I entirely forgot you, but I assure you that you are greatly mistaken. I think of you always and often sigh to think of the distance between us two loving creatures of nature. We have regular hours for all our occupations, first at 7 o'clock we go to the dancing and come home at 8, we then read our Bible and get our repeating and then play till ten then we get our music till 11 when we get our writing and accounts we sew from 12 till 1, after which I get my gramer and then work till five. At 7 we come and knit till 8 when we don't go to the dancing. This is an exact description. I must take a hasty farewell to her whom I love, reverence and doat on, and who I hope thinks the same of

MARJORY FLEMING

P.S. – An old pack of cards would be very exeptible.

In the words of Mark Twain, Marjory Fleming was 'made out of thunder-storms and sunshine, and not even her little perfunctory pieties and shop-made holinesses could squelch her spirits or put out her fires for long. Under pressure of a pestering sense of duty she heaves a shovelful of trade godliness into her journals every little while, but it does not offend, for none of it is her own: it is all borrowed, it is a convention, and custom of her environment, it is the most innocent of hypocrisies; and this tainted butter of hers soon gets to be as delicious to the reader as are the stunning and

*worldly sincerities she splatters around it every time her pen takes
a fresh breath.'*

Chilling memories from the great Russian ballerina Karsavina.

At this time I was rather afraid of Mother. It appears that, when I
was quite small, I used to have terrible fits of screaming. I choked
and went blue in the face. It usually happened in the morning at
dressing time. When my screams reached Mother's ears, she
summoned me; and Nannie reluctantly took me to her room.
Mother dipped a big sponge in cold water and squeezed it on my
naked body. The sudden shock cut my screams at once. Mother
used to describe afterwards how I stopped with a gasp in the
middle of a word.

Mother often said her love for her children was 'rational'. I
remember her stern at times and never foolish and tender. She had
a way of checking my effusions, and these checks made me doubly
timid, and were at the bottom of my occasional outbursts of
childish revolt against her. In time, however, I realized that she
would stop before no sacrifice for our sakes. Deep in my heart
there was a great admiration and pride for her. I liked watching
her dress to go out. She had a very small waist and tiny feet, of
which she was proud. I had ambitious schemes for her. 'When I
grow big I will build a grand house for Mother,' I often used to
say. When offended, I hid under a bed or a table and snapped out
repeatedly: 'I won't build you a house.' Mother's quiet answer,
'And who, if you please, wants your house?' sobered me at once. It
was like another cold douche to me.

THEATRE STREET *by Tamara Karsavina (1885–1978)*

Honoured Mother, I wish you would write to Caperny Cray to
send me my poney, and my books; and I wish that you would
come and see me as soon as possible, and bring me some candied
lemon, and figs, and cakes, and write to my Father to tell him to
send home some Sweet meats, for your dutyful son, Thomas Love
Peacock.   *Letter from the seven-year-old Peacock (1785–1866)*

CONSTANCE: Grief fills the room up of my absent child,
Lies in his bed, walks up and down with me,
Puts on his pretty looks, repeats his words,
Remembers me of all his gracious parts,
Stuffs out his vacant garments with his form;
Then have I reason to be fond of grief.
Fare you well; had you such a loss as I,
I could give better comfort than you do.
O Lord! my boy, my Arthur, my fair son!
My life, my joy, my food, my all the world!
My widow-comfort, and my sorrow's cure!

KING JOHN *by William Shakespeare (1564–1616)*

I was still young enough then to be sleeping with my Mother, which to me seemed life's whole purpose. We slept together in the first-floor bedroom on a flock-filled mattress in a bed of brass rods and curtains. Alone, at that time, of all the family, I was her chosen dream companion, chosen from all for her extra love; my right, so it seemed to me.

So in the ample night and the thickness of her hair I consumed my fattened sleep, drowsed and nuzzling to her warmth of flesh, blessed by her bed and safety. From the width of the house and the separation of the day, we two then lay joined alone. That darkness to me was like the fruit of sloes, heavy and ripe to the touch. It was a darkness of bliss and simple langour, when all edges seemed rounded, apt and fitting; and the presence for whom one had moaned and hungered was found not to have fled after all.

My Mother, freed from her noisy day, would sleep like a happy child, humped in her nightdress, breathing innocently and making soft drinking sounds in the pillow. In her flights of dream she held me close, like a parachute to her back; or rolled and enclosed me with her great tired body so that I was snug as a mouse in a hayrick.

They were deep and jealous, those wordless nights, as we curled and muttered together, like a secret I held through the waking day which set me above all others. It was for me alone that the night came down, for me the prince of her darkness, when only I would know the huge helplessness of her sleep, her dead face, and her blind bare arms. At dawn, when she rose and stumbled back to the kitchen, even then I was not wholly deserted, but rolled into the valley her sleep had left, lay deep in its smell of lavender, deep on my face to sleep again in the nest she had made my own.

The sharing of her bed at that three-year-old time I expected to last for ever. I had never known, or could not recall, any night spent away from her. But I was growing fast; I was no longer the baby; brother Tony lay in wait in his cot. When I heard the first whispers of moving me to the boys' room, I simply couldn't believe it. Surely my Mother would never agree? How could she face night without me?

My sisters began by soothing and flattering; they said, 'You're a grown big man.' 'You'll be sleeping with Harold and Jack,' they said. 'Now what d'you think of that?' What was I supposed to think? – to me it seemed outrageous. I affected a brainstorm and won a few extra nights, my last nights in that downy bed. Then the girls changed their tune: 'It'll only be for a bit. You can come back to Mum later on.' I didn't quite believe them, but Mother was silent, so I gave up the struggle and went.

I was never recalled to my Mother's bed again. It was my first betrayal, my first dose of ageing hardness, my first lesson in the gentle, merciless rejection of women. Nothing more was said, and I accepted it. I grew a little tougher, a little colder, and turned my attention more towards the outside world, which by now was emerging visibly through the mist....

CIDER WITH ROSIE *by Laurie Lee*

A poem written for one of the characters from the young Brontës' fantasy sagas.

Song to A. A.

This shall be thy lullaby
Rocking on the stormy sea,
Though it roar in thunder wild
Sleep, stilly sleep, my dark haired child.

When our shuddering boat was crossing
Elderno lake so rudely tossing
Then 'twas first my nursling smiled;
Sleep, softly sleep, my fair browed child.

Waves about thy cradle break,
Foamy tears are on thy cheek,
Yet the Ocean's self grows mild
When it bears my slumbering child.

Emily Brontë (1818–48)

Julia Strachey (1901–79) spent the early years of her life in India.

In the gruelling Indian heat and dazzling light, my mother, an unusually pretty girl of twenty-two or so, went around looking like some kind of wonderful half-butterfly, half-multi-coloured flower, with her swirling skirts of muslin figured with patterns of immense roses or hibiscus blossoms coloured brilliant pink or cinnamon, and with the dress-hems lavishly befrilled and flounced; while the whole package, so to speak, with my mother folded into the centre, was tied up and drawn very very tight half-way up, to make an elegant insect waist, around which would be twisted pink or blue or apple-green silk sashes, the long ends of which were left floating and rippling out behind, as was then the fashion. Being in love, I was totally involved in every smallest detail of my mother's *charisma*. An important part of my day was spent watching the techniques that she practised in front of the dressing-table looking-glass in the bedroom we shared, and which helped her gain such triumphant results. I would watch wide-eyed and entranced in the early morning – or in the evening if she was going out to dine – as she dressed herself, and performed her toilet, rolling up her long yellow hair into multitudes of shiny 'snail-shells' as we called them, and pinning these all up on to the crest of her upswept 'hair-do' in a gold coronet.

In the daytime, however, my mother's chief glory was her white lace parasol, flounced all over and ornamented with sundry ribbon bows; it bestowed an ethereal air upon her in my eyes, so that I verily considered she resembled the Fairy Queen herself. No less! The Fairy Queen, I should explain, was the *only* celestial or extra-terrestrial being I had ever heard tell of; for my father, a Militant Atheist if ever there was one, never permitted the words 'God', 'Jesus Christ', 'Virgin Mary' or 'Holy Ghost' to sully his lips. His conscience did not consider it permissible for these corrupt illusions to be so much as *mentioned* in the presence of an innocent child such as myself. Nevertheless, following the tendency shown by the human species to communicate in moments of emotion with some all-powerful, unseen but Gracious Divinities, I would often confide certain strong feelings in my private heart to this same Fairy Queen, sometimes thanking her warmly for delights which she had obviously provided just for me – such as sending a cloud of coloured fireflies to spangle the night-air around my head as I stood on the edge of the verandah at bedtime.   JULIA: *A Portrait by Herself and Frances Partridge*

The Sick Child

CHILD O Mother, lay your hand on my brow!
    O mother, mother, where am I now?
    Why is the room so gaunt and great?
    Why am I lying awake so late?

MOTHER Fear not at all: the night is still.
    Nothing is here that means you ill –
    Nothing but lamps the whole town through,
    And never a child awake but you.

CHILD Mother, mother, speak low in my ear,
    Some of the things are so great and near,
    Some are so small and far away,
    I have a fear that I cannot say.
    What have I done, and what do I fear,
    And why are you crying, mother dear?

MOTHER Out in the city, sounds begin.
Thank the kind God, the carts come in!
An hour or two more, and God is so kind,
The day shall be blue in the window blind,
Then shall my child go sweetly asleep,
And dream of the birds and the hills of sheep.

Robert Louis Stevenson (1850–94)

My mother, Mme Henriette Gagnon, was a charming woman and I was in love with my mother.

I must hurriedly add that I lost her when I was seven.

When I loved her at about the age of six, in 1789, I showed exactly the same characteristics as in 1828 when I was madly in love with Alberthe de Rubempré. My way of pursuing happiness was basically unchanged; there was just this difference: I was, as regards the physical side of love, just as Caesar would be, if he came back into the world, as regards the use of cannon and small arms. I would have learned very quickly, and my tactics would have remained basically the same.

I wanted to cover my mother with kisses, and without any clothes on. She loved me passionately and often kissed me; I returned her kisses with such fervour that she was often forced to go away. I abhorred my father when he came to interrupt our kisses. I always wanted to kiss her bosom. Please be kind enough to remember that I lost her in childbed when I was barely seven.

She was plump, with a faultlessly fresh complexion, she was very pretty, and I think just not quite tall enough. Her features expressed nobility and utter serenity; she was very lively, preferring to run about and do things for herself rather than give orders to her three maids, and she was fond of reading Dante's *Divine Comedy* in the original. Long afterwards I found five or six copies in different editions in her room, which had remained shut up since her death.

She died in the flower of her youth and beauty in 1790; she must have been twenty-eight or thirty.

That was when the life of my mind began.

My Aunt Séraphie dared to reproach me for not shedding enough tears. You can imagine my grief and what I was feeling! But it seemed to me that I was going to see her next day; I did not understand death.

Thus, forty-five years ago, I lost the being I loved best in the whole world.

She cannot be offended because I am taking the liberty of revealing the love I had for her; if ever I meet her again, I shall tell her about it once more. Besides, she never took any part in this love. She did not behave in the Venetian way like Mme Benzoni with the author of *Nella*. As for me, I was as criminal as possible, I was passionately in love with her charms.

THE LIFE OF HENRI BRULARD *by Stendhal*

William Cowper (1731–1800) laments his mother, who died when he was six.

Where once we dwelt our name is heard no more,
Children not thine have trod my nurs'ry floor;
And where the gard'ner Robin, day by day,
Drew me to school along the public way,
Delighted with my bauble coach, and wrapt
In scarlet mantle warm, and velvet capt,
'Tis now become a history little known,
That once we call'd the past'ral house our own.
Short-liv'd possession! but the record fair
That mem'ry keeps of all thy kindness there,
Still outlives many a storm that has effac'd
A thousand other themes less deeply trac'd.
Thy nightly visits to my chamber made,
That thou might'st know me safe and warmly laid;
Thy morning bounties ere I left my home,
The biscuit, or confectionary plum;
The fragrant waters on my cheeks bestow'd
By thy own hand, till fresh they shone and glow'd:
All this, and more endearing still than all,

Thy constant flow of love, that knew no fall,
Ne'er roughen'd by those cataracts and breaks,
That humour interpos'd too often makes;
All this still legible in mem'ry's page,
And still to be so, to my latest age,
Adds joy to duty, makes me glad to pay
Such honours to thee as my numbers may;
Perhaps a frail memorial, but sincere,
Not scorn'd in heav'n, though little notic'd here.
Could Time, his flight revers'd, restore the hours
When, playing with thy vesture's tissued flow'rs –
The violet, the pink, and jassamine –
I prick'd them into paper with a pin,
(And thou wast happier than myself the while,
Would'st softly speak, and stroke my head, and smile)
Could those few pleasant hours again appear,
Might one wish bring them, would I wish them here?
I would not trust my heart – the dear delight
Seems so to be desir'd, perhaps I might. –
But no: – what here we call our life is such,
So little to be lov'd, and thou so much,
That I should ill requite thee to constrain
Thy unbound spirit into bonds again.

from 'On Receipt of my Mother's Picture out of Norfolk'

Lady Hester Stanhope (1776–1839) is shocked at the indulgence shown by Princess Caroline towards her adopted son William Austin, who, she disapprovingly recalls in her memoirs, was dangled over the dining-table, snatching food from the guests' plates and knocking over their wine glasses in the process.

Once he cried for a spider on the ceiling, and, though they gave him all sorts of playthings to divert his attention, he would have nothing but the spider. Then there was such a calling of footmen, and long sticks, and such a to-do ... The P[rince]ss used to say to Mr Pitt, 'Don't you think he is a nice boy?' To which Pitt would reply, 'I don't understand anything about children.'

My first clear memory of my mother is of her winning the Married Ladies' race at some picnic in a crowded field. She was wearing a white blouse, a long black skirt, with a narrow-waisted black belt, and a huge picture hat. I was three. We were often at these picnics, travelling to the country by special train, the children with tin mugs hung round their necks by ribbon, and you got milk or tea, and sandwiches and cakes that weren't made by your mother. There was great cheering when she came skipping up the straight but I thought it was nothing out of the ordinary, since I knew she could do everything. Her prize was a sewing outfit in a yellow velvet case with embroidered flowers. This was such a treasure it was never used, but she would sometimes take it out and show it to me as a special treat.

Because I remember most of all some of the difficulties there were when she was old, it is pleasant to think back on her amazing agility. George came home once from school – he would have been about eight – claiming that a girl in his class, at playtime, had 'stotted' (bounced) a ball a hundred times. 'A hundred times!' mother exclaimed. 'That's nothing. Get me a ball!' We handed it over, and she stotted it two hundred times, which was more than I could count at the time. Of course there simply couldn't be anybody else's mother who could do this. Or who would even try.

Her great feat, however, was swinging the can full of water. We had this can, a receptacle of chipped blue enamel, which was used when we were sent for extra milk. When she was in the mood she could readily be persuaded to swing it round her head, half full of water, without spilling a drop. Then we would cry 'More water'. She would fill it three-quarters full, and swing away with centrifugal violence. The excitement was intense, as by this time the fevers of performance were in the air, and 'More still' we would demand. 'Make it full.' So, with the old jug brimming, she would set off again, while we watched the miracle.

'My Mother' by Alastair Dunnett (1908–   )

Ma was a tall woman who will forever for me wear long black gloves up to her elbows. On the night of the commercial travellers' ball she and my father would come into my room and cuddle me. Even now as I write this there's a sense of unbearable loss. They would have party hats on and the next morning we would wear them. Long black gloves wrapped round me, sequins from her dress sticking sideways into my cheeks. I curled her hair round and round my fingers. It was springy and my finger would go through the empty hollow of the curl. In my other hand, pressed to my nose, would be a ragged piece of cardigan that lulled me to sleep. I imagine the perfume but I remember the lipstick on her teeth. I remember her applying the lipstick and moving close to the mirror. She would press her lips together, sucking them back behind her teeth and rolling them sideways to get an even distribution of the rouge. There would be lipstick on the tea cups. Lipstick, gloves and sequins: not a bad memory of your mother. Later, visiting her grave, we would kneel on the ground and the tiny pieces of stone cut into my knee leaving the same mark as the sequins had on my cheek.

Is THAT IT? *by Bob Geldof (1954–)*

4

DISCOVERIES

Animula

'Issues from the hand of God, the simple soul'
To a flat world of changing lights and noise,
To light, dark, dry or damp, chilly or warm;
Moving between the legs of tables and of chairs,
Rising or falling, grasping at kisses and toys,
Advancing boldly, sudden to take alarm,
Retreating to the corner of arm and knee,
Eager to be reassured, taking pleasure
In the fragrant brilliance of the Christmas tree,
Pleasure in the wind, the sunlight and the sea;
Studies the sunlit pattern on the floor
And running stags around a silver tray;
Confounds the actual and the fanciful,
Content with playing-cards and kings and queens,
What the fairies do and what the servants say.
The heavy burden of the growing soul
Perplexes and offends more, day by day;
Week by week, offends and perplexes more
With the imperatives of 'is and seems'
And may and may not, desire and control.
The pain of living and the drug of dreams
Curl up the small soul in the window seat
Behind the *Encyclopaedia Britannica*.
Issues from the hand of time the simple soul
Irresolute and selfish, misshapen, lame,
Fearing the warm reality, the offered good,
Denying the importunity of the blood,
Shadow of its own shadows, spectre in its own gloom,
Leaving disordered papers in a dusty room;
Living first in the silence after the viaticum. . . .

T. S. Eliot (1888–1965)

52

A Child . . . is a Man in a small letter, yet the best copy of Adam before he tasted of Eve or the apple; and he is happy whose small practice in the world can only write this Character. He is nature's fresh picture newly drawn in oil, which time, and much handling, dims and defaces. His soul is yet a white paper unscribbled with observations of the world, wherewith, at length, it becomes a blurred notebook. He is purely happy, because he knows no evil, nor hath made means by sin to be acquainted with misery. He arrives not at the mischief of being wise, nor endures evils to come, by foreseeing them. He kisses and loves all, and, when the smart of the rod is past, smiles on his beater. Nature and his parents alike dandle him, and 'tice him on with a bait of sugar to a draught of wormwood. He plays yet, like a young prentice the first day, and is not come to his task of melancholy. His hardest labour is his tongue, as if he were loath to use so deceitful an organ; and he is best company with it when he can but prattle. We laugh at his foolish sports, but his game is our earnest; and his drums, rattles, and hobby-horses but the emblems and mocking of men's business. His father hath writ him as his own little story, wherein he reads those days of his life that he cannot remember, and sighs to see what innocence he has out-lived. The elder he grows, he is a stair lower from God; and, like his first father, much worse in his breeches. He is the Christian's example, and the old man's relapse; the one imitates his pureness, and the other falls into his simplicity. Could he put off his body with his little coat, he had got eternity without a burthen, and exchanged but one Heaven for another.

MICROCOSMOGRAPHIE *by John Earle, Bishop of Salisbury (? 1601–65)*

Manners at Table when away from Home

Little children, here ye may lere [learn],
Much courtesy that is written here.

Look thine hands be washen clean,
That no filth in thy nails be seen.

Take thou no meat till grace be said
And till thou see all things arrayed.
Look, my son, that thou not sit
Till the ruler of the house thee bid.
And at thy meat, in the beginning,
Look on poor men that thou think:
For the full stomach ever fails
To understand what the hungry ails.
Eat not thy meat too hastily,
Abide and eat easily.
Carve not thy bread too thin,
Nor break it not in twain:
The morsels that thou beginnest to touch
Cast them not in thy pouch.
Put not thy fingers in thy dish,
Neither in flesh, neither in fish;
Put not thy meat into the salt
(Into thy cellar that thy salt halt [holds])
But lay it fair on thy trencher
Before thee, that is honour.

Bite not thy meat, but carve it clean:
Be well ware no drop be seen.
When thou eatest gape not too wide,
That thy mouth be seen on every side.
And son, be ware, I rede [advise], of one thing,
Blow neither in thy meat nor in thy drink.

And cast not thy bones unto the floor,
But lay them fair on thy trencher.
Keep clean thy cloth before all
And sit thou still, whatso befall,
Till grace be said unto the end,
And till thou have washen with thy friend.
And spit not in thy basin,
My sweet son, that thou washest in;
And arise up soft and still,

And jangle neither with Jack nor Jill,
But take thy leave of thy host lowly,
And thank him with thine heart highly.
Then men will say thereafter
That 'A gentleman was here'.

Anon c. 1480

My dealings with literature go back, I suppose, some thirty and three years. We came together thus, literature and I. It was in a kitchen at midday, and I was waiting for my dinner, hungry and clean, in a tartan frock with a pinafore over it. I had washed my own face, and dried it, and I remember that my eyes smarted with lingering soap, and my skin was drawn by the evaporation of moisture on a cold day. I held in my hand a single leaf which had escaped from a printed book. How it came into that chubby fist I cannot recall. The reminiscence begins with it already there. I gazed hard at the paper, and pretended with all my powers to be completely absorbed in its contents; I pretended to ignore someone who was rattling saucepans at the kitchen range. On my left a very long and mysterious passage led to a pawnshop all full of black bundles. I heard my brother crying at the other end of the passage, and his noisy naughtiness offended me. For myself, I felt excessively 'good' with my paper; never since have I been so filled with the sense of perfect righteousness. Here was I, clean, quiet, sedate, studious; and there was my brother, the illiterate young Hooligan, disturbing the sacrosanct shop, and – what was worse – ignorant of his inferiority to me. Disgusted with him, I passed through the kitchen into another shop on the right, still conning the page with soapy, smarting eyes. At this point the light of memory is switched off. The printed matter, which sprang out of nothingness, vanishes back into the same.

THE TRUTH ABOUT AN AUTHOR *by Arnold Bennett (1867–1931)*

I can vividly remember the pleasure I derived from the Nursery History of England, illustrated by that happily still flourishing artist, George Morrow, and, a little later, from the works of Edmund Dulac.

To the enjoyment of the pictures, appreciation of the text was soon added, as thanks to the brilliant educational methods of my mother I learned to read at a very tender age. Her system, simple as it was effective, was based on a chocolate alphabet. This was spread out twice a week on the dining-room table and such letters as I recognized I was allowed to eat; later, when my knowledge of the alphabet was faultless, I was entitled to such letters as I could form into a new word. Although never strong in arithmetic I soon grasped the simple fact that the longer the word the more the chocolate, and by the time I could spell 'suffragette' without an error this branch of my education was deemed complete and a tendency to biliousness had become increasingly apparent.

ALL DONE FROM MEMORY *by Osbert Lancaster*

Though I have asked many of my acquaintances at what stage in their childhood or adolescence they became class-conscious none has ever given me a satisfactory answer. I remember how it happened to me. At the age of four and a half I caught scarlet fever; my younger brother had just been born, and I could not be nursed at home, so my parents sent me off to a public fever hospital. The ward contained twenty little proletarians, and only one bourgeois child besides myself. I did not notice particularly that the nurses and my fellow-patients had a different attitude towards me; I accepted the kindness and spoiling easily, being accustomed to it. But the respect and even reverence given to this other little boy, a clergyman's child, astonished me. 'Oh,' the nurses would cry after he had gone, 'oh, he did look a little gentleman in his pretty white pelisse when they took him away!' 'That young Matthew was a fair toff,' echoed the little pro-letarians. On my return from two months in hospital, my accent was deplored, and I learned that the boys in the ward had been very vulgar. I did not know what 'vulgar' meant; it had to be explained to me. About a year later I met Arthur, a boy of nine, who had been in the ward and taught me how to play cricket when we were convalescent together. He turned out to be a ragged errand-boy. In hospital, we had all worn the same institutional night-gowns, and I did not know that we came off such different shelves. But I suddenly realized with my first shudder of gentility that two sorts of Christians existed – ourselves, and the lower classes. GOODBYE TO ALL THAT *by Robert Graves*

The great wood engraver Thomas Bewick (1753–1828) at an early stage in his career.

I was for some time kept at reading, writing, and figures – how long, I know not, but I know that as soon as my question was done upon my slate, I spent as much time as I could find in filling with my pencil all the unoccupied spaces, with representations of such objects as struck my fancy; and these were rubbed out, for fear of a beating, before my question was given in. As soon as I reached fractions, decimals, etc., I was put to learn Latin, and in this I was for some time complimented by my master for the great progress I was making; but, as I never knew for what purpose I had to learn it, and was wearied out with getting off long tasks, I rather flagged in this department of my education, and the margins of my books, and every space of spare and blank paper, became filled with various kinds of devices or scenes I had met with; and these were often accompanied with wretched rhymes explanatory of them. As soon as I filled all the blank spaces in my books, I had recourse, at all spare times, to the gravestones and the floor of the church porch, with a bit of chalk, to give vent to this propensity of mind of figuring whatever I had seen. At that time I had never heard of the word 'drawing'; nor did I know of any other paintings beside the king's arms in the church, and the signs in Ovingham of the Black Bull, the White Horse, the Salmon, and the Hounds and Hare. I always thought I could make a far better hunting scene than the latter: the others were beyond my hand. I remember one of my master overlooking me while I was very busy with my chalk in the porch, and of his putting me very greatly to the blush by ridiculing and calling me a conjuror. My father, also, found a deal of fault for 'mis-spending my time in such idle pursuits'; but my propensity for drawing was so rooted that nothing could deter me from persevering in it; and many of my evenings at home were spent in filling the flags of the floor and the hearth-stone with my chalky designs.

After I had long scorched my face in this way, a friend, in compassion, furnished me with some paper upon which to execute my designs. Here I had more scope. Pen and ink, and the juice of the brambleberry, made a grand change. These were succeeded by a camel-hair pencil and shells of colours; and, thus supplied, I became completely set up; but of patterns, or draw-ings, I had none. The beasts and birds which enlivened the beauti-ful scenery of woods and wilds surrounding ms native hamlet, furnished me with an endless supply of subjects. I now, in the estimation of my rustic neighbours, became an eminent painter, and the walls of their houses were ornamented with an abundance of my rude productions, at a very cheap rate. These chiefly con-sisted of particular hunting scenes, in which the portraits of the hunters, the horses, and of every dog in the pack, were, in their opinion, *as well as my own*, faithfully delineated.

A MEMOIR OF THOMAS BEWICK *by Himself*

The following daydream was doomed to remain unsatisfied. Gwen Raverat, nevertheless, grew up to become a distinguished wood engraver in her own right.

It was here, at No. 31 [Kensington Square], that I discovered Bewick, one afternoon while Aunt Etty was having her rest. I remember lying on the sofa between the dining-room windows with the peacock blue serge curtains, and wishing passionately that I could have been Mrs Bewick. Of course, I should have liked still more to be Mrs Rembrandt, but that seemed too tremendous even to imagine; whereas it did not seem impossibly outrageous to think of myself as Mrs Bewick. She was English enough, and homely enough, anyhow. Surely, I thought, if I cooked his roast beef beautifully and mended his clothes and minded the children — surely he would, just sometimes, let me draw and engrave a little tailpiece for him. I wouldn't want to be known, I wouldn't sign it.

Only just to be allowed to invent a little picture sometimes. O happy, happy Mrs Bewick! thought I, as I kicked my heels on the blue sofa.

PERIOD PIECE *by Gwen Raverat (1885–1957)*

Another London scene of that time is of Duncan [Grant] standing stark naked in the back bedroom. Coming in by chance, I was amazed at the sight of him; what on earth was this strange appendage hanging between his legs? Seized by embarrassment but devoured by curiosity, I turned my back on him, bent down and, putting my head between my own legs, continued my rapt examination of his anatomy, prompted by the feeling that if I was upside down no one would spot the focus of my attention. Carried away by a smiling Vanessa, I burst into tears.

DECEIVED WITH KINDNESS *by Angelica Garnett (1918–   )*

Christy Brown, helplessly handicapped from birth, recalls a dramatic moment that was to transform his life:

I was now five, and still I showed no real sign of intelligence. I showed no apparent interest in things except with my toes – more especially those of my left foot. Although my natural habits were clean I could not aid myself, but in this respect my father took care of me. I used to lie on my back all the time in the kitchen or, on bright warm days, out in the garden, a little bundle of crooked muscles and twisted nerves, surrounded by a family that loved me and hoped for me and that made me part of their own warmth and humanity. I was lonely, imprisoned in a world of my own, unable to communicate with others, cut off, separated from them as though a glass wall stood between my existence and theirs, thrusting me beyond the sphere of their lives and activities. I longed to run about and play with the rest, but I was unable to break loose from my bondage.

Then, suddenly, it happened! In a moment everything was changed, my future life moulded into a definite shape, my mother's faith in me rewarded and her secret fear changed into open triumph.

It happened so quickly, so simply after all the years of waiting and uncertainty that I can see and feel the whole scene as if it had happened last week. It was the afternoon of a cold, grey December day. The streets outside glistened with snow; the white sparkling flakes stuck and melted on the window-panes and hung on the boughs of the trees like molten silver. The wind howled dismally, whipping up little whirling columns of snow that rose and fell at every fresh gust. And over all, the dull, murky sky stretched like a dark canopy, a vast infinity of greyness.

Inside, all the family were gathered round the big kitchen fire that lit up the little room with a warm glow and made giant shadows dance on the walls and ceiling.

In a corner Mona and Paddy were sitting huddled together, a few torn school primers before them. They were writing down little sums on to an old chipped slate, using a bright piece of yellow chalk. I was close to them, propped up by a few pillows against the wall, watching.

It was the chalk that attracted me so much. It was a long, slender stick of vivid yellow. I had never seen anything like it before, and it showed up so well against the black surface of the slate that I was fascinated by it as much as if it had been a stick of gold.

Suddenly I wanted desperately to do what my sister was doing. Then – without thinking or knowing exactly what I was doing, I reached out and took the stick of chalk out of my sister's hand – *with my left foot.*

I held it tightly between my toes, and, acting on an impulse, made a wild sort of scribble with it on the slate. Next moment I stopped, a bit dazed, surprised, looking down at the stick of yellow chalk stuck between my toes, not knowing what to do with it next, hardly knowing how it got there. Then I looked up and became aware that everyone had stopped talking and was staring at me silently. Nobody stirred. Mona, her black curls framing her chubby little face, stared at me with great big eyes and open mouth. Across the open hearth, his face lit by flames, sat my father, leaning forward, hands outspread on his knees, his shoulders tense. I felt the sweat break out on my forehead.

My mother came in from the pantry with a steaming pot in her hand. She stopped midway between the table and the fire, feeling the tension flowing through the room. She followed their stare and saw me, in the corner. Her eyes looked from my face down to my foot, with the chalk gripped between my toes. She put down the pot.

Then she crossed over to me and knelt down beside me, as she had done so many times before.

'I'll show you what to do with it, Chris,' she said, very slowly and in a queer, jerky way, her face flushed as if with some inner excitement.

Taking another piece of chalk from Mona, she hesitated, then very deliberately drew, on the floor in front of me, *the single letter* '*A*'.

'Copy that,' she said, looking steadily at me. 'Copy it, Christy.'

I couldn't.

I looked about me, looked around at the faces that were turned towards me, tense, excited faces that were at that moment frozen, immobile, eager, waiting for a miracle in their midst.

The stillness was profound. The room was full of flame and shadow that danced before my eyes and lulled my taut nerves into a sort of waking sleep. I could hear the sound of the water-tap dripping in the pantry, the loud ticking of the clock on the mantelshelf, and the soft hiss and crackle of the logs on the open hearth.

I tried again. I put out my foot and made a wild jerking stab with the chalk which produced a very crooked line and nothing more. Mother held the slate steady for me.

'Try again, Chris,' she whispered in my ear. 'Again.'

I did. I stiffened my body and put my left foot out again, for the third time. I drew one side of the letter. I drew half the other side. Then the stick of chalk broke and I was left with a stump. I wanted to fling it away and give up. Then I felt my mother's hand on my shoulder. I tried once more. Out went my foot. I shook, I sweated and strained every muscle. My hands were so tightly clenched that my fingernails bit into the flesh. I set my teeth so hard that I nearly pierced my lower lip. Everything in the room swam till the faces around me were mere patches of white. But – I drew it – *the letter* '*A*'. There it was on the floor before me. Shaky, with awkward, wobbly sides and a very uneven centre line. But it *was* the letter 'A'. I looked up. I saw my mother's face for a moment, tears on her cheeks. Then my father stooped down and hoisted me on to his shoulder.

I had done it! It had started – the thing that was to give my mind its chance of expressing itself. True, I couldn't speak with my lips, but now I would speak through something more lasting than spoken words – written words.

That one letter, scrawled on the floor with a broken bit of yellow chalk gripped between my toes, was my road to a new world, my key to mental freedom.

MY LEFT FOOT *by Christy Brown (1932–81)*

I have no remembrance of the time when I began to learn Greek, I have been told that it was when I was three years old. My earliest recollection on the subject, is that of committing to memory what my father termed vocables, being lists of common Greek words, with their signification in English, which he wrote out for me on cards. Of grammar, until some years later, I learnt no more than the inflexions of the nouns and verbs, but, after a course of vocables, proceeded at once to translation; and I faintly remember going through Aesop's *Fables*, the first Greek book which I read. The *Anabasis*, which I remember better, was the second. I learnt no Latin until my eighth year. At that time I had read, under my father's tuition, a number of Greek prose authors, among whom I remember the whole of Herodotus, and of Xenophon's *Cyropaedia* and *Memorials* of Socrates; some of the lives of the philosophers by Diogenes Laertius; part of Lucian, and Isocrates *ad Demonicum* and *ad Nicoclem*. I also read, in 1813, the first six dialogues (in the common arrangement) of Plato, from the *Euthyphron* to the *Theaetetus* inclusive: which last dialogue, I venture to think, would have been better omitted, as it was totally impossible I should understand it.

AUTOBIOGRAPHY *by John Stuart Mill (1806–73)*

Children look down upon the morning-grey
Tissue of mist that veils a valley's lap:
Their fingers itch to tear it and unwrap
The flags, the roundabouts, the gala day.
They watch the spring rise inexhaustibly –
A breathing thread out of the eddied sand,
Sufficient to their day: but half their mind
Is on the sailed and glittering estuary.
Fondly we wish their mist might never break,
Knowing it hides so much that best were hidden:
We'd chain them by the spring, lest it should broaden
For them into a quicksand and a wreck.
But they slip through our fingers like the source,
Like mist, like time that has flagged out their course.

from 'O Dreams, O Destinations' by C. Day Lewis (1904–72)

Margaret had wanted a girl, by way of variety, and was disappointed in the birth of a son. But with her usual felicity – without a thought of what the consequences might be – she soon tumbled to the idea that, if she allowed his hair to grow long and dressed him as a girl, she could satisfy her ambition; provided she never looked too closely at him in the bath.

The burden of supporting, however feebly, a male role in a cast where all the players were female (or female impersonators) was too much for me; and from this time I began to wish that I were a girl. I demanded that I should be changed into one. That was the right word to use since, with John's example before my eyes and ignorant of biological differences, it was clearly only a matter of changing one's clothes. They told me, giggling, there was a little more to it than that; and since they offered me no further explanation I determined to find out for myself. . . .

I was unlucky enough to begin my scientific experiments on a royal and public occasion; and it ended in disaster and disgrace. The Lawns, at Hove, were opened at Easter and that parade was always the most important of the year. Edward VII, who often relaxed with his friend Sassoon in his house at the bottom of First Avenue, was then in Hove and well aware that the ladies would be

wearing their new bonnets. He determined to survey them in all
their glory. My mother, Daisy and Hermione, dressed to the
nines, expectantly awaited a royal glance; and my mother felt it
was time I should make my bow. I was not in the right mood for it.
My pink satin suit was a burden to me as I was not allowed to get
it dirty, and the King kept us waiting too long for my patience. At
last Hermione, a malicious young woman, wanting to get rid of
me, advised me to go and play with a little girl in a neighbouring
group. Here was my opportunity, and I did not hesitate to take it.

I had already spied that tiny beauty, smaller even than I, but
dressed in a much more fetching way: ribbons in her hair, a white
frock like a ballet dancer's, and the most exciting frills above –
and below. Now was the time, I thought in my folly, to see if there
was any real difference between us. I sprang upon her but she was
not a passive victim. As I struggled to remove that stiff frock she
got in several blows and a nasty scratch. I found it easier after I
had thrown her to the ground. Pulling off her skirt I had begun, so
to speak, on the second layer, when the crowd drew back and the
King's party advanced upon us. We were hurriedly separated by
those in charge of us; and I have heard since that accusations and
recriminations were furiously exchanged between them. Naturally, I came in for my fair share of reproving and rebuking, but
oddly enough more on the grounds of *lèse majesté* than attempted
rape. The King himself could not have failed to have caught two of
his loyal subjects *in flagrante delicto*; but he would more likely
have laughed than frowned. For the next week I had to go every
day to the end of the Drive, and take off my cap to the statue of his
mother.

A STRACHEY CHILD *by Richard Strachey (1902–76)*

When I was a little boy I detested music. The playing of the piano,
or the voice of a trained (which means overtrained) singer, drove
me frantic.

One night I awoke in a Belgian town, and heard voices singing
and a band playing. They were rough voices, and they were
roaring with all their might a song whose vitality and glorious
rhythm made me sit up in bed to listen instead of stopping my

ears. The longer I listened the more amazed I became that such an effect could be created by music. When the tune was repeated I longed to fix it in my memory; in fact, I wanted to jump out of bed and follow the crowd, adding my own little voice to the magnificent uproar. The music came nearer, until it seemed to be under my window. Unable to control my excitement I called out for my father, who was in the next room.

'What is that tune?' I asked.

'That,' said my father, 'is called the Marseillaise. It is the finest song ever written.'

And he went over to the window and joined in the singing, beating time with his arm.

'Europe,' he said, 'was remade to that tune.'

Of all my memories of music that remains the most vivid. It is through the window of that room in Belgium that I look at the young French officer as he plays his new song to Mayor Dietrich in the drawing-room at Strasbourg; at Mireur, singing it at Montpellier; at the men of Marseilles shouting it as they drag their guns in the blazing heat along the dusty road to Paris. Through that window, and into the darkened room, come the voices of 10th August, with the tocsin singing; all the noise of the streets. I am still sitting up in the bed, trembling with excitement, when Dumouriez sings it by the Haine, and Hoche at Wissembourg, and the young Napoleon himself on the way to Italy.

What a song!

'The Marseillaise' by J. B. Morton (1893–1979)

It is curious to observe the ideas of infants. One of my aunts taking me from Mountsorrel to Swithland, entered a house at the skirts of the town, where I saw several men rather noisy, and could not conceive they were of the family. I observed also the shelves abound with crockery-ware, and could not imagine the use. The woman of the house took us into a back room, where she and my aunt seemed very familiar.

We passed on without resting; and my aunt, during this little journey, fell down, perhaps, twenty times, and generally at a stile; often lay a minute or two, and bade me look if any person was coming. I answered, 'No,' but the answer was needless; for I was scarcely able to look over a blade of grass. No damage ensued, except my being terrified.

Many years elapsed before I could unravel this mystery, which was no more than my aunt entering a public house. The crocks were the drinking cups; and, in the private room, she got so completely drunk, she could neither stand not walk.

THE HISTORY OF THE LIFE OF WILLIAM HUTTON *by Himself*

The first tutor of whom I retain any distinct memory was a German named Roelin, who used to thrash me and then smother me with caresses so that I should not complain to my father. I always faithfully kept my word to him, but nevertheless the thing was discovered, and the tutor was expelled from the house.

This man had conceived the rather ingenious idea of teaching me Greek by making me invent it for myself. That is to say, he proposed to me that we should together make a language to be used only by ourselves. I took a passionate interest in this idea. We first created an alphabet, into which he introduced Greek letters. Then we began a Dictionary, in which each French word was translated into a Greek one. All this remained in my head marvellously well, since I believed I was its inventor. I already knew a heap of Greek words, and was busy forming general rules for these words of my own creation – that is to say, I was learning Greek grammar – when the tutor was dismissed. I was then five years old.

THE RED NOTEBOOK *by Benjamin Constant (1767–1830)*

Grandson and great-grandson of Presidents of the United States, Henry Adams (1838–1918), historian and philosopher, is himself best remembered for his interpretation of the medieval spirit, Mont St Michel and Chartres, and for his autobiography, from which the following extract is taken. Adams is here describing himself.

He could not have been much more than six years old at the time –
seven at the utmost – and his mother had taken him to Quincy for
a long stay with the President during the summer. What became of
the rest of the family he quite forgot; but he distinctly remembered
standing at the house door one summer morning in a passionate
outburst of rebellion against going to school. Naturally his
mother was the immediate victim of his rage; that is what mothers
are for, and boys also; but in this case the boy had his mother at
unfair disadvantage, for she was a guest, and had no means of
enforcing obedience. Henry showed a certain tactical ability by
refusing to start, and he met all efforts at compulsion by successful, though too vehement protest. He was in fair way to win, and
was holding his own, with sufficient energy, at the bottom of the
long staircase which led up to the door of the President's library,
when the door opened, and the old man slowly came down.
Putting on his hat, he took the boy's hand without a word, and
walked with him, paralysed by awe, up the road to the town. After
the first moments of consternation at this interference in a domestic dispute, the boy reflected that an old gentleman close on eighty
would never trouble himself to walk near a mile on a hot summer
morning over a shadeless road to take a boy to school, and that it
would be strange if a lad imbued with the passion of freedom
could not find a corner to dodge around, somewhere before
reaching the school door. Then and always, the boy insisted that
this reasoning justified his apparent submission; but the old man
did not stop, and the boy saw all his strategical points turned, one
after another, until he found himself seated inside the school, and
obviously the centre of curious if not malevolent criticism. Not till
then did the President release his hand and depart.

The point was that this act, contrary to the inalienable rights of
boys, and nullifying the social compact, ought to have made him
dislike his grandfather for life. He could not recall that it had this
effect even for a moment. With a certain maturity of mind, the
child must have recognized that the President, though a tool of
tyranny, had done his disreputable work with a certain intelligence. He had shown no temper, no irritation, no personal feeling,
and had made no display of force. Above all, he had held his
tongue. During their long walk he had said nothing; he had

uttered no syllable of revolting cant about the duty of obedience and the wickedness of resistance to law; he had shown no concern in the matter; hardly even a consciousness of the boy's existence.

Till his twelfth year, the child passed his summers there, and his pleasures of childhood mostly centred in it. Of education he had as yet little to complain. Country schools were not very serious. Nothing stuck to the mind except home impressions, and the sharpest were those of kindred children; but as influences that warped a mind, none compared with the mere effect of the back of the President's bald head, as he sat in his pew on Sundays, in line with that of President Quincy, who, though some ten years younger, seemed to children about the same age. Before railways entered the New England town, every parish church showed half-a-dozen of these leading citizens, with gray hair, who sat on the main aisle in the best pews, and had sat there, or in some equivalent dignity, since the time of St Augustine, if not since the glacial epoch. It was unusual for boys to sit behind a President grandfather, and to read over his head the tablet in memory of a President great-grandfather, who had 'pledged his life, his fortune, and his sacred honor' to secure the independence of his country and so forth; but boys naturally supposed, without much reasoning, that other boys had the equivalent of President grandfathers, and that churches would always go on, with the bald-headed leading citizens on the main aisle, and Presidents or their equivalents on the walls. The Irish gardener once said to the child: 'You'll be thinkin' you'll be President too!' The casualty of the remark made so strong an impression on his mind that he never forgot it. He could not remember ever to have thought on the subject; to him, that there should be a doubt of his being President was a new idea.

THE EDUCATION OF HENRY ADAMS *by Himself*

SECRET WORLDS

The Merry-Go-Round

Jardin du Luxembourg

With roof and shadow for a while careers
the stud of horses, variously bright,
all from that land that hesitates for quite
a length of time before it disappears.
Several indeed pull carriages, with tight-
held rein, but all have boldness in their bearing;
with them a wicked scarlet lion's faring
and now and then an elephant all white.

Just as in woods, a stag comes into view,
save that it has a saddle and tied fast
thereon a little maiden all in blue.

And on the lion a little boy is going,
whose small hot hands hold on with all his might,
while raging lion's tongue and teeth are showing.

And now and then an elephant all white.

And on the horses they come riding past,
girls too, bright-skirted, whom the horse-jumps here
scarce now preoccupy: in full career
elsewhither, hitherwards, a glance they cast –

And now and then an elephant all white.

And this keeps passing by until it's ended,
and hastens aimlessly until it's done.

A red, a green, a grey is apprehended,
a little profile, scarcely yet begun. –
And now and then a smile, for us intended,
blissfully happy, dazzlingly expended
upon this breathless, blindly followed fun . . .

Rainer Maria Rilke (1875–1926)
Trs. J. B. Leishman

Arley, the Strawberry Hill Gothic home of his grandparents over-looking the Severn, was a strong imaginative force in Lord Berners' childhood. One enchantment was the Ice-house:

In the days before the general use of artificial ice, the frozen surface of one of the pools would be broken up every winter and stored away in a circular, semi-underground chamber covered with a thick layer of bracken. Once or twice, as a special treat, I was allowed to have the door of the Ice-house opened so that I might peer into the chilly depths, where the ice we had skated upon lay slumbering in its bracken nest until the time when it should emerge once more to cool our drinks and provide us with sherbets and ices.

But it was in the house itself that he found the object of greatest fascination:

. . . a tall folding screen of brightly coloured pictures cut out and pasted on at random, the joint handiwork of my mother and her sisters who, between them, must have mutilated a whole library of illustrated books and coloured prints in the course of its construction.

Under a transparent layer of yellow varnish there lay an entrancing world of flowers, birds and landscapes all jumbled together in kaleidoscopic confusion. Here you could see 'Doves of Siam, Lima mice and legless Birds of Paradise' and countless other things as well. Views of Italian lakes and towns were framed in sprays of orchids. Against a background of Swiss mountains, chamois and chalets, glittering humming-birds thrust their rapier-like beaks into the calyxes of tropical flowers. A gigantic green and crimson parakeet appeared to have alighted on the spire of Cologne cathedral, whilst a company of mediaeval knights on richly caparisoned horses caracoled in front of the Sphinx and the Pyramids. The whole thing was without rhyme or reason, but it conjured up a magical vision of some fantastic fairy paradise and, whenever I got a chance, I would creep into the drawing-room and remain before this screen in rapt attention, vainly endeavouring to memorize the innumerable objects depicted on it.

Such was the impression the screen made upon me in my early childhood. But when, many years afterwards, I came upon it again, stored away in a lumber room whither the purist taste of a later age had banished it, I was amazed to find that it was composed for the most part of political caricatures and sporting scenes. The well-remembered continental landscapes, the exotic birds and tropical flowers formed but a comparatively small portion of the whole. Neither did they, as one might suppose, feature more especially in the lower panels of the screen which, in those days, would have lain within my natural range of vision. In fact, in order to get at some of them I must have been obliged to stand on a chair.

The discovery was a surprising one, and it would seem to prove that at the time when the screen aroused my infantile enthusiasm, an inborn selective force must have already been at work, concentrating on certain things and excluding others, a selective force which continued to function in spite of the strenuous efforts of parents, nurses, governesses and schoolmasters to divert its activity into channels more favoured by themselves.

FIRST CHILDHOOD *by Lord Berners (1883–1950)*

Very, very early in my boyhood I had acquired the habit of going about alone to amuse myself in my own way, and it was only after years, when my age was about twelve, that my mother told me how anxious this singularity in me used to make her. She would miss me when looking out to see what the children were doing, and I would be called and searched for, to be found hidden away somewhere in the plantation. Then she began to keep an eye on me, and when I was observed stealing off she would secretly follow and watch me, standing motionless among the tall weeds or under the trees by the half-hour, staring at vacancy. This distressed her very much; then to her great relief and joy she discovered that I was there with a motive which she could understand and appreciate: that I was watching some living thing, an insect perhaps, but oftener a bird – a pair of little scarlet flycatchers building a nest of lichen on a peach tree, or some such beautiful thing. And as she loved all living things herself she was quite satisfied that I was not going queer in my head, for that was what she had been fearing.

FAR AWAY AND LONG AGO *by W. H. Hudson (1841–1922)*

Children's Song

We live in our own world,
A world that is too small
For you to stoop and enter
Even on hands and knees,
The adult subterfuge.
And though you probe and pry
With analytic eye,
And eavesdrop all our talk
With an amused look,
You cannot find the centre
Where we dance, where we play,
Where life is still asleep
Under the closed flower,
Under the smooth shell
Of eggs in the cupped nest
That mock the faded blue
Of your remoter heaven.

R. S. Thomas (1913–   )

All children want to crouch in their secret nests. I loved the fork of a beech tree at the head of our lane, the close thicket of a boxwood hedge in the front of the house, the soft, collapsing pile of hay in a back corner of the byre; but especially I spent time in the throat of an old willow tree at the end of the farmyard. It was a hollow tree, with gnarled, spreading roots, a soft, perishing bark and a pithy inside. Its mouth was like the fat and solid opening in a horse's collar, and, once you squeezed in through it, you were at the heart of a different life, looking out on the familiar yard as if it were suddenly behind a pane of strangeness. Above your head, the living tree flourished and breathed, you shouldered the slightly vibrant bole, and if you put your forehead to the rough pith you felt the whole lithe and whispering crown of willow moving in the sky above you. In that tight cleft, you sensed the embrace of light and branches, you were a little Atlas shouldering it all, a little Cerunnos pivoting a world of antlers.

The world grew. Mossbawn, the first place, widened. There was what we called the Sandy Loaning, a sanded pathway between old hedges leading in off the road, first among fields and then through a small bog, to a remote farmhouse. It was a silky, fragrant world there, and for the first few hundred yards you were safe enough. The sides of the lane were banks of earth topped with broom and ferns, quilted with moss and primroses. Behind the broom, in the rich grass, cattle munched reassuringly. Rabbits occasionally broke cover and ran ahead of you in a flurry of dry sand. There were wrens and goldfinches. But, gradually, those lush and definite fields gave way to scraggy marshland. Birch trees stood up to their pale shins in swamps. The ferns thickened above you. Scuffles in old leaves made you nervous and you dared yourself always to pass the badger's set, a wound of fresh mould in an overgrown ditch where the old brock had gone to earth. Around that badger's hole, there hung a field of dangerous force. This was the realm of bogeys. We'd heard about a mystery man who haunted the fringes of the bog here, we talked about man-keepers and mosscheepers, creatures uncatalogued by any naturalist, but none the less real for that. What was a mosscheeper, anyway, if not the soft, malicious sound the word itself made, a siren of collapsing sibilants coaxing you out towards bog pools lidded with innocent grass, quicksands and quagmires? They were all there and spreading out over a low, birch-screened apron of land towards the shores of Lough Beg.

That was the moss, forbidden ground. Two families lived at the heart of it, and a recluse, called Tom Tipping, whom we never saw, but in the morning on the road to school we watched his smoke rising from a clump of trees, and spoke his name between us until it was synonymous with mystery man, with unexpected scuttlings in the hedge, with footsteps slushing through long grass.   MOSSBAWN *by Seamus Heaney (1939–   )*

To a Child Dancing in the Wind

Dance there upon the shore;
What need have you to care
For wind or water's roar?
And tumble out your hair
That the salt drops have wet;
Being young you have not known
The fool's triumph, nor yet
Love lost as soon as won,
Nor the best labourer dead
And all the sheaves to bind.
What need have you to dread
The monstrous crying of wind?

W. B. Yeats (1865–1939)

The thirteen-year-old Charlotte Brontë (1816–55) is here writing to the editor of 'Magazine 1829' (her brother Branwell) in the voice of a character from their secret fantasy world of Glasstown, which predated Gondal by two years.

Sir,

It is well known that the Genii have declared that unless they perform certain arduous duties every year, of a mysterious nature, all the worlds in the firmament will be burnt up, and gathered together in one mighty globe, which will roll in solitary grandeur through the vast wilderness of space, inhabited only by the four high princes of the Genii, till time shall be succeeded by Eternity; and the impudence of this is only to be paralleled by another of their assertions, namely, that by their magic might they can reduce the world to a desert, the purest waters to streams of livid poison, and the clearest lakes to stagnant waters, the pestilential vapours of which shall slay all living creatures, except the blood-thirsty beast of the forest, and the ravenous bird of the rock. But that in the midst of this desolation the palace of the Chief Genii shall rise sparkling in the wilderness, and the horrible howl of their war-cry shall spread over the land at morning, at noontide, and night; but that they shall have their annual feast over the bones of the dead, and shall yearly rejoice with the joy of victors. I think, sir, that the horrible wickedness of this needs no remark, and therefore I haste to subscribe myself, etc.

July 14, 1829

This is the Key

This is the Key of the Kingdom
In that Kingdom is a city;
In that city is a town;
In that town there is a street;
In that street there winds a lane;
In that lane there is a yard;
In that yard there is a house;
In that house there waits a room
In that room an empty bed;
And on that bed a basket –
A Basket of Sweet Flowers:
 Of Flowers, of Flowers;
 A Basket of Sweet Flowers.

Flowers in a Basket;
Basket on the bed;
Bed in the chamber;
Chamber in the house;

House in the weedy yard;
Yard in the winding lane;
Lane in the broad street;
Street in the high town;
Town in the city;
City in the Kingdom –
This is the Key of the Kingdom;
    Of the Kingdom this is the Key.   *Anon*

It is late summer, tea-time sunlight, with long cool shadows on the enclosed lawn, and a fire of sunset already reddening on the trunks of the Scots Pines. Tea is laid in the largest room at the Farm, on a long and crowded table. On the mantelpiece are grandmother's two glass lustres, all twinkling in the window light, and the dozen prisms ready to swing and tinkle on their little swivels as soon as we ask Aunt Mary to touch them for us. . . . My heart longed for one of the triangular rods of glass; I never saw them but I broke the commandment about coveting. They were each hung, by a chain of two faceted drops of glass, from a deep ruby-red glass stand. They were heavy, and ended in a spear-point, like the cut stopper of a vinegar bottle. They caught the lamplight unexpectedly and threw entrancing little bands of white and coloured light upon the white chimney-piece – bands which shivered and flickered when, as now, the finger of an aunt had set the prisms swinging.

Not very long afterwards it penetrated even to the Farm that lustres were old fashioned and going out of favour, and when these were dismantled, oh joy of all first joys! somehow or other one of these prisms became mine, mine to have in and out of my pocket, to carry about with me, to feel the safe hard smooth sharpness of it in my hands, and, above all, to look through. To own such a crystal prism was to own a miracle, and I speak in sober maturity. All the miracles of this new century, its cars and gramophones and moving pictures in natural colour, are less than this prism was to me. For it was magic in essence, in its being and substance like a raindrop in a leaf. I felt it heavy and cool, I felt up and down its three long smooth edges, its spear-point with a neck incurved. It was a fragment of harmonious space, the space that filled the sky, lying fixed in my palm. Then I laid one of its long facets across the bridge of my nose and looked in. The world was displaced, the horizon lay before my feet, the grass with its bright yellow stars sloped down and down, and I stood upon the verge of a strange earth, but an earth in which I saw again the coloured shadows of things familiar to me. And everything there – the sky, the branches of trees, the bright leaves and flowers, the rings and fingers of my aunt's hand – was edged with coloured fire, red and gold below, and above a blue and green and a deep and exciting violet. I went from person to person begging them to look at my new world, and then excitedly snatching the prism back again to my own eyes. I walked along precariously, for my feet were in one land and level and my eyes in another, and as I walked I could feel the downward world move up to meet me. It was my first taste of ecstasy, when present experience contradicts belief. The world was not the tame world to which I had grown accustomed, but this new unbalanced moving place, where all its commonest objects were transfigured by edges of godly colours; and yet it was the same old world. I loved this prism best when we went for our compulsory walk with Minnie Groves the nursemaid. Then in the lanes a little boy might be seen straggling along at the tail of a mail-cart, bent and intent upon something which nobody else could see, his eyes looking down into a long glass prism for minutes at a time, his feet stumbling along over the gritty road as though he walked in a dream.

I kept this treasure for years.

THE SMALL YEARS *by Frank Kendon (1893–1973)*

Childhood Among the Ferns

I sat one sprinkling day upon the lea,
Where tall-stemmed ferns spread out luxuriantly,
And nothing but those tall ferns sheltered me.

The rain gained strength, and damped each lopping frond,
Ran down their stalks beside me and beyond,
And shaped slow-creeping rivulets as I conned,

With pride, my spray-roofed house. And though anon
Some drops pierced its green rafters, I sat on,
Making pretence I was not rained upon.

The sun then burst, and brought forth a sweet breath
From the limp ferns as they dried underneath:
I said: 'I could live on here thus till death';

And queried in the green rays as I sate:
'Why should I have to grow to man's estate,
And this afar-noised World perambulate?'

Thomas Hardy (1840–1928)

When my father sent me a *Robinson Crusoe* with steel engravings
I set up in business alone as a trader with savages (the wreck parts
of the tale never much interested me), in a mildewy basement
room where I stood my solitary confinements. My apparatus was
a coconut shell strung on a red cord, a tin trunk, and a piece of
packing-case which kept off any other world. Thus fenced about,
everything inside the fence was quite real, but mixed with the
smell of damp cupboards. If the bit of board fell, I had to begin the
magic all over again. I have learned since from children who play
much alone that this rule of 'beginning again in a pretend game' is
not uncommon. The magic, you see, lies in the ring or fence that
you take refuge in.

SOMETHING OF MYSELF *by Rudyard Kipling (1865–1936)*

One of my pastimes was the invention of lists of place-names; I
considered them stations on an imaginary railway, for which I
would then draw a map and prepare a timetable. In Glenora the
idea occurred to me to carry the fantasy partially into reality: I
printed the proper names on small slips of paper and deposited
them, each one held down by a slab of shale, at what seemed the
proper spot for each, along the paths in the woods. As I had
expected, as soon as my father caught sight of them, he came to
me and demanded that I go immediately and retrieve every piece

of paper. Daddypapa then suggested that they be allowed to remain until the following day. Pulling at his mustache and looking amused, he added that the name I had given the edge of the creek (dry these several weeks owing to a much-discussed drought) was Notninrivo.

Surprisingly, my father chuckled and turned to me. 'So you called the creek Notninrivo, eh? That's pretty good.'

'What's that?' said Mother.

'Nothing in the river,' he explained.

This was their own invention, crass and ridiculous. 'That's not what it means,' I objected.

Now Daddy's face became hostile. 'What do you mean, that's not what it means? What does it mean, then?'

I hung my head. It seemed impossible to explain that Notninrivo was merely the name of the preceding station spelled backward. 'You wouldn't understand,' I said.

'Will you listen to the conceited little rotter?' he cried, beside himself. 'Let's get to the bottom of this! He says the word means something else. I want to know what!'

He seized me and shook me. I hung my head still more.

'For heaven's sake, Claude, let the child alone,' said Daddymama. 'He hasn't done anything wrong.'

'It's all affectation!' he snapped. 'It's just a bid for attention.' Even as he said the words, I was aware of the awful irony in the situation. He went on shaking me. 'Come on, what does it mean?'

I shook my head. I wanted to say: 'I'll never tell you.'

Instead, I waited a moment and finally said: 'Nothing.'

He let go of me, disgusted, having proved his point. Shortly afterward I ran up into the woods and gathered all the station signs, starting with the one at the end of the bridge over the creek for Notninrivo and another one by a rotten tree stump a little farther along the path, this one for the town of O'Virninton. I had to destroy them in secret, for fear my father might discover the meaning of Notninrivo, which he must definitely never know. I carried the scraps of paper to a hidden cove down the shore and burned them. Then I ground the ashes into the wet shingle and piled several flat rocks on top of the spot.

WITHOUT STOPPING *by Paul Bowles (1910–84)*

6

CLOTHES

It was on a bright day of midwinter, in New York. The little girl who eventually became me, but as yet was neither me nor anybody else in particular, but merely a soft anonymous morsel of humanity – this little girl, who bore my name, was going for a walk with her father. The episode is literally the first thing I can remember about her, and therefore I date the birth of her identity from that day.

She had been put into her warmest coat, and into a new and very pretty bonnet, which she had surveyed in the glass with considerable satisfaction. The bonnet (I can see it today) was of white satin, patterned with a pink and green plaid in raised velvet. It was all drawn into close gathers, with a *bavolet* in the neck to keep out the cold, and thick ruffles of silky *blonde* lace under the brim in front. As the air was very cold a gossamer veil of the finest white Shetland wool was drawn about the bonnet and hung down over the wearer's round red cheeks like the white paper filigree over a Valentine; and her hands were encased in white woollen mittens.

One of them lay in the large safe hollow of her father's bare hand; her tall handsome father, who was so warm-blooded that in the coldest weather he always went out without gloves, and whose head, with its ruddy complexion and intensely blue eyes, was so far aloft that when she walked beside him she was too near to see his face. It was always an event in the little girl's life to take a walk with her father, and more particularly so today, because she had on her new winter bonnet, which was beautiful (and so becoming) that for the first time she woke to the importance of dress, and of herself as a subject for adornment – so that I may date from that hour the birth of the conscious and feminine *me* in the little girl's vague soul.

The little girl and her father walked up Fifth Avenue. . . . On Sundays after church the fashionable of various denominations paraded there on foot, in gathered satin bonnets and tall hats; but at other times it presented long stretches of empty pavement, so that the little girl, advancing at her father's side was able to see at a considerable distance the approach of another pair of legs, not as long but considerably stockier than her father's. The little girl was so very little that she never got much higher than the knees in her survey of grown-up people, and would not have known, if her father had not told her, that the approaching legs belonged to his cousin Henry. The news was very interesting, because in attendance on Cousin Henry was a small person, no bigger than herself, who must obviously be Cousin Henry's little boy Daniel, and therefore somehow belong to the little girl. So when the tall legs and the stocky ones halted for a talk, which took place somewhere high up in the air, and the small Daniel and Edith found themselves face to face close to the pavement, the little girl peered with interest at the little boy through the white woollen mist over her face. The little boy, who was very round and rosy, looked back with equal interest; and suddenly he put out a chubby hand, lifted the little girl's veil, and boldly planted a kiss on her cheek. It was the first time – and the little girl found it very pleasant.

This is my earliest definite memory of anything happening to me; and it will be seen that I was wakened to conscious life by the two tremendous forces of love and vanity.

A BACKWARD GLANCE *by Edith Wharton (1862–1937)*

In the Stuart era small boys were kept in petticoats until they were six or seven years old. In the following extract from The Lives of the Norths *the breeching of a child called Frank is described by his grandmother:*

You cannot beleeve the great concurse that was in the whole family here last Wednesday, it being the day that the taylor was to helpe dress little Frank in his breeches, in order to the making a everyday suit by it. Never had any bride that was to be drest upon her wedding night more hands about her, some the legs and some the arms, the taylor buttoning, and others putting on the sword, and so many lookers on, that had I not a ffinger amongst them I could not have seen him. . . . They are very fitt, everything, and he looks taller and prettyer than in his coats. Little Charles rejoyced as much as he did, for he jumpt all the while about him, and took notice of everything. I went to Bury and bo't everything for another suit which will be finisht upon Saturday. So the coats are to be quite left off on Sunday. . . . When he was drest he asked Buckle whether muffs were out of fashion because they had not sent him one. . . .

In her memoir Long Ago When I Was Young, *E. Nesbit (1858–1924) recalls her childhood sojourn with a French family whose daughter Marguerite became her close friend.*

I only remember one occasion on which I quarrelled with her – it was on the subject of dress. We were going to a children's party and my best blue silk was put out for me to wear.

'I wish you wouldn't wear that,' said Marguerite hesitatingly, 'it makes my grey cashmere look so old.'

Now I had nothing else to wear but a brown frock which I hated.

'Never mind,' I said hypocritically, 'it's better to be good than smart, everybody says so,' and I put on my blue silk. When I was dressed, I pranced off to the kitchen to show my finery to the cook, and under her admiring eyes executed my best curtsey. It began, of course, by drawing the right foot back; it ended in a tub of clothes and water that was standing just behind me. I floundered out somehow, and my first thought was how funny I must have looked, and in another moment I should have burst out laughing but as I scrambled out, I saw Marguerite in the doorway, smiling triumphantly, and heard her thin little voice say, 'The blue silk can't mock the poor grey cashmere now!'

An impulse of blind fury came upon me. I caught Marguerite by her little shoulders, and before the cook could interfere I had ducked her head-first into the tub of linen. Madame Lourdes behaved beautifully; she appeared on the scene at this moment, and, impartial as ever, she slapped us both, but when she heard from the cook the rights of the story, my sentence was 'bed'. 'But Marguerite', said her mother, 'has been punished enough for an unkind word.'

And Marguerite was indeed sobbing bitterly, while I was dry-eyed and still furious. 'She can't go,' I cried, 'she hasn't got a dress!'

'You have spoilt her dress,' said Madame Lourdes coolly, 'the least you can do is to lend her your brown one.' And that excellent woman actually had the courage to send her own daughter to a party in my dress, an exquisite punishment to us both.

By now I was always in a sailor suit. The hated petticoats had gone for ever some months before, but my knickerbockers instead of being kept up by braces were buttoned to a sort of red flannel corset. This was a source of grief to me and I longed for braces.

On a gloomy November day I was sitting by the dining-room window, wishing that Christmas was not such an endless time away when along the road opposite came a boy in a ragged pair of breeches without a coat. He was rattling a stick along the rickety fence that still bounded the waste ground between Avonmore Road and the back of Lisgar Terrace. As he drew nearer, whistling as he walked, I saw with admiring envy that he was wearing braces fastened by one button at the back and two buttons in front. His shirt was torn and grubby. What did it matter? This enviable boy was wearing braces and he was free. Over me came a fervid wish for freedom, and to myself I promised that once the intolerable handicap of childhood had been overcome I too would always be free. Of course, I did not express the emotion I felt in those words but with the words of age I recall that emotion, and I think I can claim that freedom has been the guiding principle by which I have lived my own life and desired it for the lives of others. Later on that November day, when Nanny sent down a nurse-maid whose name I have forgotten to fetch me up to bed, I longed to be outside somewhere in the darkness with that ragged boy.

MY LIFE AND TIMES *by Compton Mackenzie (1883–1972)*

The mountain of luggage used by the children was in part accounted for by their wardrobes. It was thought right that Mary Stuart should be more richly attired than the princesses, to mark her future position as their brother's bride. Her accounts reveal both the abundance and the formality of a royal child's wardrobe: yards of shot red and yellow taffeta for dresses, dresses of gold damask, dresses of black edged with silver, canvas and buckram to stiffen the dresses, white Florentine serge stockings, a *vasquine* or type of farthingale to hold out the dresses, shot taffeta petticoats and orange taffeta petticoats lined with red serge. Her accessories are equally elaborate: there is mention of bonnets of silver thread and black silk, orange wool to be dyed scarlet for stockings, furs to trim her clothes. Shoes are plentiful – ten pairs of ordinary shoes in the accounts of 1551, three white, three purple, two black and two red and also white, yellow, red and black velvet shoes. There are bills for exquisite embroideries on the clothes – rose leaves of gold thread for caps, and a bill for the embroidery of a device on a favour of white taffeta which Mary gave to the dauphin. There are bills for leather gloves of dog-skin and deer-skin. The accessories are in keeping with the rest: a black velvet purse to keep the combs of the queen of Scots in, a crystal mirror covered with velvet and silk ribbons, gold and silver paillettes to be sewn on to her clothes, endless chains, collars and gold belts, as well as three brass chests to hold her jewels, which included a chain of pearls and green enamel, a gold ring with a ruby in it, and jewelled buttons of many different colours and shapes.   MARY QUEEN OF SCOTS *(1542–87) by Antonia Fraser*

It was proximity of age and not similarity of temperament which drew us together. We were always dressed alike as twins, and the only difference lay in the colour of our hair ribbons and our sashes. Muriel was dark haired, dark skinned, and dark eyed, and so she wore pink hair ribbons and a pink sash; I was fair haired, fair skinned, and blue eyed, and so I wore blue hair ribbons and a blue sash. My mother treated us like a pair of dolls and we were always picturesquely dressed in full-length Kate Greenaway frocks with fichus and wide sashes, and we wore large poke bonnets. When she appeared at parties holding a little girl by each hand her friends used to say, 'How sweet your two little girls look, Mrs Starkie!' But one of the two little girls, the one with the blue hair ribbons and the blue sash, was more often than not looking anything but sweet. I hated our picturesque clothes and I longed to be dressed like other children. I passionately longed all through my childhood for a sailor suit, but my mother thought such a dress too ordinary. I used to cut out the advertisements of children dressed by the naval tailor Rowe, in sailor suits perfect in every detail, down to the whistle on a white cord tucked into the breast pocket. Some wore over their suit an overcoat called a 'reefer coat'. I longed for such a coat instead of my own coat with its little cape edged with fur. I had a large collection of these advertisements, pictures of both boys and girls. This desire for a sailor suit was never fulfilled, for I never chose my own clothes until I reached adult years, and by then I had ceased minding being different from others. But as a child I longed to be like everyone else and I used to read school stories in order to discover what other children wore and how they lived, but nowhere did I find that little girls wore full-length dresses. At parties, too, no other children wore such frocks, and Muriel and I were greatly hampered by their length. I can remember still the agony and the humiliation of running, holding up a tattered dress and frequently catching my foot in a frill which had become torn, while the other children, particularly the boys, laughed and jeered.

Sometimes our clothes were merely quaint and not even picturesque. One winter, when motoring hats and veils were the fashion for grown-ups, Muriel and I had long motoring coats and hats and thick motoring veils. I imagine that we must have looked a comic pair as we walked out with our Nurse, two little girls of six and five in full-length navy-blue double-breasted coats, flat motoring hats – surely the ugliest hat ever invented – and opaque, navy-blue, double-ninon motoring veils. It was funnier still when it is remembered that we did not even possess a motor-car at the time. Eventually, however, the veils were discarded, for I could

never remember that I was wearing mine and I used to blow my
nose through it, which did not improve its appearance.

A LADY'S CHILD *by Enid Starkie (1897–1970)*

*During the Second World War this by now distinguished French
scholar was to be seen in Oxford, resplendent in sailor suit
complete with whistle and cord: eccentric but triumphant.*

Full Moon

She was wearing the coral taffeta trousers
Someone had brought her from Isfahan,
And the little gold coat with the pomegranate blossoms,
And the coral-hafted feather fan;
And she ran down a Kentish lane in the moonlight,
And skipped in the pool of the moon as she ran.

She cared not a rap for all the big planets,
For Betelgeuse or Aldebaran,
And all the big planets cared nothing for her,
That small impertinent charlatan,
As she climbed on a Kentish stile in the moonlight,
And laughed at the sky through the sticks of her fan.

Vita Sackville-West (1892–1962)

Sharp again is my sense of not being so adequately dressed as I
should have taken thought for had I foreseen my exposure;
though the resources of my wardrobe as then constituted could
surely have left me but few alternatives. The main resource of a
small New York boy in this line at that time was the little sheath-
like jacket, tight to the body, closed at the neck and adorned in
front with a single row of brass buttons – a garment of scant grace
assuredly and compromised to my consciousness, above all, by a
strange ironic light from an unforgotten source. It was but a short
time before those days and the great Mr Thackeray had come to
America to lecture on The English Humourists, and still present to
me is the voice proceeding from my father's library, in which some

glimpse of me hovering, at an opening of the door, in passage or on staircase, prompted him to the formidable words: 'Come here, little boy, and show me your extraordinary jacket!' My sense of my jacket became from that hour a heavy one – further enriched as my vision is by my shyness of posture before the seated, the celebrated visitor, who struck me, in the sunny light of the animated room, as enormously big and who, though he laid on my shoulder the hand of benevolence, bent on my native costume the spectacles of wonder. I was to know later on why he had been so amused and why, after asking me if this were the common uniform of my age and class, he remarked that in England, were I to go there, I should be addressed as 'Buttons'. It had been revealed to me thus in a flash that we were somehow *queer*. ... Too few, I may here interject, were to remain my gathered impressions of the great humourist, but one of them, indeed almost the only other, bears again on the play of his humour over our perversities of dress. It belongs to a later moment, an occasion on which I see him familiarly seated with us, in Paris, during the spring of 1857, at some repast at which the younger of us too, by that time, habitually flocked, in our affluence of five. Our youngest was beside him, a small sister, then not quite in her eighth year, and arrayed apparently after the fashion of the period and place; and the tradition lingered long of his having suddenly laid his hand on her little flounced person and exclaimed with ludicrous horror: 'Crinoline? – I was suspecting it! So young and so depraved!'

A SMALL BOY AND OTHERS *by Henry James (1843–1916)*

My mother was a convert to Roman Catholicism, strongly religious ... There was a convent in Shoreham town and I was sent there for one or two days when my mother went away somewhere. The nuns were very nice to me and I was very happy with them but there were some things I could not understand at all. 'This is bath night,' they said to me cheerfully. I remember the bathroom. It was spacious, warm, steamy. We only had a tin bath in the bungalow. 'Now, Ralph,' said two charming nuns, 'you put on this nightgown and then get into the bath and we'll be back.' This moment, just over seventy years ago, is clearer to me now

than anything that happened last week. The nightgown was not
my own, which was, I think, oatmeal-coloured flannel and was
friendly and smelt like my teddy-bear. This nightgown was white
and it was too long for me but I put it on. 'Now, Ralph,' one said,
'get into the bath.' I sat in the bath, the white nightgown billowing
around me, refusing to sink. I was like a poached egg, surrounded
by white. The nuns did not move. Neither did I. That is all I
remember of bath night in the convent.

'The Age of Innocence' by Ralph Richardson (1902–83)

The New Vestments

There lived an old man in the Kingdom of Tess,
Who invented a purely original dress;
And when it was perfectly made and complete,
He opened the door, and walked into the street.

By way of a hat, he'd a loaf of Brown Bread,
In the middle of which he inserted his head; –
His Shirt was made up of no end of dead Mice,
The warmth of whose skins was quite fluffy and nice; –
His Drawers were of Rabbit-skins; – so were his Shoes; –
His Stockings were skins, – but it is not known whose; –
His Waistcoat and Trowsers were made of Pork Chops; –
His Buttons were Jujubes, and Chocolate Drops; –
His Coat was all Pancakes with Jam for a border,
And a girdle of Biscuits to keep it in order;
And he wore over all, as a screen from bad weather,
A Cloak of green Cabbage-leaves stitched all together.

He had walked a short way, when he heard a great noise,
Of all sorts of Beasticles, Birdlings, and Boys; –
And from every long street and dark lane in the town
Beasts, Birdles, and Boys in a tumult rushed down.
Two Cows and a half ate his Cabbage-leaf Cloak; –
Four Apes seized his Girdle, which vanished like smoke; –
Three Kids ate up half of his Pancaky Coat, –

And the tails were devour'd by an ancient He Goat; –
An army of Dogs in a twinkling tore *up* his
Pork Waistcoat and Trowsers to give to their Puppies; –
And while they were growling, and mumbling the Chops,
Ten Boys prigged the Jujubes and Chocolate Drops. –
He tried to run back to his house, but in vain,
For Scores of fat Pigs came again and again; –
They rushed out of stables and hovels and doors, –
They tore off his stockings, his shoes, and his drawers; –
And now from the housetops with screechings descend,
Striped, spotted, white, black, and grey Cats without end,
They jumped on his shoulders and knocked off his hat, –
When Crows, Ducks, and Hens made a mincemeat of that; –
They speedily flew at his sleeves in a trice,
And utterly tore up his Shirt of dead Mice; –
They swallowed the last of his Shirt with a squall, –
Whereon he ran home with no clothes on at all.

And he said to himself as he bolted the door,
'I will not wear a similar dress any more,
'Any more, any more, any more, never more!'

Edward Lear (1812–88)

Mother put the two youngest children with the next-door neighbour and marched my brother and me for a mile and a half,
muttering to herself, to Rosendale Road School, near Herne Hill.

'I've brought these two boys,' she said, giving us a push, to a
dapper little man in a tail-coat and who looked like a frosted
pen-nib. His name was Timms.

What Timms said I don't know, but I was aware of what I
looked like. Mother had a hard time making both ends meet and,
on a day like this, wanted us to be dressed in something respect-
able. The day before she put the sewing-machine on the dining-
room table, took out a paper pattern and set about making me
some trousers. . . .

She had to pay for the material for her dressmaking out of the
housekeeping money and she would raid any free material in

sight. . . . Her own bloomers were a byword: for in gay moments she would haul up her long skirts above her knees and show my father – who was always shocked – what could be done with a chair cover or something robust of that kind. 'You want me in the business instead of "that woman",' she'd say.

For she had a vengeful streak in her, and looking at our father, the impressive Managing Director, and counting his suits and knowing how she couldn't get a penny out of him for our clothes, she attacked his wardrobe. She found a pair of striped trousers of the kind worn with morning dress. Just the thing for me. Out came the scissors. Slicing the enormous trousers roughly at the knees she saw that my brother and I could get into them both at once. She was upset by our laughter. She now slashed at the trousers again and narrowed them to my size. The insoluble difficulty was the fly buttons; these she pulled round to the side of one leg; cutting and then tacking her way up the middle while they were on me at the final try-on, she sewed me up totally in front.

'I won't be able to go, Mum,' I said.

She was flabbergasted, but in her careless way, she snipped a couple of stitches in her tacking.

These were the trousers I was wearing as I stood before Mr Timms, very pleased by father's fashionable stripes and willing to show any boy who was interested the original touch of having Savile Row fly buttons down the side of one leg. What I feared was happening: the hole was lengthening in front. I could feel an alarming draught. I dared not look down. I hoped Mr Timms would not look down, as my mother chatted on and on about our family. Nothing happened. I went to my class-room; at playtime I dared not run, for fear the tacking would go. When I pulled the thread to tighten it I was left with a length of thread hanging down from the vulnerable part. When I went home after school the thread went altogether and I had to cover myself with my hand.

So my first day at Rosendale Road School began. Wearing my father's classy cut-downs I knew the distinction of our family and its awkward difference from the families of all the other children. No one else had a Managing Director's trousers on. No one else had (I was sure) our dark adventures. We were a race apart; abnormal but proud of our stripes, longing for the normality we saw around us.   A CAB AT THE DOOR by V. S. Pritchett (1900–   )

JOYS

James Kirkup (1923–   ) recalls a day by the sea.

There was sometimes a Punch and Judy show, and one summer there were nigger minstrels with ukuleles and striped trousers. I rather fancy that Shields folk thought such things were out of place on *our* sands. Then there was a man who made wonderful sculptures in the damp sand: he could do mermaids and dolphins, and castles and sailing ships and battle-cruisers, with burnt-out match-sticks for guns. I used to watch him for hours, but he did not come to Shields very often. Once, after watching him for a long while as he made a low-relief sand-picture of the Shields Town Hall – copying it from a very grubby postcard – he suddenly turned to me and asked me what I would like him to make.

'What? For *me*?' I asked, incredulous.

He didn't reply, so I said quickly:

'Make me a Music Hall, like the Empire.'

He gave me an 'old-fashioned' look.

'You *would* have to ask for something difficult, wouldn't you?' he said gruffly. I didn't know whether he was angry or not. But he made me a theatre, with hanging curtains, and tiers of boxes at the sides. There were little shells for footlights – he asked me to go and collect them myself. And in the scooped-out proscenium there was a fairy castle and a bridge and trees made of seaweed – I got that for him, too – and a paper figure of myself sitting in one of the boxes, eating an ice-cream cornet. Then he made a little lake among the trees with a big, blue mussel-shell filled with sea-water. There were crowds of people gathered round, watching him. When he had finished it all by placing a tiny celluloid swan on the lake, he turned to me and said:

'What do they call you hinney?'

I told him, and he wrote underneath, in beautiful, curling script:

'This belongs to James Falconer Kirkup.'

He made a fine flourish under my name, and added the date. I was speechless. He got up, picked up his capful of pennies and went away, and I never saw him again. Almost as soon as he had gone away, a big boy stamped his foot right in the middle of the stage. Broken-hearted, I sat beside the ruin, trying to make it right again. But it would not come right. It was drying, and crumbling away. My name, too, was crumbling away. But I sat there beside it until the sea came in, and watched the first wave wash it all away, leaving the sand smooth and empty, as if all that pleasure and wonder had never been.   THE ONLY CHILD

A child in the full health of his mind will put his hand flat on the summer turf, feel it, and give a little shiver of private glee at the elastic firmness of the globe. He is not thinking how well it will do for some game or to feed sheep upon. That would be the way of the wooer whose mind runs on his mistress's money. The child's is sheer affection, the true ecstatic sense of the thing's inherent characteristics. No matter what the things may be, no matter what they are good or no good for, there they are, each with a thrilling unique look and feel of its own, like a face; the iron astringently cool under its paint, the painted wood familiarly warmer, the clod crumbling enchantingly down in the hands, with its little dry smell of the sun and of hot nettles; each common thing a personality marked by delicious differences.

DISENCHANTMENT by C. E. Montague (1867–1928)

One incident which stands out clearly in my mind is that of the fifty-shilling train. There were at that time in London two toy-shops called Cremer. One was in New Bond Street, No. 27, I think, near Tessier's, the jeweller; another in Regent Street, somewhere between Liberty's and Piccadilly Circus.

In the window of the Regent Street shop there was a long train with people in it, and it was labelled fifty shillings. In the year 1921 it is only a small mechanical train that can be bought for fifty shillings. I can't remember whether I had reached the schoolroom when this happened, but I know I still wore a frock and had not yet reached the dignity of trousers. I used constantly to ask to go and look at this shop window and gaze at the fifty-shilling train, which seemed first to be miraculous for its size, and, secondly, for its price. Who in the world could have fifty shillings all at once?

I never went so far as thinking it was possible to possess that train; but I used to wonder whether there were people in the world who could store up fifty shillings. We were each of us given sixpence every Saturday, but it was always spent at once, nor could I calculate or even conceive how long it would take to save enough sixpences to make fifty shillings.

One evening, when we were at Coombe, in the summer, I was sent for to the drawing-room and then told to go into the dining-room. I opened the door, and there, on the floor, was the fifty-shilling train. If a fairy had flown into the room and lifted me to the ceiling I could not have thought a fact more miraculous. From that moment I knew for certain that miracles could happen and do happen, and subsequent experience has confirmed the belief.

THE PUPPET SHOW OF MEMORY *by Maurice Baring (1874–1945)*

Archie and Tina

Archie and Tina
Where are you now,
Playmates of my childhood,
Brother and sister?

When we stayed in the same place
With Archie and Tina
At the seaside,
We used

To paddle the samphire beds, fish
Crabs from the sea-pool, poke
The anemones, run,

Trailing the ribbon seaweed across the sand to the sea's edge
To throw it in as far as we could. We dug
White bones of dead animals from the sandhills, found
The jaw-bone of a fox with some teeth in it, a stoat's skull,
The hind leg of a hare.

Oh, if only; oh, if only!

Archie and Tina
Had a dog called Bam. The silver-sand
Got in his long hair. He had
To be taken home.

Oh, if only . . . !

One day when the wind blew strong
Our dog, Boy, got earache. He had
To be taken home in a jersey.

Oh what pleasure, what pleasure!

There never were so many poppies as there were then,
So much yellow corn, so many fine days,
Such sharp bright air, such seas.

Was it necessary that
Archie and Tina, Bam and Boy,
Should have been there too?
Yes, then it was. But to say now:

Where are you today
Archie and Tina,
Playmates of my childhood,
Brother and sister? Is no more than to say:

I remember
Such pleasure, so much pleasure.

Stevie Smith

'Adorable Things' from The Pillow Book of Sei Shōnagon, *lady-in-waiting at the court of the Japanese Empress during the last decade of the tenth century.*

The face of a child drawn on a melon.

An extremely plump baby, who is about a year old and has a lovely white skin, comes crawling towards one, dressed in a long gauze robe of violet with the sleeves tucked up.

A baby of two or so is crawling rapidly along the ground. With his sharp eyes he catches sight of a tiny object and, picking it up with his pretty little fingers, takes it to show to a grown-up person.

A child, whose hair has been cut like a nun's, is examining something; the hair falls over his eyes, but instead of brushing it away he holds his head to the side. The pretty white cords of his trouser-skirt are tied round his shoulders, and this too is most adorable.

A young Palace page, who is still quite small, walks by in ceremonial costume.

A little boy of about eight who reads aloud from a book in his childish voice.

E. M. Forster's aunt Laura is here remembering her childhood at Battersea Rise, home of Marianne Thornton.

I doubt if I was three years old, for we walked about the house at a very early age, and what I remember is being carried into the library at Battersea Rise one cold morning, and being put down by the glass door to watch the men rolling great balls of snow on the lawn and leaving green paths behind them as they went. It was a most fascinating sight and I stood entranced, balancing myself with outspread hands on the glass, and I remember a feeling of acute disappointment, and of being baulked, when someone came behind me and gently took my hands from the window, saying I should get them too cold if I kept them there. I obeyed but felt the men and the great snowballs were no longer so close to me as before. I have no doubt that my parents were in the group of people breakfasting at the round table in the Library, and I remember the pleasant smell of coffee and toast when I was carried to the window, but I do not know in whose arms I was borne, nor which aunt made me take my hands off the window panes but I feel sure it was not my mother. I believe that I should have said 'Need I?' to her, and that her sympathy would have set me free to stand as I liked. The wide lawn and snow-covered trees glittering in the sun with the men plodding steadily on, rolling the great snowball before them, is the very first of many beautiful landscapes that hang like pictures in my memory.

MARIANNE THORNTON *by E. M. Forster*

There was a Boy; ye knew him well, ye cliffs
And islands of Winander! – many a time,
At evening, when the earliest stars began
To move along the edges of the hills,
Rising or setting, would he stand alone,
Beneath the trees, or by the glimmering lake;
And there, with fingers interwoven, both hands
Pressed closely palm to palm and to his mouth
Uplifted, he, as through an instrument,
Blew mimic hootings to the silent owls,
That they might answer him. – And they would shout
Across the watery vale, and shout again,
Responsive to his call, – with quivering peals,
And long halloos, and screams, and echoes loud
Redoubled and redoubled; concourse wild
Of jocund din! And, when there came a pause
Of silence such as baffled his best skill:
Then, sometimes, in that silence, while he hung
Listening, a gentle shock of mild surprise
Has carried far into his heart the voice
Of mountain-torrents; or the visible scene
Would enter unawares into his mind
With all its solemn imagery, its rocks,
Its woods, and that uncertain heaven received
Into the bosom of the steady lake

from 'The Prelude' by William Wordsworth (1770–1850)

[Saturday] had yet another characteristic feature, namely, that during May we used to go out on Saturday evenings after dinner to the 'Month of Mary' devotions.

As we were liable, there, to meet M. Vinteuil, who held very strict views on 'the deplorable untidiness of young people, which seems to be encouraged in these days', my mother would first see that there was nothing out of order in my appearance, and then we would set out for the church. It was in these 'Month of Mary' services that I can remember having first fallen in love with hawthorn-blossom. The hawthorn was not merely in the church, for there, holy ground as it was, we had all of us a right of entry; but, arranged upon the altar itself, inseparable from the mysteries in whose celebration it was playing a part, it thrust in among the tapers and the sacred vessels its rows of branches, tied to one another horizontally in a stiff, festal scheme of decoration; and they were made more lovely still by the scalloped outline of the dark leaves, over which were scattered in profusion, as over a bridal train, little clusters of buds of a dazzling whiteness. Though I dared not look at them save through my fingers, I could feel that the formal scheme was composed of living things, and that it was Nature herself who, by trimming the shape of the foliage, and by adding the crowning ornament of those snowy buds, had made the decorations worthy of what was at once a public rejoicing and a solemn mystery.

When, before turning to leave the church, I made a genuflection before the altar, I felt suddenly, as I rose again, a bitter-sweet fragrance of almonds steal towards me from the hawthorn-blossom, and I then noticed that on the flowers themselves were little spots of a creamier colour, in which I imagined that this fragrance must lie concealed, as the taste of an almond cake lay in the burned parts, or the sweetness of Mlle. Vinteuil's cheeks beneath their freckles. . . .

That year my family fixed the day of their return to Paris rather earlier than usual. On the morning of our departure I had had my hair curled, to be ready to face the photographer, had had a new hat carefully set upon my head, and had been buttoned into a velvet jacket; a little later my mother, after searching everywhere for me, found me standing in tears on that steep little hillside close to Tansonville, bidding a long farewell to my hawthorns, clasping their sharp branches to my bosom, and (like a princess in a tragedy, oppressed by the weight of all her senseless jewellery) with no gratitude towards the officious hand which had, in curling those ringlets, been at pains to collect all my hair upon my forehead; trampling underfoot the curl-papers which I had torn from my head, and my new hat with them. My mother was not at all moved by my tears, but she could not suppress a cry at the sight of my battered headgear and my ruined jacket. I did not, however, hear her. 'Oh, my poor little hawthorns,' I was assuring them through my sobs, 'it is not you that want to make me unhappy, to force me to leave you. You, you have never done me any harm. So I shall always love you.' And, drying my eyes, I promised them that, when I grew up, I would never copy the foolish example of other men, but that even in Paris, on fine spring days, instead of paying calls and listening to silly talk, I would make excursions into the country to see the first hawthorn-trees in bloom.

SWANN'S WAY *by Marcel Proust (1871–1922)*

The Little Dancers

Lonely, save for a few faint stars, the sky
Dreams; and lonely, below, the little street
Into its gloom retires, secluded and shy.
Scarcely the dumb roar enters this soft retreat;
And all is dark, save where come flooding rays
From a tavern-window: there, to the brisk measure
Of an organ that down in an alley merrily plays,
Two children, all alone and no one by,
Holding their tattered frocks, through an airy maze
Of motion lightly threaded with nimble feet
Dance sedately: face to face they gaze,
Their eyes shining, grave with a perfect pleasure.

Laurence Binyon (1869–1943)

*Down was the house in Kent belonging to Gwen Raverat's grand-
father, Charles Darwin.*

There was no bathroom at Down, nor any hot water, except in the
kitchen, but there were plenty of housemaids to run about with
the big brown-painted bath-cans. And just as everything else at
Down was perfect, so there too was the most beautiful, secret,
romantic lavatory, that ever was known; at the end of a long
passage and up several steps. It had the only window which
looked out over the orchard, and was always full of a dim green
light. You looked down into the tops of the apple trees; and when
I read *Romeo and Juliet* (which was the first Shakespeare I read
for myself) the line: 'That tips with silver all these fruit-tree tops',
always made me think of that window. But the place of all others,
where the essence of the whole house was concentrated, was in the
cupboard under the stairs, by the garden door. It was full of
ancient tennis rackets, smaller than those we use now; and para-
sols and croquet mallets, and it was there that the exquisite,
special smell of the house was strongest.

PERIOD PIECE *by Gwen Raverat*

My thrill of the week was to visit a little shop on Lansdowne Hill
in the early dusk of winter afternoon and receive a rolled-up
bundle of 'Comic Papers', *Chips* and *Comic Cuts*, the *Rainbow*,
the *Gem* and the *Magnet* – I hold them, as I did with everything, to
my nose, the smell is excruciating – damp paper, newsprint; I feel I
shall burst. Ahead of me stretches the evening with my grandmother; the gas lit, the fire burning, the papers unrolled and
untied, the peace and security of the literary life, though even then
I am depressed by the knowledge that nothing I shall find inside
will come up to the sensation of opening them.

ENEMIES OF PROMISE *by Cyril Connolly (1903–74)*

I should like to rise and go
Where the golden apples grow; –
Where below another sky
Parrot islands anchored lie,
And, watched by cockatoos and goats,
Lonely Crusoes building boats; –
Where in sunshine reaching out
Eastern cities, miles about,
Are with mosque and minaret
Among sandy gardens set,
And rich goods from near and far
Hang for sale in the bazaar; –
Where the Great Wall round China goes,
And on one side the desert blows,
And with bell and voice and drum,
Cities on the other hum; –
Where are forest, hot as fire,
Wide as England, tall as a spire,
Full of apes and coco-nuts
And the Negro hunters' huts . . .
Where among the desert sands
Some deserted city stands,
All its children, sweep and prince,
Grown to manhood ages since,
Not a foot in street or house,
Not a stir of child or mouse,
And when kindly falls the night,
In all the town no spark of light.
There I'll come when I'm a man
With a camel caravan;
Light a fire in the gloom
Of some dusty dining-room;
See the pictures on the walls,
Heroes, fights, and festivals;
And in a corner find the toys
Of the old Egyptian boys.

Robert Louis Stevenson

In July came a night of magic. . . . Roused at ten o'clock at night, we were taken down to the shore to see the phosphorescent lights. They had been described to us, but I had been unable to imagine them beforehand. Light sprang out of the dark wet sand as we walked on it; we trod as saints tread, rayed in light. We rushed into the sea and a trail of brightness followed us; the water broke in light before us. We could not believe it; we could not have enough of it. Small waves broke gleaming, rolled in in darkness outlined in a lace of light. We leapt in and out, scattering the darkness, spreading the light like creators, like makers of the world. I wandered away from Judy and from Alethea, in an ecstasy of fantasy. I was Lucifer, the light-bringer. I was God making the world. 'Let there be light! Let there be light! Let there be light!' I shouted, dancing on the wet sand to make it so. 'Let there be light, light, light!' Curves, arcs, sweeps of light, coming and going so often as I willed it, trod it, danced it, stamped it. My mother's voice came faintly down the shore in the mild darkness, but it seemed to have nothing to do with me. 'Darling, where are you? Priscilla!' I was alone in primal chaos, in a darkness which I alone could make ordered and light. The waves, milder than the mild air of night, rolled in from the shallow sea. The smell of mussels came faintly from a stranded sandbank, the salty water lingered on my legs. 'Let there be light light light!' A part of me is there still, dancing in solitary luxury a great pattern of light across the darkness of the flat wet sand.

A LATE BEGINNER *by Priscilla Napier*

Child's Evening

Stand motionless upon Atlantic sand,
Only lengthened shadows on the beach, now lonely,
Show through diamond brilliance that the sun is low
Down beneath a striped sea town
Green and white-rayed as it might be seen
Slatted through a blind; sea is in her matted
Hair, sea is on the wave-worn stair.
Wide the slippery slope-slide
Warm rail beneath her salted arm,

Alone walking. Who goes there? One.
Stare, pausing, at the black shade and stone's glare,
Bright, but a little airier than in the midday light.

There is nothing in the moment but the present,
Were she not a child then there would always be
The future in the present. But her Now is golden,
Floating in transparent dazzling sky without a thorn.

Diana Witherby (1915–   )

At the age of eleven, I began Euclid, with my brother as my tutor.
This was one of the great events of my life, as dazzling as first love.
I had not imagined that there was anything so delicious in the
world. After I had learned the fifth proposition, my brother told
me that it was generally considered difficult, but I had found no
difficulty whatever. This was the first time it had dawned upon me
that I might have some intelligence. From that moment until
Whitehead and I finished *Principia Mathematica*, when I was
thirty-eight, mathematics was my chief interest, and my chief
source of happiness.

THE AUTOBIOGRAPHY OF BERTRAND RUSSELL *(1872–1970)*

These weekly [dancing] classes of Miss Thieler's took place in the
late morning, or early afternoon. Only as a pupil is one to know
the sensation of ballroom dancing in sunshine. Long dusty dazzling shafts slanted on to us through the pointed windows of the
Molesworth Hall. The sun was made theatrical and unlikely by
the pertinacious drumming of the piano. . . .
    On benches placed round against the dado, or (if not too shy)
on the platform at the end of the room, the mothers, nurses and
governesses took their seats. They had had first to peel off from us
the many wrappings in which little girls braved the weather on
their way to Miss Thieler's. Over our shivery muslins, under our
top-coats, would be several jerseys and a tied-across shawl. Thick
stockings went over openwork stockings, and often gaiters were
buttoned on top of this. In those days, everybody subscribed to

the idea that children were perishable. Even little boys arrived in a mobled state. In fact, South Dublin children bound for Miss Thieler's were to be recognized by their abnormal size....

Just as she never spared us, she never flattered our mothers or keepers seated around the walls. And this, in the part of our city where we were constantly flattered, did more than anything to exalt her – what a famous dancing-teacher she was! Happy (but rare) the mother who could go home saying, 'Miss Thieler was pleased today with my little girl.'

As we trickled into our places across the floor, we little girls as white as the ballerinas of Swan Lake, but with the action of clumsy cygnets, I suppose we all felt (I felt certainly) that something psychic inside each child or the day had already determined whether that child, today, should be a duffer or be able to dance.

I was a crack polka-dancer, springing around the floor: I had been taught that step in the drawing-room at home. Unhappily, the jerkiness of the polka infected everything else I tried – for weeks together I could not learn to waltz. I was not even allowed to take a partner, but, for interims that held up the entire class, had to go round the floor in a single file of duffers while Miss Thieler, head fallen wearily sideways, beat the pads of her hands together 'One two *three*, four five *six*—!' at each turn of the bar and end of the bar. The piano, meanwhile, with an insulting loud slowness played.

This was dreadful. She kept us duffers in such *tenue* that I dared not even hold my head forward to let my hair flop curtains over my burning cheeks. A feeling of doom and of inability was drawn tight like a wire noose round my brain. Then, one morning, at the dreadful height of such minutes, a spring released itself in my inside. My feet and body released themselves, without warning, from inside the noose of my consciousness. Like a butterfly free of the chrysalis, like a soul soaring out of the body, I burst from the file of duffers and went spinning smoothly, liquidly round the floor by myself. I waltzed. The piano dropped its disdainful note and quickened and melted in sympathy. I felt no floor under my feet: this was my dream of being able to fly. I *could* fly – I could waltz. So much the sun of heaven was in my eyes that I saw nothing. All round me surprise, and something more than surprise, created a sort of unheard cheer. Though I was a vain child I felt no pride: the experience was too pure. Like a top from a lick of the magic whip I spun on and on in my course, till I slowed, staggered, was giddy and flopped down.

'So you've managed to learn to waltz,' my governess said as we walked home. 'I thought you could, if you tried.'

SEVEN WINTERS *by Elizabeth Bowen (1899–1973)*

8

OFF TO SCHOOL

The morning came, without any warning, when my sisters surrounded me, wrapped me in scarves, tied up my bootlaces, thrust a cap on my head, and stuffed a baked potato in my pocket.

'What's this?' I said.

'You're starting school today.'

'I ain't. I'm stopping 'ome.'

'Now, come on, Loll. You're a big boy now.'

'I ain't.'

'You are.'

'Boo-hoo.'

They picked me up bodily, kicking and bawling, and carried me up to the road.

'Boys who don't go to school get put into boxes, and turn into rabbits, and get chopped up Sundays.'

I felt this was overdoing it rather, but I said no more after that. I arrived at the school just three feet tall and fatly wrapped in my scarves. The playground roared like a rodeo, and the potato burned through my thigh. Old boots, ragged stockings, torn trousers and skirts, went skating and skidding around me. The rabble closed in; I was encircled; grit flew in my face like shrapnel. Tall girls with frizzled hair, and huge boys with sharp elbows, began to prod me with hideous interest. They plucked at my scarves, spun me round like a top, screwed my nose, and stole my potato.

I was rescued at last by a gracious lady – the sixteen-year-old junior-teacher – who boxed a few ears and dried my face and led me off to The Infants. I spent that first day picking holes in paper, then went home in a smouldering temper.

'What's the matter, Loll? Didn't he like it at school, then?'

'They never gave me the present!'

'Present? What present?'

'They said they'd give me a present.'

'Well, now, I'm sure they didn't.'

'They did! They said: "You're Laurie Lee, ain't you? Well, just you sit there for the present." I sat there all day but I never got it. I ain't going back there again!'

But after a week I felt like a veteran and grew as ruthless as anyone else. Somebody had stolen my baked potato, so I swiped somebody else's apple. The Infant Room was packed with toys such as I'd never seen before – coloured shapes and rolls of clay, stuffed birds and men to paint. Also a frame of counting beads which our young teacher played like a harp, leaning her bosom against our faces and guiding our wandering fingers....

The beautiful assistant left us at last, and was replaced by an opulent widow. She was tall, and smelt like a cart-load of lavender; and wore a hair net, which I thought was a wig. I remember going close up and having a good look – it was clearly too square to be hair.

'What are you staring at?' the widow inquired.

I was much too soft-hearted to answer.

'Go on. Do tell. You needn't be shy.'

'You're wearing a wig,' I said.

'I can assure you I'm not!' She went very red.

'You are. I seen it,' I said.

The new teacher grew flustered and curiously cross. She took me upon her knee.

'Now look very close. Is that really a wig?'

I looked hard, saw the net, and said, 'Yes.'

'Well, really!' she said, while the Infants gaped. 'I can assure you it's *not* a wig! And if you only could watch me getting dressed in the morning you'd know it wasn't one either.'

She shook me from her knee like a sodden cat, but she'd stirred my imagination. To suggest I might watch her getting dressed in the morning seemed to me both outrageous and wonderful.

CIDER WITH ROSIE *by Laurie Lee*

Georgie Porgie, pudding and pie,
Kissed the girls and made them cry;
When the boys came out to play,
Georgie Porgie ran away. *Anon*

Frank Lahiffe loved Mary O'Dwyer as well. It was an intolerable triangle. She probably loathed both of us, but, at the age of four, I was not in the least interested in her feelings. The nuns compounded my heartache by placing Mary in a desk between Lahiffe and me. Learning my letters, I would trace the 'D' with my finger. It was cut from sandpaper and stuck on light blue cardboard. We would close our eyes and feel the shape of the 'D' while mouthing its sound. 'Duh,' I muttered with the others, but my eyes were slits of guile, partly open to facilitate my observation of the nun. When she looked away, I darted to the next desk and planted a kiss on Mary's knee. She sat there, eyes clamped tight, now muttering, 'Fuh.'

Lahiffe, more absorbed by his rival than his alphabet, then repeated my manoeuvre, kissing la O'Dwyer's other knee. She burst into tears. 'Mary O'Dwyer, stop being a cissy,' said the nun, not bothering to enquire into the reasons for the four-year-old's distress. 'Guh,' said Lahiffe and I.

IS THAT IT? *by Bob Geldof*

Erich Kästner (1899–1974) is chiefly remembered for his ever-popular Emil and the Detectives. *The following is taken from his authobiography,* When I was a Little Boy.

The school did not frighten me. I did not know any cheerful-looking schools. Doubtless they had to be as they were. And Herr Bremser, the stout pleasant teacher who welcomed the mothers and fathers and the new pupils did not frighten me at all. . . .

Herr Bremser put us in rows according to size, and took down our names. The parents stood close-packed along the walls and in the gangways, nodding and smiling encouragingly to their sons and holding the paper cones of sweets. This in fact was their chief task. They held small, medium or giant cones in their hands, compared the size of each other's cones and were proud or envious accordingly. You should have seen mine! It was as gaily coloured as a hundred picture postcards, as heavy as a coal bucket, and reached right up to the tip of my nose. I sat contentedly in my place, beaming at my mother and feeling a prince of cone-owners. Some of the little boys were crying in the most heart-rending fashion and running to their excited mammas.

But it was all over soon. Herr Bremser bade us goodbye and parents, children and paper cones set out noisily for home. I carried my cone of sweets like a flag-standard before me. Now and then I laid it down on the pavement and rested. From time to time my mother seized it and carried it for a bit. We sweated like furniture removers. Even a sweet load is still a load.

In this way we helped each other along through Glacis Strasse, Bautzener Strasse, across the Albert Platz and into Königsbrücker Strasse. From Luisen Strasse onwards I refused to let the cone out of my hands any more. It was a triumphal procession. Passers-by and neighbours stared. Children stopped and ran after us, swarming round us like bees that smell honey. 'And now let's go to Fräulein Haubold!' I said to my mother from behind my cone.

Fräulein Haubold was the manageress of a branch of a well-known dyer's in the ground floor of our tenement house, and I spent many hours in the quiet, spotless room. It smelled of freshly ironed clothes, chemically cleaned gloves and starched blouses. Fräulein Haubold was an elderly spinster, and we liked one another very much. I had heard that she said nice things about me, so she deserved the glorious sight better than anyone else. That went without saying.

My mother opened the door. With the paper cone and its red bow of ribbon pressed against my face I mounted the step into the shop, but as I could see nothing through the cone and its bow, I stumbled, and the tip of the cone broke off. I stood as still as a pillar of salt – a pillar of salt clutching a funnel of sweets whose contents poured in a steady rustling stream over my laced boots. I raised the cone as high as I could. This was not difficult because it was getting lighter and lighter. Finally I found myself holding nothing but a brightly coloured bottomless cardboard funnel. I lowered it and looked down at the ground. I was standing ankle deep in sweetmeats – chocolate creams, dates, Easter hares, figs, oranges, tartlets, waffles and golden cockchafers. The children who were following us giggled. My mother covered her face with her hands. Fräulein Haubold gripped the counter. What an abundance of sweetness! And I was standing in the middle of it.

You can shed tears over chocolates and sweets, especially when they happen to be yours. We hurriedly stuffed the sticky wreckage of sweets and fruit into my beautiful new brown leather school satchel and tottered through the shop, out of the back door to the well of the stairs, and up to our flat. Tears obscured the childish heaven. The contents of the paper cone were glued together in one sticky mass in the satchel. Two presents had melted into one. My mother had bought the beautiful paper cone and filled it with good things. My father had made the satchel. When he came home in the evening he cleaned it. Then he took his sharp saddler's knife and cut out a little bag for me. It was a little bag with an adjustable strap and was made of the same indestructible leather as the satchel. I carried my mid-morning snack to school in it ever afterwards.

In school itself there was only one difficulty. I was dreadfully inattentive. School was too slow for me. I was bored stiff. So I carried on entertaining conversations with my neighbours in front, behind and beside me. Clearly young men of seven have a lot to tell each other. Herr Bremser, easy-natured though he was, found my love of chattering most disturbing. His efforts to make thirty little Dresdeners into good readers were sadly hampered by the fact that one-third of the class was carrying on unlawful conversations, and that I was the ringleader. Finally he lost patience one day and told me angrily that if I did not mend my ways he would write to my parents about me.

When I came home at midday I imparted this interesting information. 'If I don't mend my ways,' I repeated, still out on the landing taking off my satchel, 'he will write a letter to you. His patience is at an end.' My mother was really horrified at this account of things, and still more by the coolness with which I repeated it. She took me very seriously to task, and I promised her that I would behave better. I could not guarantee that I would become attentive there and then and for ever, but I would not disturb the other pupils in future. That was a fair offer.

And the next day my mother went to Herr Bremser unknown to me. When she had told him everything he laughed. 'You don't say so!' he cried. 'What an odd boy. Any other child would have simply waited and said nothing until his parents got the letter.'

The village school at Larling consisted of two lofty rooms known, reasonably enough, as Big Room and Little Room. ... The Little Room, in which I found myself, was the domain of a Miss Parrot. She was a large woman with a pillow bosom, hennaed hair and gold-rimmed glasses. Behind her back she was known to us all as 'Polly'.

I was by no means the youngest pupil in her class but I was certainly one of the smallest. I was placed in a double desk in the front row beside a boy in a grey, knitted jumper who whispered to me that his name was Gordon. 'Mine's Col,' I whispered back and promptly earned myself a rap on the head from Miss Parrot's long ruler. She then commanded us to be silent for prayers. I stole a peep behind me. The other children had all closed their eyes and clasped their hands under their noses so I did the same. 'Our Father,' said Miss Parrot briskly.

Like sprinters at the sound of the gun the class was off. 'Ar - Farth - wi - chartin - Evven - allo - be - Thy - Name - Thy - Kingdumcum - Thywillbedone - on - earthasitisinEvven. ...' I opened and closed my lips but I didn't deceive Miss Parrot even though I bawled 'Amen' as lustily as anyone. She frowned and leant down towards me. 'Don't you *know* The Lord's Prayer?' she asked in a shocked voice.

I shook my head and flushed pink to the tips of my ears. There was a sound of sipped breath from the expectant class behind me. What was going to happen? Perhaps the floor would open and the devil would swallow me up.

'Then you must learn it – *at once*!' said Miss Parrot, opening her eyes so wide that a rim of white appeared all around each iris.

The class breathed again. I nodded dumbly.

'Say "Yes, Miss,"' said Miss Parrot.

'Yes, Miss,' I murmured.

I was presented with a slate and a slate pencil and was moved to protest that at home I was used to pen and ink. I was made to understand that ink was a Big Room privilege. In the Little Room it was slates. I quickly mastered the new medium and under Gordon's expert tuition learnt how to produce an excruciating squeak by first rubbing the point of my slate pencil across my scalp and then applying it to my slate. My formal education had begun.   ONE HAND CLAPPING *by Colin Middleton Murry (1926–)*

We were day-boys, William and I, at dispensaries of learning the number and succession of which today excite my wonder; we couldn't have changed oftener, it strikes me as I look back, if our presence had been inveterately objected to, and yet I enjoy an inward certainty that, my brother being vividly bright and I quite blankly innocuous, this reproach was never brought home to our house. It was an humiliation to me at first, small boys though we were, that our instructors kept being instructresses and thereby a grave reflection both on our attainments and our spirit. A bevy of these educative ladies passes before me, I still possess their names; as for instance that of Mrs Daly and that of Miss Rogers (previously of the 'Chelsea Female Institute', though at the moment of Sixth Avenue this latter), whose benches indeed my brother didn't haunt, but who handled us literally with gloves — I still see the elegant objects as Miss Rogers beat time with a long black ferule to some species of droning chant or chorus in which we spent most of our hours; just as I see her very tall and straight and spare, in a light blue dress, her firm face framed in long black glossy ringlets and the stamp of the Chelsea Female Institute all over her. Mrs Daly, clearly the immediate successor to the nebulous Miss Bayou, remains quite substantial — perhaps because the sphere of her small influence has succeeded in not passing away, up to this present writing; so that in certain notes on New York published a few years since I was moved to refer to it with emotion as one of the small red houses on the south side of Waverley Place that really carry the imagination back to a vanished social order. They carry mine to a stout red-faced lady with grey hair and a large apron, the latter convenience somehow suggesting, as she stood about with a resolute air, that she viewed her little pupils as so many small slices cut from the loaf of life and on which she was to dab the butter of arithmetic and spelling, accompanied by way of jam with a light application of the practice of prize-giving. I recall an occasion indeed, I must in justice mention, when the jam really was thick — my only memory of a schoolfeast, strange to say, throughout our young annals: something uncanny in the air of the schoolroom at the unwonted evening or late afternoon hour, and tables that seemed to me prodigiously long and on which the edibles were chunky and sticky. The stout red-faced lady must have been Irish, as the name she bore imported — or do I think so but from the indescribably Irish look of her revisited house? It refers itself at any rate to a New York age in which a little more or a little less of the colour was scarce notable in the general flush.

A SMALL BOY AND OTHERS *by Henry James*

The Schoolboy

I love to rise in a summer morn
When the birds sing on every tree;
The distant huntsman winds his horn,
And sky-lark sings with me.
O! what sweet company.

But to go to school in a summer morn,
O! it drives all joy away;
Under a cruel eye outworn,
The little ones spend the day
In sighing and dismay.

Ah! then at times I drooping sit,
And spend many an anxious hour,
Nor in my book can I take delight,
Nor sit in learning's bower,
Worn thro' with the dreary shower.

How can the bird that is born for joy
Sit in a cage and sing?
How can a child, when fears annoy,
But droop his tender wing,
And forget his youthful spring?

O! father and mother, if buds are nip't
And blossoms blown away,
And if the tender plants are strip'd
Of their joy in the springing day,
By sorrow and care's dismay,

How shall the summer arise in joy,
Or the summer fruits appear?
Or how shall we gather what griefs destroy,
Or bless the mellowing year,
When the blasts of winter appear?

William Blake

Hours and hours later three o'clock was near, and it was time for the school concert. A few mothers, towers of hat, had been wandering stiffly round the grounds since lunch. ... In the after-lunch break I had had a practice on the platform. It took twenty-two steps to walk round the grand piano. I was to play with Miss Pearl. I was sorry it was not Miss Dóbrée, because Miss Pearl did not smell so nice; but she let me climb up and put my head inside the piano while she played some notes.

So I was to start the concert. Why not Denys Roberts? He was the really young one. I caught sight of my sister in the audience, and she gave me a friendly smile. I knew this was decent of her, as she was already in Upper Fifth. One or two of her friends smiled too, and the result of this was to make me walk up on the platform with unsuitable stumping gait, to show I was not afraid, even trying to be funny, it must have seemed – my everlasting bad habit when shy, or feeling things against me. As long as I could dispel the little-boy suggestion. I adjusted the lanyard of my whistle so that it showed. Sitting on the platform at the piano, the stool was ridiculously high: my feet were far from the ground. Miss Pearl smelt of disinfectant. The piece was much too potty for me, I felt. Mostly slow octaves, while Miss Pearl did rather more difficult things in the bass. To show it was easy I smiled at the audience. They smiled back. 'Attend to the music, dear,' Miss Pearl whispered. I did, but to show that this was not enough to absorb me, I kicked my right leg in time for the last few bars. All over. And clapping! I had done it. They would say 'Well done.' There were some of my teachers in the aisle. I almost ran off the platform; and then I really did run down the aisle. Forgetting everything in my relief, I came to a stop in a long slide, which seemed as if it was never going to stop. I had not meant it.

'Not in front of the audience, dear.'

I don't know who said it, but instead of applauding me, they were reproving me. Baby-ish show-off – and I knew it. ... I had not done well. Where was Miss Pegler? She would understand. I suddenly felt really wretched. I sat at the back with the rest of the kindergarten, on the floor. None of the mistresses spoke to me – I might have been buried underground: and Miss Pegler wasn't there.

Soon we were being signalled for, and I knew what it was – the form picture. I had forgotten – the midsummer term photograph; and I had been looking forward to it. Perhaps everything would be all right. There were chairs on the grass – and there of course was Miss Pegler. I ran up to her as hard as I could go.

Suddenly I was running *back*, even faster, to the cloak-room. I had forgotten Joseph, the sailor, left in the satchel, and brought to school specially for this. Everybody was in position, but with a push and clamber I was up on the chair, standing next to Miss Pegler.

'Are you sure you want to have him in the photograph?'

What did she mean?

'Well, then, stand behind Kathleen, and don't push, not even in the slightest.' Did she think, too, that I had been stupid in the concert? 'I'm not pushing,' I said in a threatening voice. The photograph was over, and suddenly they were all looking at me. Monica was pointing at me.

"Why, he's got a dolly,' she was saying, in her fearful voice, like tin.

'It's NOT.'

'It's a DOLL.'

'It's not – it's a sailor – the largest toy soldier in the world. It's one of my crew.'

'It's a doll.' Some of the others took it up. But I was running and crying at the same time. 'It's not – not –not.' Nobody heard. I got my satchel out of the cloak-room and put Joseph carefully in the bottom. And then I began to run steadily, not crying any more, across the Common, down Nightingale Lane, for home.

STEPS TO IMMATURITY *by Stephen Potter (1900–69)*

Hare's schoolmaster was the father of Francis Kilvert, the diarist.

Aunt Lucy and the Maurices had long urged my mother to send me to school, and perhaps in many ways my terrible fits of naughtiness made it desirable, though they chiefly arose from nervousness, caused by the incessant 'nagging' I received at home from everyone except my mother and Lea. But the choice of the school to which I was sent at nine years old was very unfortunate.

The greater portion of Mr Kilvert's scholars – his 'little flock of lambs in Christ's fold' – were a set of little monsters. All infantine immoralities were highly popular, and – in such close quarters – it would have been difficult for the most pure and high-minded boy to escape from them. The first evening I was there, at nine years old, I was compelled to eat Eve's apple quite up – indeed, the Tree of the Knowledge of Good and Evil was stripped absolutely bare: there was no fruit left to gather.

THE STORY OF MY LIFE *by Augustus Hare (1834–1903)*

At Miss Budd's we began morning-school with a hymn. In reward for I know not what good or bad behaviour one or other of us might be called upon to choose this hymn, and my choice on these occasions would fall upon 'All things bright and beautiful'; possibly because it was the only one I could remember in my sudden embarrassment. But indeed I liked it, in as far as one can like a hymn, for it had a scent of the country which distinguished it from its fellows. 'The rushes that we gather by the stream-side every day' opened up a vista of enchantment and adventure to a London child along which he could wander happily through the Arithmetic lesson. 'A very pleasing choice,' Miss Budd would say, 'but we will omit the third verse, for unfortunately it is not quite true of those of us here today. We do *not* make a habit of gathering rushes. Now, Miss Florence, please, omitting the third verse.' And Miss Florence Budd at the piano would strike the appropriate chord. Unimaginative Miss Budds. I had gathered rushes and fallen into that stream a hundred times.

IT'S TOO LATE NOW *by A. A. Milne (1882–1956)*

A dillar, a dollar,
A ten o'clock scholar.
What makes you come so soon?
You used to come at ten o'clock,
But now you come at noon.

Anon

In school 'time was all withdrawn'. This was brought home to me
by a curious experience one dreary morning. I was seated with my
school-fellows at a long table, copying again and again 'Alfred
Tennyson is a poet', my writing getting steadily worse as the hated
statement was repeated. Doubt began – perhaps people had
denied that he was a poet? Glancing up at the school clock to see
how far off it still was to the lunch-interval at a quarter to eleven, I
beheld a miracle. As I looked, the big hand slipped from ten past
ten to twenty past! If the sun had done a similar turn in the sky I
could not have been more astonished. And it was not an answer to
a prayer like Joshua's, though it might well have been. I watched
to see what would happen next: the clock resumed its usual duty
at twenty past, and nobody noticed anything. We had lunch-time
by the clock, and I was too glad of this to point out what I had
seen. But thenceforward all clocks for me lost something of their
authority.

A LONDON CHILD OF THE 1870s *by M. V. Hughes (b. 1866)*

Timothy Winters

Timothy Winters comes to school
With eyes as wide as a football-pool,
Ears like bombs and teeth like splinters:
A blitz of a boy is Timothy Winters.

His belly is white, his neck is dark,
And his hair is an exclamation-mark.
His clothes are enough to scare a crow
And through his britches the blue winds blow.

When teacher talks he won't hear a word
And he shoots down dead the arithmetic-bird,
He licks the patterns off his plate
And he's not even heard of the Welfare State.

Timothy Winters has bloody feet
And he lives in a house on Suez Street,
He sleeps in a sack on the kitchen floor
And they say there aren't boys like him any more.

Old Man Winters likes his beer
And his missus ran off with a bombardier,
Grandma sits in the grate with a gin
And Timothy's dosed with an aspirin.

The Welfare Worker lies awake
But the law's as tricky as a ten-foot snake,
So Timothy Winters drinks his cup
And slowly goes on growing up.

At Morning Prayers the Master helves
For children less fortunate than ourselves,
And the loudest response in the room is when
Timothy Winters roars 'Amen!'

So come one angel, come on ten:
Timothy Winters says 'Amen
Amen amen amen amen.'
Timothy Winters, Lord.
                    Amen.

                              Charles Causley (1917–)

In this episode Pu Yi, last Emperor of China, is eight years old.

One summer's day in the third year of the Republic [1914] eight
eunuch guards, armed with ceremonial spears, marched in file
towards the Palace of Mind Nurture. Behind them, a team of

bearers carried Pu Yi in the yellow palanquin. When this procession, which took place morning and afternoon on every school-day, reached the entrance to the palace, two junior eunuchs of the presence escorted Pu Yi to the schoolroom. It was simply furnished with a few tables and chairs. A vase of flowers and some hanging character scrolls were the only decoration. There was also a large foreign clock with a pendulum. The ritual in the schoolroom never varied. Pu Yi sat at his own table, facing southwards, as an emperor always should. The two eunuchs stood like figurines, one on either side of him. 'Call them,' said Pu Yi, pointing towards the door.

The eunuchs went to the door and ushered in a second procession. First came a eunuch carrying a pile of books, then came an imperial tutor, and last of all, Pu Yi's fellow-pupils. They were his brother, Pu Chieh, and Yu Chung, son of Prince Pu Lun who, by every right, should have been emperor. Pu Chieh and Yu Chung knelt before Pu Yi and then went to sit at a table with the tutor, leaving Pu Yi to sit by himself.

It was time for the English lesson to begin. The tutor rose and handed round copies of their only English textbook, *Alice in Wonderland*. Facing each page of the story was a Chinese translation, the work of an earnest missionary. Pu Yi became fascinated by the adventures of Alice. He saw her as a young English concubine who had fallen down a deep well into the underworld of the Forbidden City. Unlocking gates and parting curtains, Alice dared to enter the hidden palaces and gardens of what was also called the Purple City. There she met frog footmen who, clearly, were eunuchs in disguise. To her horror, she was confronted by the Venerable Buddha. Sometimes the Venerable Buddha was the Duchess, who beat her little boy mercilessly for sneezing; and sometimes she was the Queen of Hearts, who walked in processions and sentenced people to death for the slightest offence. 'Off with her head,' the Queen of Hearts cried when Alice failed to kowtow to her. Both the Duchess and the Queen of Hearts left Pu Yi in no doubt that the young eunuchs and concubines of this underworld court were there to be beaten and tortured.

THE PUPPET EMPEROR *by Brian Power (1918–)*

This time tomorrow, where shall I be?
Not in this academy!...

No more Latin, no more French,
No more sitting on a hard school bench.

No more dirty bread and butter,
No more water from the gutter.

No more maggots in the ham,
No more filthy bread and jam.

No more milk in dirty old jugs,
No more cabbage boiled with slugs.

No more spiders in my bath,
Trying hard to make me laugh.

No more beetles in my tea,
Making googly eyes at me.

No more going to – (the headmaster)'s door,
Coming back and feeling sore.

No more lessons stuffed with rice,
No more cabbages full of lice.
All at home is dear and nice.
Breaking up, and going away,
NOT TOMORROW, BUT TODAY!

Anon

9

ENCOUNTERS

The naturalist and surgeon Francis Buckland (1826–80) showed a marked precocity.

When Frank Buckland was little more than four years old a clergyman had travelled from Devonshire to Oxford to bring Dr Buckland some 'very curious fossils'. On the production of these treasures Dr Buckland called to his son, who was playing in the room, 'Frankie, what are these?' 'They are the vertebrae of an ichthyosaurus,' lisped the child, who could not yet speak plain. The dumbfounded clergyman returned home crestfallen.

LIFE OF FRANK BUCKLAND *by George C. Bompas*

When I was eleven years old, my health compelled my parents to take a villa at San Remo for the winter, and during that period Mr Horace Round, the great authority on heraldry and genealogy, came for a few days' visit. In appearance he was hirsute and solid, in the manner of the late nineteenth-century Englishman. Just before he left, he suddenly asked 'Are the young people interested in genealogies too?' and then, before there was time to answer him, slid with abandon down the whole length of the banisters. This unexpected behaviour on the part of one who was normally dignified, and by no means young, made us children laugh, and my father subsequently reproved us, saying 'Don't laugh! These Great Men have their Little Idiosyncracies.'

LEFT HAND RIGHT HAND! *by Osbert Sitwell (1892–1969)*

Stravinsky's earliest musical memory was of the country,

where my parents, like most people of their class, spent the summer with their children. I can see it now. An enormous

peasant seated on the stump of a tree. The sharp resinous tang of
fresh-cut wood in my nostrils. The peasant simply clad in a short
red shirt. His bare legs covered with reddish hair, on his feet birch
sandals, on his head a mop of hair as thick and as red as his beard
– not a white hair, yet an old man. He was dumb, but he had a way
of clicking his tongue very noisily, and the children were afraid of
him. So was I. But curiosity used to triumph over fear. The
children would gather round him. Then, to amuse them, he would
begin to sing. This song was composed of two syllables, the only
ones he could pronounce. They were devoid of any meaning, but
he made them alternate with incredible dexterity in a very rapid
tempo. He used to accompany this clucking in the following way:
pressing the palm of his right hand under his left armpit, he would
work his left arm with a rapid movement, making it press on the
right hand. From beneath the red shirt he extracted a succession of
sounds which were somewhat dubious but very rhythmic, and
which might be euphemistically described as resounding kisses.
This amused me beyond words, and at home I set myself with zeal
to imitate this music – so often and so successfully that I was
forbidden to indulge in such an indecent accompaniment. The
two dull syllables which alone remained thus lost all their attrac-
tion for me.

CHRONICLE OF MY LIFE *by Igor Stravinsky (1882–1971)*

... the first things which I can genuinely remember are connected
with an illness which I had when I was about three. It was a very
severe attack of scarlet fever which also affected my kidneys and
in those days scarlet fever was a dangerous disease. ... At one
moment my illness took a turn for the worse and I was, so it was
said, upon the point of death. They called in Sir William Jenner,
the Queen's doctor and a descendant of the Jenner who invented
inoculation. He was a kindly man and I was fascinated by the
shape of his nose. He prescribed a draught of the most appalling
taste. I drank it down, but on his second visit – presumably next
day – I sat up in bed with a second dose in the glass in my hand
unable to drink it despite all the urging of my mother and Sir
William. At last I said to them – according to my mother, with

considerable severity – 'If you will *all* go out of the room, I will drink it.' I do not really remember that, but I do vividly remember the sequel. I remember sitting up in bed alone and the resignation with which I drank the filthy stuff, and the doctor and my mother coming back into the room and praising me. Sir William sat down on my bed and said that I had been so good that I would be given what I wanted. What did I want? 'A pigeon pie,' I said, 'with the legs sticking out.' 'You cannot,' he explained and his explanation was not unexpected by me, 'be given a pigeon pie with the legs sticking out just yet, but you will be given one as soon as you are quite well. But isn't there something – not to eat – which you would like now?' I remember looking carefully into his kindly old face and saying: 'I should like to pull your nose.' He said that I might, and gently, not disrespectfully, but as a kind of symbol or token, serious but also, I believe, deep down amused, I pulled Sir William Jenner's nose.

SOWING *by Leonard Woolf (1880–1969)*

in Just –

in Just –
spring   when the world is mud –
luscious the little
lame balloonman

whistles   far   and wee
and eddieandbill come
running from marbles and
piracies and it's
spring

when the world is puddle-wonderful

the queer
old balloonman whistles
far   and   wee
and bettyandisbel come dancing
from hop-scotch and jump-rope and

it's
spring
and
    the
        goat-footed
balloonman   whistles
far
and
wee

e. e. cummings (1894–1962)

One of the pleasantest stories about Oliver Goldsmith (?1730–74) is told by the dramatist George Colman the Younger in his Random Records:

I was only five years old when Goldsmith took me on his knee, while he was drinking coffee, one evening, with my father, and began to play with me; which amiable act I returned with the ingratitude of a peevish brat, by giving him a very smart slap on the face; it must have been a tingler, for it left the marks of my little spiteful paw upon his cheek. This infantile outrage was followed by summary justice, and I was locked up by my indignant father in an adjoining room, to undergo solitary imprisonment in the dark. Here I began to howl and scream most abominably, which was no bad step towards liberation, since those who were inclined to pity me might be likely to set me free, for the purpose of abating a nuisance.

At length a generous friend appeared to extricate me from jeopardy, and that generous friend was no other than the man I had so wantonly molested by assault and battery – it was the tender-hearted Doctor himself, with a lighted candle in his hand, and a smile upon his countenance, which was still partially red from the effects of my petulance. I sulked and sobbed, and he fondled and soothed, till I began to brighten. Goldsmith, who in regard to children was like the Village Preacher he has so beautifully described, for 'Their welfare pleased him, and their cares

distress'd', seized the propitious moment of returning good
humour – so he put down the candle, and began to conjure. He
placed three hats, which happened to be in the room, upon the
carpet, and a shilling under each: the shillings, he told me, were
England, France, and Spain. 'Hey, presto, cockolorum!' cried the
Doctor, and lo! on uncovering the shillings, which had been
dispersed each beneath a separate hat, they were all found con-
gregated under one. ... Astonishment might have amounted to
awe for one who appeared to me gifted with the power of performing miracles, if the good nature of the man had not obviated
my dread of the magician. ...

One day I was sitting with my sister Galya in Marinsky Park,
reading Stevenson's *Treasure Island*. Galya was also reading; her
summer hat lay beside her on the bench, its green ribbon stirring
in the wind.

Earlier it had rained but now the rain had nearly stopped and
only a few drops pattered off the lilacs.

Galya was a short-sighted and extremely trusting girl whose
equanimity it was almost impossible to upset.

A child with bows in her hair and a skipping rope had stopped
in front of us and was distracting me by her skipping. I shook the
lilac tree. A small shower descended noisily on to the child and
Galya. The little girl stuck out her tongue at me and ran away;
Galya only brushed the drops off her page and continued to read.

It was at this moment that I saw the man who for years to come
was to poison my mind with dreams of an unattainable destiny.

A tall midshipman with a calm, sunburned face came striding
lightly down the path. A straight black cutlass hung from his shiny
belt. Black ribbons with bronze anchors on them fluttered in the
breeze. His uniform was all black, the vivid gold of the insignia
alone relieving its austerity.

In our land-locked Kiev where we hardly ever saw a sailor, he
was a visitor from the remote and legendary world of sailing
ships, from the Frigate Pallada, from the world of all the oceans,
all the ports, all the winds, all the fascination of the life of those

who toil at sea. His antique black-hilted cutlass had come to
Marinsky Park straight out of Robert Louis Stevenson.

The midshipman walked past, the sand crunching under his
feet. I stood up and followed him. Galya was too short-sighted to
notice my disappearance.

The man was the embodiment of all my ocean-going dreams. I
had often imagined the sea, stormy or misty or calm in the gold
evening, and myself on a distant voyage, with the whole world
swiftly shifting and changing before my eyes like the patterns in a
kaleidoscope. Good gracious, if someone had only thought of
making me a birthday present of so much as a bit of rust off an
anchor! I would have treasured it like a jewel.

The midshipman looked round. Inscribed on the narrow ribbon of his cap was the mysterious word 'Azimuth'. I learned later
that this was the name of a training ship of the Baltic fleet.

I followed him down street after street. He saluted infantry
officers with a careless grace which made me ashamed of our
land-lubbing soldiery.

After looking back several times he finally stopped at a corner
of a street and beckoned me over.

'Tell me, boy,' he said with an amused smile, 'why have I got
you in tow?'

I blushed and couldn't get out a word.

'I know, he wants to be a sailor,' he guessed, for some reason
referring to me in the third person.

'I'm short-sighted,' I said despondently.

He put his lean hand on my shoulder.

'Let's go to the Kreshchatik.'

We walked side by side. Not daring to look up I could only see
the dazzling gloss on his stout, polished boots.

When we got to the Kreshchatik, he took me to the Samadeni
Café and ordered two pistachio ices and two glasses of water. The
waiter put them down on a small three-legged table with a marble
top. The marble was very cold and had figures scribbled all over it:
the stock exchange brokers used to gather in the café and work
out their profits and losses on the tables.

We ate our ices in silence. The midshipman drew from his
wallet the photograph of a magnificent corvette fully rigged and
with a large funnel. Handing it to me, he said:

'Take this to remember me by. It's my ship. I sailed in her to Liverpool.'

Then he firmly shook my hand and walked out. I stayed on until the sweating businessmen in boaters who sat at the next table began to stare. Then I stumbled out and ran all the way to Marinsky Park. There was no one on the bench. Galya had gone. I realized that the midshipman had felt sorry for me and learned for the first time that pity leaves a bitter aftertaste.

STORY OF A LIFE *by Konstantin Paustovsky (1892–1968)*

The following curious encounter is described by Dickens' close friend and biographer, John Forster.

The house called Gadshill-place stands on the strip of highest ground in the main road between Rochester and Gravesend. Often had we travelled past it together, years and years before it became his home; and never without some allusion to what he told me when first I saw it in his company, that amid the recollections connected with his childhood it held always a prominent place, for, upon first seeing it as he came from Chatham with his father, and looking up at it with much admiration, he had been promised that he might himself live in it, or in some such house, when he came to be a man, if he would only work hard enough. Which for a long time was his ambition. The story is a pleasant one, and receives authentic confirmation at the opening of one of his essays on travelling abroad, when as he passes along the road to Canterbury there crosses it a vision of his former self.

> So smooth was the old high road, and so fresh were the horses, and so fast went I, that it was midway between Gravesend and Rochester, and the widening river was bearing the ships, white sailed or black-smoked, out to sea, when I noticed by the wayside a very queer small boy.
>
> 'Holloa!' said I, to the very queer small boy, 'where do you live?'
>
> 'At Chatham,' says he.
>
> 'What do you do there?' says I.
>
> 'I go to school,' says he.

I took him up in a moment, and we went on. Presently, the very queer small boy says, 'This is Gads-hill we are coming to, where Falstaff went out to rob those travellers, and ran away.'

'You know something about Falstaff, eh?' said I.

'All about him,' said the very queer small boy. 'I am old (I am nine), and I read all sorts of books. But *do* let us stop at the top of the hill, and look at the house there, if you please!'

'You admire that house?' said I.

'Bless you, sir,' said the very queer small boy, 'when I was not more than half as old as nine, it used to be a treat for me to be brought to look at it. And now I am nine, I come by myself to look at it. And ever since I can recollect, my father, seeing me so fond of it, has often said to me, *If you were to be very persevering and were to work hard, you might some day come to live in it.* Though that's impossible!' said the very queer small boy, drawing a low breath, and now staring at the house out of the window with all his might.

I was rather amazed to be told this by the very queer small boy; for that house happens to be *my* house, and I have reason to believe that what he said was true.

THE LIFE OF CHARLES DICKENS *(1812–70)*

Each December I stayed with my Aunt Georgie, my mother's sister, wife of Sir Edward Burne-Jones, at The Grange, North End Road. At first I must have been escorted there, but later I went alone, and arriving at the house would reach up to the open-work iron bell-pull on the wonderful gate that let me into all felicity. When I had a house of my own, and The Grange was emptied of meaning, I begged for and was given that bell-pull for my entrance, in the hope that other children might also feel happy when they rang it.

At The Grange I had love and affection as much as the greediest, and I was not very greedy, could desire. There were most wonderful smells of paints and turpentine whiffing down from the big studio on the first floor where my Uncle worked; there was the society of my two cousins, and a sloping mulberry tree which we used to climb for our plots and conferences. There was a rocking-horse in the nursery and a table that, tilted up on two chairs, made a toboggan-slide of the best. There were pictures finished or half finished of lovely colours; and in the rooms chairs and cupboards such as the world had not yet seen, for William Morris (our Deputy 'Uncle Topsy') was just beginning to fabricate these things.

It was a jumble of delights and emotions culminating in being allowed to blow the big organ in the studio for the beloved Aunt, while the Uncle worked, or 'Uncle Topsy' came in full of some business of picture-frames or stained glass or general denunciations. . . .

As a rule Morris took no notice of anything outside what was in his mind at the moment. But I remember one amazing exception. My cousin Margaret and I, then about eight, were in the nursery eating pork-dripping on brown bread, which is a dish for the Gods, when we heard 'Uncle Topsy' in the hall calling, as he usually did, for 'Ned' or 'Georgie'. The matter was outside our world. So we were the more impressed when, not finding the grown-ups, he came in and said he would tell us a story. We settled ourselves under the table which we used for a toboggan-slide and he, gravely as ever, climbed on to our big rocking-horse. There, slowly surging back and forth while the poor beast creaked, he told us a tale full of fascinating horrors, about a man who was condemned to dream bad dreams. One of them took the shape of a cow's tail waving from a heap of dried fish. He went away as abruptly as he had come. Long afterwards, when I was old enough to know a maker's pains, it dawned on me that we must have heard the Saga of Burnt Njal, which was then interesting him. In default of grown-ups, and pressed by need to pass the story between his teeth and clarify it, he had used us.

SOMETHING OF MYSELF *by Rudyard Kipling*

*Walter Scott formed an affectionate attachment to Marjory Flem-
ing, the child prodigy. As a contemporary records, at the age of
seven she would make the novelist recite nursery rhymes she had
taught him:*

He used to say when he came to Alibi Crackaby he broke down.
Pin-Pan, Musky-Dan, Tweedle-um, Twodle-um, made him roar
with laughter. He said Musky-Dan especially was beyond endurance, bringing up an Irishman and his hat fresh from the Spice
Islands and odoriferous Ind; she getting quite bitter in her dis-
pleasure at his ill behaviour and stupidness. Then he would read
ballads to her in his own glorious way, the two getting wild with
excitement over 'Gil Morrice', or 'The Baron of Smailholm', and
he would take her on his knee, and make her repeat Constance's
speeches in *King John*, till he swayed to and fro sobbing his fill.

The year before she died, when in Edinburgh, she was at a
Twelfth Night supper at Scott's, in Castle Street. The company
had all come – all but Marjorie; and all were dull because Scott
was dull. 'Where's that bairn? What can have come over her? I'll
go myself and see!' and he was getting up, and would have gone,
when the bell rang, and in came Duncan Roy and his henchman
Dougal, with the Sedan chair, which was brought right into the
lobby, and its top raised. And there in its darkness and dingy old
cloth sat Maidie in white, her eyes gleaming, and Scott bending
over her in ecstasy –'hung over her enamoured'. 'Sit ye there, my
dautie, till they all see you,' and forthwith he brought them all.
You can fancy the scene. And he lifted her up and marched to his
seat with her on his stout shoulder, and set her down beside him;
and then began the night, and such a night. Those who knew Scott
best said, that night was never equalled. Maidie and he were the
stars; and she gave them Constance's speeches, and Helvellyn –
the ballad much in vogue – and all her repertoire, Scott showing
her off, and being ofttimes rebuked by her for his intentional
blunders.

Next morning I found myself in a new and strange world. The
house to my childish eyes appeared of vast size: it consisted of a

long range of rooms on the ground, built of brick, with brick floors and roof thatched with rushes. . . . A little distance from the house were the kitchen, bakery, dairy, huge barns for storing the produce, and wood-piles big as houses, the wood being nothing but stalks of the cardoon thistle or wild artichoke, which burn like paper, so that immense quantities had to be collected to supply fuel for a large establishment.

Two of the smallest of us were handed over to the care of a sharp little native boy, aged about nine or ten years, who was told to take us out of the way and keep us amused. The first place he took us to was the great barn, the door of which stood open; it was nearly empty just then, and was the biggest interior I had ever seen; how big it really was I don't know, but it seemed to me about as big as Olympia, or the Agricultural Hall, or the Crystal Palace would be to any ordinary little London boy. No sooner were we in this vast place than we saw a strange and startling thing – a man, sitting or crouching on the floor, his hands before him, the wrists tied together, his body bound with thongs of raw hide to a big post which stood in the centre of the floor and supported the beam of the loft above. He was a young man, not more than twenty perhaps, with black hair and a smooth, pale, sallow face. His eyes were cast down, and he paid no attention to us, standing there staring at him, and he appeared to be suffering or ill. After a few moments I shrank away to the door and asked our conductor in a frightened whisper why he was tied up to a post there. Our native boy seemed to be quite pleased at the effect on us, and answered cheerfully that he was a murderer – he had committed a murder somewhere, and had been caught last evening, but as it was too late to take him to the lock-up at the village, which was a long distance away, they had brought him here as the most convenient place, and tied him in the barn to keep him safe. Later on they would come and take him away.

Murder was a common word in those days, but I had not at that time grasped its meaning; I had seen no murder done, nor any person killed in a fight; I only knew that it must be something wicked and horrible. Nevertheless, the shock I had received passed away in the course of that first morning in a new world; but what I had seen in the barn was not forgotten: the image of that young man tied to the post, his bent head and downward gaze, and ghastly face shaded by lank black hair, is as plain to me now as if I had seen him but yesterday.

FAR AWAY AND LONG AGO *by W. H. Hudson*

I remember when Lytton Strachey came to stay with us. We children were much impressed by his uncannily distinguished appearance. We marvelled at the silky length of his beard, we mutely adored, and felt that here was indeed a wonder and a mystery. I think he must have been charming to us. I can still hear him reading aloud to us in his exquisitely modulated voice, and can remember the sheer bliss it was to listen – though I have forgotten what book he was reading from. He told us he was so weak before breakfast that he found it impossible to lift a match. This curious statement amazed and puzzled me (how well I understand it now!) and it seemed to me there must be more to follow.

THE SEVENTH CHILD *by Romilly John (1906–   )*

On one memorable occasion, my father and I had been travelling to London, to take in a visit to a museum and lunch at Snow's. We got into a compartment in which there was already one passenger: an old man with a long white beard and dressed, from head to foot, in black corduroy, and wearing a funny, floppy tie, of a style that would have quite defeated my mother. We sat opposite him. He was reading a book, holding it very close to his eyes, so that I could see both sides of the dust-jacket. On the back, there was the photograph of the reader opposite, there could be no doubt about it, the faces and the flowing beards matched, and there were the black corduroy and funny tie, of course in miniature, like a dwarf replica, and in black-and-white that missed the high colour of the face and the forget-me-not blue eyes. On the front was the name of the author: Aloysius (which I mentally pronounced, never having encountered a name so extraordinary, *Alloyshus*) Horn, and the title of the book, which I cannot remember. I was immensely excited by this discovery: here we were sitting opposite a man, almost in touching distance, who had written a book.

What is more, he was reading the book that he had written. Indeed, so engrossed was he in it that he seemed to be quite unaware of our presence. I wanted my father to share in my amazing discovery, so I nudged him on the forearm. He looked up, rather crossly, from the *Westminster Gazette*; but when, with an expressive, and, as I hoped, discreet, movement of the head, I indicated the book held up high with the bearded face on the back, and the same bearded face, in bright colours, and multiplied by ten, behind it, I could see at once that his interest had been aroused. Unlike me, he was sitting at an oblique angle to the reader, so that, instead of having one full-face superimposed upon another full-face much magnified, he could see partly round the side of the book and get a glancing view of the face in majestic, bearded semi-profile: the sage totally absorbed in his own printed words. After knocking out his pipe and then filling it again – an operation I knew well as being designed to gain time before he decided what to do next – he cleared his throat, and, in a bold effort to separate the photograph from the living face (the blue eyes were now watering slightly), he tapped the reader on the knee, and asked, rather engagingly: 'I seem to have seen your face somewhere before' (he had, indeed, a few seconds earlier, on the back of the dust-jacket). 'Excuse my indiscretion, but are you not Aloysius Horn (he pronounced it *Alloishus* – I had to give my father credit for having picked up a thing or two, almost as if he hadn't noticed) the well-known traveller?' (This was quite a new revelation of my father's charms, for I had never known him to talk like a blurb before, and had forgotten, for the moment, that he too was, vaguely, in the publishing line). Our *vis-à-vis* did not seem in the least bit put out by this direct approach; on the contrary, he seemed almost to have expected it (perhaps he had travelled all the way from Hastings, or at least from Wadhurst, without anyone getting into his compartment, so that the book had rested on the seat beside him, still with the back cover facing up). Smiling most affably, he acknowledged, in a very high-pitched voice, that he was indeed Aloysius Horn; 'the well-known traveller' was not actually spoken, but was implied in the slight pause that followed this self-identification.

The rest of the journey was spent most agreeably, I think for all three concerned. The traveller-author talked about his travels and his books – this was the latest one, only just out, to catch the Christmas readership and then there were a lot more to come. Then they talked about South Africa, Bechuanaland, Basutoland, Matabeleland, Swaziland, Somaliland, Egypt, and the Soudan – my father was now getting at least one country a turn ahead of the bearded author, rattling down the homeward track, roughly in the order of his own rather chaotic African career and, as he tended to equate literature with travel, and admired both Conrad and Kipling, he was obviously excited thus to meet the living combination of the two. Aloysius Horn seemed equally pleased; his journey had turned out well worthwhile, and, perhaps in the following years, he would make regular trips to and from Tunbridge Wells, in the hope of a repeat performance. All the while, I looked on in wonder; my father had grown several feet in my esteem, and I was actually seeing a real author and was listening to him talking about his work. I knew my father too was unusually pleased, for he spent the rest of the day, in London, addressing me as 'old boy' (I was eleven) and humming Gilbert and Sullivan tunes, always a sign that he was in exceptionally good humour.

STILL LIFE *by Richard Cobb (1917–   )*

10

PLAY

Franklin Hyde

Who caroused in the Dirt and was corrected by His Uncle.

His Uncle came on Franklin Hyde
Carousing in the Dirt.
He Shook him hard from Side to Side
And Hit him till it Hurt,
Exclaiming, with a Final Thud,
'Take that! Abandoned Boy!
For Playing with Disgusting Mud
As though it were a Toy!'

Moral

From Franklin Hyde's adventure, learn
To pass your Leisure Time
In Cleanly Merriment, and turn
From Mud and Ooze and Slime
And every form of Nastiness –
But, on the other Hand,
Children in ordinary Dress
May always play with Sand.

Hilaire Belloc (1870–1953)

An early extract from William A. Owens' account of his struggle to survive a childhood of near starvation on the flatlands of East Texas.

All that spring I spent my days in the field, sleeping, waking, crying when I was hungry or needed changing. When I was big enough to crawl, my mother tied me to a stake to keep me from going off into the woods where there were snakes and scorpions and long blue santafees with yellow stingered legs. Where the rows were long, she tied me in the middle of the field. When she was plowing and Monroe planting, she staked me between them, where one or the other could keep an eye on me.

My toys were the dirt, and a stick to dig the dirt. No one could live closer to the earth than I did. I dug the sand, I rolled in it, I covered myself with it. Before my first year had passed I had eaten the peck of dirt everyone, Pin Hook people said, is entitled to. I had learned the feel, the smell, the taste of earth.

THIS STUBBORN SOIL *by William A. Owens (1905–)*

German toys and models surrounded Peter from the first: every imaginable toy gun of the time, and soldiers and forts, and boats, and a musical box, little choppers, sabres, drums. And as live toys, dwarfs were given him to play with. Artemon Matveyef made him a present of a little gilt carriage drawn by tiny ponies, and when he went out in it two dwarfs went on his right hand and two on his left, while a fifth dwarf rode on a little horse behind him. On the 19th September, 1675, the child rode thus in procession in his carriage to the monastery of Serge-Troitsky. He was then three years old. Boys of his own age, though not all of his lineage, were brought in to play with him, among them some whom he kept with him for the rest of his life. They fought battles, destroyed kingdoms, built cities upon the nursery floor, the infant Peter rehearsing there his whole life and career.

PETER THE GREAT *(1672–1725) by Stephen Graham*

With France at war Louis's favourite toys were naturally soldiers. A goldsmith of Nancy had made him an army all in silver: pikemen, halberdiers, musketeers, troopers, gunners with their model pieces of ordnance of the six calibres used in France, pioneers with their tools, all correct in every detail. He also had a tiny set of gold cannon drawn by a team of fleas.

LOUIS XIV *(1638–1715) by Vincent Cronin*

The future Frederick the Great (1712–86) was less enchanted by soldiery.

Now, one of the first things his father planned to give his son pleasure was a miniature soldier company, a regiment of little boys which the prince was to command as soon as he should be drilled and taught a soldier's duty. The seven-year-old colonel was dressed in a tight blue bit of coat and a cocked hat, as exactly like his father as possible, but there the likeness ended, for little Fritz did not care in the least for soldiers, took no interest in drilling, and had no pride whatever in his smart regiment. He was so much happier playing his flute, and would much rather make music than war. WHEN THEY WERE CHILDREN *by Amy Steedman*

It was the primordial cave (and not what Freudian mystics might suppose) that lay behind the games I played when I was four. A big cretonne-covered divan, white with black trefoils, in one of the drawing rooms at Vyra rises in my mind, like some massive product of a geological upheaval before the beginning of history. . . .

With the help of some grown-up person, who would use first both hands and then a powerful leg, the divan would be moved several inches away from the wall, so as to form a narrow passage which I would be further helped to roof snugly with the divan's bolsters and close up at the ends with a couple of its cushions. I then had the fantastic pleasure of creeping through that pitch-dark tunnel, where I lingered a little to listen to the singing in my ears – that lonesome vibration so familiar to small boys in dusty hiding places – and then, in a burst of delicious panic, on rapidly thudding hands and knees I would reach the tunnel's far end, push its cushion away, and be welcomed by a mesh of sunshine on the parquet under the canework of a Viennese chair and two gamesome flies settling by turns. A dreamier and more delicate sensation was provided by another cave game, when upon awakening in the early morning I made a tent of my bedclothes and let my imagination play in a thousand dim ways with shadowy snow-slides of linen and with the faint light that seemed to penetrate my penumbral covert from some immense distance, where I fancied that strange, pale animals roamed in a landscape of lakes. The recollection of my crib, with its lateral nets of fluffy cotton cords, brings back, too, the pleasure of handling a certain beautiful, delightfully solid, garnet-dark crystal egg left over from some unremembered Easter; I used to chew a corner of the bedsheet until it was thoroughly soaked and then wrap the egg in it tightly, so as to admire and re-lick the warm, ruddy glitter of the snugly enveloped facets that came seeping through with a miraculous completeness of glow and colour.

SPEAK, MEMORY by Vladimir Nabokov (1899–1977)

Harston House was – at least in part – a lovely William and Mary house, and it had a large old-fashioned garden very suited to hide-and-seek, with an orchard, a stream and a big pond containing an island, and there was a fountain on the front lawn. We would fix a cup to the handle of a walking stick, and the water so obtained tasted very cold and very pure. The fountain was about two feet deep and a yard across. Once my elder brother Raymond fell in at the age of three, and when asked how he had got out he replied with bravura, 'I struck out for the shore.'

A SORT OF LIFE by Graham Greene (1904–   )

Rough

My parents kept me from children who were rough
Who threw words like stones and who wore torn clothes.
Their thighs showed through rags. They ran in the street
And climbed cliffs and stripped by the country streams.

I feared more than tigers their muscles like iron,
Their jerking hands and their knees tight on my arms.
I feared the salt coarse pointing of those boys
Who copied my lisp behind me on the road.

They were lithe, they sprang out behind hedges
Like dogs to bark at my world. They threw mud
While I looked the other way, pretending to smile.
I longed to forgive them, but they never smiled.

Stephen Spender (1909–   )

The hunt was over. A rug was spread in the shade of some young birch-trees and the whole company disposed themselves in a circle on the rug. Gavrilo, the butler, having stamped down the lush green grass around him, was wiping plates and taking out of the box plums and peaches wrapped in leaves. The sun shone through the green branches of the young birches and cast round quivering medallions of light on the pattern of the rug, on my legs and even on Gavrilo's perspiring bald head. A light breeze fluttering through the foliage of the trees on to my hair and burning face refreshed me beyond measure.

When we had had our share of ice-cream and fruit it was no use sitting on the rug any longer so in spite of the scorching heat of the oblique rays of the sun we got up and proceeded to play games.

'Well, what shall it be?' said Lyuba, screwing her eyes up in the sun and hopping about on the grass. 'Let's play Robinson!'

'No . . . that's too dull,' said Volodya, sprawling on the grass and chewing some leaves. 'It's always Robinson! If you must do something, we'd better build a summer-house.'

Volodya was obviously putting on airs: probably he was proud of having ridden the hunter and was pretending to be very tired. Or perhaps even at that age he was too matter-of-fact and had too little imagination really to enjoy playing at Robinson, which consisted in performing scenes from *The Swiss Family Robinson* which we had read not long before.

'Please do . . . why won't you do what we want?' the girls insisted. 'You can be Charles, or Ernest, or the father, whichever you like,' said Katya, trying to pull him up from the ground by the sleeve of his jacket.

'I really don't want to – it's a silly game!' said Volodya, stretching himself and at the same time smiling smugly.

'It would have been better to stay at home if no one wants to play,' declared Lyuba in tears.

She was an awful cry-baby.

'All right, come along then; only please don't cry. I can't stand it!'

Volodya's condescension afforded us very little satisfaction: on the contrary his lazy bored look destroyed all the fun of the game. When we sat on the ground and pretending we were going fishing began to row with all our might Volodya sat with folded arms in an attitude which had nothing in common with the attitude of a fisherman. I told him so but he retorted that by waving our arms about more vigorously or less we should not gain or lose anything, and should not travel any the further. I could not help agreeing with him. When I pretended to go hunting and set off into the woods with a stick over my shoulder Volodya lay down on his back with his hands behind his head and told me he would pretend to be coming too. Such talk and behaviour had a damping effect on the game and were extremely distasteful, the more so because in one's secret heart one had to admit that Volodya was right.

I knew myself that not only could I not kill a bird with a stick but that I could not even make it fire. It was just a game. Once you begin arguing like that it becomes equally impossible to ride out for a drive on chairs; and, I thought, Volodya must remember how in the long winter evenings we covered an arm-chair with a shawl to turn it into a carriage. One of us sat in front as the coachman, someone else was a footman, and the girls sat in the middle. Three chairs were the horses – and we were off. And what adventures we used to meet on the way, and how gaily and swiftly those winter evenings passed! . . . If you only go by what's real there won't be any games. And if there are no games, what is left?

CHILDHOOD by Leo Tolstoy (1828–1910)

Henry and Mary

Henry was a young king,
   Mary was his queen;
He gave her a snowdrop
   On a stalk of green.

Then all for his kindness
   And all for his care
She gave him a new-laid egg
   In the garden there.

'Love, can you sing?'
                                      'I cannot sing.'
'Or tell a tale?'
                                      'Not one I know.'
'Then let us play at queen and king
As down the garden walks we go.'

Robert Graves

Walks in Kensington Gardens were dull. Non-being made up a
great proportion of our time in London. The walks – twice every
day in Kensington Gardens – were so monotonous. . . .
    We sailed boats, of course. There was the great day when my
Cornish lugger sailed perfectly to the middle of the pond and then
with my eyes upon it, amazed, sank suddenly; 'Did you see that?'
my father cried, coming striding towards me. We had both seen it
and both were amazed. To make the wonder complete, many
weeks later in the spring, I was walking by the pond and a man in a
flat-boat was dredging the pond of duckweed, and to my
unspeakable excitement, up he brought my lugger in his dredging
net; and I claimed it; and he gave it to me, and I ran home with this
marvellous story to tell. Then my mother made new sails; and my
father rigged it, and I remember seeing him fixing the sails to the
yard-arm after dinner; and how interested he became and said,
with his little snort, half laughing, something like 'Absurd – what
fun it is doing this!'   A SKETCH OF THE PAST *by Virginia Woolf*

*In this fragment from 'The History of the Year 1829' Charlotte
Brontë records the genesis of the 'plays' or games that were to
develop into the secret worlds of Angria and Gondal.*

Once Papa lent my sister Maria a book. It was an old geography
book; she wrote on its blank leaf, 'Papa lent me this book.' This
book is a hundred and twenty years old; it is at this moment lying
before me. While I write this I am in the kitchen of the Parsonage,
Haworth; Tabby, the servant, is washing up the breakfast things,
and Anne, my youngest sister (Maria was my eldest), is kneeling

on a chair, looking at some cakes which Tabby has been baking for us. Emily is in the parlour, brushing the carpet. Papa and Branwell are gone to Keighley. Aunt is upstairs in her room, and I am sitting by the table writing this in the kitchen. . . . Our plays were established: 'Young Men', June 1826; 'Our Fellows', July 1827; 'Islanders', December 1827. These are our three great plays, that are not kept secret. Emily's and my bed plays were established the 1st of December 1827; the others, March 1828. Bed plays mean secret plays; they are very nice ones. All our plays are very strange ones. Their nature I need not write on paper, for I think I shall always remember them. The 'Young Men's' play took its rise from some wooden soldiers Branwell had; 'Our Fellows' from *Aesop's Fables*; and the 'Islanders' from several events which happened. I will sketch out the origin of our plays more explicitly if I can. First, 'Young Men'. Papa bought Branwell some wooden soldiers at Leeds; when Papa came home it was night and we were in bed, so next morning Branwell came to our door with a box of soldiers. Emily and I jumped out of bed, and I snatched up one and exclaimed, 'This is the Duke of Wellington! This shall be the Duke!' When I had said this, Emily likewise took up one and said it should be hers; when Anne came down, she said one should be hers. Mine was the prettiest of the whole, and the tallest and the most perfect in every part. Emily's was a grave-looking fellow, and we called him 'Gravey'. Anne's was a queer little thing, very much like herself, and we called him 'Waiting-Boy'. Branwell chose his and called him 'Buonaparte'.

In her introduction to 'Tales of the Islanders' Charlotte takes the account a little further.

June the 31st, 1829.

The play of the 'Islanders' was formed in December 1827, in the following manner. One night, about the time when the cold sleet and stormy fogs of November are succeeded by the snow-storms, and high piercing night winds of confirmed winter, we were all sitting round the warm blazing kitchen fire, having just concluded a quarrel with Tabby concerning the propriety of lighting a candle, from which she came off victorious, no candle having been produced. A long pause succeeded, which was at last broken by Branwell saying, in a lazy manner, 'I don't know what to do.' This was echoed by Emily and Anne.

Tabby. 'Wha ya may go t'bed.'

Branwell. 'I'd rather do anything than that.'

Charlotte. 'Why are you so glum tonight, Tabby? Oh! Suppose we had each an island of our own.'

Branwell. 'If we had I would choose the Island of Man.'

Charlotte. 'And I would choose the Isle of Wight.'

Emily. 'The Isle of Arran for me.'

Anne. 'And mine shall be Guernsey.'

We then chose who should be chief men in our islands. Branwell chose John Bull, Astley Cooper, and Leigh Hunt; Emily, Walter Scott, Mr Lockhart, Johnny Lockhart; Anne, Michael Sadler, Lord Bentinck, Sir Henry Halford. I chose the Duke of Wellington and two sons, Christopher North and Co., and Mr Abernethy. Here our conversation was interrupted by the, to us, dismal sound of the clock striking seven, and we were summoned off to bed. The next day we added many others to our list of men, till we got almost all the chief men of the kingdom. After this, for a long time, nothing worth noticing occurred. In June 1828 we erected a school on a fictitious island, which was to contain 1000 children. The manner of the building was as follows. The island was fifty miles in circumference, and certainly appeared more like the work of enchantment than anything real. . . .

THE LIFE OF CHARLOTTE BRONTË *by Elizabeth Gaskell*

New Hampshire

Children's voices in the orchard
Between the blossom- and the fruit-time:
Golden head, crimson head,
Between the green tip and the root.
Black wing, brown wing, hover over;
Twenty years and the spring is over;
To-day grieves, to-morrow grieves,

Cover me over, light-in-leaves;
Golden head, black wing,
Cling, swing,
Spring, sing,
Swing up into the apple-tree.

from 'Landscapes' by T. S. Eliot

My mother's general principles of first treatment were, to guard me with steady watchfulness from all avoidable pain or danger; and, for the rest, to let me amuse myself as I liked, provided I was neither fretful nor troublesome. But the law was, that I should find my own amusement. No toys of any kind were at first allowed; – and the pity of my Croydon aunt for my monastic poverty in this respect was boundless. On one of my birthdays, thinking to overcome my mother's resolution by splendour of temptation, she bought the most radiant Punch and Judy she could find in all the Soho bazaar – as big as a real Punch and Judy, all dressed in scarlet and gold, and that would dance, tied to the leg of a chair. I must have been greatly impressed, for I remember well the look of the two figures, as my aunt herself exhibited their virtues. My mother was obliged to accept them; but afterwards quietly told me it was not right that I should have them; and I never saw them again.

Nor did I painfully wish, what I was never permitted for an instant to hope, or even imagine, the possession of such things as one saw in toy-shops. I had a bunch of keys to play with, as long as I was capable only of pleasure in what glittered and jingled; as I grew older, I had a cart, and a ball; and when I was five or six years old, two boxes of well-cut wooden bricks. With these modest, but, I still think, entirely sufficient possessions, and being always summarily whipped if I cried, did not do as I was bid, or tumbled on the stairs, I soon attained serene and secure methods of life and motion; and could pass my days contentedly in tracing the squares and comparing the colours of my carpet; – examining the knots in the wood of the floor, or counting the bricks in the opposite houses; with rapturous intervals of excitement during the filling of the water-cart, through its leathern pipe, from the dripping iron post at the pavement edge; or the still more admirable proceedings of the turncock, when he turned and turned till a fountain sprang up in the middle of the street. But the carpet, and what patterns I could find in bed covers, dresses, or wall-papers to be examined, were my chief resources, and my attention to the particulars in these was soon so accurate, that when at three and a half I was taken to have my portrait painted by Mr Northcote, I had not been ten minutes alone with him before I asked him why there were holes in his carpet.

PRAETERITA *by John Ruskin (1819–1900)*

Jean-Jacques Rousseau and a young cousin have been sent to board at Bossey with a Pastor Lambercier 'to learn Latin and all that sorry nonsense as well that goes by the name of education'.

Outside the gate into the courtyard, on the left as you came in, was a terrace on which we often sat of an afternoon, although it was fully exposed to the sun. In order to provide some shade, however, M. Lambercier had a walnut tree planted there. Its planting was carried out with all solemnity; we two boarders were its godparents, and whilst the hole was being filled we each held the tree with one hand, singing triumphal songs. Now for its watering a kind of trench was left all round it, and every day my cousin and I eagerly watched the watering ceremony, which confirmed us in our natural belief that it was a finer thing to plant a tree on a terrace than a flag in the breech. We resolved, therefore, to win that glory for ourselves and share it with no one.

For that purpose we went and cut a slip from a young willow, and planted it on the terrace some eight or ten feet from the sacred walnut. Nor did we omit to dig a trench round our tree, but the difficulty was to obtain the wherewithal to fill it. For our water was brought from a considerable distance, and we children were not allowed to run out and fetch it. Nevertheless our willow could not thrive without it, and for some days we resorted to every sort of device for getting it, to such good effect that it budded beneath our eyes, putting out little leaves whose growth we measured hour by hour, in the firm belief that, though it was not a foot high, it would not be long before it cast us a shade.

Now our tree was our sole preoccupation, and we went about in a sort of fever, incapable of applying ourselves to our lessons or to anything else. Our elders, therefore, unable to make out the cause of the trouble, kept us more confined than ever; and the fatal moment drew near when our water would give out. We were desperate at the thought of watching our tree parch to death. Finally invention's mother, necessity, suggested a way of keeping it alive and saving ourselves from death by despair. Our plan was to make an underground tunnel which would secretly bring to the willow some of the water which was given to the walnut tree. Feverishly we undertook our enterprise, but at first it did not succeed; the runnel filled up with dirt, and everything went wrong. But nothing deterred us: '*Labor omnia vincit improbus.*' We dug away more earth and deepened our trench to give the water a flow; and we cut some boxes into little narrow boards, putting some of them flat at the bottom and propping others at angles at each side to make a triangular channel for our stream. Where it flowed in we planted thin sticks at intervals to form a grating or trap that would hold up the fine earth and stones, and keep the channel free for the water. Then we carefully covered our work, treading the soil well down, and on the day when it was completed waited in an ecstasy of alternate hope and fear for watering time. After centuries of delay the hour came round at last, and M. Lambercier emerged, as usual, to witness the ceremony, throughout which we both stood behind him, to hide our tree. For, most fortunately, he had his back to it.

A few seconds after the first bucket was poured in we saw a trickle of water flow into our trench. At this sight our caution deserted us, and we set up such shouts of joy that M. Lambercier turned round; which was a pity since he had just been observing with delight how good the soil was around his tree and how greedily it absorbed the water. Shocked, however, to see it providing for two trenches, he also set up a shout. Then, taking a closer look, he discovered our trick and sent straight for a mattock, which quickly knocked a few of our boards flying. 'An aqueduct! an aqueduct!' he cried, and rained down his merciless blows on every side. Each one of them pierced us to the heart. In a moment the boards, the runnel, the trench, and the willow were all destroyed, and the earth all round was ploughed up. But, in the course of all this frightful business, the only words uttered were his cries of 'An aqueduct! an aqueduct!' as he knocked everything to pieces.

It may be supposed that the incident had unpleasant consequences for the young architects. But not so. That was all. M. Lambercier did not utter a word of reproach, did not look sternly upon us, and never mentioned the matter at all, though we heard his full-throated laugh ring out shortly afterwards from his sister's room. You could hear M. Lambercier's laugh from afar. What was even more surprising, however, was that when the first shock was over, we were not very distressed ourselves. We planted another tree in another place, and often reminded one another of the first one's unhappy fate, by significantly repeating 'An aqueduct! an aqueduct!' Before that time I had had occasional bouts of conceit and fancied myself an Aristides or a Brutus; but this was my first well-defined attack of vanity. To have built an aqueduct with our own hands and set a cutting to compete with a large tree seemed to me the very height of glory, the meaning of which I understood better at ten than did Caesar at thirty.

THE CONFESSIONS *by Jean-Jacques Rousseau (1712–78)*

All shod with steel,
We hissed along the polished ice in games
Confederate, imitative of the chase
And woodland pleasures, – the resounding horn,
The pack loud chiming, and the hunted hare.
So through the darkness and the cold we flew,
And not a voice was idle; with the din
Smitten, the precipices rang aloud;
The leafless trees and every icy crag
Tinkled like iron; while far distant hills
Into the tumult sent an alien sound
Of melancholy not unnoticed, while the stars
Eastward were sparkling clear, and in the west
The orange sky of evening died away.

Not seldom from the uproar I retired
Into a silent bay, or sportively
Glanced sideway, leaving the tumultuous throng,
To cut across the reflex of a star
That fled, and, flying still before me, gleamed
Upon the grassy plain; and oftentimes,
When we had given our bodies to the wind,
And all the shadowy banks on either side
Came sweeping through the darkness, spinning still
The rapid line of motion, then at once
Have I, reclining back upon my heels,
Stopped short; yet still the solitary cliffs
Wheeled by me – even as if the earth had rolled
With visible motion her diurnal round!
Behind me did they stretch in solemn train,
Feebler and feebler, and I stood and watched
Till all was tranquil as a dreamless sleep.

from 'The Prelude' by William Wordsworth

Oscar Wilde's younger son remembers his father.

It was only during these early years that I knew my father; after
1895 I never saw him again. Most small boys adore their fathers,
and we adored ours; and as all good fathers are, he was a hero to
us both. He was so tall and distinguished and, to our uncritical
eyes, so handsome. There was nothing about him of the monster
that some people who never knew him and never even saw him
have tried to make him out to be. He was a real companion to us,
and we always looked forward eagerly to his frequent visits to our
nursery. Most parents in those days were far too solemn and
pompous with their children, insisting on a vast amount of usually
undeserved respect. My own father was quite different; he had so
much of the child in his own nature that he delighted in playing
our games. He would go down on all fours on the nursery floor,
being in turn a lion, a wolf, a horse, caring nothing for his usually
immaculate appearance. And there was nothing half-hearted in
his methods of play. One day he arrived with a toy milk-cart

drawn by a horse with real hair on it. All the harness undid and took off, and the churns with which the cart was filled could be removed and opened. When my father discovered this he immediately went downstairs and came back with a jug of milk with which he proceeded to fill the churns. We then all tore round the nursery table, slopping milk all over the place, until the arrival of our nurse to put an end to that game. . . .

When he grew tired of playing he would keep us quiet by telling us fairy stories, or tales of adventure, of which he had a never-ending supply. He was a great admirer of Jules Verne and Stevenson, and of Kipling in his more imaginative vein. The last present he gave me was *The Jungle Book*; he had already given me *Treasure Island* and Jules Verne's *Five Weeks in a Balloon*, which were the first books I read through entirely by myself. He told us all his own written fairy stories suitably adapted for our young minds, and a great many others as well. There was one about the fairies who lived in the great bottles of coloured water that chemists used to put in their windows, with lights behind them that made them take on all kinds of different shapes. The fairies came down from their bottles at night and played and danced and made pills in the empty shop. Cyril once asked him why he had tears in his eyes when he told us the story of *The Selfish Giant*, and he replied that really beautiful things always made him cry.

SON OF OSCAR WILDE *by Vyvyan Holland (1886–1967)*

On a visit to Seend, Angelica Garnett becomes seriously ill with a throat infection.

These days, such an infection is quickly controlled by drugs, and the normally healthy child hardly experiences illness. At that time, however, the doctor could do little but watch and wait for one's natural vigour to reassert itself. Every illness had its initial moments of malaise together with an inner certainty of imminent collapse and a deep reluctance to admit it. Then there was the relief of going to bed, followed by headaches, pain, nausea and sensations of the strangest kind. On this occasion Vanessa was trapped at Seend while I lay in a state of timeless suspension in the

old nursery in the back part of the house. Vague feminine presences hovered round me; Ellen the housemaid and another
woman sat murmuring by the fire when they supposed me asleep.
Their shadows engulfed the ceiling, while floors and walls no
longer seemed solid, but approached and retreated like the waves
of the sea. Small objects became large, amongst them my head,
stretched to enormous size. Never hungry, I was yet fed from
plates with double walls containing hot water to keep the food
warm, stoppered with little corks on a chain. So familiar did I
become with the garlands decorating their edges that I could
easily reproduce their dull green, pink and blue at this moment.
The doctor too left an indelible impression: he sprang up by the
bed like a jack-in-the-box, jocose in the old-fashioned manner,
and yet full of vague menace since he evidently knew too much
about me. I didn't like the way he talked to Vanessa, mentioning
all sorts of things about my body as though I were not there. Had
he been young and smiling I might not have minded, but he was
small and stout with a double chin, dressed in black with a stiff
wing-collar: he was absurd, but had to be propitiated. One day I
made some cotton-wool eggs and, pretending I had laid them
myself, I drew them out from under my bottom and offered them
to him as the first fruits of my convalescence, though I knew quite
well that I should have got better without his help. I remember his
astonishment, as though the gesture were improper, and the
awkward bonhomie with which he passed it off.

DECEIVED WITH KINDNESS

I was almost constantly engaged in some mischievous prank or
other; but with a detail of these it would be wearisome to load my
narrative; they were occasioned by the overflowings of an active,
wild disposition. At one time, in imitation of the savages
described in *Robinson Crusoe* – or some other savages – I often,
in a morning, set off *stark naked* across the fell, where I was joined
by some associates, who, in like manner, ran about like mad
things, or like Bedlamites who had escaped. Climbing the tall trees
at Eltringham for rook nests, at the hazard of breaking our necks

or our bones, was another piece of business which employed our attention. . . .

I have often since shuddered at the thoughts of doing these and such like desperate acts, and wondered how I escaped; but neither caution nor fear had at that time taken a place in the mind; on the contrary, any uncommon or frightful exploit had charms in it that I could not resist. One of these pranks, however, attracted the attention of the neighbourhood, brought me into a great dilemma, and occasioned me a severe beating. I engaged a constant associate, Josh. Liddell, who was ever ready at my command to help me, as soon as I communicated any design to him. I had discovered two oxen in a little savannah or bit of grazing ground, surrounded by hazel and other bushes, near the brink of the river. Thither we went in order to enjoy so tempting a sight as to see them plunge overhead into the flood. When all was ready, we suddenly, with long branches in our hands, sprang upon them from the bushes overhanging the precipice, the danger of which they did not see; and they were plunged, with such a *delightful dash*, overhead into the river! They, however, happened to be no worse for it; for they were driven down by the rapid current of the flood, and landed safely at a distance below. This exploit, happening on a Sunday afternoon, was an aggravation of the crime.

A MEMOIR OF THOMAS BEWICK *by Himself*

Autobiographical Note

Beeston, the place, near Nottingham;
We lived there for three years or so.
Each Saturday at two o'clock
We queued up for the matinée,
All the kids for streets around
With snotty noses, giant caps,
Cut down coats and heavy boots,
The natural enemies of cops
And schoolteachers. Profane and hoarse
We scrambled, yelled and fought until
The Picture Palace opened up

And then, like Hamelin children, forced
Our bony way into the Hall.
That much is easy to recall;
Also the reek of chewing-gum,
Gob-stoppers and liquorice,
But of the flickering myths themselves
Not much remains. The hero was
A milky, wide-brimmed hat, a shape
Astride the arched white stallion.
The villain's horse and hat were black.
Disbelief did not exist
And laundered virtue always won
With quicker gun and harder fist
And all of us applauded it.
Yet I remember moments when
In solitude I'd find myself
Brooding on the sooty man,
The bristling villain, who could move
Imagination in a way
The well-shaved hero never could,
And even warm the nervous heart
With something oddly close to love.

Vernon Scannell (1922–   )

On [one] occasion my father took us up to London to visit a friend of his. The name meant nothing to me but the memory of that visit is still extraordinarily vivid. Weg and I were shown into a long white room and told to 'amuse' ourselves. We looked around us with some trepidation. The floor was covered with toys: wooden bricks, toy soldiers, model railways, all scattered in profusion. While we were gazing at them doubtfully, a door at the far end of the room opened quietly and a small, plump-faced man with the bluest eyes I had ever seen came in on his hands and knees. His head was just about on the same level as ours. 'Hello,' he said. 'So you've come to play with me, have you? That's fine, fine.'

In a twinkling he had us both organized. I was to be the commander of the Red army; Weg of the Blue; while he rushed round frantically winding up clockwork trains, constructing bridges and fortifications, firing pencils out of toy cannons. It was all highly hysterical – quite unlike any grown-up behaviour I had ever known. And then, almost without our noticing it, he had slipped away.

Eventually my father appeared to collect us and take us home. The little plump man appeared once again and handed us each a book. Weg's was called *Floor Games*, mine was *Little Wars*. Inside each he had written our names and underneath 'With love from H. G. Wells'. Throughout my childhood I used those books just as their author would have wished them to be used – as practical hand-books. I drew and scribbled all over them and it was years before I was able to link them and that magical afternoon with the author of what had by then become one of my favourite novels, *The War of the Worlds*.

ONE HAND CLAPPING *by Colin Middleton Murry*

In his memoir Seven Summers, *the Indian novelist Mulk Raj Anand (1905–) describes one of the games that helped to while away a long childhood convalescence.*

Another sport which Rukmani and I played together was the dyeing of sparrows. . . . The game consisted in first catching some sparrows. Rukmani and I would sit down by the threshold of the verandah and sprinkle some lentils before us, first a little way away to tempt the sparrows, then, when they came to peck at the grains, a little nearer us, and, when we had won their confidence, still nearer, till the sparrows became so unafraid of us as to come and eat out of our hands. In this way we would ensnare a sparrow and dye it in a little cup of liquid dye we kept ready by us. Then we would release it and it would fly away, coloured a vivid green. Next day we would use a deep crimson dye and the next day yellow or blue. In the seven days of the week we would colour the seven sparrows we caught in the seven colours of the rainbow. And our happiness knew no bounds as we saw these sparrows, transformed by our hands, fly all over the barracks, confusing the sepoys, who looked with hands over their eyes at the queer phenomenon of sparrows which had become different overnight. And when these little coloured birds alighted in our own courtyard, we shrieked with joy and our mothers affected to share our pleasure in the colours that we had set free in the heights of the sky.

Miss Boustead was Commander-in-Chief of the Sloane Square Wolf Cubs, an elite corps of which I was a junior member. She was a woman built on generous lines and when she turned out in an immense khaki skirt and wide-brimmed scouting hat, with her whistle on a lanyard and her long-service decorations, she made a formidable figure. Miss Boustead's ideas on Cub training were single-minded and resulted in one activity only. She formed up her platoon at Sloane Square Underground Station and led us, by public transport, to Wimbledon Common. Once out in open country Miss Boustead would choose some suitable clearing or glen and stand in it with her legs akimbo. She would then give the order, 'Cubs, scatter!' Ours was not to reason why, and each loyal Cub rushed into the middle distance and flung himself into the undergrowth. It was then a Cub's task to advance, squirming on his belly, taking advantage of every bit of ground cover, daring a dash in full view whenever the Commander's head was turned, towards the bulky figure in the clearing. The rules were simple. The Cub who got between Miss Boustead's legs before she spotted him was awarded the box of Cadbury's Assorted. I shall always feel grateful to Miss Boustead for organizing the only form of competitive sport I have ever enjoyed.

CLINGING TO THE WRECKAGE *by John Mortimer (1923–)*

11

SORROWS

Lady Sarashina (born in 1008) remembers leaving her home in the province of Takasue to return to Kyoto, capital of Heian Japan.

I was brought up in a part of the country so remote that it lies beyond the end of the Great East Road. What an uncouth creature I must have been in those days! Yet even shut away in the provinces I somehow came to hear that the world contained things known as Tales, and from that moment my greatest desire was to read them for myself. To idle away the time, my sister, my stepmother, and others in the household would tell me stories from the Tales, including episodes about Genji, the Shining Prince; but, since they had to depend on their memories, they could not possibly tell me all I wanted to know and their stories only made me more curious than ever. In my impatience I got a statue of the Healing Buddha built in my own size. When no one was watching, I would perform my ablutions and, stealing into the altar room, would prostrate myself and pray fervently, 'Oh, please arrange things so that we may soon go to the Capital, where there are so many Tales, and please let me read them all.'

On the third day of the Ninth Month, when I was twelve years old, we left our house and moved to a place called Imatachi in preparation for our journey to the Capital. The house where I had played for so many years was dismantled and one could see into the rooms from outside. Everything was in great disorder. As I stepped into the carriage to leave for the last time, the sun had just set and the sky was shrouded with mist. Looking into the house, I caught sight of the Healing Buddha standing there alone – that Buddha before whom I had prayed so often in secret. At the thought of abandoning him I began weeping quietly.

The temporary house in Imatachi was a simple place with a thatched roof; in the absence of a proper fence and latticed shutters, our servants had hung up some blinds and curtains. To the south was a wide plain; the sea was close on both sides, and in the evening a beautiful mist covered the entire landscape. I found it so charming that I got up early in the morning and gazed about, thinking how sad it would be to leave this place even though we had been here for only a few days.

We left on the fifteenth, a dark, wet day, and, having crossed the border, lodged at a place called Ikata in the province of Shimōsa. It was raining so hard that our cottage was almost afloat, and I was far too frightened to sleep. Looking out, I saw a hillock rising from a bare plain, and on it grew three isolated trees. We spent the next day drying our things that had got soaked and waiting for the other members of the party to catch up with us.

On the seventeenth we set off early in the morning. As we were being ferried across a deep river, one of the boatmen told us that this was the site of a mansion belonging to the Chieftain of Mano, whose workmen used to weave thousands upon thousands of rolls of cloth and then bleach them in these waters. The four great pillars that stood in the river were said to be his ancient gateposts. Some members of our party composed poems for the occasion and I made up this one for myself.

> Had not the gateposts in the river thus stood firm
> But crumbled with the years,
> What trace would now remain to tell me of the past?

That evening we stayed in Kuroto Beach, where the white dunes stretched out far in the distance. A bright moon hung over the dense pine groves, and the wind soughed forlornly in the branches. The scene inspired us to write poems. Mine was,

> Had I not stayed awake this night,
> When should I have seen the moon –
> This Autumn moon that lights Kuroto Beach?

We left early in the morning and by nightfall had reached Kagami Rapids on Futoi River, the border between Shimōsa and Musashi. We stayed at Matsusato Ford, while our men spent the entire night ferrying our luggage to the other side of the river.

It was here at the provincial border that my nurse, whose husband had recently died, gave birth to her baby. This meant that she could no longer travel to the Capital in our company. I was longing for her that night, and so my elder brother carried me in his arms to the hut where she lay. Our own lodging was a makeshift place, but at least it had blinds and hangings to protect us from the wind. My nurse, having no husband, had been lodged in a rough, primitive hut. The roof was merely a piece of rush matting and through it shone the moon, lighting up every corner of the room. I could read the suffering in her face as she lay there, so white and pure, covered with a dress of crimson cloth and looking completely transparent in the moonlight. She had not seen me for some time and began weeping as she stroked my hair. I found it hard to abandon her there, but my brother was in a hurry to take me back. On our return I was utterly wretched; her face, still vivid in my memory, made me so sad that even the sight of the moon could not console me and I went to bed wilted with sorrow.

On the following morning our carriages were ferried to the other side of the river and we, too, went across. Now the people who had accompanied us on the first part of our journey made their farewells and returned to the east, while those of us who were continuing to the Capital stayed for a while by the river. At this parting of the ways we all wept bitterly, and even my childish heart was full of grief.

AS I CROSSED A BRIDGE OF DREAMS *by Lady Sarashina*

I was three years old when we moved to West View. I remember being taken by my mother one day to look at a house. It was empty and dirty and cold and a woman caretaker showed us empty dirty rooms. Later I was told we were going to live there and dismay chilled me, as if I were going to live in an unknown house of the dead with that terrible caretaker. I remember then a day – another fragment of the ruins of time – when from the window of May's house next door I watched in woe the incessant heavy rain as strange men carried our furniture into a big removal van. Abandoned and forlorn I saw my world dismantled and gone.

Then I remember a door opening – the dining-room door of West View – and I saw my mother laughing and welcoming me. I 'saw' my mother that day for the first time, laughing and happy as she held out her arms to her little girl. The room she was in was fresh and clean, and there was a Christmas-tree, fragrant, and hung with glittering beautiful marvels, coloured glass balls and tinsel, and a soap teddy-bear and a little doll made of sugar, and twisted candles, red and blue and orange; inexhaustible, countless treasures of beauty hung on that lovely tree. Incredible transformation! The two pictures would not mix, the two houses were not the same house, but different houses; and in some inexplicable sense our new house was the same place as our old house, as if with the familiar pieces of furniture we had brought the place itself with us.

FAREWELL HAPPY FIELDS *by Kathleen Raine (1908–)*

The Toys

My little Son, who looked from thoughtful eyes,
And moved and spoke in quiet grown-up wise,
Having my law the seventh time disobeyed,
I struck him, and dismissed
With hard words and unkissed,
– His Mother, who was patient, being dead.
Then, fearing lest his grief should hinder sleep,
I visited his bed,
But found him slumbering deep,
With darkened eyelids, and their lashes yet
From his late sobbing wet.
And I, with moan,
Kissing away his tears, left others of my own;
For on a table drawn beside his head,
He had put, within his reach,
A box of counters and a red-veined stone,
A piece of glass abraded by the beach,

And six or seven shells,
A bottle with bluebells,
And two French copper coins, ranged there,
    with careful art,
To comfort his sad heart.
So when that night I prayed
To God, I wept, and said:
Ah, when at last we lie with trancéd breath,
Not vexing Thee in death,
And Thou rememberest of what toys
We made our joys,
How weakly understood
Thy great commanded good,
Then fatherly not less
Then I whom Thou has moulded from the clay,
Thou'lt leave Thy wrath, and say,
'I will be sorry for their childishness.'

from 'The Unknown Eros' by Coventry Patmore (1823–96)

My little world was enlarged, too, by a visit every Christmas to the pantomime at Drury Lane. My father was an admirable companion on these jaunts, for the boyish, unsophisticated side of him came uppermost, and the dignity of 'the cloth' was forgotten. When the two robbers of *Babes in the Wood* quarrelled, beginning with fretful slaps at each other and working up, through swords, battle-axes, pistols, to a thunderous duel with cannons – exchanging huge cardboard cannonballs at point-blank range – my father's uninhibited laughter (he had a falsetto laugh, contrasting oddly with his fine baritone voice) grew almost as hysterical as my own.

To *Peter Pan*, on the other hand, my reaction was negative. I was not a great one for fairies or the whimsical, and I knew beforehand that Peter Pan flew on wires. Besides, I had just suffered one of those public embarrassments which turn everything sour for a small boy. The visit to *Peter Pan* was to be this year's treat for the Christ Church choir boys. I was never a member of the choir myself, but I had been invited to go with them and attend the dinner-party before the theatre in the house of Miss

Price, one of my father's richest parishioners and a considerable patroness of his. When we arrived at Hyde Park Gardens, Miss Price took me aside and told me that at dinner, when she gave me a sign, I was to hand round a box of chocolate cigars and cigarettes which would be lying on a side table. All anxiously, for I did not know at what point of dinner it was deemed correct to smoke a chocolate cigar, and hardly tasting what I ate, I awaited the signal. Miss Price glanced at me. I leapt up, but was instantly recalled to the table. It had not been the signal. Twice again this happened, to my increasing humiliation. When finally our hostess did give the sign, I had totally lost my nerve and failed to respond. Guessing my predicament, she said gently, 'Will you hand round the cigarettes now, Cecil?' I obeyed, but without pleasure: once again I had muffed things, made a fool of myself – and in front of a crowd of boys. It seems a trivial incident now. But it shows how early (I was only eight or nine when it occurred) a sense of failure had begun to set in, dormant most of the time but flaring up within me at my slightest *faux-pas* or incompetence.

THE BURIED DAY *by C. Day Lewis*

I do not remember my sisters' presence at the first of these Christmas Trees – a very magnificent one, with a crowd of guests. Doubtless they were there; but I happened (aged six) to be preoccupied with love and jealousy. For many months my parents had been happy to entertain (in consequence, I believe, of some strained relations with her family) a young lady whose wooer, a Captain E., had brought her a Christmas gift, which she, in dissatisfaction, promptly threw at his head. Both parties being noted for passionate tempers, all looked for a violent scene, and I in my childish hope for final rupture. They were married some short while later, the bride insisting on a chaise with four greys and a couple of postillions. As the equipage rolled off I waved with the rest from the porch: but my little handkerchiefing was wet, and I fled back through the house to sob out my woe in the stable on the neck of our demure mare Jessie, friend of the family.

MEMORIES AND OPINIONS *by 'Q'*
(Sir Arthur Quiller-Couch (1863–1944))

I used to stay at Battersby for a day or two sometimes, while my godson and his brother and sister were children. . . .

I was there on a Sunday, and observed the rigour with which the young people were taught to observe the Sabbath; they might not cut out things, nor use their paint-box on a Sunday, and this they thought rather hard, because their cousins the John Pontifexes might do these things. Their cousins might play with their toy train on Sunday, but though they had promised that they would run none but Sunday trains, all traffic had been prohibited. One treat only was allowed them – on Sunday evenings they might choose their own hymns.

In the course of the evening they came into the drawing-room, and, as an especial treat, were to sing some of their hymns to me, instead of saying them, so that I might hear how nicely they sang. Ernest was to choose the first hymn, and he chose one about some people who were to come to the sunset tree. I am no botanist, and do not know what kind of tree a sunset tree is, but the words began, 'Come, come, come; come to the sunset tree for the day is past and gone'. The tune was rather pretty and had taken Ernest's fancy, for he was unusually fond of music and had a sweet little child's voice which he liked using.

He was, however, very late in being able to sound a hard 'c' or 'k', and, instead of saying 'Come', he said 'Tum, tum, tum'.

'Ernest,' said Theobald, from the armchair in front of the fire, where he was sitting with his hands folded before him, 'don't you think it would be very nice if you were to say "come" like other people, instead of "tum"?'

'I do say tum,' replied Ernest, meaning that he had said 'come'.

Theobald was always in a bad temper on Sunday evening. Whether it is that they are as much bored with the day as their neighbours, or whether they are tired, or whatever the cause may be, clergymen are seldom at their best on Sunday evening; I had already seen signs that evening that my host was cross, and was a little nervous at hearing Ernest say so promptly 'I do say tum', when his papa had said he did not say it as he should.

Theobald noticed the fact that he was being contradicted in a moment. He got up from his armchair and went to the piano.

'No, Ernest, you don't,' he said, 'you say nothing of the kind, you say "tum", not "come". Now say "come" after me, as I do.'

'Tum,' said Ernest, at once; 'is that better?' I have no doubt he thought it was, but it was not.

'Now, Ernest, you are not taking pains; you are not trying as you ought to do. It is high time you learned to say "come", why, Joey can say "come", can't you, Joey?'

'Yeth, I can,' replied Joey, and he said something which was not far off 'come'.

'There, Ernest, do you hear that? There's no difficulty about it, nor shadow of difficulty. Now, take your time, think about it, and say "come" after me.'

The boy remained silent a few seconds and then said 'tum' again.

I laughed, but Theobald turned to me impatiently and said, 'Please do not laugh, Overton; it will make the boy think it does not matter, and it matters a great deal'; then, turning to Ernest, he said, 'Now, Ernest, I will give you one more chance, and if you don't say "come" I shall know that you are self-willed and naughty.'

He looked very angry, and a shade came over Ernest's face, like that which comes upon the face of a puppy when it is being scolded without understanding why. The child saw well what was coming now, was frightened, and, of course, said 'tum' once more.

'Very well, Ernest,' said his father, catching him angrily by the shoulder. 'I have done my best to save you, but if you will have it so, you will,' and he lugged the little wretch, crying by anticipation, out of the room. A few minutes more and we could hear screams coming from the dining-room, across the hall which separated the drawing-room from the dining-room, and knew that poor Ernest was being beaten.

'I have sent him up to bed,' said Theobald, as he returned to the drawing-room, 'and now, Christina, I think we will have the servants in to prayers,' and he rang the bell for them, red-handed as he was.

THE WAY OF ALL FLESH *by Samuel Butler (1835–1902)*

Compton Mackenzie's parents were both on the stage, which often posed a problem for his mother, who had to choose between her career with her husband, and life with her little sons.

This Holy Week of 1889 was to bring her a difficult test. They would be travelling on Easter Sunday in order to open at some theatre on Easter Monday. I do not know if my father had yet made the Gaiety Theatre, Dublin, his regular venue for Easter Monday, but Ireland may well have been where they were going. For the last night of that precious week it had been promised that we children should be allowed to sit up to the incredible hour of eight o'clock. Some time before seven there was the sound of two hansom-cabs coming along Avonmore Road. They stopped before our door and presently appeared a Mr Coward and a Lady Cregeen to say that they had brought a second hansom in order to take my father and mother out to dinner at the Hotel Victoria in Northumberland Avenue. . . .

'Oh, I don't think we *can* come,' said my mother. 'It's the children's last night.'

But Coward was insistent.

'I'll put that right,' he declared.

Then my father said to my mother that he thought they ought to go. I have supposed later that Coward, a wealthy man, was one of my father's backers for his ambition to lease a London theatre for a season, and that he did not feel he could well refuse his invitation. I can recall as if it were yesterday the agony of apprehension in which I listened to this conversation and heard my mother at last surrender. I can see her now walking upstairs to her room to divest herself of the tea-gown she was wearing, that much loved garment symbolic of her intention to be at home.

As they were going out of the front door Coward turned to me to put it right by pressing into my hand half a sovereign.

The door closed. The jingle of the hansom-cabs and trot of the horses' hooves grew less and less audible until silence fell. Then I went up to my bedroom and as I climbed the stairs I thought, not in so many words exactly of course, but with the equivalent surge of emotion:

'You can never again in life afford to depend on the love of somebody, you must always be prepared henceforth to be disappointed, and then if you are disappointed you will be able to bear it because you knew it might happen.'

When I reached my bedroom I opened the window and flung that golden ten-shilling piece out into the deep April dusk.

MY LIFE AND TIMES

Agatha Christie (1890–1976) is on holiday with her parents and elder sister.

Father and Madge made a good many excursions on horseback, and in answer to my entreaties one day I was told that on the morrow I should be allowed to accompany them. I was thrilled. My mother had a few misgivings, but my father soon overruled them.

'We have a Guide with us,' he said, 'and he's quite used to children and will see to it that they don't fall off.'

The next morning the three horses arrived, and off we went. We zigzagged along up the precipitous paths, and I enjoyed myself enormously perched on top of what seemed to me an immense horse. The Guide led it up, and occasionally picking little bunches of flowers, handed them to me to stick in my hatband. So far all was well, but when we arrived at the top and prepared to have lunch, the Guide excelled himself. He came running back to us bringing with him a magnificent butterfly he had trapped. *'Pour la petite mademoiselle,'* he cried. Taking a pin from his lapel he transfixed the butterfly and stuck it in my hat! Oh, the horror of that moment! The feeling of the poor butterfly fluttering, struggling against the pin. The agony I felt as the butterfly fluttered there. And of course I couldn't *say* anything. There were too many conflicting loyalties in my mind. This was a kindness on the part of the Guide. He had brought it to me. It was a special kind of present. How could I hurt his feelings by saying I didn't like it? How I wanted him to take it off! And all the time, there was the butterfly, fluttering, dying. That horrible flapping against my hat. There is only one thing a child can do in these circumstances. I cried.

The more anyone asked me questions the more I was unable to reply.

'What's the matter?' demanded my father. 'Have you got a pain?'

My sister said, 'Perhaps she's frightened at riding on the horse.'

I said No and No. I wasn't frightened and I hadn't got a pain.

'Tired,' said my father.

'No,' I said.

'Well, then, what *is* the matter?'

But I couldn't say. Of course I couldn't say. The Guide was standing there, watching me with an attentive and puzzled face. My father said rather crossly:

'She's too young a child. We shouldn't have brought her on this expedition.'

I redoubled my weeping. I must have ruined the day for both him and my sister, and I knew I was doing so, but I couldn't stop. All I hoped and prayed that presently he, or even my sister, would *guess* what was the matter. Surely they would look at that butterfly, they would see it, they would say, 'Perhaps she doesn't like the butterfly on her hat.' If *they* said it, it would be all right. But I couldn't *tell* them. It was a terrible day. I refused to eat any lunch. I sat there and cried, and the butterfly flapped. It stopped flapping in the end. That ought to have made me feel better. But by that time I had got into such a state of misery that nothing *could* have made me feel better.

We rode down again, my father definitely out of temper, my sister annoyed, the Guide still sweet, kindly and puzzled. Fortunately, he did not think of getting me a second butterfly to cheer me up. We arrived back, a most woeful party, and went into our sitting-room where mother was.

'Oh dear,' she said, 'what's the matter? Has Agatha hurt herself?'

'I don't know,' said my father crossly. 'I don't know what's the matter with the child. I suppose she's got a pain or something. She's been crying ever since lunch-time, and she wouldn't eat a thing.'

'What is the matter, Agatha?' asked my mother.

I couldn't tell her. I only looked at her dumbly while tears still rolled down my cheeks. She looked at me thoughtfully for some minutes, then said, 'Who put that butterfly in her hat?'

My sister explained that it had been the Guide.

'I see,' said mother. Then she said to me, 'You didn't like it, did you? It was alive and you thought it was being hurt?'

Oh, the glorious relief, the wonderful relief when somebody knows what's in your mind and tells it to you so that you are at last released from that long bondage of silence. I flung myself at her in a kind of frenzy, thrust my arms round her neck and said, 'Yes, yes, yes. It's been flapping. It's been *flapping*. But he was so kind and he meant to be kind. I couldn't *say*.'

She understood it all and patted me gently. Suddenly the whole thing seemed to recede in the distance.

'I quite see what you felt,' she said. 'I know. But it's over now, and so we won't talk about it any more.'

AN AUTOBIOGRAPHY

As we dance round a-ring-a-ring,
A maiden goes a-maying;
And here a flower, and there a flower,
Through mead and meadow straying:
O gentle one, why dost thou weep? –
Silver to spend with; gold to keep;
Till spin the green round World asleep,
And Heaven its dews be staying.

Anon.

When my grandmother died, my mother's devoted nurse took over the running of The Postern. 'Nanny' was a somewhat remarkable personage, wrinkled, small and rheumy-eyed. . . . She sang old nursery-rhymes that I have never heard again; and, on my visits to The Postern, she would order the kitchen-maid to catch half a dozen flies, and drown them in a glass of water. The inanimate flies were then scattered across a plate of table-salt, which had the miraculous effect of restoring them to life and enabling them, after they had scraped and groomed themselves, to spread their wings and dart away. This strange scientific experiment I followed with unfailing interest. But Nanny also offered me more conventional treats; and one evening she escorted me to the Crystal Palace, to see the latest Christmas pantomime. It was there I fell in love, and first suffered the exquisite agonies of a wild romantic longing.

We had already arrived at the transformation-scene; Bengal-lighting bathed the stage, all rosy pinks, celestial blues and dreamily dissolving yellows; and behind gauzy veils, which slowly melted and lifted, a mysterious and beautiful young woman, *'un être, qui n'était que lumière, or et gaze'* – I assume she was the Fairy Princess – moved out between the canvas drops, her face radiantly transfigured by the changing colours of her background. I felt a sharp pang; I was keenly aware of the distance that divided us; I longed – how I could not imagine – to incorporate my life with hers. I knew that I should presently forget her face; and the prospect of forgetting and losing her – of returning to my own colourless existence – made my anguish doubly poignant. We were near the end of the pantomime; and perhaps, if the curtain had gone down, I should have borne my loss more bravely. But, at this moment, Nanny jerked my elbow and said that the time had come to catch our train. Having caught it and dismounted on a dark platform, we finished our journey in a decrepit four-wheeler, rattling through suburban streets. I remember the acrid smell of the cab and the salty taste of tears, as they drenched my nose, found their way into my mouth or, slipping around its corners, wet my chin.

THE MARBLE FOOT *by Peter Quennell*

My first experience of Weltschmerz, if that is what it was, must have come to me at the very early age of five or six. Behind the house in Lexham Gardens was a long parallelogram enclosed by the house on the north and on the other three sides by three grimy six-foot walls. It was a typical London garden of that era, consisting of a worn parallelogram of grass surrounded by narrow gravel paths and then narrow beds of sooty, sour London soil against the walls. Each child was given a few feet of bed for his own personal 'garden' and there we sowed seeds or grew pansies bought off barrows in the Earls Court Road. I was very fond of this garden and of my 'garden' and it was here that I first experienced a wave of that profound, cosmic melancholia which is hidden in every human heart and can be heard at its best – or should one say worst? – in the infant crying in the night and with no language but a cry. It happened in this way.

Every year in the last week of July or the first of August, the whole Woolf family went away for a summer holiday to the country. It was a large-scale exodus. First my mother went off and looked at houses. Then we were told that a house had been 'taken'. When the day came, six, seven, eight, and eventually nine children, servants, dogs, cats, canaries, and at one time two white rats in a bird-cage, mountains of luggage were transported in an omnibus to the station and then in a reserved 'saloon' railway carriage to our destination. I can remember country houses in Wimbledon, Henley, Tenby, Penmaenmawr, Speldhurst, and Whitby which carry me back in memory to my fifth year. And I can remember returning one late, chilly September afternoon to Lexham Gardens from our holiday and rushing out eagerly to see the back garden. There it lay in its grimy solitude. There was not a breath of air. There were no flowers; a few spindly lilac bushes drooped in the beds. The grimy ivy drooped on the grimy walls. And all over the walls from ivy leaf to ivy leaf were large or small spider-webs, dozens and dozens of them, quite motionless, and motionless in the centre of each web sat a large or a small, a fat or a lean spider. I stood by myself in the patch of scurfy grass and contemplated the spiders; I can still smell the smell of sour earth and ivy; and suddenly my whole mind and body seemed to be overwhelmed in melancholy. I did not cry, though there were, I think, tears in my eyes; I had experienced for the first time, without understanding it, that sense of cosmic unhappiness which comes upon us when those that look out of the windows be darkened, when the daughters of music are laid low, the doors are shut in the street, the sound of the grinding is low, the grasshopper is a burden, and desire fails.

The second occasion on which I felt the burden of a hostile universe weigh down my spirit must have been when I was about eight years old. We had arrived in Whitby for our summer holidays and found ourselves in a large, new red-brick house on a cliff overlooking the sea. After tea I wandered out by myself to explore the garden. The house and garden were quite new for the garden was almost bare. Along the side facing the sea ran a long low mound or rampart. I sat there in the sunshine looking down on the sparkling water. It smelt and felt so good after the long hours in the stuffy train. And then suddenly quite near me out of a hole in the bank came two large black and yellow newts. They did not notice me and stretched themselves out to bask in the sun. They entranced me and I forgot everything, including time, as I sat there with those strange, beautiful creatures surrounded by blue sky, sunshine, and sparkling sea. I do not know how long I had sat there when, all at once, I felt afraid. I looked up and saw that an enormous black thunder cloud had crept up and now covered more than half of the sky. It was just blotting out the sun, and, as it did so, the newts scuttled back into their hole. It was terrifying and, no doubt, I was terrified. But I felt something more powerful than fear, once more that sense of profound, passive, cosmic despair, the melancholy of a human being, eager for happiness and beauty, powerless in face of a hostile universe. As the great raindrops began to fall and the thunder to mutter and growl over the sea, I crept back into the house with a curious muddle of fear, contempt, scepticism, and fatalism in my childish mind.

SOWING *by Leonard Woolf*

Another example of childhood angst:

I must have been about eleven. The scene again took place at table, but this time my mother and I were alone. I had been at school that morning. What had happened? Possibly nothing.

. . . Then why did I suddenly break down? Why did I again feel, as I fell convulsively sobbing into mamma's arms, that indefinable anguish, the very same exactly that I had felt at my little cousin's death? It was as though the special sluice-gate of some unknown, unbounded, mystic sea had suddenly been opened and an overwhelming flood poured into my heart. I was not so much unhappy as terrified; but how was I to explain it to my mother? All she could distinguish between my sobs were, repeated again and again, these blind despairing words:

'I'm not like other people . . . not like other people!'

IF IT DIE . . . by André Gide (1860–1951)

A child's capacity for forgiveness is here shown under the extreme provocation of a sadistic beating from his grandfather.

'Lexei!' called grandfather. 'Come nearer! Come! Don't you hear me speaking to you? Look and see what a flogging is. . . . One!'

With a mild flourish he brought the rod down on the naked flesh, and Sascha set up a howl.

'Rubbish!' said grandfather. 'That's nothing! . . . But here's something to make you smart.'

And he dealt such blows that the flesh was soon in a state of inflammation and covered with great red weals, and my cousin gave a prolonged howl. . . .

'I won't do it again,' squealed Sascha, in a dreadfully thin, weak voice, unpleasant to hear. 'Didn't I tell – didn't I tell about the tablecloth?'

Grandfather answered calmly, as if he were reading the Psalter:

'Tale-bearing is no justification. The informer gets whipped first, so take that for the tablecloth.'

Grandmother threw herself upon me and seized my hand, crying: 'I won't allow Lexei to be touched! I won't allow it, you monster!' And she began to kick the door, calling: 'Varia! Varvara!'

Grandfather darted across to her, threw her down, seized me and carried me to the bench. I struck at him with my fists, pulled his sandy beard, and bit his fingers. He bellowed and held me as in a vice. In the end, throwing me down on the bench, he struck me on the face.

I shall never forget his savage cry: 'Tie him up! I'm going to kill him!' nor my mother's white face and great eyes as she ran along up and down beside the bench, shrieking:

'Father! You mustn't! Let me have him!'

Grandfather flogged me till I lost consciousness, and I was unwell for some days, tossing about, face downwards, on a wide, stuffy bed, in a little room with one window and a lamp which was always kept burning before the case of ikons in the corner. Those dark days had been the greatest in my life. In the course of them I had developed wonderfully, and I was conscious of a peculiar difference in myself. I began to experience a new solicitude for others, and I became so keenly alive to their sufferings and my own that it was almost as if my heart had been lacerated, and thus rendered sensitive. . . .

Very soon after this, as suddenly as if he had fallen from the ceiling, grandfather appeared, and sitting on the bed, laid his ice-cold hands on my head.

'How do you do, young gentleman? Come! answer me. Don't sulk! Well? What have you to say?'

I had a great mind to kick away his legs, but it hurt me to move. His head, sandier than ever, shook from side to side uneasily; his bright eyes seemed to be looking for something on the wall as he pulled out of his pocket a gingerbread goat, a horn made of sugar, an apple and a cluster of purple raisins, which he placed on the pillow under my very nose.

'There you are! There's a present for you.'

And he stooped and kissed me on the forehead. Then, stroking my head with those small, cruel hands, yellow-stained about the crooked, claw-like nails, he began to speak.

'I left my mark on you then, my friend. You were very angry. You bit me and scratched me, and then I lost my temper too. However, it will do you no harm to have been punished more severely than you deserved.'. . .

Bending his withered, well-knit body towards me, he began to tell me in vigorous and powerful language, with a felicitous choice of words, about the days of his childhood. His green eyes were very bright, and his golden hair stood rakishly on end as, deflecting his high-pitched voice, he breathed in my face. . . .

As he spoke he seemed to increase in size like a cloud before my very eyes, being transformed from a small, wizened old man to an individual of fabulous strength. Had he not pulled a great grey barge up the river all by himself? Now and again he jumped up from the bed and showed me how the bargees travelled with the towing-rope round them, and how they pumped water, singing fragments of a song in a bass voice; then, youthfully springing back on the bed, to my ever-increasing astonishment, he would continue hoarsely and impressively. . . .

Several times people put their heads in at the door to call him, but each time I begged him not to go.

And he laughingly waved them away, saying, 'Wait a bit.'

He stayed with me and told me stories until it was almost dark, and when, after an affectionate farewell, he left me, I had learned that he was neither malevolent nor formidable. It brought the tears into my eyes to remember that it was he who had so cruelly beaten me, but I could not forget it.

MY CHILDHOOD *by Maxim Gorky (1868–1936)*

12

DREAMS AND VISIONS

I have seen
A curious child, who dwelt upon a tract
Of inland ground, applying to his ear
The convolusions of a smooth-lipped shell;
To which, in silence hushed, his very soul
Listened intensely; and his countenance soon
Brightened with joy; for from within were heard
Murmurings . . .

from 'The Excursion' by William Wordsworth

All appeared new and strange at first, inexpressibly rare and delightful and beautiful. I was a little stranger which at my entrance into the world was saluted and surrounded with innumerable joys. My knowledge was Divine; I knew by intuition those things which since my apostasy I collected again by the highest reason. My very ignorance was advantageous. I seemed as one brought into the estate of innocence. All things were spotless and pure and glorious; yea, and infinitely mine and joyful and precious. I knew not that there were any sins, or complaints or laws. I dreamed not of poverties, contentions, or vices. All tears and quarrels were hidden from mine eyes. Everything was at rest, free and immortal. I knew nothing of sickness or death or exaction. In the absence of these I was entertained like an angel with the works of God in their splendour and glory; I saw all in the peace of Eden; heaven and earth did sing my Creator's praises, and could not make more melody to Adam than to me. All Time was Eternity, and a perpetual Sabbath. Is it not strange that an infant should be heir of the whole world, and see those mysteries which the books of the learned never unfold?

The corn was orient and immortal wheat which never should be reaped nor was ever sown. I thought it had stood from everlasting to everlasting. The dust and stones of the street were as precious as gold: the gates were at first the end of the world. The green trees when I saw them first through one of the gates transported and ravished me; their sweetness and unusual beauty made my heart to leap, and almost mad with ecstasy, they were such strange and wonderful things. The Men! O what venerable and reverend creatures did the aged seem! Immortal Cherubims! And young men glittering and sparkling angels, and maids strange seraphic pieces of life and beauty! Boys and girls tumbling in the street were moving jewels: I knew not that they were born or should die. But all things abided eternally as they were in their proper places. Eternity was manifest in the Light of the Day, and something infinite behind everything appeared, which talked with my expectation and moved my desire. The City seemed to stand in Eden or to be built in Heaven. The streets were mine, the temple was mine, the people were mine, their clothes and gold and silver were mine, as much as their sparkling eyes, fair skins, and ruddy faces. The skies were mine, and so were the sun and moon and stars, and all the world was mine; and I the only spectator and enjoyer of it.

CENTURIES OF MEDITATIONS *by Thomas Traherne (1637–74)*

... I remember being taken, when I was about four years old, with two cousins of my age, up the hill, past the semi-detached houses, past the larger and older ones with carriage gates and gate-stop latches that clicked, over the railway bridge, up again past the last houses of all, and I remember being lifted over a fence between oak trees into a field of buttercups. At first we just stood. For a few moments the world stood still with us. The miracle that stupidly wise people fail to understand happened. The sun waited in the sky. Then, moved by a common instinct, together we spread out our arms and ran in among the buttercups, hugging, snatching, wading, gathering, shouting and shouted at, trampling disastrous lanes far out into the centre of the field. It was sheer greed of gold.

THE SUBURBAN CHILD *by James Kenward (1908–)*

The Boy

I'd like, above all, to be one of those
who drive with wild black horses through the night,
torches like hair uplifted in affright
when the great wind of their wild hunting blows.
I'd like to stand in front as in a boat,
tall, like a long floating flag unrolled.
And dark, but with a helmet made of gold,
restlessly flashing. And behind to ride
ten other looming figures side by side,
with helmets matching mine for changefulness,
now clear as glass, now old and lustreless.
And one to stand by me and blow us space
with the brass trumpet that can blaze and blare,
blowing a black solitude through which we tear
like dreams that speed too fast to leave a trace.
Houses behind us fall upon their knee,
alleys cringe crookedly before our train,
squares break in flight: we summon and we seize:
we ride, and our great horses rush like rain.

Rainer Maria Rilke, trs. J. B. Leishman

. . . early one morning, with the sun across the trees, we heard a
double call, and in an instant, recognizing, we ran to hang out of
the window. In the woods between Combourne and Hor-Den we
had, with all the insurgent earth, found our spirit's voice. It was
the cuckoo, who resolved everything. The Mallions Woods answered him faintly half a mile away, Pine Woods and Mabs Wood
heard, then Little Combourne and Ladys Den and the woods on
Winchet Hill.

In a day or two the whole under-sky was hollow, ringing with
its call and echo and answer; there was nothing in the earth and
the still, even face of the sky, but this mysterious voice. This is
sober matter-of-fact. Before I was eight I found I could not bear to
hear it and remain alone. How little we were, and how lost, when

the big world broke into voice and called that soft, monotonous, hazy call, here and a mile away, and nothing answered it but empty silence and its own echoes. It is terrible to be in an ecstasy of joy alone. All the hordes of life were united in a single cry, earth was no longer a mass of separate lives, but one spirit, crying out to be heard; and all its answer was its own voice repeated from some sunken valley on the other side of the hill.

I was in the children's gardens, alone on the top of our hill, when first the cuckoo's voice assured me of that secret spirit in our woods. I had surmised it before, but now that it was vocal I listened with a growing fear. At last I could not bear it. Dropping my spade, I tore down the path past the summerhouse and green-house to be near the cheerful mortal sounds of kitchen and scullery. Yet when I arrived there I only wondered at my own fears, and though I could not go back to the garden, I would not go indoors. THE SMALL YEARS *by Frank Kendon*

Tell Me, Tell Me, Smiling Child

Tell me, tell me, smiling child,
What the past is like to thee?
'An Autumn evening, soft and mild,
With a wind that sighs mournfully.'

Tell me, what is the present hour?
'A green and flowery spray,
Where a young bird sits gathering its power
To mount and fly away.'

And what is the future, happy one?
'A sea beneath a cloudless sun;
A mighty, glorious, dazzling sea
Stretching into infinity.'

Emily Brontë

I can remember a dream I had, which must have come to me about that time; it impressed itself deeply on my imagination. I dreamt one night that I went out for a walk alone in the garden, and when I got to the bottom of the steps that led up to it, I stopped, overcome with fright. In front of me, quite close to the tunnel one has to go through, there was a barrel of lime; and on it I saw two horrible little demons, dancing about with a surprising quickness of movement – surprising because they wore flat-irons on their feet. All of a sudden their flashing eyes fell on me, and thereupon, apparently much more frightened of me that I was of them, they jumped down off the barrel and took refuge in the linen-room, just in front of them. Their nervousness encouraged me to go and see what they were up to, so I went up to the linen-room window; there they were, the poor little demons, running about over the tables in a frantic effort to get out of sight. Sometimes they would come up to the window, looking anxiously to see if I was still there; and finding that I went on watching them, they began to run to and fro as if in desperation. There was nothing very extraordinary, to be sure, about this dream of mine; but I suppose God allowed me to remember it for a special purpose. He wanted me to see that the soul, when in a state of grace, has nothing to fear from the spirits of evil; they are cowards, so cowardly that they run away at a glance from a child.

AUTOBIOGRAPHY OF A SAINT
by Thérèse de Lisieux (1873–97)

In the following episode James Kirkup is not yet three.

The ground out in the backyard was made of a kind of coarse concrete, full of tiny shells and pebbles – shingle from our sands. The little stones, worn smooth by the pounding of the North Sea breakers, had been made even smoother by the passage of countless colliers' boots and housewives' shoes. The stones were mostly brown in colour, but there were also yellow and black and white and striped ones, and others that were the brown-blue shade of a ripe black eye; there were also well-rubbed fragments of old brick, and bits of green, dull bottle-glass, both pale and dark. These, with jagged portions of broken shells, were all conglomerated in a hard, smooth, cement-roughened mass that looked dull when dry but shone and sparkled when it rained or when my father or Mr Battey 'scrubbed the yard' – a weekly ritual – with great pailfuls of tap-water and a stiff-bristled yard broom. I had soon noticed, on the beach, how stones and shells and seaweed shone when they were wet, and how disappointingly dull they were when dry. Our backyard was like having a section of the beach on our own scullery doorstep – but fixed, and hard, and immovable, despite the great tides of tap-water my father regularly sluiced over it.

Among all these variegated pebbles there was one that stood out. It was in a dark corner of the yard, near Mrs Battey's green-painted coal-house door. This pebble was slightly smaller than the rest, but it was bright scarlet. It was the only one of its kind, and its brilliant red had earned it the name of 'The Blood-stone'. It certainly was not a real bloodstone, which is dark green, flecked with red. Nor could it possibly have been a ruby, or a cat's eye, as some asserted, for it was opaque. It was most mysterious. Children used to come from near and far, lifting the 'sneck' of our back door, and shouting: 'Mrs Battey! Mrs Kirpick!' (they could never get our name right); 'can we come in and see the Blood-stone?' They would come in and stand or crouch in a silent, awestruck ring round the little crimson stone. Some adventurous soul might try to dig it out with a pen nib or a penknife, and my heart, as I stood watching them from the kitchen window, would contract with anxiety; but nothing would shift it; the children would stare at it and discuss it in hushed whispers, nodding their heads with 'old-fashioned' seriousness. It gave great renown and distinction to our backyard, and though I went very much in awe of the Bloodstone, I was very proud of it. I always treated it with great respect – I would never have dreamed of *walking* on it, for example – and I fully believed it had magic properties, though I never wished to test them, for I was sure that any sort of magic would be unpleasant and alarming.

Many were the tales and prohibitions it inspired. Some said it was the tooth out of a Chinese donkeyman's head, and others that a coalman had spat it out, red-hot. . . . Some said it was a scarlet bean, that sprouted diamonds once every hundred years. Some swore it was giant's blood. But all were agreed that it was fatal to stand on it, or to touch it, unless you had spat on it first. If you were to touch it without spitting on it, you would drop down dead, or your finger would fall off. I can still see a little circle of crouching backsides – tightly stretched little breeches and knickers – sometimes no knickers at all – and potato-holed stockings – gathered round the Bloodstone, and can hear that chorus of infant spitting as they made the stone safe to touch.

One day, playing on my own in the backyard, in the chill shadow of the coalhouses and the rain-water tubs, I suddenly realized, as I crawled over the palm-denting ground, that I had inadvertently put my hand on – the Bloodstone! a shudder of fright went through me as I slowly lifted my hand and revealed the terrible stone – smooth, sinister, brilliant, like an open wound that can never be healed. It was a feeling much worse than when you put your hand in 'mess' or in a dog's 'business' or on one of the great, shining half-crowns of spit that illuminated, with a grisly radiance, the dark kerbs of the front street. I went cold, and my hand seemed to burn where the stone had touched it. I sat there, unable to warn my mother, who was singing happily as she worked in the scullery; I couldn't make a sound: I just couldn't bring myself to tell her that I was about to drop dead.

I saw the whole yard very clearly – the tall brick walls that led up dizzily to the dark-blue sky, the broken clouds, the smoke from the river drifting faster than the moving clouds, the seagulls smoothly rocking in the wind from the sea. I saw the swollen blisters – there were several new ones – on the sides of the rain-water barrels, and I longed to burst some of them. I reached out and burst a big, juicy one, then another, and another and another. The familiar oily, tarry smell came from them. By the time I had burst half a dozen I began to admit to myself that though I had touched the Bloodstone without spitting on it first, I had not dropped down dead. Cautiously, I spat on the Bloodstone, just for luck . . . better late than never. Then I got up and ran to my mother and flung myself into her arms. Even she, who was used to my successive attacks of paralysed shyness and wild demonstrativeness, was puzzled by my outburst of tears and laughter. I couldn't tell her what had happened. But just as I had known at once what ghosts were, so at that moment in the backyard I knew what death would be like – an unspeakable moment of realization which we can share with no one, for the shock of knowledge takes us out of ourselves, and puts us far away, on our own, lonelier than ever, and far beyond the reach even of those we know and love best.

THE ONLY CHILD

About now somebody gave me *Hookeybeak the Raven and other tales*, illustrated by Wilhelm Busch. . . . Hookeybeak the Raven enthralled me. It began:

> Here's Tommy Tit, who's gathering berries in the wood;
> Here's Hookeybeak the Raven – that Raven wasn't good.

I suppose my first attempt at meditation was inspired by Hookeybeak. 'That Raven wasn't good,' I used to murmur to myself over and over again. The mischief in which Hookeybeak delighted was pictured and related in verse for some two dozen pages until on the last page Hookeybeak, in making a mess of Aunt Matilda Tabitha's knitting, managed to hang himself,

> But round his neck, oh horror! was caught the worsted
> thread,
> And Hookeybeak fell down that day, and hung till stiff
> and dead.
> And Aunt Matilda Tabitha she said to Tommy Tit:
> 'You see, he wasn't good, my dear, and here's the end of
> it!'

These lines played upon my fancy with an elegiac emotion I should not feel so sharply again for quite a long time. It was to comfort my sorrow that I repeated over and over again 'That Raven wasn't good'. As the ancient Greeks were awed by the emotion of watching the protagonist in a tragedy moving towards his doom without being able to deflect him from his fatal course, so I, reading the story of Hookeybeak, was powerless to prevent his end. 'That Raven wasn't good.' His end was ineluctable.

MY LIFE AND TIMES *by Compton Mackenzie*

*Two accounts of the same episode: one in a poem by Thomas
Hardy and the other from the biography written as from the pen
of his second wife Florence, but largely dictated to her by the poet
in his old age.*

The Self-Unseeing

Here is the ancient floor,
Footworn and hollowed and thin,
Here was the former door
Where the dead feet walked in.

She sat here in her chair,
Smiling into the fire;
He who played stood there,
Bowing it higher and higher.

Childlike, I danced in a dream;
Blessings emblazoned that day;
Everything glowed with a gleam;
Yet we were looking away!

Thomas Hardy

Though healthy he was fragile, and precocious to a degree, being
able to read almost before he could walk, and to tune a violin
when of quite tender years. He was of ecstatic temperament,
extraordinarily sensitive to music, and among the endless jigs,
hornpipes, reels, waltzes, and country-dances that his father
played of an evening in his early married years, and to which the
boy danced a *pas seul* in the middle of the room, there were three
or four that always moved the child to tears, though he strenuously tried to hide them.

THE LIFE OF THOMAS HARDY *by Florence Emily Hardy*

The imagining of tales (about grown-up people, 'real people', I called them – children always seemed to me incompletely realized) had gone on in me since my first conscious moments; I cannot remember the time when I did not want to 'make up' stories. But it was in Paris that I found the necessary formula. Oddly enough, I had no desire to write my stories down (even had I known how to write, and I couldn't yet form a letter); but from the first I had to have a book in my hand to 'make up' with, and from the first it had to be a certain sort of book. The page had to be closely printed, with rather heavy black type, and not much margin. Certain densely printed novels in the early Tauchnitz editions, Harrison Ainsworth's for instance, would have been my richest sources of inspiration had I not hit one day on something even better: Washington Irving's 'Alhambra'. . . . There was richness and mystery in the thick black type, a hint of bursting overflowing material in the serried lines and scant margin. To this day I am bored by the sight of widely spaced type, and a little islet of text in a sailless sea of white paper.

Well – the 'Alhambra' once in hand, making up was ecstasy. At any moment the impulse might seize me; and then, if the book was in reach, I had only to walk the floor, turning the pages as I walked, to be swept off full sail on the sea of dreams. The fact that I could not read added to the completeness of the illusion, for from those mysterious blank pages I could evoke whatever my fancy chose. Parents and nurses, peeping at me through the cracks of doors (I always had to be alone to 'make up'), noticed that I often held the book upside down, but that I never failed to turn the pages, and that I turned them at about the right pace for a person reading aloud as passionately and precipitately as was my habit.

There was something almost ritualistic in the performance. The call came regularly and imperiously; and though, when it caught me at inconvenient moments, I would struggle against it conscientiously – for I was beginning to be a very conscientious little girl – the struggle was always a losing one. I had to obey the furious Muse; and there are deplorable tales of my abandoning the 'nice' playmates who had been invited to 'spend the day', and rushing to my mother with the desperate cry: 'Mamma, you must go and entertain that little girl for me. *I've got to make up.*'

A BACKWARD GLANCE *by Edith Wharton*

There was a man of double deed
Who sowed his garden full of seed;
And when the seed began to grow,
'Twas like a garden full of snow;
And when the snow began to fall,
Like birds it was upon the wall;
And when the birds began to fly,
'Twas like a shipwreck in the sky;
And when the sky began to crack,
'Twas like a stick upon my back;
And when my back began to smart,
'Twas like a pen-knife in my heart;
And when my heart began to bleed,
Then I was dead – and dead indeed.

Anon

Command: that was the function for which I already felt myself to be secretly ready; and I still see the exact spot, among the periwinkles behind the summerhouse, where I practised those attitudes which, in a commander, must become second nature. With one foot raised and planted upon an outcropping root of the lime-tree, right hand on hip, chin up, I stood, rigid with authority, and whistled. I have never seen a general whistle on parade, but in those days I had not seen soldiers at all in the flesh; and there is no doubt that whistling does give to the whistler a scornful, superior look of unconcern, which could well – who knows? – impress the troops.

It must also have been about this time that I had a recurring dream, repeating itself in each sharp detail, in which I died, shot through the chest, on the field of battle, in the moment of victory. I subsided into the arms of an officer; the anxious staff, red-coated and gold-braided, hung over me; I knew that the battle was won and that the credit of it was mine; and then I woke up. Dreams, as well as day-dreams, pointed to a splendid, possibly a heroic, career.

That I should some day be shot through the chest turned out to be true enough, but there were then no aide-de-camp's arms to break my fall, the British Army was in full retreat, and I was not in command of it. But I was not to know that; and being sensible enough to realize that even those of us born to command must begin at the bottom, I decided to consult Mr Walker upon the first steps to be taken.

Mr Walker was an under-gardener, but had served his time as a soldier, a 'private' soldier, which sounded to me rather select and exclusive. . . . Mr Walker had a red beard, and was busy trenching celery in the dull stretch of kitchen-garden by the potting-shed on the fateful day when he destroyed, at a blow and for ever, my splendid aspirations.

The conversation began well enough, with the choice of a regiment. Mr Walker had served in the Norfolks, but had the detachment not to insist that his own was the only regiment worthy of my consideration. In fact, he did not hesitate. The Lancers, he said, were the thing for me (we did not go into the niceties of weighing the 5th against the 9th or the 12th, the 16th or 17th against the 21st). Planting his spade firmly into the wormy soil, so as to leave both hands free, he described in the air an isosceles triangle, with its apex turned down. I have forgotten with what red or yellow, or blue or gold, this triangle was so resplendent; but it represented that part of a lancer's uniform which would cover my chest, and he easily persuaded me that there was no more beautiful chest-covering in the whole British Army. . . .

The regiment decided upon, I came to my main point, the question of promotion. To my surprise, Mr Walker saw no advantages in the privacy of a 'private' soldier. I was to start as an officer. I became a Captain in no time, and a Major in Mr Walker's next breath, and almost immediately afterwards as fine a gentleman (we both hoped) as Mr Walker's own Colonel had been. My spell as a Brigadier-General took longer, since the meaning of a brigade had to be explained, but, that grasped, I rose rapidly to Major-General and commanded, hand on hip, a division. . . .

Promoted full General, I believed myself to be within one step of my destiny and was taken aback to learn, for the first time, of the existence of Field-Marshals. Mr Walker lingered lovingly over these, and told me that Lord Wolseley was the greatest soldier of them all. Then was he the Commander-in-Chief? I asked.

Then and there the blow fell. 'Nobody,' said Mr Walker, 'can be Commander-in-Chief except His Royal Highness himself.' All was over; a military career, so ardently looked forward to, was not for me. There was no future in it. Yet Mr Walker, hitherto so sympathetic, having destroyed a noble ambition in a couple of seconds, took up his spade and calmly went on trenching celery.

A VICTORIAN BOYHOOD *by L. E. Jones (1885–1969)*

Tartary

If I were Lord of Tartary,
   Myself and me alone,
My bed should be of ivory,
   Of beaten gold my throne;
And in my court should peacocks flaunt,
And in my forests tigers haunt,
And in my pools great fishes slant
   Their fins athwart the sun.

If I were Lord of Tartary,
   Trumpeters every day
To all my meals should summon me,
   And in my courtyards bray;
And in the evenings lamps should shine
Yellow as honey, red as wine,
While harp and flute and mandoline
   Made music sweet and gay.

If I were Lord of Tartary,
   I'd wear a robe of beads,
White, and gold, and green they'd be –
   And small, and thick as seeds;
And ere should wane the morning star,
I'd don my robe and scimitar,
And zebras seven should draw my car
   Through Tartary's dark glades.

Lord of fruits of Tartary,
    Her rivers silver-pale!
Lord of the hills of Tartary,
    Glen, thicket, wood, and dale!
Her flashing stars, her scented breeze,
Her trembling lakes, like foamless seas,
Her bird-delighting citron-trees
    In every purple vale!

Walter de la Mare

A clock was entirely an object of luxury in the African highlands. All the year round you could tell, from the position of the sun, what the time was, and as you had no dealings with railways, and could arrange your life on the farm according to your own wishes, it became a matter of no importance. But this was a very fine clock. In the midst of a cluster of pink roses, at every full hour, a cuckoo here flung up its little door and threw itself forward to announce the hour in a clear insolent voice. Its apparition was every time a fresh delight to the young people of the farm. From the position of the sun, they judged accurately when the moment for the midday call was due, and by a quarter to twelve I could see them approaching the house from all sides, at the tail of their goats, which they dared not leave behind. The heads of the children and of the goats swam through the bush and long grass of the forest like heads of frogs in a pond.

They left their flocks on the lawn and came in noiselessly on their bare feet; the bigger ones were about ten years and the youngest two years. They behaved very well, and kept up a sort of self-made ceremonial for their visits, which came to this: that they could move about freely in the house so long as they did not touch anything, nor sit down, nor speak unless spoken to. As the cuckoo rushed out on them, a great movement of ecstasy and suppressed laughter ran through the group. It also sometimes happened that a very small herdboy, who did not feel any responsibility about the goats, would come back in the early morning all by himself, stand for a long time in front of the clock, now shut up and silent, and address it in Kikuyu in a slow sing-song declaration of love, then gravely walk out again. My houseboys laughed at the herdboys, and confided to me that the children were so ignorant that they believed the cuckoo to be alive.

OUT OF AFRICA *by Karen Blixen (1885–1962)*

How many miles to Babylon?
   Threescore miles and ten.
Can I get there by candle-light?
   Yes, and back again.
If your heels are nimble and light,
   You may get there by candle-light.

Anon

My mother and her sisters were true Victorians; not in a general way frightened of battle, murder, and sudden death, but perfectly terrified of insects. Opening her first Egyptian orange to find it full of life, she had been unable to eat another orange for several years. There had been a shattering moment on her first day in our newly built house in Zamalek, when a praying mantis alighted in her open cabin trunk. With a wild cry she shut the lid and locked the trunk and piled it high with heavy dictionaries until my father's return from work. . . .

The discovery of a scorpion in the nursery toy-cupboard was, I think, kept from her.

'Come and look, Nanny, what there is! A tiny little lobster in one of the dolls' teacups.'

There it sat, registering apparent good will, and caused a furore. Mohammed and Ahmed were summoned; and even they looked serious and alarmed and repeatedly shook out their long galabiehs during the hunt. Once, thrillingly, there was a cobra at the grotto, and earlier still, on a picnic to the pyramids, May had been found by Nanny to be playing with a scorpion, poking it idly with a small stick, totally unaware of its potency. She was forcibly impressed with the narrowness of this escape.

'Within three inches of death,' she kept saying to Nanny at

nursery breakfast next morning, 'I was within *three inches* of death.'

'Oh well,' Nanny said comfortably, 'I daresay we've all had narrower escapes than we know.' She poured May out another cup of tea. The sun streamed in through the open fly-netted sewing-room window. 'Elbows off the table, William Badenough,' for William's second name, which was Goodenough, was a source of endless nursery wit.

All the same, it was an impressive thought, and I was impressed too, although death at this time held no terrors. All was clearly arranged in my mind. When the summons came I would carefully climb up an endless long ladder stretching high into the brilliance of the blue Egyptian sky. Far below, the goats, poor fellows, would all be streaming off disappointedly over the Zamalek bridge in the general direction of Em-baba. The judgment seat of God was, inexplicably, sited at the tram stop on the near side of the bridge. Emphatically numbered amongst the sheep, I would be wearing my best lace petticoat, a flannel petticoat with scalloped edges, and a pair of best knickers with pink ribbon threaded through them. Closely behind me would follow May, clad in her Sunday dark blue skirt and white blouse, carrying my best dress and pink sash over one arm. (No one in their senses climbs ladders wearing their best dress.) On a sort of crystal railway platform at the top we should pause, while May put on my dress and tied my sash. Here a slight doubt rose, the perennial question of whether or not one wears a hat. Could Heaven be classified as church or home? What May did after discharging her essential function was also a little uncertain, but she probably faded into the middle distance where she would for ever remain, peacefully turning down celestial night-nursery beds.

My own course was perfectly clear. Saint Peter (and what has he done to deserve an eternity of conciergehood?) would fling back the gates and I would be received, amidst universal enthusiasm, into the presence of God. It would be like going down into the drawing-room in the evenings, only more so.

A LATE BEGINNER *by Priscilla Napier*

The Hunter

When I was but thirteen or so
　　I went into a golden land;
Chimborazo, Cotopaxi
　　Took me by the hand.

My father died, my brother too,
　　They passed like fleeting dreams,
I stood where Popocatapetl
　　In the sunlight gleams.

I dimly heard the master's voice
　　And boys far-off at play,
Chimborazo, Cotopaxi
　　Had stolen me away.

I walked in a great golden dream
　　To and fro from school –
Shining Popocatapetl
　　The dusty streets did rule.

I walked home with a gold dark boy
　　And never a word I'd say,
Chimborazo, Cotopaxi
　　Had taken my speech away:

I gazed entranced upon his face
　　Fairer than any flower –
O shining Popocatapetl
　　It was thy magic hour:

The houses, people, traffic seemed
　　Thin fading dreams by day,
Chimborazo, Cotopaxi
　　They had stolen my soul away!

W. J. Turner (1889–1946)

My father was a man of wide culture, to whom, in the words of
the Psalms, all things were full of the goodness of the Lord. But the
regime made a solemn background to a child's life. He was
conscious of living in a world ruled by unalterable law under the
direct eye of the Almighty. He was a miserable atom as compared
with Omnipotence, but an atom, nevertheless, in which Omnipotence took an acute interest. The words of the Bible, from daily
family prayers and long Sabbath sessions, were as familiar to him
as the story of Jack and the Beanstalk. A child has a natural love of
rhetoric, and the noble scriptural cadences had their own meaning
for me, quite apart from their proper interpretation. The consequence was that I built up a Bible world of my own and placed it in
the woods.

From it I excluded the more gracious pictures, the rejoicing
'little hills', the mountains that 'clapped their hands', Elim with its
wells and palm trees, the 'streams of water in the south' of the
126th Psalm. These belonged properly to the sunny Border. But
for the rest, Israel warred in the woods, Israelitish prophets ken-
nelled in the shale of the burns, back-sliding Judah built altars to
Baal on some knoll under the pines. I knew exactly what a
heathenish 'grove' was: it was a cluster of self-sown beeches on a
certain 'high place'. The imagery of the Psalms haunted every
sylvan corner. More, as I struggled, a confused little mortal, with
the first tangles of Calvinistic theology, I came to identify abstrac-
tions with special localities. The Soul, a shining cylindrical thing,
was linked with a particular patch of bent and heather, and in that
theatre its struggles took place, while Sin, a horrid substance like
black salt, was intimately connected with a certain thicket of
brambles and spotted toadstools.

MEMORY HOLD-THE-DOOR *by John Buchan (1875–1940)*

Fern Hill

Now as I was young and easy under the apple boughs
About the lilting house and happy as the grass was green,
    The night above the dingle starry,
        Time let me hail and climb
    Golden in the heydays of his eyes,
And honoured among wagons I was prince of the apple towns
And once below a time I lordly had the trees and leaves
        Trail with daisies and barley
    Down the rivers of the windfall light.

And as I was green and carefree, famous among the barns
About the happy yard and singing as the farm was home,
    In the sun that is young once only,
        Time let me play and be
    Golden in the mercy of his means,
And green and golden I was huntsman and herdsman, the calves
Sang to my horn, the foxes on the hills barked clear and cold,
        And the sabbath rang slowly
    In the pebbles of the holy streams.

All the sun long it was running, it was lovely, the hay
Fields high as the house, the tunes from the chimneys, it was air
    And playing, lovely and watery
        And fire green as grass.
    And nightly under the simple stars
As I rode to sleep the owls were bearing the farm away,
All the moon long I heard, blessed among stables, the nightjars
        Flying with the ricks, and the horses
        Flashing into the dark.

And then to awake, and the farm, like a wanderer white
With the dew, come back, the cock on his shoulder: it was all
    Shining, it was Adam and maiden,
        The sky gathered again
    And the sun grew round that very day.

So it must have been after the birth of the simple light
In the first, spinning place, the spellbound horses walking warm
    Out of the whinnying green stable
        On to the fields of praise.

And honoured among foxes and pheasants by the gay house
Under the new made clouds and happy as the heart was long,
    In the sun born over and over,
        I ran my heedless ways,
      My wishes raced through the house high hay
And nothing I cared, at my sky blue trades, that time allows
In all his tuneful turning so few and such morning songs
    Before the children green and golden
        Follow him out of grace,

Nothing I cared, in the lamb white days, that time would take me
Up to the swallow thronged loft by the shadow of my hand,
    In the moon that is always rising,
        Nor that riding to sleep
    I should hear him fly with the high fields
And wake to the farm forever fled from the childless land.
Oh as I was young and easy in the mercy of his means,
        Time held me green and dying
      Though I sang in my chains like the sea.

Dylan Thomas (1914–53)

13

NEW HORIZONS

One of the queerest incidents of my early education was when a
French actor, Dalès, was invited to give me lessons in elocution. . . .

'I suppose, M. Dalès,' my father once said to him, 'you could
give lessons in dancing too.'

Dalès was a stout old gentleman of over sixty; with a profound
consciousness of his own merits but an equally profound sense of
modesty, he answered that he could not judge of his own talents,
but that he often gave hints to the ballet-dancers at the Opera.

'Just as I supposed,' remarked my father, offering him his
snuff-box open — a favour he would never have shown to a
Russian or German tutor. 'I should be much obliged if you would
make him dance a little after the declamation; he is so stiff.' . . .

And now you must imagine my small room on a dismal winter
evening, with the water running down the frozen windows over
the sandbags, two tallow candles burning on the table, and us two
face to face. On the stage Dalès spoke in a fairly natural voice, but,
in giving a lesson, he thought himself bound to get away as far as
possible from nature. He recited Racine in a sing-song voice, and
made a parting, like the parting of an Englishman's back hair, at
the caesura of each line, so that every verse came out in two pieces
like a broken stick.

Meanwhile he made the gestures of a man who has fallen into
the water and cannot swim. He made me repeat each verse several
times and constantly shook his head: 'Not right at all! Listen to
me! *"Je crains Dieu, cher Abner"*' — now came the parting; he
closed his eyes, shook his head slightly, and added, repelling the
waves with a languid movement of the arm, '*"et n'ai point d'autre
crainte."*'

Then the old gentleman, who 'feared nothing but God', would
look at his watch, put away his books, and take hold of a chair.

This chair was my partner.

Is it surprising that I never learned to dance? These lessons did not last long: within a fortnight they were brought to an end by a very tragic event.

I was at the theatre with my uncle, and the overture was played several times without the curtain rising. The front rows, wishing to show their familiarity with Paris customs, began to make the noise which is made in Paris by the back rows only. A manager came out in front of the curtain; he bowed to the left, he bowed to the right, he bowed to the front, and then he said: 'We ask for all the indulgence of the audience; a terrible misfortune has befallen us: Dalès, a member of our company' – and here the manager's speech was interrupted by genuine tears – 'has been found dead in his room, poisoned by the fumes from the stove.'

Such were the forcible means by which the Russian system of ventilation delivered me from lessons in elocution, from spouting Racine, and from dancing a solo with the partner who boasted four legs carved in mahogany.

CHILDHOOD, YOUTH AND EXILE by Alexander Herzen (1812–70)

My uncle, John A. Quarles, was also a farmer, and his place was in the country four miles from Florida. He had eight children and fifteen or twenty negroes and was also fortunate in other ways, particularly in his character. I have not come across a better man than he was. I was his guest for two or three months every year, from the fourth year after we removed to Hannibal till I was eleven or twelve years old. . . .

The farmhouse stood in the middle of a very large yard and the yard was fenced on three sides with rails and on the rear side with high palings; against these stood the smoke-house; beyond the palings was the orchard; beyond the orchard were the negro quarters and the tobacco fields. The front yard was entered over a stile made of sawed-off logs of graduated heights; I do not remember any gate. In a corner of the front yard were a dozen lofty hickory trees and a dozen black walnuts, and in the nutting season riches were to be gathered there.

Down a piece, abreast the house, stood a little log cabin against the rail fence; and there the woody hill fell sharply away, past the barns, the corn-crib, the stables and the tobacco-curing house, to a limpid brook which sang along over its gravelly bed and curved and frisked in and out and here and there and yonder in the deep shade of overhanging foliage and vines – a divine place for wading, and it had swimming pools, too, which were forbidden to us and therefore much frequented by us. For we were little Christian children and had early been taught the value of forbidden fruit.

In the little log cabin lived a bedridden white-headed slave woman whom we visited daily and looked upon with awe, for we believed she was upward of a thousand years old and had talked with Moses. The younger negroes credited these statistics and had furnished them to us in good faith. We accommodated all the details which came to us about her; and so we believed that she had lost her health in the long desert trip coming out of Egypt and had never been able to get it back again. She had a round bald place on the crown of her head and we used to creep around and gaze at it in reverent silence and reflect that it was caused by fright through seeing Pharaoh drowned. We called her 'Aunt' Hannah, Southern fashion. She was superstitious, like the other negroes; also, like them, she was deeply religious. Like them, she had great faith in prayer and employed it in all ordinary exigencies, but not in cases where a dead certainty of result was urgent. Whenever witches were around she tied up the remnant of her wool in little tufts, with white thread, and this promptly made the witches impotent. . . .

In my schoolboy days I had no aversion to slavery. I was not aware that there was anything wrong about it. No one arraigned it in my hearing; the local papers said nothing against it; the local pulpit taught us that God approved it, that it was a holy thing and that the doubter need only look in the Bible if he wished to settle his mind – and then the texts were read aloud to us to make the matter sure; if the slaves themselves had an aversion to slavery they were wise and said nothing. In Hannibal we seldom saw a slave misused; on the farm never.

There was, however, one small incident of my boyhood days which touched this matter, and it must have meant a good deal to me or it would not have stayed in my memory, clear and sharp,

vivid and shadowless, all these slow-drifting years. We had a little
slave boy whom we had hired from someone, there in Hannibal.
He was from the eastern shore of Maryland and had been brought
away from his family and his friends halfway across the American
continent and sold. He was a cheery spirit, innocent and gentle,
and the noisiest creature that ever was, perhaps. All day long he
was singing, whistling, yelling, whooping, laughing – it was mad-
dening, devastating, unendurable. At last, one day, I lost all my
temper and went raging to my mother and said Sandy had been
singing for an hour without a single break and I couldn't stand it
and *wouldn't* she please shut him up. The tears came into her eyes
and her lip trembled and she said something like this:

'Poor thing, when he sings it shows that he is not remembering
and that comforts me; but when he is still I am afraid he is
thinking and I cannot bear it. He will never see his mother again; if
he can sing I must not hinder it, but be thankful for it. If you were
older you would understand me; then that friendless child's noise
would make you glad.'

It was a simple speech and made up of small words but it went
home, and Sandy's noise was not a trouble to me any more. She
never used large words but she had a natural gift for making small
ones do effective work. ... She has come handy to me several
times in my books, where she figures as Tom Sawyer's Aunt Polly.
I fitted her out with a dialect and tried to think up other improve-
ments for her but did not find any.

THE AUTOBIOGRAPHY OF MARK TWAIN *(1835–1910)*

There was presently talk at home of my sitting for a scholarship
for a place at the Strand School, a secondary school at Streatham.
... Miss H. had been nagging my father about scholarships; and
because of the Ruskin 'prize' he was impressed and I was in a state
of euphoric self-confidence.

Soon, Father and I were on a bus going to Streatham. I was
going to sit for the examination. I was impressed by being at a
school where there was a dining hall and where boys could buy
buns, chocolate and drink cocoa in the break. They also wore long
trousers. There was a touch of Greyfriars in this. I was sick with

fright and had had diarrhoea, of course, but I felt I could rely on my genius. But when I sat down to the examination papers I found that my genius was not being called upon. I could answer scarcely any of the questions and I could only hope to get by in Scripture. There was a question about Noah and the Ark; something about the numbers of people aboard, size and location of the ark, the duration of the flood, and how many times the dove flew in and out with what in its beak? I had inherited my father's dislike of a fact. I ignored the question and wrote at full speed a dramatic eye-witness account of the Flood, ending with that favourite device – a Lament. I made the drowning millions lament. A month later I heard the inevitable news: the genius, the inhabitant of a higher plane, had failed to win a scholarship.

A CAB AT THE DOOR *by V. S. Pritchett*

I believe I can tell the particular little chance that filled my head first with such Chimes of Verse, as have never since left ringing there: For I remember when I began to read, and to take some pleasure in it, there was wont to lie in my Mothers Parlour (I know not by what accident, for she her self never in her life read any Book but of Devotion) but there was wont to lie *Spencers* Works [*The Faerie Queene*]; this I happened to fall upon, and was infinitely delighted with the Stories of the Knights, and Giants, and Monsters, and brave Houses, which I found every where there: (Though my understanding had little to do with all this) and by degrees with the tinckling of the Rhyme and Dance of the Numbers, so that I think I had read him all over before I was twelve years old, and was thus made a Poet as irremediably as a Child is made an Eunuch.

from 'Of Myself' by Abraham Cowley (1618–67)

In 1890, when I was ten years old, I was put under the care of a tutor who came daily to Lexham Gardens to teach me and my elder brother, Herbert. . . .

One of the pleasant things about Mr Floyd was that he was one of those very rare people who never mind looking ridiculous. He taught us to play fives against a wall on the verandah and he also taught us singlestick, and as he was very tall and we were very small, the spectacle was extraordinarily absurd. But to see Mr Floyd at his best was to see him reading Caesar with my canary sitting on the top of his head. I had a canary, called Chickabiddy, who was so tame that the door of his cage was never shut during the day and he used to fly about the room. I had taught him to come and perch on one's head if one called 'Chickabiddy, Chickabiddy', and it used to be a game we played for two of us to stand at opposite ends of a room and make him fly backwards and forwards very rapidly from head to head. Mr Floyd became very fond of him and he took a liking to Mr Floyd's head. Mr Floyd had a habit of walking up and down the room as he taught us, and Chickabiddy would sit the whole time on his head. The moment would come – eagerly awaited by us – when Chickabiddy would make a mess on the top of Mr Floyd's head. If he was aware of the evacuation, he wiped the mess off with a piece of blotting-paper without interrupting the lesson. Sometimes he did not feel what had happened, and then I, as owner of the bird, said: 'I am afraid, Sir, Chickabiddy has made a mess', and Mr Floyd would say very politely: 'Thank you, my boy', and wipe the mess off with the blotting-paper.

SOWING *by Leonard Woolf*

Some words of advice from Lady Mary Wortley Montagu (1689–1762) to her daughter, the Countess of Bute.

Louvere, Jan. 10, 1752

My Dear Child,

I am extremely concerned to hear you complain of ill health, at a time of life when you ought to be in the flower of your strength. I hope I need not recommend to you the care of it: the tenderness you have for your children is sufficient to enforce you to the utmost regard for the preservation of a life so necessary to their well being. I do not doubt your prudence in their education: neither can I say any thing particular relating to it at this distance, different tempers requiring different management. In general, never attempt to govern them (as most people do) by deceit: if they find themselves cheated, even in trifles, it will so far lessen the authority of their instructor, as to make them neglect all their future admonitions. And, if possible, breed them free from prejudices; those contracted in the nursery often influence the whole life after, of which I have seen many melancholy examples. ... If your daughters are inclined to love reading, do not check their inclination by hindering them of the diverting part of it; it is as necessary for the amusement of women as the reputation of men; but teach them not to expect or desire any applause from it. Let their brothers shine, and let them content themselves with making their lives easier by it, which I experimentally know is more effectually done by study than any other way. Ignorance is as much the fountain of vice as idleness, and indeed generally produces it. People that do not read, or work for a livelihood, have many hours they know not how to employ; especially women, who commonly fall into vapours, or something worse. I am afraid you'll think this letter very tedious: forgive it as coming from your most affectionate mother.

M.W.

On a Sunday I went to the woods to watch Monroe make a steam engine with a whistle. He had found a five-gallon coal oil can on the road. He had tried to make the iron teakettle on the stove whistle. The oil can was bigger and better.

He took us to a place where a sandy-bottomed branch wound in and out among tall oak trees. While Dewey and Cleaver built a fire, he put water in the can and plugged the spout with a whistle whittled from a hickory limb. After long waiting, steam rose and boiled out, but there was no whistle – only the sound like a boiling teakettle.

Monroe whittled a whistle with a smaller opening and plugged the spout. This time there was a whistle, but it was watery when it should have been clear and sharp.

Again Monroe whittled and plugged. By now the fire had

burned down to a bed of red hot coals. The can hissed and sizzled when he put it on. Steam began to build up. There was a rumbling, and the can lifted, first on one side and then on the other. We watched the whistle and waited. This time the sound had to be good.

'It's leaking.'

Not steam but a fine spray of water was coming through the whistle, and the can was beginning to bounce.

'Get away,' Monroe yelled.

We watched a side of the can cave in like bent paper. Then we ran and hid behind trees.

I was close enough to see the can, bouncing and turning, with all sides drawn in, and steam coming out in a fine thin whistle. Then the whistle was lost in a rumbling and the can rose up, straight into the branches high overhead, and burst with a crack and a spray of boiling water.

We were out of reach, but close enough to see what might have happened to us.

THIS STUBBORN SOIL *by William A. Owens*

A medical examination at school had revealed the fact that I was short-sighted. The doctor took me solemnly between his knees, looked into my face, and said, 'If you don't get some glasses, you'll be blind by the time you are fifteen, and I shall tell your parents so.'

I was rather proud of this distinction. Fifteen! That was so far ahead that it meant nothing to me, except a sort of twilight at the end of life. My parents thought otherwise, and one Saturday afternoon I was taken, via a steep road called Pig Hill, to a chemist's shop on Lavender Hill, Clapham, opposite the first theatre that I was ever to enter, 'The Shakespeare'. Behind the shop was a room where my eyes were tested in the rough and ready way customary in those days. The chemist hung an open framework that felt like the Forth Bridge around my ears and on my nose. Lenses were slotted into this, and twisted about, while I was instructed to read the card of letters beginning with a large 'E'.

I remember still the astonishment with which I saw the smaller letters change from a dark blur into separate items of the alphabet. I thought about it all the following week, and found that by screwing up my eyes when I was out of doors I could get to some faint approximation of that clarity, for a few seconds at a time.

This made me surmise that the universe which hitherto I had seen as a vague mass of colour and blurred shapes might in actuality be much more concise and defined. I was therefore half prepared for the surprise which shook me a week later when, on the Saturday evening, we went again to the shop on Lavender Hill, and the chemist produced the bespoken pair of steel-rimmed spectacles through which I was invited to read the card. I read it, from top to bottom! I turned, and looked in triumph at Mother, but what I saw was Mother intensified. I saw the pupils of her eyes, the tiny feathers in her boa necklet; I saw the hairs in Father's moustache, and on the back of his hand. Jack's cap might have been made of metal, so hard and clear did it shine on his close-cropped head, above his bony face and huge nose. I saw *his* eyes too, round, inquiring, fierce with a hunger of observation. He was studying me with a gimlet sharpness such as I had never before been able to perceive.

Then we walked out of the shop, and I stepped on to the pavement, which came up and hit me, so that I had to grasp the nearest support – Father's coat. 'Take care, now, take care!' he said indulgently (though he disapproved of all these concessions to physical weakness). 'And mind you don't break them!' . . .

The excitement of this optical stimulation may have put me into a mild fever, for my sleep at night was peopled with great globes of flashing light; and in the daytime I felt my cheeks burning. The second self, the observing self, stepped forward to an even sharper alertness, and I moved under its guidance as though entranced.

Such was my condition one evening after school, when I was sitting at the kitchen table, drawing on a sheet of paper an underground labyrinth, and peopling its corridors and recesses with tiny matchstick figures, a line for the body, four lines for the limbs, and an open dot for the head. This was a pastime to which I had been long addicted but I could now pursue it more minutely.

Tonight, however, I was restless, and I wearied of the game. Bedtime loomed ahead, and I had no inclination to start a new game. Mother or Jack would soon be driving me upstairs. At the moment, they were absent from the kitchen. I looked about me and saw nothing. I was tired and not unwilling to go to bed. I looked up at the Swiss clock, in its wooden case on the high shelf over the stove. And I read the time!

At first I could not believe my eyes. The family had wasted hours trying to instruct me in the mystery of the clock face. I was just as dull over this as in the spelling of simple words. The impact on my mind in that instant was so sharp that I have remembered the position of the clock-hands ever since. The time was twenty minutes past six, and the gaslight above the table, over which I leaned and stared, hissed with an occasional impure splutter.

Then, still incredulous, I turned my attention to other objects in the kitchen. On the sewing machine lay Jack's library book, a dirty brown object disguised in a uniform binding with gilt numbers on the back. I picked it up, opened it at the first page, and began to read *The Swiss Family Robinson.*

It is an understatement to say that I began to read. I stepped into another life. I was one of that family on the wrecked ship, passing through the barrier of words, enlarging my small suburban existence by this new dimension. I could not know what was happening, or the scope of this vast inheritance. I heard the sea breaking on the shore of that fortunate island and I shared with Fritz, Ernest, Jack and Franz in establishing ourselves under the palm trees, and in offering up thanksgiving for our safety. I have never lost that island. . . .

Mother found me sitting at the table, with the book in front of me, and my breathing body in front of the book. Then Jack followed her, and both of them stood watching for some moments before I jerked my head, saw them, and broke the spell.

'I can read,' I said.

OVER THE BRIDGE *by Richard Church (1893–1972)*

In my opinion painters owe to Giotto, the Florentine painter, exactly the same debt they owe to nature, which constantly serves them as a model and whose finest and most beautiful aspects they are always striving to imitate and reproduce. . . . And yet this great man, who started life in the year 1276 in the village of Vespignano, fourteen miles out in the country from the city of Florence, was the son of a poor peasant farmer called Bondone, who gave him the name of Giotto and then brought him up just like any other boy of his class.

By the time he reached the age of ten Giotto showed in all his boyish ways such unusually quick intelligence and liveliness that he delighted not only his father but all who knew him, whether they lived in the village or beyond. Bondone used to let him look after some sheep; and while the animals grazed here and there about the farm, the boy, drawn instinctively to the art of design, was always sketching what he saw in nature, or imagined in his own mind, on stones or on the ground or the sand. One day Cimabue was on his way from Florence to Vespignano, where he had some business to attend to, when he came across Giotto who, while the sheep were grazing near by, was drawing one of them by scratching with a slightly pointed stone on a smooth clean piece of rock. And this was before he had received any instruction except for what he saw in nature itself. Cimabue stopped in astonishment to watch him, and then he asked the boy whether he would like to come and live with him. . . . After he had gone to live there, helped by his natural talent and instructed by Cimabue, in a very short space of time Giotto not only captured his master's own style but also began to draw so ably from life that he made a decisive break with the crude traditional Byzantine style and brought to life the great art of painting as we know it today, introducing the technique of drawing accurately from life, which had been neglected for more than two hundred years.

THE LIVES OF THE ARTISTS *by Giorgio Vasari (1511–74)*

Like all children, I used to ask a great many questions. Aunt Flora was patient in answering them, but she was inclined to take her revenge by giving me information that was incorrect or misleading. When I asked her what was really the matter with my grandfather, she told me quite gravely that he was bewitched, that he was under a spell. I asked her if a counter-spell, a magic charm, could be found, would he get all right again? She said Yes.

The idea lay for some days incubating in my brain until one day I happened to read in a volume of Russian Fairy Stories about a man who was delivered from a ban the Ice-Maiden had laid upon him by being crowned with a wreath of snowdrops. It seemed a simple matter. I asked my grandmother if it had ever been tried and was told not to talk nonsense. But by that time I had already discovered that, when grown-ups told one not to talk nonsense, it was in nine cases out of ten merely a device for setting aside an embarrassing suggestion. I began to harbour the gravest suspicions, and finally became convinced that, for some reason or other, my poor grandfather was being deliberately held in thrall.

Come what might, I was determined to make the experiment, which was facilitated by its happening to be the snowdrop season. I gathered a large bunch of those self-righteous little flowers and, with the help of some wire and some cotton thread, I managed to construct a clumsy wreath. Secreting myself in the library with my talisman, I waited until the sound of snoring announced the fact that my grandfather had fallen asleep. I then stole into his room on tiptoe, succeeded in deftly placing the wreath on the old gentleman's head, and returned to my hiding-place to await the result.

Shortly afterwards I heard my grandmother enter the room. Her startled exclamation at the strange vision of my grandfather sitting with his mouth open, snoring loudly and decked out like Ophelia, must have roused him from his slumbers, for it was followed by a bellow of rage and a great commotion.

I guessed that my experiment had failed. My hopes of being acclaimed as a miracle-worker were dashed to the ground. I was now terrified by what I had done, for I realized that, after having mentioned the subject of snowdrops to my grandmother, I should at once be suspected. I fled to Aunt Flora's room as to the horns of the altar, and besought her protection. She was, I fancy, amused by my account of the unfortunate experiment, and no doubt she felt a trifle guilty for having put the idea in my head, and for having been indirectly the cause of all the trouble. Knowing also that, however good my intentions may have been, they would most certainly be misjudged by the rest of the family, she willingly undertook my defence, and I got off with a caution never again under any circumstances to enter my grandfather's room without permission.

FIRST CHILDHOOD *by Lord Berners*

14

TRAVELS

Mr Salteena, 'an elderly man of 42', and his young friend Ethel have been invited to stay with Bernard Clarke in his country house.

Starting Gaily

When the great morning came Mr Salteena did not have an egg for his brekfast in case he should be sick on the jorney.

What top hat will you wear asked Ethel.

I shall wear my best black and my white alpacka coat to keep off the dust and flies replied Mr Salteena.

I shall put some red ruge on my face said Ethel because I am very pale owing to the drains in this house.

You will look very silly said Mr Salteena with a dry laugh.

Well so will you said Ethel in a snappy tone and she ran out of the room with a very superier run throwing out her legs behind and her arms swinging in rithum.

Well said the owner of the house she has a most idiotick run.

Presently Ethel came back in her best hat and a lovly velvit coat of royal blue. Do I look nice in my get up she asked.

Mr Salteena survayed her. You look rarther rash my dear your colors dont quite match your face but never mind I am just going up to say goodbye to Rosalind the housemaid.

Well dont be long said Ethel. Mr S. skipped upstairs to Rosalinds room. Good-bye Rosalind he said I shall be back soon and I hope I shall enjoy myself.

I make no doubt of that sir said Rosalind with a blush as Mr Salteena silently put 2/6 on the dirty toilet cover.

Take care of your bronkitis said Mr S. rarther bashfully and he hastily left the room waving his hand carelessly to the housemaid.

Come along cried Ethel powdering her nose in the hall let us get into the cab. Mr Salteena did not care for powder but he was an unselfish man so he dashed into the cab. Sit down said Ethel as the cabman waved his whip you are standing on my luggage. Well I am paying for the cab said Mr S. so I might be allowed to put my feet were I like.

They traveled 2nd class in the train and Ethel was longing to go first but thought perhaps least said soonest mended. Mr Salteena got very excited in the train about his visit. Ethel was calm but she felt excited inside. Bernard has a big house said Mr S. gazing at Ethel he is inclined to be rich.

Oh indeed said Ethel looking at some cows flashing past the window. Mr S. felt rarther disheartened so he read the paper till the train stopped and the porters shouted Rickamere station. We had better collect our traps said Mr Salteena and just then a very exalted footman in a cocked hat and olive green uniform put his head in at the window. Are you for Rickamere Hall he said in impressive tones.

Well yes I am said Mr Salteena and so is this lady.

Very good sir said the noble footman if you will alight I will see to your luggage there is a convayance awaiting you.

Oh thankyou thankyou said Mr S. and he and Ethel stepped along the platform. Outside they found a lovely cariage lined with olive green cushions to match the footman and the horses had green bridles and bows on their manes and tails. They got gingerly in. Will he bring our luggage asked Ethel nervously.

I expect so said Mr Salteena lighting a very long cigar.

Do we tip him asked Ethel quietly.

Well no I dont think so not yet we had better just thank him perlitely.

Just then the footman staggered out with the bagage. Ethel bowed gracefully over the door of the cariage and Mr S. waved his hand as each bit of luggage was hoisted up to make sure it was all there. Then he said thankyou my good fellow very politely. Not at all sir said the footman and touching his cocked hat he jumped actively to the box.

I was right not to tip him whispered Mr Salteena the thing to do is to leave 2/6 on your dressing table when your stay is over.

Does he find it asked Ethel who did not really know at all how to go on at a visit. I beleeve so replied Mr Salteena anyhow it is quite the custom and we cant help it if he does not. Now my dear what do you think of the sceenery.

Very nice said Ethel gazing at the rich fur rug on her knees. Just then the cariage rolled into a beautifull drive with tall trees and big red flowers growing amid shiny dark leaves. Presently the haughty coachman pulled up with a great clatter at a huge front door with tall pillers each side a big iron bell and two very clean scrapers. The doors flung open as if by majic causing Ethel to jump and a portly butler appeared on the scene with a very shiny shirt front and a huge pale face. Welcome sir he exclaimed good naturedly as Mr Salteena alighted rarther quickly from the viacle and please to step inside.

Mr Salteena stepped in as bid followed by Ethel. The footman again struggled with the luggage and the butler Francis Minnit by name kindly lent a hand. The hall was very big and hung round with guns and mats and ancesters giving it a gloomy but a grand air. The butler then showed them down a winding corridoor till he came to a door which he flung open shouting Mr Salteena and a lady sir.

A tall man of 29 rose from the sofa. He was rarther bent in the middle with very nice long legs fairish hair and blue eyes. Hullo Alf old boy he cried so you have got here all safe and no limbs broken.

THE YOUNG VISITERS by Daisy Ashford (1881–1972),
written at the age of nine.

> Sally go round the moon, Sally,
> Sally go round the sun.
> Sally go round the ominlebus
> On a Sunday afternoon.   *Anon*

An entreaty from Master Boscawen, aged three, to his father, the Admiral.

July, 1748.

Dear, dear Papa,

Pray come home, I have made you a great many ships to come in, and Mama says you will bring me something pretty, and pray do Papa, for I am very good Your dutyful son,

E.H.B.

I had a boat, and the boat had wings;
    And I did dream that we went a flying
Over the heads of queens and kings,
    Over the souls of dead and dying,
Up among the stars and the great white rings,
    And where the Moon on her back is lying.

                                                    Anon

One of the stories which my mother told me was about the adventures of Raja Rasalu, a bloodcurdling narrative of how a young prince issued forth from his palace against the wishes of his parents, fought the demons, became an ascetic and finally won the hand of a fairy princess by defeating her father at chess.

The heroic character of this tale, with its mixture of exalted and noble passions, refined thought and actions, had kept me breathless and tense with excitement as various episodes of its long narrative were told me. It fired my imagination so that when on subsequent evenings my mother asked me which tale I should like her to recite, I would generally choose the story of the adventures of Raja Rasalu.

And some days later, buckling the wooden sword which Godu, the carpenter, had made for me, to a band round my waist, I set out exactly as Rasalu had done, without asking my parents' permission, and adventured into the hills across the old river bed, a quarter of a mile away from home.

I was talking to myself as I sped along, hopping over splinters and stones in the desolate river bed. The brownish ochre hills towered there beyond my gaze, sun-kissed and soaked in a vast quietude, like the remote fortress homes of the Pathans. And, ascending the hills by a pathway that had been cut by the Pathan goatherds through the bushes and the cacti, the scrub and the grey osiers which grew in sheer abundance over the crags, I reached the summit of a minor incline. Then I descended the slope of a dell, exerting myself on my own in a highly dramatic, imaginary fight with every monstrous cactus that came my way, cutting and slashing with a fine, absorbed bravery of which the towering purple hills were the silent and awestruck witnesses. I stood here for a moment, the panting and triumphant master of all that I surveyed among the summits of the copper-coloured crags, and, with a dull ache at the back of my head, waited to think of the possibility of further adventures.

Through the deeps of stillness about me, disturbed only by a soft breeze in the hot sunny afternoon, I could hear the sound of water. I looked round and on the slopes of the dell at my feet I saw a crystal-clear pool issuing from some natural spring. I descended towards it through a little valley full of lush, tall grass, poppies, mushrooms and wild anemones. My heart pulled back with a sudden fear as I approached the water. But, recalling that Rasalu was very bold and not at all afraid of the wilds and forests, I took a palmful of water and drank to quench my thirst.

Then, still bound in the spell of my fancies, I capered here and there, exploring for the nest of a bird which I heard cooing with a deep, resonant voice. But I could not locate it and sat down to rest under the scanty shade of a berry tree. The shrill cries of vultures haunted the landscape and filled it with the dread of a terrible desolation, especially as I had heard that vultures fed on corpses and lived in lonely places, haunted by jinns.

I got up and ran.

Hardly had I gone three steps when I heard a sudden, sinister whistle and saw, on one side, a long cobra creep out of a bush with its terrible, glistening black body and push its hood up with a flicker of its split tongues, as if it were full of a merciless anger and hate.

I stood transfixed for a moment and could not even shriek.

But the snake dipped its head and went its way into the bush grass where the frogs croaked.

I ran, shaking, terror-stricken and dumb.

SEVEN SUMMERS *by Mulk Raj Anand*

My dear Fanny . . .

 I have so many interruptions that I cannot manage to fill a
Letter in one day – since I scribbled the song we have walked
through a beautiful Country to Kirkcudbright – at which
place I will write you a song about myself –

> There was a naughty Boy,
>   A naughty boy was he,
> He would not stop at home,
>   He could not quiet be –
>   He took
>   In his Knapsack
>   A Book
>   Full of vowels
>   And a shirt
>   With some towels –
>   A slight cap
>   For night cap –
>   A hair brush,
>   Comb ditto,
>   New Stockings
>   For old ones
>   Would split O!
>   This Knapsack
>   Tight at's back
>   He rivetted close
> And followéd his Nose
>   To the North,
>   To the North,
> And follow'd his nose
>   To the North.

> There was a naughty boy
>   And a naughty boy was he,
> For nothing would he do
>   But scribble poetry –
>   He took

An inkstand
In his hand
And a Pen
Big as ten
In the other,
And away
In a Pother
He ran
To the mountains
And fountains
And ghostes
And Postes
And witches
And ditches
And wrote
In his coat
When the weather
Was cool,
Fear of gout,
And without
When the weather
Was warm –
Och the charm
When we choose
To follow one's nose
To the north,
To the north,
To follow one's nose
To the north!

There was a naughty boy
And a naughty boy was he,
He kept little fishes
In washing tubs three
In spite
Of the might
Of the Maid
Nor afraid

Of his Granny-good –
He often would
Hurly burly
Get up early
And go
By hook or crook
To the brook
And bring home
Miller's thumb,
Tittlebat
Not over fat,
Minnows small
As the stall
Of a glove,
Not above
The size
Of a nice
Little Baby's
Little fingers –
O he made
'Twas his trade
Of Fish a pretty Kettle
A Kettle –
A Kettle
Of Fish a pretty Kettle
A Kettle!

There was a naughty Boy,
And a naughty Boy was he,
He ran away to Scotland
The people for to see –
Then he found
That the ground
Was as hard,
That a yard
Was as long,
That a song
Was as merry,

That a cherry
Was as red –
That lead
Was as weighty,
That fourscore
Was as eighty,
That a door
Was as wooden
As in England –
So he stood in his shoes
And he wonder'd,
He wonder'd,
He stood in his shoes
And he wonder'd.

[Newton Stewart, July 4.]

My dear Fanny, I am ashamed of writing you such stuff, nor would I if it were not for being tired after my day's walking, and ready to tumble into bed so fatigued that when I am asleep you might sew my nose to my great toe and trundle me round the town, like a Hoop, without waking me. Then I get so hungry a Ham goes but a very little way and fowls are like Larks to me – A Batch of Bread I make no more ado with than a sheet of parliament; and I can eat a Bull's head as easily as I used to do Bull's eyes. I take a whole string of Pork Sausages down as easily as a Pen'orth of Lady's fingers. Ah dear I must soon be contented with an acre or two of oaten cake a hogshead of Milk and a Clothes-basket of Eggs morning noon and night when I get among the Highlanders. . . .

John Keats (1795–1821) to his sister Fanny, 1818

Midnight on the Great Western

In the third-class seat sat the journeying boy,
    And the roof-lamp's oily flame
Played down on his listless form and face,
Bewrapt past knowing to what he was going,
    Or whence he came.

In the band of his hat the journeying boy
    Had a ticket stuck; and a string
Around his neck bore the key of his box,
That twinkled gleams of the lamp's sad beams
    Like a living thing.

What past can be yours, O journeying boy,
    Towards a world unknown,
Who calmly, as if incurious quite
On all at stake, can undertake
    This plunge alone?

Knows your soul a sphere, O journeying boy,
    Our rude realms far above,
Whence with spacious vision you mark and mete
This region of sin that you find you in,
    But are not of?

Thomas Hardy

Osbert Sitwell recalls a visit to the home of his nurse, Davis.

When I paid my first visit I was three years of age. Davis's father
was a cobbler in a small village near Newbury in Berkshire, and
she was going home to spend a few days with her parents, who
were both very old. Since I refused to be parted from her for an
instant, she – though it must have spoilt her holiday – nevertheless, in accordance with the principle of appeasement which she
had adopted where I was concerned ('Anything for peace, Master
Osbert!'), arranged to take me with her. . . .

    Certainly every detail of my stay lives in my memory; our
arrival, very tired, at the cottage on an evening of timeless June,
the long shadows of the trees on our way there, and how I woke
up the next morning, very early, because of the excitement of the
change, and how at that hour the light of the sun still lay flat as
feathers along the ledges of the windows. Presently the rays
slanted downwards, and there were signs of activity. Life seemed
very intimate and enclosed here, after the larger houses to which I

was accustomed; warm and compact and lacking in any sense of fear. There were no creaking boards, no inexplicable rustlings, no feeling of interruption if one ran into an empty room. Every noise here made explicit its meaning. I heard now, as I lay beside Davis who was still fast asleep, the sounds that accompanied her father's getting-up, the washings and splashings and crinkling tug of clothes being put on, then his going downstairs, moving about, lighting the fire and washing the dishes. Soon after, I heard the sizzling of bacon as he crisped it on a fork before the fire for my breakfast – for, I do not know why, he, not his wife, did this part of the cooking –, and then there reached me the talking of rustic voices below.

From contrast with the surroundings I had left, the primitive conditions of this cottage existence seemed to offer a new kind of idyllic comfort, composed of warmth and simple ease. Everything I saw, I touched, I ate, possessed a new value for me. Even the waking-up so early was in itself a joy, I comprehended, as I lay there in bed, touching the warm reality of Davis's body, for I stretched out a foot against her leg. . . .

After I had been dressed and had eaten the bacon, so crisp and delicious, I was allowed to sit in the workshop, full of the smell of leather, and watch the old cobbler hammering at his last and listen to him talking through the din to his friends. . . . Then, after that, there were the walks, accompanied by the angelic host – fair-haired and round-eyed – of Davis's numerous nephews and nieces, through the flat, flowery meadows so different from the abrupt, dramatic country to which I was used. As a rule shy of other children, with these I was at my ease, for I loved all beings and all things belonging to Davis.

LEFT HAND RIGHT HAND!

Summer holidays at Trebetherick

> Then before breakfast down toward the sea
> I ran alone, monarch of miles of sand,
> Its shining stretches satin-smooth and vein'd.
> I felt beneath bare feet the lugworm casts
> And walked where only gulls and oyster-catchers

Had stepped before me to the water's edge.
The morning tide flowed in to welcome me,
The fan-shaped scallop shells, the backs of crabs,
The bits of driftwood worn to reptile shapes,
The heaps of bladder-wrack the tide had left
(Which, lifted up, sent sandhoppers to leap
In hundreds round me) answered 'Welcome back!'
Along the links and under cold Bray Hill
Fresh water pattered from an iris marsh
And drowned the golf-balls on its stealthy way
Over the slates in which the elvers hid,
And spread across the beach. I used to stand,
A speculative water engineer –
Here I would plan a dam and there a sluice
And thus divert the stream, creating lakes,
A chain of locks descending to the sea.
Inland I saw, above the tamarisks,
From various villas morning breakfast smoke
Which warned me then of mine; so up the lane
I wandered home contented, full of plans,
Pulling a length of pink convolvulus
Whose blossoms, almost as I picked them, died.
   Bright as the morning sea those early days!
Though there were tears, and sand thrown in my eyes,
And punishments and smells of mackintosh,
Long barefoot climbs to fetch the morning milk,
Terrors from hissing geese and angry shouts,
Slammed doors and waitings and a sense of dread,
Still warm as shallow sea-pools in the sun
And welcoming to me the girls and boys.
   Wet rocks on which our bathing dresses dried;
Small coves, deserted in our later years
For more adventurous inlets down the coast:
Paralysis when climbing up the cliff –
Too steep to reach the top, too far to fall,
Tumbling to death in seething surf below,
A ledge just wide enough to lodge one's foot,
A sea-pink clump the only thing to clutch,

Cold wave-worn slate so mercilessly smooth
And no one near and evening coming on –
Till Ralph arrived: 'Now put your left foot here.
Give us your hand' . . . and back across the years
I swing to safety with old friends again.
Small seem they now, those once tremendous cliffs,
Diminished now those joy-enclosing bays.
　　Sweet were the afternoons of treasure-hunts.
We searched in pairs and lifted after showers
The diamond-sparkling sprays of tamarisk:
Their pendent raindrops would release themselves
And soak our shirt-sleeves. Then upon the links
Under a tee-box lay a baffling clue:
A foursome puffing past the sunlit hedge
With rattling golf-bags; all the singing grass
Busy with crickets and blue butterflies;
The burnet moths, the unresponsive sheep
Seemed maddeningly indifferent to our plight . . .
'Oh, hurry up, man: why, we're third from last.'
And in the Oakleys' garden after tea
Of splits and cream under old apple boughs,
With high tide offering prospects of a bathe,
The winners had their prizes.

from 'Summoned by Bells' by John Betjeman (1906–84)

Letters home from Wolfgang Amadeus Mozart (1756–91).

Wörgl, December 13th, 1769

Dearest Mamma!
　　My heart is completely enchanted with all these pleasures, because it is so jolly on this journey, because it is so warm in the carriage and because our coachman is a fine fellow who, when the road gives him the slightest chance, drives so fast. Papa will have already described the journey to Mamma. The reason why I am writing to Mamma is to show her that I

know my duty and that I am with the deepest respect her devoted son

Wolfgang Mozart

Rome, April 14th, 1770

Praise and thanks be to God, I and my wretched pen are well and I kiss Mamma and Nannerl [Mozart's sister] a thousand or 1000 times. I only wish that my sister were in Rome, for this town would certainly please her, as St Peter's church and many other things in Rome are *regular*. The most beautiful flowers are now being carried past in the street – so Papa has just told me. I am a fool, as everyone knows. Oh, I am having a hard time, for in our rooms there is only one bed and so Mamma can well imagine that I get no sleep with Papa. I am looking forward to our new quarters. I have just now drawn St Peter with his keys and with him St Paul with his sword and St Luke with my sister and so forth. I have had the honour of kissing St Peter's foot in St Peter's church and as I have the misfortune to be so small, I, that same old dunce,

Wolfgang Mozart,

had to be lifted up.

Naples, June 16th, 1770

I too am still alive and always merry as usual and I simply love travelling. I have now been on the Mediterranean too. I kiss Mamma's hand and Nannerl 1000 times and am your Simple Simon of a son and Jack Pudding of a brother.

I remember going to Carlton House, when George IV lived there, as quite a little child before a dinner the King gave. In the year '26 (I think) George IV asked my Mother, my Sister and me down to Windsor for the first time; he had been on bad terms with my poor father when he died, – and took hardly any notice of the poor widow and little fatherless girl, who were so poor at the time of his (the Duke of Kent's) death, that they could not have travelled back to Kensington Palace had it not been for the kind assistance of my dear Uncle, Prince Leopold. We went to Cumberland Lodge, the King living at the Royal Lodge. Aunt Gloucester was there at the same time. When we arrived at the Royal Lodge the King took me by the hand, saying: 'Give me your little paw.' He was large and gouty but with a wonderful dignity and charm of manner. He wore the wig which was so much worn in those days. Then he said he would give me something to wear, and that was his picture set in diamonds, which was worn by the Princesses as an order to a blue ribbon on the left shoulder. I was very proud of this, – and Lady Conyngham pinned it on my shoulder.

Lady Maria Conyngham, then quite young, and Lord Graves were desired to take me a drive to amuse me. I went with them, and Baroness (then Miss) Lehzen (my governess) in a pony carriage and 4, with 4 grey ponies (like my own), and was driven about the Park and taken to Sandpit Gate where the King had a Menagerie – with wapitis, gazelles, chamois, etc., etc. Then we went (I think the next day) to Virginia Water, and met the King in his phaeton in which he was driving the Duchess of Gloucester, – and he said 'Pop her in', and I was lifted in and placed between him and Aunt Gloucester, who held me round the waist. (Mamma was much frightened.) I was greatly pleased, and remember that I looked with great respect at the scarlet liveries, etc. (the Royal Family had crimson and green liveries and only the King scarlet and blue in those days). We drove round the nicest part of Virginia Water and stopped at the Fishing Temple. Here there was a large barge and everyone went on board and fished, while a band played in another! There were numbers of great people there, amongst whom was the last Duke of Dorset, then Master of the Horse. The King paid great attention to my Sister, and some people fancied he might marry her!! She was very lovely then – about 18 – and had charming manners, about which the King was extremely particular. I afterwards went with Baroness Lehzen and Lady Maria C. to the Page Whiting's cottage. . . . Here I had some fruit and amused myself by cramming one of Whiting's children, a little girl, with peaches. I came after dinner to hear the band play in the Conservatory, which is still standing, and which was lit up by coloured lamps – the King, Royal Family, etc., sitting in a corner of the large saloon.

MEMOIRS OF QUEEN VICTORIA'S EARLY YEARS *by Herself*

The Beach

Louder than gulls the little children scream
Whom fathers haul into the jovial foam;
But others fearlessly rush in, breast high,
Laughing the salty water from their mouths –
Heroes of the nursery.

The horny boatman, who has seen whales
And flying fishes, who has sailed as far
As Demerara and the Ivory Coast,
Will warn them, when they crowd to hear his tales,
That every ocean smells alike of tar.

Robert Graves

I have an image of us all crossing the Channel. The sea was monstrously rough on that occasion, and I am told there was not one passenger on board who didn't suffer as I did. That smell of boats, reinforced doubtless by subsequent experiences, rises again to my nose – as leaning desperately forward I look from time to time along the smitten row of my half-brothers. Dorelia I also see, and can remember feeling anxious about. Children do not expect grown-ups to be ill. They feel bewildered and sorry for themselves at the sight of those on whom they depend groaning under a weakness similar to their own; the security of the universe seems to be shaken.

There had been a lot of kidnapping going on about this time, and an eager look-out was being kept for the miscreants. I do not know where the children were taken; perhaps they were bartered in some eastern town inaccessible to the law. At any rate, Dorelia had no sooner stepped on board than she fell under grave suspicion. As I have said, her appearance was certainly un-English: it should therefore surprise no one that she was at once concluded to be a Chinese kidnapper – an idea only too well substantiated by the roaring trade she was obviously carrying on. If the conscientious detective required still further proof, he had only to glance at the fiery-looking gentleman with a beard (most likely a disguise) who accompanied her, and who seemed exactly cut out for the part of European agent to a Chinese kidnapping business. And then, the children themselves: in some cases it was impossible to tell if they were boys or girls – from the waist downwards they appeared to be boys, but this appearance was hotly disputed by their pink dresses and long hair. The steamboat officials were quite of the detective's way of thinking. It was monstrous that one woman should have so many infants, all entitled by their age to travel free. How these deductions were ultimately confounded by Augustus's plausible account of us all I leave to the imagination: I only hope they were able to preserve their confidence in logic by assuring each other that they had been somehow taken in.

THE SEVENTH CHILD *by Romilly John*

An early effort from a future Pulitzer Prize-winner.

Chacago

Chacago. ditto
the land of
the free.
It is on lake
Mich'gan, and
not on the sea.
It has some
fine houses
in the suberbs
I'm told
And its people
are rolling in
silver and
gold.

In the city
it'self there
are
warehouses
large.
The folks go
on the lake
in sail boat
and barge.
But for all
of its beauty
I'de rather
go home.
To Boston,
Charles River,
and the
State houses
dome.

Amy Lowell (1874–1925), aged nine

My Mother said that I never should
Play with the gypsies in the wood,
The wood was dark; the grass was green;
In came Sally with a tambourine.

I went to the sea – no ship to get across;
I paid ten shillings for a blind white horse;
I up on his back and was off in a crack,
Sally tell my Mother I shall never come back.

Anon

15

THE SCHOLAR

To hear our children recite the classics so fluently, like the sound of pouring water from a vase. Ah, is this not happiness?

Chin Shengt'an

An eighteenth-century letter from an Eton schoolboy.

My dear Mama,

I wright to tell you I am very retched, and my chilblains is worse agen. I have not made any progress and I do not think I shall. i am very sorry to be such expense to you, but i do not think this schule is very good. One of the fellows has taken the crown of my new hat for a target, he has burrowed my watch to make wheal, with the works, but it won't act – me and him have tried to put the works back, but we think some wheels are missing as they won't fit. I hope Matilda's cold is better i am glad she is not at a schule. I think I have got the consumption the boys at the place are not gentlemen but of course you did not know that when you sent me hear, i will try not to get bad habits.

The trousers have worn out at the knee, i think the tailor must have cheated you, the buttons have come off, and they are loos at the back i don't think the food is good but I should not mind if I was stronger. The peace of meet i sent you is off the beef we had on Sunday but on other days it is more stringey. There are black beetles in the kitchen and sometimes they cook them in the dinner which can't be wholesome when you are not strong. Dear mama I hope you and papa are well and dont mind my being uncomfortable because i dont think i shall last long please send me some more money as i owe 8d if you think you can't spare it i can

burrow it of a boy who is going to leave at the half-quarter
and then he won't ask for it again but perhaps you wd not
like me to be obliged to his parents as they are trades people
and I think you deal at their shop i did not mention it or i
dare say they would have put it down in the bill.

Your loving but retched son

T.H.

*Part of a history of England from the pen of the young Jane
Austen (1775–1817).*

MARY

This woman had the good luck of being advanced to the throne of
England, in spite of the superior pretensions, Merit, and Beauty of
her Cousins Mary Queen of Scotland and Jane Grey. Nor can I
pity the Kingdom for the misfortunes they experienced during her
Reign, since they fully deserved them, for having allowed her to
succeed her Brother — which was a double peice of folly, since they
might have foreseen that as she died without children, she would
be succeeded by that disgrace to humanity, that pest of society,
Elizabeth. Many were the people who fell martyrs to the protes-
tant Religion during her reign; I suppose not fewer than a dozen.
She married Philip King of Spain who in her sister's reign was
famous for building Armadas. She died without issue, and then
the dreadful moment came in which the destroyer of all comfort,
the deceitful Betrayer of trust reposed in her, and the Murderess of
her Cousin succeeded to the Throne.—

ELIZABETH

It was the peculiar misfortune of this Woman to have bad Ministers — Since wicked as she herself was, she could not have committed such extensive mischeif, had not these vile and abandoned
Men connived at, and encouraged her in her Crimes. I know that
it has by many people been asserted and beleived that Lord
Burleigh, Sir Francis Walsingham, and the rest of those who filled
the cheif offices of State were deserving, experienced, and able

Ministers. But oh! how blinded such writers and such Readers must be to true Merit, to Merit despised, neglected and defamed, if they can persist in such opinions when they reflect that these men, these boasted men were such scandals to their Country and their sex as to allow and assist their Queen in confining for the space of nineteen years, a *Woman* who if the claims of Relationship and Merit were of no avail, yet as a Queen and as one who condescended to place confidence in her, had every reason to expect assistance and protection; and at length in allowing Elizabeth to bring this amiable Woman to an untimely, unmerited, and scandalous Death. Can any one if he reflects but for a moment on this blot, this everlasting blot upon their understanding and their Character, allow any praise to Lord Burleigh or Sir Francis Walsingham? Oh! what must this bewitching Princess whose only freind was then the Duke of Norfolk, and whose only ones now Mr Whitaker, Mrs Lefroy, Mrs Knight and myself, who was abandoned by her son, confined by her Cousin, abused, reproached and vilified by all, what must not her most noble mind have suffered when informed that Elizabeth had given orders for her Death! Yet she bore it with a most unshaken fortitude, firm in her mind; constant in her Religion; and prepared herself to meet the cruel fate to which she was doomed, with a magnanimity that would alone proceed from conscious Innocence. ... She was executed in the Great Hall at Fotheringay Castle (sacred Place!) on Wednesday the 8th of February 1586 – to the everlasting Reproach of Elizabeth, her Ministers, and of England in general.

I was at school under a master who was entirely at the mercy of the new notions that daily occurred to him. He introduced games quite fresh to us, he taught us to fence and to do the lesser circle on the horizontal bar; he sailed model yachts for us on the foulest canal in Europe; he played us into school to a march of his own composing performed on a harmonium by himself; he started a debating society and an amateur dramatic club. He even talked about our honour, and, having mentioned it, audaciously left many important things to its care – with what frightful results I forget. Once he suffered the spell of literature, read us a poem of his own, and told us that anyone who tried could write poetry. As it were to prove his statement, he ordered us all to write a poem on the subject of Courage within a week, and promised to crown the best poet with a rich gift. Having been commanded to produce a poem on the subject of Courage, I produced a poem on the subject of Courage in, what seemed to me, the most natural manner in the world. I thought of lifeboats and fire-engines, and decided on lifeboats for the mere reason that 'wave' and 'save' would rhyme together. A lifeboat, then, was to save the crew of a wrecked ship. Next, what *was* poetry? I desired a model structure which I might copy. Turning to a school hymn-book, I found —

> A little ship was on the sea,
>   It was a pretty sight;
> It sailed along so pleasantly
>   And all was calm and bright.

That stanza I adopted, and slavishly imitated. In a brief space a poem of four such stanzas was accomplished. I wrote it in cold blood, hammered it out word after word, and was much pleased with the result. On the following day I read the poem aloud to myself, and was thrilled with emotion. The dashing cruel wave that rhymed with save appeared to me intensely realistic. I failed to conceive how any poem could be better than mine. The sequel is that only one other boy besides myself had even attempted verse. One after another, each sullenly said that he had nothing to show. (How clever *I* felt!) Then I saw my rival's composition; it dealt with a fire in New York and many fire-engines; I did not care for it; I could not make sense of much of it; but I saw with painful clearness that it was as far above mine as the heaven was above the earth. . . .

'Did you write this yourself?' The master was addressing the creator of New York fire-engines.

'Yes, sir.'

'All of it?'

'Yes, sir.'

'You lie, sir.'

It was magnificent for me. The fool, my rival, relying too fondly on the master's ignorance of modern literature, had simply transcribed entire the work of some great American recitation-monger. I received the laurel, which I fancy amounted to a shilling.

Nothing dashed by the fiasco of his poetry competition, the schoolmaster immediately instituted a competition in prose. He told us about M. Jourdain, who talked prose without knowing it, and requested us each to write a short story upon any theme we might choose to select. I produced the story with the same ease and certainty as I had produced the verse. I had no difficulty in finding a plot which satisfied me; it was concerned with a drowning accident at the seaside, and it culminated – with a remorseless naturalism that even thus early proclaimed the elective affinity between Flaubert and myself – in an inquest. It described the wonders of the deep, and I have reason to remember that it likened the gap between the fin and the side of a fish to a pocket. In this competition I had no competitor. I, alone, had achieved fiction. I watched the master as he read my work, and I could see from his eyes and gestures that he thought it marvellously good for the boy. He spoke to me about it in a tone which I had never heard from him before and never heard again, and then, putting the manuscript in a drawer, he left us to ourselves for a few minutes.

'I'll just read it to you,' said the big boy of the form, a daring but vicious rascal. He usurped the pedagogic arm-chair, found the manuscript, rapped the ruler on the desk, and began to read. I protested in vain. The whole class roared with laughter, and I was overcome with shame. I know that I, eleven, cried. Presently the reader stopped and scratched his head; the form waited.

'Oh!' he exclaimed. 'Fishes have pockets! Fishes have pockets!'

The phrase was used as a missile against me for months.

The master returned with his assistant, and the latter also perused the tale.

'Very remarkable!' he sagely commented – to be sage was his foible, 'very remarkable, indeed!'

Yet I can remember no further impulse to write a story for at least ten years. Despite this astonishing success, martyrdom, and glory, I forthwith abandoned fiction and went mad on water-colours.   THE TRUTH ABOUT AN AUTHOR *by Arnold Bennett*

Elizabeth Drewery remembers life in an East Anglican village school at the turn of the century.

I started at the age of five. My mother insisted I should have my hair cut short like a boy. That was to keep a clean head. I also had to wear thick hobnail boots. They were quite fashionable at that time, and many girls wore them. We were summoned to school by the ringing of the bell. Mr Whitehead was my master, and he was very strict but very thorough in all he taught. When he wanted us to learn something new, he would write it on a large blackboard in chalk; and it was not rubbed off until we all knew it by heart. When we were about eleven years we had to walk, once a week, to the Old School, Snape – the girls for cookery lessons and the boys for woodwork. We children were brought up in the hard way. Each afternoon, after school closed, I had to run home, get a pail and go on a field and pick up so many bushels of stones – three large pails to the bushel. And sometimes my mother would give me a penny for sweets. At school I had many failures, but I worked up to the top standard and left at the age of fourteen. I left on a Friday; and by the next I was on my way in a carrier's cart with my little tin box to seek my own living. I went to a doctor's house at Alderton near Woodbridge, and kept there for three and a half years.

ASK THE FELLOWS WHO CUT THE HAY
by George Ewart Evans (1909–88)

A description of schooldays in the Malinke tribe of French Guinea.

Immediately after breakfast my sister and I would start out for school, carrying our exercise-books and note-books in a satchel made of raffia....

Once in school, we went straight to our seats, boys and girls sitting side by side, our quarrels over; and, as soon as we had sat down, we became all ears, and sat absolutely still, so that the teacher used to give his lessons in an impressive silence. I should just like to have seen what would have happened if we had so much as stirred in our seats. Our teacher moved like quicksilver: he never remained long in the same place; he was here, there and everywhere. His flow of talk would have bewildered less attentive pupils. But we were remarkably attentive, and we found it no strain to be so. Young though we were, we all regarded our school work as something deadly serious. Everything we learned was strange and unexpected; it was as if we were learning about life on another planet; and we never grew tired of listening. Even if it had been otherwise, the silence could not have been more absolute under the strict discipline of a master who seemed to be every-where at once and who would never have given us an opportunity to let our attention wander or to interrupt. But as I have said, an interruption was out of the question: it simply did not occur to us. And so we tried to attract the teacher's attention as little as possible: for we lived in constant dread of being sent out to the blackboard.

This blackboard was our nightmare. Its dark, blank mirror was the exact reflection of the amount of our knowledge. We knew very little, and the little we knew was very shaky: the slightest thing could upset it. Now if we did not want to be the recipients of several strokes of the cane, we had to go to the blackboard and take the chalk in our hands and pay our debt in kind. Here the tiniest detail was of the utmost importance: the wretched black-board magnified every mistake. If we made one of our downward strokes not exactly of the same height as the others, we were required either to do an extra lesson on Sunday, or we had to go to the teacher during break, and receive, in the class that was always known as the infants', an unforgettable beating on our bare backsides. Irregular downward strokes used to horrify our teacher: he would examine our exercise-books under a magnifying-glass, and for each irregularity he discovered we got a stroke. I remember him well, a man like quicksilver; and he wielded his stick with joyous abandon!

THE DARK CHILD *by Camara Laye (1924–   )*

The Birched Schoolboy

On Monday in the morning when I shall rise
At vi. of the clock, it is the gise
To go to school without a-vise
I had rather go twenty mile twice!
    What availeth it me though I say nay?

My master looketh as he were mad:
'Where hast thou been, though sorry lad?'
'Milking ducks, my mother bade:'
It was no marvel that I were sad.
    What availeth it me though I say nay?

My master peppered my arse with well good speed:
It was worse than fennel seed;
He would not leave till it did bleed.
Much sorrow has been for his deed!
    What availeth it me though I say nay?

I would my master were a wat [hare]
And my book a wild cat,
And a brace of greyhounds in his top.
I would be glad for to see that!
    What availeth it me though I say nay?

I would my master were an hare,
And all his bookis houndis were,
And I myself a jolly hunter:
To blow my horn I would not spare!
For if he were dead I would not care.
    What availeth it me though I say nay?

Anon., c. 1490

Darling Mama, –
    I like it rather better than I expected. They have killed a
large snake by stoning it, and Gumbleton has skinned it,
such nasty work, and peged it on a board covered with

butter and pepper, and layed it out in the sun to dry. It is going to be stuffed. Do you know I have been in the vault under the church. It is so dark. There are great big coffins there. The boy's chief game is robbers. Give love and 8 thousand kisses to Lea [his nurse] and love to the Grannies. Good-bye darling Mama.

Frederick Leuis has been very ill of crop. Do you know what that is? I have been to the school-feast at Mr Clutter-buck's. It was so beautiful. All the girls were seated round little round tables, amongst beds of geraniums, heltrope, verbenas, and balm of Gilead. We carried the tea and were called in to grapes and gooseberries, and we played at thread-the-needle and went in a swing, and in a flying boat. God-bye Mamma.

Augustus Hare, aged nine

Cultural divisions in a Guatemalan school.

Miss McMillan was our English grammar teacher. Her pedagogi-cal method with Underdeveloped Peoples was to tell stories.

'Now Fishy-wishy, as you all know, lived in a small pond at the edge of the deep dark woods. We *all* know what a *pond* is, don't we? *That's* right. In this pond there also lived two close friends of Fishy-wishy's, Frogsy-wogsy and Baby turtle. Now who can tell me what a *turtle* is? Raise your hands now. Tor-*tu*ga, that's right. *My*, we're wide awake this morning. . . .'

I don't think any of us really minded these inane fables, which we could listen to with half an ear while thinking of something else. (The dullards in the class sat out the hour in a benign haze.) We far preferred Fishy-wishy to the slavish rote-learning in our Spanish courses, and so did our best to encourage Miss McMillan. At the start of each lesson we pleaded with her to tell us if Fishy-wishy was punished for missing school, or if Frogsy-wogsy and Baby turtle made up after their quarrel. I imagine Miss McMillan saw through our deception but went along because she had as little enthusiasm for the fine points of English grammar as we did. RITES *by Victor Perera (1937–   )*

Robert Louis Stevenson's father reacted understandingly to this cri de coeur *by removing his thirteen-year-old son from Spring Grove.*

Ma chere Maman, –

Jai recu votre lettre Aujourdhui et comme le jour prochaine est mon jour de naisance je vous écrit ce lettre. Ma grande gatteaux est arrivé il leve 12 livres and demi le prix etait 17 shillings. Sur la soirée de Monseigneur Faux il y etait quelques belles feux d'artifice. Mais les polissons entrent dans notre champ et nos feux d'artifice et handkerchiefs disappeared quickly, but we charged them out of the field. Je suis presque driven mad par une bruit terrible tous les garcons kik up comme grand un bruit qu'il est possible. I hope you will find your house at Mentone nice. I have been obliged to stop from writing by the want of a pen, but now I have one, so will continue.

My dear papa, you told me to tell you whenever I was miserable. I do not feel well, and I wish to get home. Do take me with you.

R. Stevenson.

'Why have you such a slope-shouldered, belly-protuberant, stooping and deformed appearance? Answer me that, oh ye faithless and hunchbacked generation!'

The headmaster of my prep school looked very much like God. He had long, white, slightly curly hair, and was old and beautiful. He wore a dark suit which had shortish trousers showing the tops of his highly polished black boots. He also spoke in God's prose, a mixture of the Old Testament and Rudyard Kipling's *Just So Stories*.

'Draw nigh and hearken to me, oh litter of runts and weaklings. I say unto you that you are round-shouldered through the wearing of braces! Unbutton your braces and cast them from you. Each boy to acquire a dark-blue elastic belt with a snake buckle, to be slotted neatly into the loops provided at the top of school shorts.'

'Dear Mummy,' I wrote, in the compulsory letter home, 'I don't like it here at all. I know it said braces on the clothes list, but we're not allowed braces any more. In fact we have to cast them from us. Noah told us this in assembly' (we were expected to call the staff by their nicknames; the headmaster's was 'Noah'). 'Could you send me a dark-blue belt with a snake buckle as quickly as you can?'

'What, gasping for breath, ye red-faced and pop-eyed generation?' Noah looked at us with amused contempt at the following week's assembly. 'Why do you show such clear signs of stomach contraction? Why are you an offence to the eye, all tied up like parcels? I say unto you, there will be no more belts or the wearing thereof. Abandon belts! Each boy to equip himself with a decent pair of sturdy elastic braces!'

'Dear Mummy,' I wrote, 'I still don't like it here. Would you please send me a new pair of braces as soon as you can? I cast mine aside and now I can't find them. And now I have to cast aside my belt....'

Noah was also tremendously keen on iodine lockets. These were small china bottles, full of iodine, tied to a tape which, if worn round the neck at all times, would, he was persuaded, prevent any known disease from bunions to botulism. We were all issued with these charms, which we used to fight with like conkers.

'I have noticed that some boys,' Noah looked sadly around him at assembly and sounded puzzled, 'have taken to wearing small pieces of broken china slung about their necks on a ribbon. I take this to be a primitive superstition, and calculated to ward off the evil eye. "Ham" will be giving us a talk with lantern-slides on African tribes who still cling to such irrational beliefs. This school is a Christian community. Cast aside the amulets, resist the mumbo-jumbo, or behold I will strike ye with my rod and terrible will be the striking thereof!'

I can't remember Noah taking a great part in our education. He bought a little carillon of bells which he hung outside the dining-room and he used to summon us in to Sunday supper by playing tunes on them. He enjoyed this exercise and long after supper was over, indeed long after lights had been turned out, he would stand in the passage in his dark suit and highly polished boots, delicately picking out tune after tune with a small hammer, smiling benevolently.   CLINGING TO THE WRECKAGE by John Mortimer

There was a boy, sufficiently unpopular, whose last term it was, and whose friend I was supposed to be. When the man with a barrow of sweets called on the last week of term it was a custom, which was invariable and sacred, that those who were leaving should spend more than the sixpence doled out to them each week and buy a sweet however small for everyone in the school. Having bought them he had to go round, seek each person out, and force a sweet on him however much, in deference to custom, anyone might protest he had had enough. My friend bought sweets but offered none to a soul.

It must have been absurd to watch the school prowling round, not asking but very much expecting the offer which never came. At last they revolted. They all set on him and it was while he was running away before they caught up that I felt it was my duty to suffer with him because I was his friend. What helped to bring me to this pass was that he ran by me into the gymnasium with forty of them howling after and I, who had been so full up to that time of the story of Judas, I believe it haunts all little boys, went in after them to stand up for my friend. . . .

They were screaming at him, hating in him everything they hated, exulting in the revenge they were going to have through him on the whole term, on everything which had gone wrong for each one of them. Reading this you may think they were going to do something terrible but this is not the case; all they wanted was to carry out the traditional mass punishment and that was, believe it or not, to all of them pile themselves up and lie on top of him.

I forget how I got in but at last they leaped, we lay down, and they piled up on us with groans and shrieks of rage at first and then of pain. I found what I had suspected, that those at the bottom get hurt least, and so it ended except that I was so proud; I thought it so brave and, I remember well, so Christ-like.

PACK MY BAG by Henry Green (1905–73)

The tutor was a slave-attendant who accompanied the boy through the streets, as to and from school, and was responsible for his behaviour. Socrates is talking to a boy named Lysis.

'Tell me one more thing. Do your parents let you control your own life, or is that another thing they don't let you do?'

'Of course they don't.'

'So someone is in charge of you.'

'Yes, my tutor here.'

'A slave?'

'Oh yes. He belongs to us.'

'How odd to put a free man under the control of a slave! How does your tutor exercise his authority over you?'

'By conducting me to school, I suppose.'

Lysis by Plato

At school I was popular, for I had embarked on the career which was to occupy me for the next ten years of 'trying to be funny'. I was neither good nor bad at games; my favourite exercise was to take a short piece of pointed wood in my hand and walk for hours through the long summer grasses round the playing fields, calling at imaginary ports, tunnelling the hay, chewing sorrel, and following my faint tracks in the silver grass as a liner follows a trade route. Inside my desk a cardboard shoebox perforated with holes supported a brood of looper caterpillars. Who can forget that smell of caterpillars, the smell of wet cardboard, drying leaves and insect excrement, the odour of northern childhood?...

I went on 'trying to be funny' till I was seventeen. This horrible process was my defence mechanism. It was the shell I was secreting as a protection from the outside world: by making people laugh I became popular, and I became feared as well. 'Go on, be funny!' some boy would command, and I would clown away or recite my poems and parodies, with their echoes of Mark Twain and Stephen Leacock. 'Connolly's being funny', the word would go round, and soon I would have collected a crowd. I revelled in this, and would grow funnier and funnier till I passed quite naturally into tears. 'Connolly's not funny now. He's gone too far', and the group would break up and leave me, except for some friend who remained to puzzle over the psychology of the manic-depressive. 'But you were being quite funny a moment ago.' 'Oh, Boo-Hoo-Hoo. I wish I was dead.' 'Oh, shut up, Connolly.' 'Oh, go away. I hate you.' Then a master would come by and comfort me. I would be handed, still hysterical, to the matron, and the inevitable case-history would be gone over. (*p*) 'It's his grand-mother. (*pp*) She spoils him.'

ENEMIES OF PROMISE *by Cyril Connolly*

Holiday

When the boys came out of school they threw up their
    caps,
And the air was striped with their spinning.

When the girls came out of school they pulled off their
    stockings,
And the roof-tops streamed with long black banners.

When the boys and girls came out of school
All the bells of the town choked with their chiming.

When the boys walked in the streets their shoes purred on
    the asphalt,
And the corners were bright as butterflies.

When the girls walked in the streets their legs shone in
    shop-windows,
And the cinema-queues trembled with love.

When the boys and girls walked in the streets
It was like a cathedral decked with worshippers.

And when the boys and girls went back to school
All the clocks of the town wrung their rusted hands.

Julian Mitchell (1935–   )

James Lees-Milne (1908–   ) approaches his first boarding school in the company of his mother.

There are of course few more agreeable ways of spending a hot summer's afternoon than that of ambling in an open four-wheeler through the Home Counties. But on this occasion my mother's pleasure was lessened by anxiety as to where precisely we were heading for, and extreme irritation with our driver's insubordination; mine was entirely dispelled by a sudden access of homesickness and downright misery. By the time we had wandered through the town and into a lane between water meadows my mother's emotions had subsided – quick to anger she was quicker still to sweetness – whereas mine were if anything accentuated. In sensing this state of affairs she tried by every means to cheer me up, giving vent to a parent's usual catalogue of platitudes. The happiest time of my life was now dawning. The term always went by in a flash. I would soon be making the friends of a lifetime. 'Which reminds me,' she added, in a rather portentous and uncharacteristic tone, 'your father would wish me to give you a little, just a little piece of advice. About life generally.' She paused, and then suddenly corrected herself. 'On the whole, it might be better if you asked the headmaster to explain all about the disgusting side of it.' And then half to herself and half aloud, she added, 'Not that I myself have ever found it *exactly* that.'

I of course had not the faintest idea what she was talking about. At that particular moment every side of life appeared to me so disgusting that no amount of explanation by all the headmasters in England could possibly improve it. Life to me meant weeks, months and even years of banishment from home. For the second time that day I burst into uncontrollable sobs. This sound evidently had some pejorative effect upon the cabby, because he cracked his whip and for the first time the old horse broke into an uncomfortable jog trot.

When I had slightly recovered I noticed that we were passing through a rusty pair of open gates. Ahead stretched an uphill drive lined with clumps of faded ponticums. At the end of it as though barring the way to eternity straddled the vast red brick mausoleum of my dying hopes, covered with virginia creeper and fire escapes. Out of the front door of this lugubrious edifice were streaming dozens of grey-flannelled, becapped midgets, dressed exactly alike, carrying cricket bats and pads, interspersed with a few white-flannelled giants in striped jackets and straw boaters. As I learned afterwards, the 4th of June happened to be a half-holiday, and the exodus of boys and masters on to the playing field coincided with our ill-fated arrival. The spectacle before us was now too much for my tender-hearted mother. 'How hideous!' she exclaimed. 'How perfectly hideous! How could the de Frevilles . . . ? She gave an ill-concealed gulp and a few silent tears blazed a trail down her faintly rouged cheeks. The remark had an electrical effect upon the cabby. He actually gave a snort and lashed the hollow flanks of the old horse, which suddenly plunged into a lolloping canter just as we were approaching the carriage sweep.

My mother and I, both now sobbing uncontrollably, were pitchforked by the unexpected jolt against the tuck-box. Instantly there was a harsh sound of rending woodwork. The tuck-box gave a wobble, then a lurch and disappeared through the floor boards, which clattered to the ground, our feet with them. The noise was alarming, the spectacle exceedingly humiliating. The two of us, shocked beyond measure, had no alternative to running inside the carriage as fast as our legs could carry us. Any other course would have invited instant and perhaps fatal injury, for we would have been knocked down by the seat we had precipitately left and then been crushed by the axle or the wheels. But the faster we ran and the louder we shouted to that brute of a cabby, who never once so much as turned his head in our direction, the more the old horse took the bit between its teeth. Round and round the sweep we went, and over and over the remains of the tuck-box, of which the contents – for the lid and bottom had broken off with the fall – made a ghastly contusion on the drive. Strawberries, petits-beurres biscuits, asparagus, cream and pheasants' feathers were churned into the gravel by a succession of wheels, and human and equine feet. My mother had the presence of mind to seize me by the arm and pull me along with her, or I should inevitably have been lost. Just before we completed the fourth round of the sweep one of the white-flannelled giants managed to catch hold of the bridle and, by dint of being dragged several yards along the gravel to the absolute detriment of his immaculate ducks, brought the sweating horse to a standstill.

The scene witnessed by the entire school was indescribable. My mother was hauled from the wreckage in a fit of hysterical giggles. Her dress was torn to shreds and her long hair was down to her waist. My plight was even more pitiable. In the mêlée I had completely lost my trousers. In fact it was a mercy that they had come off truly and properly: a miracle that the trailing extremities had not got caught in the wheel spokes, and possibly squeezed or throttled me to death. The two of us were then stretched on the grass and restored by the matron with sal volatile. All this while the abominable cabby was bending over us, making demands in dumb show for his fare and reparation money for the damage to his victoria.

The final ignominy was having to explain who we were. It transpired that my mother had failed to notify the headmaster that we were coming that afternoon. And although in later years she strenuously denied it, I have often wondered whether she had ever entered me for the school in the first place, or merely assumed that the headmaster would welcome any stray child whose parents dropped in on the off chance. Welcome me, or rather accept me he did. The kindest thing he could have done would have been to send us both packing there and then. As it was, the boys who witnessed our arrival never allowed me to forget it.

ANOTHER SELF

16

BIRDS AND BEASTS

The Yak

As a friend to the children commend me the Yak.
You will find it exactly the thing:
It will carry and fetch, you can ride on its back,
Or lead it about with a string.
The Tartar who dwells on the plains of Thibet
(A desolate region of snow)
Has for centuries made it a nursery pet,
And surely the Tartar should know!
Then tell your papa where the Yak can be got,
And if he is awfully rich
He will buy you the creature – or else he will *not*.
(I cannot be positive which.)

Hilaire Belloc

. . . I can remember, with the utmost distinctness, an animal, almost before I can remember human beings. Henry Moat's brother, Bill, was a fisherman, and used to bring over to see us from Whitby a tame seal. He had caught it during a whaling cruise, and it now lived in the backyard of his ancestral house at Whitby. It can be imagined with what mingled pride, pleasure and interest my sister and I made the acquaintance of this new friend, who flopped about the sands after us in the most flattering way, used suddenly to come up and poke his nose at the back of his master's knee so that he would nearly fall down, and would then bellow loudly for fish. . . . The reader may wonder how such a slippery customer was conveyed to us. . . . Unlikely as it sounds, by train, and then by cab. Bill was a well-known character in Whitby, and was allowed to take his seal with him in a third-class carriage. He would have charge of its head, a porter would help him by pushing from below, and the sleek creature would ride beside him, giving a delicious breath of the ocean – and of fish – to the whole of the compartment. Once arrived at Scarborough, they would then take a cab, sent by my mother, the seal again sitting beside him, and looking round with interest at place and people.

LEFT HAND RIGHT HAND! *by Osbert Sitwell*

At La Roque I had lessons from Monsieur Tabourel, the schoolmaster of Saint-Ouen, in the *commune* of Blancmesnil. . . . Monsieur Tabourel's teaching was far from exciting. It was during one of his lessons that a privet hawk-moth chose the time for coming out of its chrysalis. I had reared the caterpillar and was keeping the chrysalis carefully in a small narrow uncovered box, in which it lay, looking like a mummy in its sarcophagus. I used to examine it every day, but never perceived the smallest change, and I should perhaps have despaired if it had not been for the little convulsive movements this semblance of a creature made when I tickled its abdomen with the nib of my pen. It was really alive then! Now on that day, as Monsieur Tabourel was correcting my sums, my eyes fell on the box. O Proteus! What did I see? Wings! Great green and pink wings beginning to stir and quiver!

Overwhelmed with admiration, with joy, dancing with enthusiasm, I could not help seizing, for want of a better divinity, old Tabourel's fat paw.

'Oh, Monsieur Tabourel! Look! Oh, if I had only known . . .'

I stopped short just in time, for what I had been meaning to say was: 'If I had only known that while you were explaining those deadly sums, one of the mysteries of life, so great a one, so long expected, was going on at my very elbow! . . .' A resurrection like Lazarus's! A metamorphosis, a miracle I had never yet beheld. . . .

Monsieur Tabourel was a man of education; calmly, but with a shade of astonishment or blame or something disapproving in his voice:

'What!' said he; 'didn't you know that a chrysalis is the envelope of a butterfly? Every butterfly you see has come out of a chrysalis. It's perfectly natural.'

At that I dropped Monsieur Tabourel's hand. Yes indeed, I

knew my *natural* history as well, perhaps better than he. . . . But because it was natural, could he not see that it was marvellous? Poor creature! From that day, I took a dislike to him and a loathing to his lessons.

IF IT DIE . . . *by André Gide*

Four letters from Piero de' Medici (1471–1503) to his father, Lorenzo the Magnificent (1449–92).

Magnificent Father,

Lucrezia and I are trying who can write best. She writes to grandmother Lucrezia, I, my father, to you. The one who obtains what he asks for will win. Till now Lucrezia has had all she wished for. I, who have always written in Latin in order to give a more literary tone to my letters, have not yet had that pony you promised me; so that I am laughed at by all. See to it therefore, Your Magnificence, that she should not always be the winner.

26th May, 1479

Magnificent Father mine,

That pony does not come, and I am afraid that it will remain so long with you that Andrea will cause it to change from a beast to a man, instead of curing its hoof. – We are all well and studying. Giovanni is beginning to spell. By this letter you can judge where I am in writing; as for Greek I keep myself rather in exercise by the help of Martino than make any progress. Giuliano laughs and thinks of nothing else; Lucrezia sews, sings, and reads; Maddalena knocks her head against the wall, but without doing herself any real harm; Luisa begins to say a few little words; Contessina fills the house with her noise. . . . Nothing is wanting to us save your presence.

Magnificent Father mine,

I fear that some misfortune has happened to that pony, for had it been well I know you would have sent it to me as you promised. I beg of you therefore as a grace that you will take this fear from me; for I think of it night and day, and until the pony comes I shall have no peace. In case that one cannot come be pleased to send me another. For, as I have already written to you, I am here on foot, and sometimes it is necessary for me to go in the company of my friends. See to this therefore, Your Magnificence.

Magnifico Patri meo,

I cannot tell you, Magnificent Father, how glad I am to have the pony, and how his arrival incites me to work. If I desire to praise him, *Ante diem clauset componet vesper Olympo.* He is so handsome and so perfect that the trumpet of Maronius would hardly suffice to sing his praises. You may think how I love him; particularly when his joyous neighs resound and rejoice all the neighbourhood. I owe you and I send you many thanks for such a fine gift and I shall try and repay you by becoming what you wish. I promise you that I shall try with all my heart.

Three Turkeys fair their last have breathed
And now this worled for ever leaved
Their Father and their Mother too
Will sigh and weep as well as you
Mourning for their osprings fair
Whom they did nurse with tender care
Indeed the rats their bones have crunched
To eternity are they launched
There graceful form and pretty eyes
Their fellow pows did not despise
A direful death indeed they had
That would put any parent mad
But she was more than usual calm
She did not give a singel dam
She is as gentel as a lamb
Here ends this melancholy lay
Farewell poor Turkeys I must say

Marjory Fleming, aged eight

As for the queer collection of objects that by now I may have amassed in my corner, I could tell a story about each of them if I had the face to do so. But it is difficult to share with another the peculiar sense of their value – how it is that a mossed stone, one of a hundred, or a handful of duckweed squeezed out like a sponge, or a bunch of crisp and crackling 'everlastings', may have appealed to one as striking and desirable, apt for possession. They are collected and bestowed with care – but not of these will I speak. There was a small covered basket, however, about three inches deep, of which something may be said, though it has been kept a secret hitherto. We had brought that basket from home, from far away, on the journey to Earlham, and nobody but the children knew what it contained. A beetle, very large, black as ebony, with a little earth for it to burrow in on the way – it was a beetle that we had brought hither, intending to set it free in the garden at Earlham. And now was the moment; the beetle stepped forth upon alien ground, doubtfully paced and paused; and I cannot forget the incident, now that the crunch of the gravel and the dry smell of the box-borders is about me again, at ten o'clock of a fine summer morning. The beetle may finally have advanced along Wilberforce's Walk, which ran in a straight vista down the edge of the shrubbery in this quarter. Wilberforce perhaps, on just such a morning, once strolled there with Uncle Joseph John, plotting the holy war upon the slave-driver; the path was named after him. It was long and straight and shady; the two friends in their broad-brimmed hats could just have walked abreast; and you would have seen them pass out into sunshine at the far end, as they turned to follow the path which made the circuit of the lawn.

EARLHAM *by Percy Lubbock (1879–1965)*

Pinch
Said the chaffinch
To the nightingale
As it sat on the rail
Along the flowering current of the electric main.

Unpublished poem by John Fairbairn (1934–   ), written at the age of five

Sergei Aksakov (1791–1859) recalls the ecstatic experience of the arrival of spring when, as a delicate child, he stayed at his father's country house on the eastern Russian steppes.

In the middle of Lent a rapid thaw set in. The snow began to melt quickly and water appeared everywhere. . . . Though confined to the house – for in wet weather I was not allowed even to stand on the steps – I followed none the less closely each stage of advancing spring. . . .

The starlings and larks arrived; and then the wild birds, called 'game' by sportsmen, began to appear. My father told me, with delight, that he had seen swans flying so high that they were scarcely visible, and long skeins of wild geese. Evseich had seen divers and mallards alighting on the pond, rock-pigeons about the stackyard, thrushes and lapwings round the springs. How many sensations for me! How I shouted for joy! The floods rose and rose, and no time was lost in raising the sluices. And I was not there! The weather was too bad, I did not venture even to ask leave to go; but my father's description did something to satisfy my curiosity. Every day my reports became more frequent, more important, and more tantalizing. At last Evseich, in wild excitement, declared that birds of every kind were there in such multitudes that they were jostling each other; and the limits of my endurance had been reached. It was no longer possible for me to hear all this and not see it; and backed by my father's approval and my own tears and eager entreaties, I wrung from my mother permission to go out, on condition that I was well wrapped up, for the wind blew damp and piercing. I was allowed to sit on the little veranda, just opposite the river and looking out on the garden. The inner door was still blocked up; and Evseich carried me round the house, as there was water and mud everywhere. And indeed, one who has never seen it can form no idea of what I then saw going on in the sky, on the earth, and on the water; nor can it be seen now in the same place, because the number of migratory birds is less nowadays.

The river had left its banks, and covered the trees and bushes on both sides; next, it had spread over half the garden and united with the lake in the 'Jackdaw Wood'. The edges of the water were crowded with wild birds of every kind; a multitude of ducks were swimming on the water, between the drowned tops of the bushes; and, all the time, large and small flocks of different birds were on the move – some flying high and steadily, others low and often alighting, and others moving from one point to another. The air was full of their calls, cries, and whistles. I did not know what bird was flying or walking there before me, or what importance it had; nor could I distinguish their calls; I was awestruck and stunned by the spectacle. My father and Evseich, who were standing beside me, were much excited themselves. Each kept pointing out birds to the other, and named them, often deciding by the note, for only the nearer birds could be distinguished by their plumage. 'Pintails! pintails!' cried Evseich in a flurry, 'flocks and flocks! And mallards too, I declare, beyond counting!' And then my father struck in: 'Can't you hear the snipe, how they're drumming? But they're terribly high up. And look at the rollers playing over the wheat-field, a perfect cloud of them! What a host of ruffs too! I never in my life saw such flocks!' Though I could not then understand the scene before me, and only looked and listened while my pulse seemed now to stop, and now to beat like a hammer, yet it all came before me later, as it does now, clear and distinct; and it gave me then, as it gives me now, unutterable delight. And to think that the sportsman alone is capable of understanding this fully! I, while yet a child, was a sportsman at heart; so my feelings on my return to the house may be guessed. I seemed, and could not but seem, a crazy half-witted creature: my eyes were wild, I could see nothing and heard not a word of what was said to me. Clasping my father's hand, I kept my eyes fixed on his face; I could not bear to speak to anyone else, or on any other subject than what we had just seen. My mother was angry, and threatened that she would not let me go out unless I became sensible and cleared my head at once of ducks and snipe. Good heavens, how utterly impossible!

YEARS OF CHILDHOOD

Along the outside of the front fence ran the country road, dusty in the summertime and a good place for snakes – they liked to lie in it and sun themselves; when they were rattlesnakes or puff adders we killed them; when they were black snakes or racers or belonged to the fabled 'hoop' breed we fled without shame; when they were 'house snakes' or 'garters' we carried them home and put them in Aunt Patsy's work basket for a surprise; for she was prejudiced against snakes, and always when she took the basket in her lap and they began to climb out of it it disordered her mind. She never could seem to get used to them; her opportunities went for nothing. And she was always cold towards bats, too, and could not bear them; and yet I think a bat is as friendly a bird as there is. My mother was Aunt Patsy's sister and had the same wild superstitions. A bat is beautifully soft and silky; I do not know any creature that is pleasanter to the touch or is more graceful for caressings, if offered in the right spirit. I know all about these coleoptera because our great cave, three miles below Hannibal, was multitudinously stocked with them and often I brought them home to amuse my mother with. It was easy to manage if it was a school day because then I had ostensibly been to school and hadn't any bats. She was not a suspicious person but full of trust and confidence; and when I said, 'There's something in my coat pocket for you', she would put her hand in. But she always took it out again, herself; I didn't have to tell her. It was remarkable the way she couldn't learn to like private bats. The more experience she had the more she could not change her views.

THE AUTOBIOGRAPHY OF MARK TWAIN

Julia Strachey recalls an alarming encounter in India.

I shall never forget the afternoon when I got my first sight of a cobra.

I was walking with my parents along a path that ran beside railings to the railway station. An old man holding a flute was squatting beside the path. On the ground beside him stood a tall rush-plaited basket with no lid to it. Only a narrow hole at the top. As we neared him the old man raised the flute to his lips and started to play a slow, rhythmical tune upon it. My parents, who recognized that a snake-charming performance was about to begin, came to a halt in front of the old fellow, thinking no doubt that the coming entertainment would delight me.

'Oh look, Ju! Look, look . . . you must see this!'

I looked and saw the neat little head of a serpent rise up with slow elegance from out the aperture at the top of the basket. As it rose ever higher and higher, the serpent started swaying his glittering black length from side to side in time to the flute music.

Had this been all of the performance I should have been well satisfied. But no! This kind of snake (which I had not come across before, and whose name of course was Cobra) had a peculiar – an exceptional – talent. I soon noticed that while the creature was so gracefully swaying from side to side to the rhythm of the flute, something weird and uncanny was happening at the same time. The narrow neat head began puffing itself out sideways – more and more and more. And still the head continued to swell! It was like a nightmare. It swelled. And swelled. And swelled. Changing its shape, changing its size, swelling larger and LARGER, ballooning itself up into the most infernal puffery – it became a black and glittering dinner plate, a grotesque deformity. Meanwhile a baleful hook-and-eye design began to manifest itself, slashed out big and bold across the snake's weirdly transformed head (if head it could still be called, for it had now reached unrecognizable proportions). I had never seen anything like this happen before. And now the monstrous shape began hollowing and caving itself in, in a most uncanny way. Then I noticed with a start how its own former little modest snake face with the small beady eyes was now to be seen perched high up on the very *top* of this new giant face!

I had never before seen a spectacle so wicked and ferocious, so full of evil intent. I recognized Black Magic. A Demon casting straight at us a destructive spell. My heart twisted over and plummeted down into my boots, for I grasped intuitively that this crazed thing was actively menacing me, that all its abnormal contortions were aimed at destroying me!

'There's nothing to be afraid of! It's only dancing!' my mother and father tried to reassure me, looking down and seeing me between them in floods of tears.

Dancing it may have been! But this was plainly a ritual Dance of Death! And what can you do against that?

JULIA

Three deranged aunts, with differing manifestations of madness, provide a bizarre background to a childhood in Wales.

There were thousands of jackdaws everywhere in the town, and our garden was always full of them. Sensing that my mad aunts presented no danger, they were completely tame. They would tap on the windows to be let into the house and go hopping from room to room in search of scraps.

Weekly the great ceremony took place of the baking of the jackdaw cake. For this, co-operation was forced upon my three aunts, as the ingredients had to be decided upon and bought: eggs, raisins, candied peel and sultanas required to produce a cake of exceptional richness. Li did the shopping, because Polly was supposed not to leave the house and Annie was too confused to be able to buy what was necessary, put down her money, and pick up the change.

Each aunt took it in turns to bake and ice the cake and to decorate the icing. While they were kept busy doing this they seemed to me quite changed. Annie wore an ordinary dress and stopped laughing, Li ceased to cry, and Polly's fits were quieter than on any other day. While the one whose turn it was did the baking, the others stood about in the kitchen and watched, and they were as easy to talk to as at other times they were not.

On Saturday mornings at ten o'clock the cake was fed to the jackdaws. This had been happening for years, so that by half past nine the garden was full of birds, anything up to a hundred of them balancing and swinging with a tremendous gleeful outcry on the bushes and the low boughs of the trees. This was the great moment of the week for my aunts, and therefore for me. The cake would be cut into three sections and placed on separate plates on the kitchen table, and then at ten the kitchen windows were flung wide to admit the great black cataract of birds. For some hours after this weekly event the atmosphere was one of calm and contentment, and then the laughter and weeping would start again.

Jackdaw Cake by Norman Lewis (1912–)

The common cormorant or shag
Lays eggs inside a paper bag
The reason you will see no doubt
It is to keep the lightning out
But what these unobservant birds
Have never noticed is that herds
Of wandering bears may come with buns
And steal the bags to hold the crumbs.

Anon

Giuseppe di Lampedusa (1896–1957) recollects his childhood winter home at Santa Margherita.

One would open a door on a passage and glimpse a perspective of rooms dim in the shade of half-pulled shutters, their walls covered with French prints representing Bonaparte's campaigns in Italy; at the top of the stairs leading to the second floor was a door that was almost invisible, so narrow was it and flush with the wall, and behind this was a big room crammed with old pictures hung right up to the very top of the walls, as in prints of the Paris *Salon* in the eighteenth century. One of the ancestral portraits in the first room was hinged, and behind lay my uncle's gun-rooms, for he was a great shot.

The trophies shut in glass cabinets were local only: pheasants, disconsolate-looking woodcock, moorhen from the Belice; but a big bench with scales, little measures for preparing cartridges, glass-fronted cupboards full of multi-coloured cartridge-cases, coloured prints showing more dangerous adventures (I can still see a bearded explorer in white fleeing screaming before the charge of a greenish rhinoceros). . . . On the walls also hung prints and photographs of shooting-dogs, pointers and setters, showing the calm of all canine faces. The guns were ranged in big racks, ticketed with numbers corresponding to a register in which were recorded the shots fired from each. It was from one of these guns, I think a lady's, with two richly damascened barrels, that I fired, in the garden, the first and last shots of my sporting career; one of the bearded keepers forced me to shoot at some innocent redbreasts;

two fell, unfortunately, with blood on their tepid grey plumage; and as they were still quivering the keeper wrung their necks with his fingers.

In spite of my readings of '*Victoires et Conquêtes*' and '*L'épée de l'intrépide général rougie du sang des ennemis de l'Empire*' this scene horrified me: apparently I only like blood when metamorphosed into printer's ink. I went straight to my father, to whose orders this slaughter of the Innocents was due, and said that never again would I fire on any creature.

Ten years later I was to kill a Bosnian with a pistol and who knows how many other Christians by shellfire. But it never made a tenth of the impression on me as those two wretched redbreasts.

I held out my smeared hand to my well-loved poodle Tom which was following me, and I can still see the kind but reproachful way with which it raised half its black lip, as well-brought-up dogs do when they want to show their disgust, though without offending their masters.   TWO STORIES AND A MEMORY

As the grown-ups were kind to children, the children were kind to animals. Kindness circulated – like a currency. There was an understanding, part of the unwritten constitution of Suburbia, that kindness received involved the obligation to pass it on. If a horse and cart drew up there was a scramble to fetch sugar-lumps. If a cat came over the fence there was an appeal for milk, and children spent a great deal of their time tip-toeing with saucers of milk towards cats who really only needed a quiet place where they could curl up and sleep the sleep of the overfilled.

THE SUBURBAN CHILD *by James Kenward*

Open war was declared at length between Aunt Esther and myself. I had a favourite cat called Selma, which I adored, and which followed me about at Lime wherever I went. Aunt Esther saw this, and at once insisted that the cat must be given up to her. I wept over it in agonies of grief: but Aunt Esther insisted. My mother was relentless in saying that I must be taught to give up my own way and pleasure to others; and forced to give it up if I would

not do so willingly, and with many tears, I took Selma in a basket
to the Rectory. For some days it almost comforted me for going to
the Rectory, because then I possibly saw my idolized Selma. But
soon there came a day when Selma was missing: Aunt Esther had
ordered her to be . . . hung!

THE STORY OF MY LIFE *by Augustus Hare*

*Seven-year-old Frank Buckland records in his diary the Duke of
Wellington's visit to Oxford in June 1834 for his installation as
Chancellor of the University.*

On Saturday the Duke's beautiful carriage came into the quad-
rangle, and the Duke got out to call upon the Dean. One of the
choristers asked if the harness was of gold. The coachman had a
wig and cocked hat.

Buckland later wrote: A live turtle was sent down from London, to be dressed for the banquet in Christ Church Hall. My
father tied a long rope round the turtle's fin, and let him have a
swim in 'Mercury', the ornamental water in the middle of the
Christ Church 'quad', while I held the string. I recollect, too, that
my father made me stand on the back of the turtle while he held
me on (I was then a little fellow), and I had a ride for a few yards as
it swam round and round the pond. As a great treat I was allowed
to assist the cook to cut off the turtle's head in the college kitchen.
The head, after it was separated, nipped the finger of one of the
kitchen boys who was opening the beast's mouth. This same head
is now in my museum.

Uncle Yusia was fond of instructing us on how to kill jackals by
sneezing at them. When spending the night in the desert, he used
to lie down with his head on the knapsack which contained his
food and pretend to go to sleep. The jackals crept up with their
tails between their legs. When the boldest got its teeth into the
knapsack and started cautiously pulling it out, my uncle gave an
ear-shattering sneeze, and immediately, so he said, the timid

jackal dropped dead of heart failure, without giving so much as a squeal.

We believed him because we heard him sneeze every morning in preparation for the new day: the windows rattled and the cat, panic-stricken, hurtled about the room looking for shelter.

STORY OF A LIFE *by Konstantin Paustovsky*

The Song of the Mischievous Dog

There are many who say that a dog has his day,
And a cat has a number of lives;
There are others who think that a lobster is pink,
And that bees never work in their hives.
There are fewer, of course, who insist that a horse
Has a horn and two humps on its head,
And a fellow who jests that a mare can build nests
Is as rare as a donkey that's red.
Yet in spite of all this, I have moments of bliss,
For I cherish a passion for bones,
And though doubtful of biscuit, I'm willing to risk it,
And love to chase rabbits and stones.
But my greatest delight is to take a good bite
At a calf that is plump and delicious;
And if I indulge in a bite at a bulge,
Let's hope you won't think me too vicious.

Dylan Thomas, aged eleven

Essay by an anonymous child of ten.

The bird that I am going to write about is the Owl. The Owl cannot see at all by day and at night is as blind as a bat.

I do not know much about the Owl, so I will go on to the beast which I am going to choose. It is the Cow. The Cow is a mammal. It has six sides – right, left, an upper and below. At the back it has a tail on which hangs a brush. With this it sends the flies away so that they do not fall into the milk. The head is for the purpose of growing horns and so that the mouth can be somewhere. The horns are to butt with, and the mouth is to moo with. Under the cow hangs the milk. It is arranged for milking. When people milk, the milk comes and there is never an end to the supply. How the cow does it I have not yet realized, but it makes more and more. The cow has a fine sense of smell; one can smell it far away. This is the reason for the fresh air in the country.

The man cow is called an ox. It is not a mammal. The cow does not eat much, but what it eats it eats twice, so that it gets enough. When it is hungry it moos, and when it says nothing it is because its inside is all full up with grass.

17

SIN

I am holding to the nose of my infant brother a flask of eau-de-Cologne. He seizes it, tilts it, and at one gulp swigs down a fair portion of its contents. I stare. He stares back. Can all be well with him? All is not well. A second later a muffled choking roar announces his inner consternation. Julia his nurse appears. I bleat: 'He *drank* it. I meant him just to smell it.' Her face turns pale as junket, and his is now dark plum colour. As she charges from the room with him she flings across her shoulder:

'You may have been the death of him.'

Well, I have been the death of him. I hurry away and creep under my bed, and there, in my best cotton frock, entomb myself, inhaling the peppery smell of carpet and carpet dust, and listening as from the world of shades to far-off voices interspersed with dreadful silences. I am due to go to Henley Regatta – prime treat of the year; but they can call and call, I will never come out. Presently the vibration of the car rises, diminishes, and fades along the drive. My father is headed for the Umpire's Launch; he cannot brook delay. But can my mother and Helen really have accompanied him, indifferent to or unaware of the fatality? I practise saying sincerely to my parents: 'It was an accident.' The memory of Boy's congested outraged face is lacerating. 'You gave me poison to drink,' it says, '*on purpose.*'

The silence now seems absolute. Perhaps Julia has charged with him to Nanny Green, her friend, expert in croup and other mysteries, who lives near by ... or to the doctor ... or the undertaker....

Time passes. Then I hear sounds impossible to associate with domestic tragedy. Shrieks and peals, with deep gardeners' voices interspersed. The maids are in splits in the kitchen, at their elevenses: a not uncommon occurrence whenever their employers are abroad. The day is not doom-laden, but ordinary. The call of nature obliges me to emerge. I gaze from the bathroom window and see my brother setting forth as usual in his pram, with Julia at the helm. He looks his customary outdoor self – an infant version of Mithras, Sun God, rayed round by the layers of a *broderie anglaise* sun hat, tied in a dashing bow beneath his chins. I hurry down to join them in the garden. He is unequivocally pleased to see me, and seems devoid of rancour or of mortal symptoms. 'Wherever have you been?' exclaims Julia sharply, eyeing me. 'They had to go without you.' I am silent, sheepish. She does not demur when I grip the handle of the pram and start to push. 'I told your mother,' she says presently, 'you felt a wee bit sicky after breakfast. It might be as well for you to stay here quiet with Birdie Boy and me.' I remain dumb. 'And who's his favourite sis-sis?' she cries, addressing her impassive charge.

THE SWAN IN THE EVENING *by Rosamond Lehmann (1901–   )*

I was subject, as a child, to outbursts of temper so tumultuous, so unbridled as to cause those who witnessed them to expect at any moment an attack of apoplexy. I often regret that I am unable any longer to lose my temper in so spectacular a fashion. . . . A really good display of fury is always impressive; there is something mystical, something demonic in its quality. There is no doubt that, during my early childhood, the violence of my temper was very useful in preserving me from punishment. It certainly did so on the occasion of my first and only experience of corporal chastisement.

This took place when I threw my mother's spaniel out of the window. Let me hasten to assure dog-lovers that this action was not inspired by innate cruelty or even by a hatred for dogs in general. It was due, rather, to a false association of ideas, an erroneous form of reasoning to which the human mind is particularly prone. I had heard somebody say that if you threw a dog into water it would instinctively swim. Reflection upon this biological fact led me to wonder if a dog, when thrown into the air, would also instinctively fly. Happening to see my mother's spaniel lying near an open window on the first floor, I felt that here was a good opportunity to make the experiment. It was a fat dog, and I had some difficulty in lifting it up on to the window-sill. After giving it an encouraging pat, I pushed it off. I watched the unfortunate animal gyrating in the air, its long ringleted ears and tail spread out by centrifugal force. (Incidentally it bore a strong resemblance to Elizabeth Barrett Browning.) But it appeared to be making no effort whatever to fly.

My mother was excusably infuriated by what appeared to be an act of wanton cruelty (although the animal had fallen unscathed into a lilac bush) and I failed to convince her of the scientific aspect of the experiment. She made up her mind to cross the education Rubicon and to give me my first thrashing. This was the occasion on which she appealed in vain to my father. By the time she had selected a convenient implement (which happened to be a bed-room slipper) I fancy her resolution had already weakened. She set about it in a half-hearted fashion. Nevertheless, the first blow acted upon me as a spark in a powder magazine. With empurpled face, foaming at the mouth, I wrested the slipper from her hand and began belabouring her throat and bosom with such violence that she ended by flying in terror from the room.

FIRST CHILDHOOD *by Lord Berners*

No royal child could be more scrupulously cared for than I was in my early years. I was idolized by everyone around me and, what is rarer, always treated as a beloved son, never as a spoiled child. Never once, until I left my father's house, was I allowed to run out alone into the road with the other children. They never had to repress or to indulge in me any of those wayward humours that are usually attributed to Nature, but which are all the product of education alone. I had the faults of my years. I was a chatterer, I was greedy, and sometimes I lied. I would have stolen fruit or sweets or any kind of eatable; but I never took delight in being naughty or destructive, or in accusing other people or torturing poor animals. However, I do remember once having made water in one of our neighbour's cooking-pots while she was at church; her name was Mme Clot. I will even admit that the thought of it still makes me laugh, because Mme Clot, although a good woman on the whole, was the grumpiest old body I have ever met. And that is a brief and truthful account of all my childish misdeeds.

THE CONFESSIONS *of Jean-Jacques Rousseau*

Edmund Verney writes to his son at Mr Blackwell's school at Bicester.

Child,   September, 1682

I received a letter from your master Mr Blackwell, who complains of you in your business, and that you are idly and evilly inclined, and particularly that you jointly with some other, as bad as yourself, have late mischiefed a tablet or two of his, and that you rise in the nights which was made to rest and sleep in. . . .

You have much deceived me, your father, who blinded with love to you, thought you no less than a young saint, but now to my grief perceive that you are growing very fast to be an old devil. . . .

All these matters drew my thoughts to the subject of idolatry, which was severely censured at the missionary meeting. I cross-examined my Father very closely as to the nature of this sin, and pinned him down to the categorical statement that idolatry consisted in praying to any one or anything but God himself. Wood and stone, in the words of the hymn, were peculiarly liable to be bowed down to by the heathen in their blindness. I pressed my Father further on this subject, and he assured me that God would be very angry, and would signify His anger, if anyone, in a Christian country, bowed down to wood and stone. I cannot recall why I was so pertinacious on this subject, but I remember that my Father became a little restive under my cross-examination. I determined, however, to test the matter for myself, and one morning, when both my parents were safely out of the house, I prepared for the great act of heresy. I was in the morning-room on the ground-floor, where, with much labour, I hoisted a small chair on to the table close to the window. My heart was now beating as if it would leap out of my side, but I pursued my experiment. I knelt down on the carpet in front of the table and looking up I said my daily prayer in a loud voice, only substituting the address 'O Chair!' for the habitual one.

Having carried this act of idolatry safely through, I waited to see what would happen. It was a fine day, and I gazed up at the slip of white sky above the houses opposite, and expected something to appear in it. God would certainly exhibit his anger in some terrible form, and would chastize my impious and wilful action. I was very much alarmed, but still more excited; I breathed the high, sharp air of defiance. But nothing happened; there was not a cloud in the sky, not an unusual sound in the street. Presently I was quite sure that nothing would happen. I had committed idolatry, flagrantly and deliberately, and God did not care.

The result of this ridiculous act was not to make me question the existence and power of God; those were forces which I did not dream of ignoring. But what it did was to lessen still further my confidence in my Father's knowledge of the Divine mind. My Father had said, positively, that if I worshipped a thing made of wood, God would manifest his anger. I had then worshipped a chair, made (or partly made) of wood, and God had made no sign whatever. My Father, therefore, was not really acquainted with the Divine practice in cases of idolatry.

FATHER AND SON *by Edmund Gosse*

The Story of Little Suck-a-Thumb

One day, Mamma said: 'Conrad dear,
I must go out and leave you here.
But mind now, Conrad, what I say,
Don't suck your thumb while I'm away.
The great tall tailor always comes
To little boys that suck their thumbs,
And ere they dream what he's about,
He takes his great sharp scissors out
And cuts their thumbs clean off, – and then,
You know, they never grow again.'

Mamma had scarcely turn'd her back,
The thumb was in, Alack! Alack!
The door flew open, in he ran,
The great, long, red-legg'd scissor-man.

Oh! children, see! the tailor's come
And caught out little Suck-a-Thumb.
Snip! Snap! Snip! the scissors go;
And Conrad cries out – Oh! Oh! Oh!
Snip! Snap! Snip! They go so fast,
That both his thumbs are off at last.

Mamma comes home; there Conrad stands,
And looks quite sad, and shows his hands, –
'Ah!' said Mamma 'I knew he'd come
To naughty little Suck-a-Thumb.'

STRUWWELPETER *by Heinrich Hoffmann (1809–74)*

I was still in petticoats, and was sitting on a stool in the yard while my father was busy about the beehives. Suddenly a pretty little creature settled on my hand, and I watched it with delight as it crawled about. Then all at once I began to shriek. The pretty little creature was a bee, which had a good right to be angry when the pastor was robbing him of the honey-filled combs in his hive, and to sting the robber's little son in revenge! My cries brought the whole household round me, and everyone pitied me. The servant-girl took me in her arms and tried to comfort me with kisses, while my mother reproached my father for beginning to work at the hives without first putting me in a place of safety. My misfortune having made me so interesting an object, I went on crying with much satisfaction, till I suddenly noticed that, although the tears were still pouring down, the pain had disappeared. My conscience told me to stop, but in order to be interesting a bit longer I went on with my lamentations, so getting a lot more comforting than I really needed. However, this made me feel such a little rogue that I was miserable over it all the rest of the day.

MEMOIRS OF CHILDHOOD AND YOUTH *by Albert Schweitzer*

St Augustine of Hippo (354–430) agonizes in his Confessions *over childhood delinquencies.*

There was a pear-tree near our vineyard, loaded with fruit that was attractive neither to look at nor to taste. Late one night a band of ruffians, myself included, went off to shake down the fruit and carry it away, for we had continued our games out of doors until well after dark, as was our pernicious habit. We took away an enormous quantity of pears, not to eat them ourselves, but simply to throw them to the pigs. Perhaps we ate some of them, but our real pleasure consisted in doing something that was forbidden. . . .

We were tickled to laughter by the prank we had played, because no one suspected us of it although the owners were furious. Why was it, then, that I thought it fun not to have been the only culprit? Perhaps it was because we do not easily laugh when we are alone. True enough: but even when a man is all by himself and quite alone, sometimes he cannot help laughing if he thinks or hears or sees something especially funny. All the same, I am quite sure that I would never have done this thing on my own.

My God, I lay all this before you, for it is still alive in my memory. By myself I would not have committed that robbery. It was not the takings that attracted me but the raid itself, and yet to do it by myself would have been no fun and I should not have done it. This was friendship of a most unfriendly sort, bewitching my mind in an inexplicable way. For the sake of a laugh, a little sport, I was glad to do harm and anxious to damage another; and that without thought of profit for myself or retaliation for injuries received! And all because we are ashamed to hold back when others say 'Come on! Let's do it!'

Bertrand Russell recalls his state of mind at the age of five.

I was, in fact, unusually prone to a sense of sin. When asked what was my favourite hymn, I answered 'Weary of earth and laden with my sin'. On one occasion when my grandmother read the parable of the Prodigal Son at family prayers, I said to her afterwards: 'I know why you read that – because I broke my jug.' She used to relate the anecdote in after years with amusement, not realizing that she was responsible for a morbidness which had produced tragic results in her own children.

Mark Twain was not similarly encumbered by conscience.

My mother had a good deal of trouble with me but I think she enjoyed it. She had none at all with my brother Henry, who was two years younger than I, and I think that the unbroken monotony of his goodness and truthfulness and obedience would have been a burden to her but for the relief and variety which I furnished in the other direction. I was a tonic. I was valuable to her. I never thought of it before but now I see it. I never knew Henry to do a vicious thing toward me or toward anyone else – but he frequently did righteous ones that cost me as heavily. It was his duty to report me, when I needed reporting and neglected to do it myself, and he was very faithful in discharging that duty....

Henry never stole sugar. He took it openly from the bowl. His mother knew he wouldn't take sugar when she wasn't looking, but she had her doubts about me. Not exactly doubts, either. She knew very well I *would.* One day when she was not present Henry took sugar from her prized and precious old-English sugar bowl, which was an heirloom in the family – and he managed to break the bowl. It was the first time I had ever had a chance to tell anything on him and I was inexpressibly glad. I told him I was going to tell on him but he was not disturbed. When my mother came in and saw the bowl lying on the floor in fragments she was speechless for a minute. I allowed that silence to work; I judged it would increase the effect. I was waiting for her to ask, 'Who did that?' – so that I could fetch out my news. But it was an error of calculation. When she got through with her silence she didn't ask anything about it – she merely gave me a crack on the skull with her thimble that I felt all the way down to my heels. Then I broke out with my injured innocence, expecting to make her very sorry that she had punished the wrong one. I expected her to go something remorseful and pathetic. I told her that I was not the one – it

was Henry. But there was no upheaval. She said, without emotion: 'It's all right. It isn't any matter. You deserve it for something
that you are going to do that I shan't hear about.'

It was in the Old Rectory that I first knew fear. We had been given
a book of English fairy stories illustrated only too effectively by
Arthur Rackham. Page after page of horror met me. On one page
the giant Cormoran towered over a village, a clutch of screaming
peasants tied to his great belt by their necks. On another they
hung by their hair from hooks in his larder, with eyes protruding
from their contorted and emaciated faces. The giant had come
into our house, and round every corner I expected to meet him, to
be grabbed and swept away to that fearful larder. The top storey
of the house was the most terrifying to me, for I felt certain that he
lived up there, and I would clutch our nurse's hand and huddle
against her whenever we went there. I never told her why.

When I was about four years old I did my first drawing. It was
an unskilful rendering of my brother sitting on his pot; but feeling
rather pleased with it I took it to my mother. The result was
terrifying. In a second she changed into a mad thing, her eyes
shone with ferocity, and picking up a tortoiseshell hairbrush she
threw herself at me. 'Ah you nasty little thing,' she screamed, 'ah,
you dirty little boy; ah, ah, ah, take that, take that and that!' and
the blows seemed to hit me everywhere. The physical pain I forgot
soon enough. But I never forgot the demented figure who was my
mother, changed so swiftly, so unaccountably, into another
being. Nobody could tell me why. Evidently I had sinned most
terribly.

If Dick or I wanted to go to the lavatory, our request always had
to be camouflaged in such a way as to avoid embarrassment. We
were told to refer to it as the Poogeally. It was quite a nice name,
so we used it readily enough, and it was only many years later that
I discovered it was really the French 'Puis j'y aller?' which my
mother had introduced in order to bring decorum to so humble an
act.   ACROSS THE STRAITS *by Kyffin Williams (1918–)*

My school days began, but I played truant day after day, and the maidservant had to lead me as a prisoner to school. Although small of figure I was a good athlete, and so often fighting that some of my relatives thought that prize fighting was of a certainty to be my future vocation....

Strange that I was not a bad scholar, and that I passed all my standards with ease. In the last year of my school days I became captain of the school's football team, and was honoured and trusted by being allowed to take charge of the ball, but owing to making private use of the same, and practising in secret with boys of other schools, I was requested by the Committee to forfeit my trust, although I might still continue captain as aforesaid. If I had been contented with these innocent honours, and had not been so ambitious to excel in other and more infamous parts all would have been well, and my schooldays would have been something of of a credit to me. But unfortunately, at this time, I organized a band of robbers, six in number, and all of good families and comfortable homes. It was our wont to enter busy stores, knowing that small boys would not be attended to until the grown people had finished their purchases. Then we would slyly take things up for a curious examination, at the same time watching a favourable opportunity to surreptitiously appropriate them. When accosted by the shopman as to our wants we would innocently ask the price of some article we had agreed on, and receiving answer, would quietly leave the premises. This went on for some time, and I had nefariously profited by a large assortment of miscellaneous articles, such as paints, brushes, books, bottles of scent and various other items that could not be preserved, such as sweets and confectionery. How this continued for six weeks speaks well for our well-laid plans and our dexterity in the performance of them....

At home I was cured of thieving by what I thought at that time to be a very remarkable incident – no more or less than the result of witchcraft. One day my grandmother happened to be standing before the fire cooking, and above the fireplace was a large mirror, towards which her eyes were turned. Thinking this a favourable opportunity to rifle the sugar basin, I lost no time in making the attempt; but my fingers had scarcely closed on a large lump when the old lady, without in the least turning her head, cried in a shrill voice, 'You dare!' For my life I could not account for this discovery, and it sent such a shock through me that I never again attempted in the old lady's presence to be other than honest. She could close her eyes in the arm chair and even breathe audibly, but I never had the confidence to make another attempt. But this incident at home had no detrimental effect on my courage abroad.

THE AUTOBIOGRAPHY OF A SUPER-TRAMP
by W. H. Davies (1871–1940)

Colonel Jack, a little pickpocket, is perplexed over how to deal with a tremendous windfall of four gold guineas.

. . . I had really more Wealth than I knew what to do with, for Lodging I had none, nor any Box or Drawer to hide my Money in, nor had I any Pocket, but such, *as I say*, was full of Holes; I knew no Body in the World, that I cou'd go and desire them to lay it up for me; for being a poor naked, ragged Boy, they would presently say, I had robb'd some Body, and perhaps lay hold of me, and my Money would be my Crime, *as they say*, it often is in Foreign Countries: And now as I was full of Wealth, behold! I was full of Care, for what to do to secure my Money I could not tell, and this held me so long, and was so vexatious to me the next Day, that I truly sat down and cried. . . .

When my crying was over, the Case was the same; I had the Money still, and what to do with it I could not tell, at last it came into my Head, that I would look out for some Hole in a Tree, and see to hide it there, till I should have occasion for it: Big with this Discovery, as I then thought it, I began to look about me for a Tree; but there were no Trees in the Fields about *Stepney*, or *Mile-End* that look'd fit for my Purpose, and if there were any, that I began to look narrowly at, the Fields were so full of People, that they wou'd see if I went to hide any Thing there, and I thought the people eyed me as it were, and that two Men in particular follow'd me, to see what I intended to do.

This drove me farther off, and I cross'd the Road at *Mile-End*, and in the middle of the Town went down a Lane that goes away to the *Blind Beggars* at *Bednal-Green*; when I came a little way in the Lane, I found a Foot Path over the Fields, and in those Fields several Trees for my Turn, as I thought; at last one Tree had a little Hole in it, pretty high out of my Reach, and I climb'd up the Tree to get to it, and when I came there, I put my Hand in, and found, (as I thought) a Place very fit, so I placed my Treasure there and was mighty well satisfied with it, but behold, putting my Hand in again to lay it more commodiously as I thought, of a sudden it slipp'd away from me, and I found the Tree was hollow, and my little Parcel was fallen in quite out of my Reach, and how far it might go in, I knew not; so, that in a Word, my Money was quite gone, irrecoverably lost, there could be no Room, so much as to hope ever to see it again, for it was a vast great Tree.

As young as I was, I was now sensible what a Fool I was before, that I could not think of Ways to keep my Money, but I must come thus far to throw it into a Hole where I could not reach it; well, I thrust my Hand quite up to my Elbow, but no Bottom was to be found, or any end of the Hole or Cavity; I got a Stick off the Tree, and thrust it in a great Way, but all was one; then I cry'd, nay, roar'd out, I was in such a Passion, then I got down the Tree again, then up again, and thrust in my Hand again till I scratch'd my Arm and made it bleed, and cry'd all the while most violently: Then I began to think I had not so much as a Halfpenny of it left for a Halfpenny Roll, and I was hungry, and then I cry'd again: Then I came away in Despair, crying and roaring like a little Boy that had been whipp'd, then I went back again to the Tree, and up the Tree again, and thus I did several Times.

The last Time I had gotten up the Tree, I happen'd to come down not on the same Side that I went up and came down before, but on the other Side of the Tree, and on the other side of the Bank also; and behold the Tree had a great open Place in the Side of it close to the Ground, as old hollow Trees often have; and looking into the open Place, to my inexpressible Joy, there lay my Money, and my linnen Rag, all wrapp'd up just as I had put it into the Hole: For the Tree being hollow all the Way up, there had been some Moss or light Stuff, (which I had not Judgment enough to know) was not firm, and had given way when it came to drop out of my Hand, and so it had slipp'd quite down at once.

I was but a Child, and I rejoic'd like a Child, for I hollow'd quite
out aloud when I saw it; then I run to it and snatch'd it up, hug'd
and kiss'd the dirty Rag a hundred Times; then danc'd and jump'd
about, run from one End of the Field to the other, and in short, I
knew not what, much less do I know now, what I did, tho' I shall
never forget the Thing, either what a sinking Grief it was to my
Heart when I thought I had lost it, or what a Flood of Joy
o'erwhelm'd me when I had got it again.

THE LIFE OF COLONEL JACK *by Daniel Defoe (1660–1731)*

18

RED-LETTER DAYS

The first big festival that I can remember was Peace Day in 1919. It was a day of magical transformations, of tears and dusty sunlight, of bands, processions, and buns by the cartload; and I was so young I thought it normal. . . .

We had all been provided with fancy-dress, and that seemed normal too. Apart from the Squire's contribution Marjorie had been busy for weeks stitching up glories for ourselves and the neighbours. No makeshift, rag-bag cobbling either; Marjorie had worked as though for a wedding.

On the morning of the feast Poppy Green came to the house to try on her angel's dress. She was five years old and about my size. She had russet curls like apple peelings, a polished pumpkin face, a fruity air of exploding puddings, and a perpetual cheeky squint. I loved her, she was like a portable sweet-shop. This morning I watched my sisters dress her. She was supposed to represent a spirit. They'd made her a short frilly frock, a tinfoil helmet, cardboard wings, and a wand with a star. When they'd clothed her they stood her up on the mantelpiece and had a good look at her. Then they went off awhile on some other business and left us alone together.

'Fly!' I commanded. 'You've got wings, ain't you?'

Poppy squirmed and wiggled her shoulders.

I grew impatient and pushed her off the mantelpiece, and she fell with a howl into the fireplace. Looking down at her, smudged with coal and tears, her wand and wings all crumpled, I felt nothing but rage and astonishment. She should have been fluttering round the room. CIDER WITH ROSIE *by Laurie Lee*

I was under the charge of two nurses, one Russian and the other German. Vera Artamonovna and Mme Proveau were two very good-natured women, but I got weary of watching them all day, as they knitted stockings and wrangled together. So, whenever I could, I escaped to the part of the house occupied by the Senator – my uncle, the former ambassador, was now a Senator and was generally called by this title – and there I found my only friend, my uncle's valet, Calot.

I have seldom met so kind and gentle a creature as this man. Utterly solitary in Russia, separated from all his own belongings, and hardly able to speak our language, he had a woman's tenderness for me. I spent whole hours in his room, and, though I was often mischievous and troublesome, he bore it all with a good-natured smile. He cut out all kinds of marvels for me in cardboard, and carved me many toys of wood; and how I loved him in return! In the evenings he used to take picture-books from the library and bring them up to my nursery – *The Travels* of Gmelin and Pallas, and another thick book called *The World in Pictures*, which I liked so much and looked at so long, that the leather binding got worn out: for two hours together Calot would show me the same pictures and repeat the same explanations for the thousandth time.

Before my birthday party, Calot shut himself up in his room, and I could hear mysterious sounds of a hammer and other tools issuing from it. He often walked quickly through the passage, carrying a glue-pot or something wrapped up in paper, but each time he left his room locked. I knew he was preparing some surprise for me, and my curiosity may be imagined. I sent the servant's children to act as spies, but Calot was not to be caught napping. We even managed to make a small hole in the staircase, through which we could look down into the room; but we could see nothing but the top of the window and the portrait of Frederick the Great, with his long nose and a large star on his breast, looking like a sick vulture. At last the noises stopped, and the room was unlocked – but it looked just as before, except for snippings of gilt and coloured paper on the floor. I was devoured by curiosity; but Calot wore a pretence of solemnity on his features and never touched the ticklish subject.

I was still suffering agonies of impatience when the great day arrived. I awoke at six, to wonder what Calot had in store for me;

at eight Calot himself appeared, wearing a white tie and white waistcoat under his blue livery, but his hands were empty! I wondered how it would all end, and whether he had spoilt what he was making. The day went on, and the usual presents were forthcoming: my aunt's footman had brought me an expensive toy wrapped up in a napkin, and my uncle, the Senator, had been generous also, but I was too restless, in expectation of the surprise, to enjoy my happiness.

Then, when I was not thinking of it, after dinner or perhaps after tea, my nurse said to me: 'Go downstairs for a moment, there is someone there asking for you.' 'At last!' I thought, and down the bannisters I slid on my arms. The drawing-room door flew open; I heard music and saw a transparency representing my initials; then some little boys, disguised as Turks, offered me sweets; and this was followed by a puppet-show and parlour fireworks. Calot was very hot and very busy; he kept everything going and was quite as excited as I was myself.

No presents could rank with this entertainment. I never cared much for *things*; the bump of acquisitiveness was never, at any age, highly developed in me. The satisfaction of my curiosity, the abundance of candles, the silver paper, the smell of gunpowder – nothing was wanting but a companion of my own age. But I spent all my childhood in solitude and consequently was not exacting on that score.

CHILDHOOD, YOUTH AND EXILE *by Alexander Herzen*

Letter from the five-year-old Dante Gabriel Rossetti (1828–82).

Dear Aunt Eliza,

We went to a fancy fair in the Regent's Park where I bought a box of paints, Maria, an album, and Christina, two fishes and a hook. The fair was for the benefit of a Charity School. I have been reading Shakespeare's Richard the 3rd for my amusement, and like it exceedingly. I, Maria, and William know several scenes by heart. I have bought a picture of Richard and Richmond fighting and I gilded it after which I cut it out with no white. My Aunt came yesterday and gave Maria a pretty little basket it was worked in flowers of green card.

> I remain, my dear Aunt,
> Your affectionate Nephew
> Gabriel C. D. Rossetti

James Kirkup remembers his Aunt Lyallie and her sons:

She had a little black Pomeranian dog called Rosie who was a most affectionate animal; she would run to welcome me whenever I climbed my Granny's steep, canvas-covered back stairs, and would jump on to my lap when I sat down, and lick my face with her rough little pink tongue.

'Puir little beastie!' my Granny would say to her, as she supped a saucer of tea. Rosie was sometimes teased by my Aunt Lyallie's three strapping sons, whom I adored for their dashing sense of fun, their animal spirits, their 'gift of the gab', and their adventurous lives. Two of them were in the Coldstream Guards, and had been to India. The youngest, whom I think I liked best of all, had a marvellous, full-hearted laugh.

'If only I could laugh like that!' I used to think. But I never could. This cousin was an excitable, animated, sensitive young man who played the fiddle very well. I used to like to sit on the 'clippy' mat in front of my Granny Johnson's kitchen fire and listen to him practising scales and playing *The Minstrel Boy*, or *We'll Reel the Keel Row*. He and my mother, who was a sweet singer, were the first to awaken my passion for music and dancing. I would sit quietly waiting in my Granny's house, hoping, if he was out, that he would come in soon and play his fiddle. I would sit watching him shave and brushing his teeth: that in itself was a marvel, for he would put his toothbrush up the chimney and brush his teeth with soot. They were the whitest teeth I've ever seen. Then he would light a Woodbine and spend a long time polishing his shoes and combing his hair: that house always smelt of shaving-soap, and shoe-polish, and hair-oil and cigarettes. Then, after a cup of tea — there was always a pot of tea being 'mashed' at my Granny Johnson's – he would say, while I listened with bated breath:

'Well, I think I'll have a bit scrape at the old fiddle.'

And I would sit trembling with expectancy while he opened the violin-case, took out his fiddle and rosined his bow. The inside of the violin-case was beautiful and strange. It was lined with royal-blue velvet, and there were two little boxes inside, where the waist of the violin came, full of pegs and bits of rosin. There was a larger box at the narrow end, in which he kept a tangle of 'Cathedral' strings. And how elegant was the rosewood bow, inlaid with ivory and mother-of-pearl! Then he would set up his little, rickety gilt music-stand, and draw his bow across the strings, producing chords that sent shivers down my back, after which he would begin practising his scales and exercises while I looked on spell-bound, listening to every note, watching his left-hand crab up and down the strings, and his right hand rising and falling and suddenly plucking a thrilling *pizzicato*. It was all enchantment, and I looked upon him as a magician, his handsome, pointed face cradled on the chin-rest, and a long lock of dark hair falling over his brow. Then from time to time he would look at me and give me a prodigious wink, and smile dazzlingly and go on playing; I thought this was the cleverest thing of all, to be able to play, and wink at the same time. He played for a while in a picture palace with a pianist who accompanied the last of the silent moving pictures. Later on, when I read about Paganini, I would think of my cousin Tom – thin, volatile, tall and wild – and remember his clever hands, his grin, and his devilish wink.

THE ONLY CHILD

March 13

My dearest, dearest Mamma, today is my 12th birthday. How well I remember many happy birthdays at Stoke, when before breakfast I had a wreath of snowdrops, and at dinner a little pudding with my name in plums. . . . I will try this new year to throw away self and think less how to please it. Good-bye dear Mamma.

Augustus Hare

From the Diary of Smith Minor:

St James's School,
September 1884

Sunday. – We went for the choir expedition last Thursday. It was *great fun*. We went to London by the 8.35 train. We missed the train!! So we went by the 8.53. We got to London at 10.15. We then went to the mint we first saw the silver melted and made into thick tablets, then we saw it rolled out into thin bits then cut stamped and weighed then we had a very good luncheon and went to the Tower. We first saw the Bloody Tower were the little Princes were murdered then we saw the jewels the warder said the Queen's crown was worth over £1,000,000 then we saw the armory and the torture's, then we went to Madame Tussaus it is quite a large building now with a large stairkes then we had tea and went home.

LOST DIARIES *by Maurice Baring*

A blind child's first experience of the sea.

One warm day, there was a series of explosions at the front gate. At first, I thought someone was setting off firecrackers, but then I realized that what I heard was a motorcar engine idling and repeatedly backfiring. We heard such engine sounds all the time – mixed in with the clip-clop of victoria horses, the clatter of handcarts, and the clink and ponk-ponk of bicycle bells and car klaxons – but they were always the sounds of passing traffic. No vehicle, it seemed, ever stopped in front of the school.

'Mr Ras Mohun wants us all at the front gate!' Bhaskar cried, running into the boys' dormitory. 'There's a lorry! We are really going to Juhu Beach!'

We had heard Mr Ras Mohun mention the visit to Juhu Beach as a 'red-letter day'. We had all talked about going to the seaside, without knowing exactly what it was. Abdul had once remarked, 'Mahim Sea Beach is not the seaside, and there is no stuffed sand or stuffed ocean for the blind to feel. They have to take us to Juhu Beach to show us what it is.'

'Why are we going in a lorry?' I asked now.

'Because there are no trams to Juhu Beach, you son of an owl,' Abdul said. 'It's really far.'

The lorry had no seats, so we all sat on the floor, the boys on one side and the girls on the other. I wanted to run around – perhaps try to sit with Paran – but Mr Ras Mohun was addressing us from the front of the lorry.

'Boys and girls, this is our first annual holiday at Juhu Beach,' he said. 'Juhu Beach is on the Arabian Sea, and we have a day's holiday there because of a special gift from Mrs Thomas and the American Marathi Mission. It will take us quite some time to reach Juhu Beach. I want you to stay in your places, because the ride to Juhu Beach is bumpy.'

To help us pass the time, Miss Mary led us in a new song. It really had only one line: 'John Brown's Whiskey Bottle Number One Hundred and One'. Each time we sang it, we would sing out one number less than the time before. The song sounded naughty and festive to us, and we felt we were really on an annual holiday.

At Juhu Beach, I heard a sound I'd never heard before – a gigantic roar alternating with the sound of a huge amount of water rushing out. The sound was very different from Mahim Sea Beach, which was quiet, like a canal in Lahore. (It was actually an inlet.) I wanted to run toward the sound and touch it – to feel what it was really like – but the Sighted Master herded us boys into the boys' shack. He gave us each a pair of bathing drawers and we got into them.

'Now you can do what you like,' the Sighted Master said. 'But don't go beyond the rope in the water.'

I hesitated for a moment, wondering if there were wired lanes and how, amid the roar and the rush, I would hear the Sighted Master ringing the bell on the other side of the rope, but the partially sighted boys started running towards the roar and the rush, calling back, 'Abdul! Reuben! Vedi! There is nothing in the way! You can run, too!'

I ran toward the roar and the rush. The air smelled of salt and coconut. There was hot, grainy, dry ground underfoot. It was so hot that I could scarcely bear to put my feet on it, so I had to run fast, and couldn't stop to examine it. Suddenly, I was in the water, being carried out. It closed over my head. I forgot everything. I felt

I'd never been so happy. A jolt opened my mouth. I was rapidly swallowing water that tasted of tears – buckets of them. I was flung back, choking. Again the water closed over my head. The water retreated. I lay on the water, wondering if the sea could take me all the way to the Punjab. Then I came up against the rope, as thick as the one we used for the tug-of-war, and I heard the Sighted Master calling to me, 'That's far enough! Come back! You'll drown!'

We spent the day bathing in the water and running around on the new ground. I couldn't get over the way it shifted around, almost like the water. We could go into the water as often as we liked, and when we ran we just had to keep the sound of the ocean to our left or right, depending on which way we were facing. The school compound and the racing track suddenly shrank in my mind, like a woollen sock Mamaji had knitted for me which became so small after Heea's ayah washed it that I could scarcely get my hand in it.

At one point, we had a picnic – Mr Ras Mohun, the Sighted Master, Mrs Ras Mohun, Heea, the Matron, and all the boys and girls. We all sat down on bedsheets. For the first time, I was able to sit next to Deoji and eat with him. The food was not mutton and toast but thick, heavy potato-filled bread, with a chewy relish made of pickled mango skin.

VEDI *by Ved Mehta (1934–   )*

A Boy's Song

Where the pools are bright and deep,
Where the grey trout lies asleep,
Up the river and o'er the lea,
That's the way for Billy and me.

Where the blackbird sings the latest,
Where the hawthorn blooms the sweetest,
Where the nestlings chirp and flee,
That's the way for Billy and me.

Where the mowers mow the cleanest,
Where the hay lies thick and greenest;

There to trace the homeward bee,
That's the way for Billy and me.

Where the hazel bank is steepest,
Where the shadow falls the deepest,
Where the clustering nuts fall free,
That's the way for Billy and me.

Why the boys should drive away
Little sweet maidens from the play,
Or love to banter and fight so well,
That's the thing I never could tell.

But this I know, I love to play,
Through the meadow, among the hay;
Up the water and o'er the lea,
That's the way for Billy and me.

James Hogg (1770–1835), the 'Ettrick Shepherd'

I had gone to bed, but was prevented from sleeping by strange rumours – a thrill of agitation that ran through the house from top to bottom, accompanied by waves of harmonious sound. No doubt I had noticed some preparations during the day. No doubt I had been told there was to be a ball that evening. But could I have any idea what a ball was? I had not given the matter a thought and had gone to bed as usual. But now came these strange rumours. . . . I listened, trying to catch some sound that would be more distinct, trying to understand what was happening. I strained my ears with all my might and main. Finally, unable to resist any longer, I got up and groped my way out of the room along the dark passage, till I reached the lighted staircase. My room was on the third floor. The waves of sound rose from the first; I felt I must go and see; and as I got nearer, creeping downstairs step by step, I began to distinguish the sounds of voices, the rustling of dresses, whispering and laughter. Nothing wore its usual look; I felt as if I was going to be suddenly initiated into another life – a mysterious, differently real, more brilliant, more exciting life, which began only after little boys had gone to bed. The passages on the second floor were deserted; the party was downstairs. Should I go on? I should be caught if I did. I should certainly be punished for not going to sleep, for having ventured to look. I slipped my head between the iron bars of the banisters to take a peep. At that very moment some of the guests were arriving – an officer in uniform, a lady all in ribbons and silk; she was holding a fan in her hand; the man-servant – my friend Victor – whom I did not recognize at first because of his knee-breeches and white stockings, was standing by the open door of the drawing-room and announcing the guests. All of a sudden someone pounced down on me – it was my nurse Marie, who was trying to peep like me and had ensconced herself a little lower down, at the first turn of the stairs. She seized me in her arms and I thought at first she was going to carry me back to my room and shut me up; but no, on the contrary, she took me down to the place where she had been watching and from which it was just possible to catch a tiny whiff of the festivities below. I heard the music perfectly now. I saw the gentlemen whirling round to the sound of invisible instruments, with beautifully dressed ladies, who were all far more lovely than in the daytime. Then the music ceased; the dancers stopped; and there was a noise of voices instead of the sound of instruments. My nurse was on the point of taking me back to bed, when just at that moment one of the lovely ladies who was standing leaning by the door and fanning herself caught sight of me. She came up to where I was and kissed me, laughing because I did not recognize her. She was evidently the friend I had seen that morning calling on my mother; but all the same I was not really and truly sure of it. When I got back to my bed, my brain was in a turmoil, and before sinking into sleep, I thought in a confused way – there is reality and there are dreams; and there is *another* reality as well.

IF IT DIE . . . *by André Gide*

When I was very small, I was invited to tea by Roger [Fry] at Dalmeny Avenue, in London. Several other little girls were there as well as his bearded, deep-voiced sister, Margery, who kept house for him. Expecting the spread of jellies, cakes and biscuits that were usually put before children, we each sat down to a plate bare of all but a baked potato. Discovering that these were made of cardboard, everyone but myself burst into tears. Somehow aware that this was what the grown-ups called a joke, I opened mine and found it filled with hundreds and thousands, multi-coloured sweets the size of a pin's head, impossible to eat without scattering them all over the floor – indeed impossible to eat at all. Dismayed that their attempt to amuse us had fallen so flat, poor Margery bustled away to get the real tea, hidden behind a curtain, and the rest of the evening, no doubt spent more normally, was forgotten by me.   DECEIVED WITH KINDNESS *by Angelica Garnett*

Monday, 12 February [1872]

This is Boosie Evans' birthday, and at 6.30 eight of the children came to tea at my rooms, for I had arranged my yearly children's party today to celebrate the event. . . .

The children were a little shy when they first came in, and were standing together at the opposite side of the room. 'Come round here and warm yourselves. You needn't be afraid of me.' 'No, sir,' replied Sena Anthony quickly and frankly, 'we're too fond of you to be afraid of you.' How easy it is to amuse children and make them happy. They were overwhelmed with admiration of one of the attar of rose bottles which Emmie brought from Hyderabad. Then they were seized with awe at the sight of a lock of hair which I cut from the mane of the great lion at the Clifton Zoological Gardens when he was asleep, in August 1865. But one of the things which amused and interested them most was an old letter lock off my hat box.

I offered a sovereign to whoever could open it. They tried a long time, but the reward was not claimed. They were very indignant and angry with themselves for not being able to open it when I told them the cabalistic word was 'pat'. 'And you were patting your pussy all the while, if we had only thought about it and noticed it,' said one of the children, alluding to my tabby cat who was lying in my arm chair beside me. First came buns, bread and butter, and tea poured out by Boosie amid great fun. Crackers and looking at picture books. They played bagatelle and the Race

Game. Then came a grand fiery snap dragon. And lastly I told them tales till midnight, the story of Faithful Eric and the wolves, and the story of the fright Emmie had in the night at Hyderabad. Dear children, what a pleasure it is to have them. I am never so happy as when I have these children about me. And they behave so nicely, like little gentlewomen, much better than most young ladies. I should be very sorry to spend six hours in the company of many young ladies of my acquaintance, whereas tonight I was as sorry when 12 o'clock came as the children, and missed them sadly when all the bright faces trooped out into the dark night together to their homes in the village, with Goodnight and thanks and courtesies, and left me alone in my silent room.

Wherever I may go I shall never find such children again.

Diary of the Revd Francis Kilvert (1840–79)

At the period when we were living in the first-floor apartment overlooking the Place Grenette, before 1790 or, to be exact, until the middle of 1789, my uncle the young lawyer had a very pleasant little apartment on the second floor, at the corner of the Place Grenette and the Grande-Rue. He used to joke with me and let me watch him take off his fine clothes and put on his dressing-gown, at nine o'clock in the evening, before supper. This was a delicious moment for me, and I would walk downstairs in front of him to the first floor delightedly, carrying the silver candlestick. My aristocratic family would have felt itself disgraced if the candle-stick had not been of silver. It is true that it contained no noble wax candle, for it was customary then to use tallow. But we had this tallow sent from Briançon, with great care, packed in a case; it had to be made of goat's fat, and was ordered at the right time from a friend living in the mountains there. I can still see myself watching the tallow being unpacked and eating bread-and-milk from a silver bowl; I was always struck by the odd noise of the spoon scraping against the bottom of the bowl, which was wet with milk. The relations between my family and this Briançon friend were almost those of host and guest, as in Homer, a natural consequence of the distrust and barbarism which were then wide-spread.

My uncle, young, brilliant and frivolous, was said to be the most attractive man in the town, to such a degree that many years later Mme Delaunay, wishing to vindicate her virtue, in spite of numerous lapses, could say: 'However, I never yielded to M. Gagnon junior!'

My uncle, I say, made game of the gravity of his father, who showed great surprise at meeting him in society wearing rich clothes for which he had not paid. 'I made myself scarce,' my uncle added as he told me the story.

One evening, in spite of everybody (but who raised objections in 1790?), he took me to the theatre. They were playing *Le Cid*.

'Why, the child's crazy,' my excellent grandfather remarked when I got back; his love of literature had prevented him from objecting seriously to my visit to the theatre. So I saw *Le Cid* acted, but, I fancy, in costumes of sky-blue satin with white satin shoes.

As he recited the stanzas, or at some other point, wielding his sword with too much fervour, the Cid hurt himself near the right eye.

'He very nearly put out his eye,' people were saying round me. I was in the second box on the right, in the first tier.

Another time my uncle was kind enough to take me to the *Caravan of Cairo* (he found me rather in the way of his manoeuvres with the ladies, and I was well aware of this). I was beside myself with excitement over the camels. *The Infanta of Zamora*, in which a poltroon or a cook sang an arietta wearing a helmet with a rat for a crest, made me wild with delight. This seemed to me the height of comedy.

I said to myself, very vaguely no doubt and not as clearly as I am setting it down here: 'Every moment of my uncle's life is as delicious as these we are now enjoying together at the theatre. Surely the finest thing in the world is to be a charming fellow like my uncle.' It never entered my five-year-old head that my uncle might not be quite as happy as I was at seeing the caravan of camels file past.

THE LIFE OF HENRI BRULARD *by Stendhal*

... we had one memorable initiation at Geneva. We went to our first play. It was Labiche's *Le Voyage de Monsieur Perrichon*, that amusing parable illustrating the undeniable truth that we are less grateful to those who save us than to those we save. We had read the play with Georges, and had no trouble in following it, but we should have liked any play on that occasion, seen from those plush chairs, in that gilded and overhanging box. I have long since lost all sense of, or taste for, the glamour of Empires and Alhambras and Café Royals, which never ceased to enchant and to inspire a Degas, a Manet, or a Sickert. But on that night the curves and the curlicues, the pilasters and the cornices, and all those festive protuberances that distinguish a theatre or opera house from any other place of assembly, had their full effects upon my inexperience. The revelation of that evening, however, was for me neither the humours of M. Perrichon nor the charm of theatre-baroque. It was Gilda's bosom. For, curiously, there was a double bill for our entertainment, M. Perrichon being followed by *Rigoletto*. I had seen plenty of ladies in low dresses, including Daisy Orde; but never before had my eye been caught and held by a silky sheen, as of white satin, such as rose and fell with the breathing of this exquisite creature. Could this indeed be skin, I wondered, that shimmered and glistened so, or was it some subtle material, cunningly fitted? I had young eyes; I could not be deceived: this was indeed a woman's own skin; and I carried with me from that memorable evening a new understanding of what the heroes of our story-books may have seen in their heroines. If all Princesses and beautiful maidens had chests like Gilda's, their price in hazards and miseries may not have been too high after all. I did not discuss Gilda's chest (as I thought of it) with anybody, not even with my brother. This was not delicacy about the feminine form, but shyness, and perhaps a little slyness, about my secret possessions. For in some indefinable way I had a conviction that the tactile value (as Mr Berenson might have put it) of Gilda's chest was for me alone. I have often, in maturer years, had the same most acceptable impression of being the sole possessor of a sudden beauty, whether found in a woman, a mountain, or a William and Mary façade.

A VICTORIAN BOYHOOD *by L. E. Jones*

Boxing Day in Tientsin in the 1920s.

All winter long, from November to February, the cold winds blew from the Interior. The river and the canals and creeks froze. Everything was still. One by one, the pedlars disappeared to hide like moths in secret places, until only the tea pedlar was left at our corner. By Christmas-time even he had gone.

On Boxing Day a carnival was always held at the ice-skating rink. The first item on the programme was a fancy dress parade for children. My mother was determined that one of us should win it and she put all her imagination into designing the oddest of costumes for us. One year she decided that I was to be a Christmas tree. On the day of the carnival I had to stand in the middle of the bedroom while the elaborate process of dressing me went on. First I was sewn into a green felt garment. Then prickly fir branches were fixed on to it so that they stuck out in all directions. Lastly, tinsel, glass globes, stars and crackers were hung all over me. Barely able to see through my decorations, I was propped into a rickshaw and taken to the rink. But, by the time I had put on my skates and stepped on to the ice, we discovered that the fancy dress parade had just ended. Furious, my mother went to see the carnival committee. Fearing what she might do, and perhaps feeling a little sorry for me when they saw me under my branches, the committee came to a compromise and its chairman, Mr Peebles, made an announcement over the loudspeaker. 'Ladies and gentlemen, we are sure you will not want to miss seeing Mrs Power's son Brian in his remarkable costume. He will now skate once round the rink.'

A gramophone played the Viennese waltz 'Gold and Silver' and off I went, blushing with embarrassment and skating very slowly with my arms outstretched in case any of my decorations should drop off. The corners of the rink were the worst part and twice I nearly fell. Somehow I reached the committee box, where my proud mother was standing. Mr Peebles presented me with a consolation prize of a box of chocolates and the audience clapped. My ordeal was over for another year.

THE FORD OF HEAVEN *by Brian Power*

Charlie Chaplin's stage début.

What other facts besides drink were involved I do not know, but a year after my birth my parents separated. Mother did not seek alimony. Being a star in her own right, earning twenty-five pounds a week, she was well able to support herself and her children. Only when ill-fortune befell her did she seek relief; otherwise she would never have taken legal steps.

She had been having trouble with her voice. It was never strong, and the slightest cold brought on laryngitis which lasted for weeks; but she was obliged to keep working, so that her voice grew progressively worse. She could not rely on it. In the middle of singing it would crack or suddenly disappear into a whisper, and the audience would laugh and start booing. The worry of it impaired her health and made her a nervous wreck. As a consequence, her theatrical engagements fell off until they were practically nil.

It was owing to her vocal condition that at the age of five I made my first appearance on the stage. Mother usually brought me to the theatre at night in preference to leaving me alone in rented rooms. She was playing the Canteen at Aldershot at the time, a grubby, mean theatre catering mostly to soldiers. They were a rowdy lot and wanted little excuse to deride and ridicule. To performers, Aldershot was a week of terror.

I remember standing in the wings when Mother's voice cracked and went into a whisper. The audience began to laugh and sing falsetto and to make catcalls. It was all vague and I did not quite understand what was going on. But the noise increased until Mother was obliged to walk off the stage. When she came into the wings she was very upset and argued with the stage manager who, having seen me perform before Mother's friends, said something about letting me go on in her place.

And in the turmoil I remember him leading me by the hand and, after a few explanatory words to the audience, leaving me on the stage alone. And before a glare of footlights and faces in smoke, I started to sing, accompanied by the orchestra, which fiddled about until it found my key. It was a well-known song called 'Jack Jones' that went as follows:

Jack Jones well and known to everybody
Round about the market, don't yer see,
I've no fault to find with Jack at all,
Not when 'e's as 'e used to be.
But since 'e's had the bullion left him
'E has altered for the worst,
For to see the way he treats all his old pals
Fills me with nothing but disgust.
Each Sunday morning he reads the *Telegraph*,
Once he was contented with the *Star*.
Since Jack Jones has come into a little bit of cash,
Well, 'e don't know where 'e are.

Half-way through, a shower of money poured on to the stage. Immediately I stopped and announced that I would pick up the money first and sing afterwards. This caused much laughter. The stage manager came on with a handkerchief and helped me to gather it up. I thought he was going to keep it. This thought was conveyed to the audience and increased their laughter, especially when he walked off with it and me anxiously following him. Not until he handed it to Mother did I return and continue to sing. I was quite at home. I talked to the audience, danced, and did several imitations including one of Mother singing her Irish march song that went as follows:

Riley, Riley, that's the boy to beguile ye,
Riley, Riley, that's the boy for me.
In all the Army great and small,
There's none so trim and neat
As the noble Sergeant Riley
Of the gallant Eighty-eight.

And in repeating the chorus, in all innocence I imitated Mother's voice cracking and was surprised at the impact it had on the audience. There was laughter and cheers, then more money-throwing; and when Mother came on the stage to carry me off, her presence evoked tremendous applause. That night was my first appearance on the stage and Mother's last.

MY AUTOBIOGRAPHY *by Charlie Chaplin (1889–1977)*

The Wedding

The Abbey was indeed thronged next day when Ethel and Bernard cantered up in a very fine carrage drawn by two prancing steeds who foamed a good deal. In the porch stood several clean altar boys who conducted the lucky pair up the aile while the organ pealed a merry blast. The mighty edifice was packed and seated in the front row was the Earl of Clincham looking very brisk as he was going to give Ethel away at the correct moment. Beside him sat Mr Salteena all in black and looking bitterly sad and he ground his teeth as Ethel came marching up. There were some merry hymns and as soon as Ethel and Bernard were one the clergyman began a sermon about Adam and Eve and the serpent and Mr Salteena cried into his large handkerchief and the earl kept on nudging him as his sniffs were rarther loud. Then the wedding march pealed fourth and doun the church stepped Ethel and Bernard as husband and wife. Into the cab they got and speedelly dashed off to the Gaierty. The wedding refreshments were indeed a treat to all and even Mr Salteena cheered up when he beheld the wedding cake and sparkling wines. Then the earl got up and made a very fine speech about marrage vows and bliss and he quoted several good bits from the bible which got a lot of applause. Bernard replied in good round terms. I thank your lordship for those kind remarks he said in clear tones I expect we shall be as happy as a lark and I hope you will all be ditto some day. Here Here muttered a stray lady in the crowd and down sat Bernard while Ethel went up to change her wedding garment for a choice pink velvit dress with a golden gurdle and a very chick tocque. Bernard also put on a new suit of blue stripe and some silk socks and clean under clothing. Hurah hurah shouted the guests as the pair reappeard in the aforesaid get ups. Then everybody got a bag of rice and sprinkled on the pair and Mr Salteena sadly threw a white tennis shoe at them wiping his eyes the while. Off drove the happy pair and the guests finished up the food. The happy pair went to Egypt for there Honymoon as they thought it would be a nice warm spot and they had never seen the wondrous land. Ethel was a bit sick on the boat but Bernard braved the storm in manly style. However Ethel had recovered by the time they got to Egypt and here we will leave them for a merry six weeks of bliss while we return to England.   THE YOUNG VISITERS *by Daisy Ashford*

19

FATHERS

No man can tell but he that loves his children how many delicious accents make a man's heart dance in the pretty conversation of these dear pledges: their childishness, their stammering, their little angers, their innocence, their imperfections, their necessities, are so many emanations of joy and comfort to him that delights in their persons and society; but he that loves not his wife and children feeds a lioness at home, and broods a nest of sorrows.

XXV SERMONS *by Jeremy Taylor (1613–67)*

Sir Thomas More (1478–1535) addressed the following lines 'To His Sweetest Children' (Margaret, Elizabeth, Cecilia and John).

I have given you, forsooth, kisses in plenty and but few stripes. If ever I have flogged you 'twas but with a peacock's tail.

An early lesson for the great Renaissance goldsmith and sculptor Benvenuto Cellini (1500–71).

The child was born during the night after All Saints' Day, at exactly half past four, in the year 1500. The midwife knew that they were expecting a girl and as soon as she had washed the baby she wrapped it up in some fine white linen and then came up very, very softly to my father and said: 'I've brought you a wonderful present – and one you didn't expect.'

My father was a true philosopher; he had been pacing the room and when the midwife came to him he said: 'Whatever God gives is dear to me.' Then, drawing back the swaddling clothes, he saw with his own eyes the son that no one had expected. He clasped his old hands together, and with them lifted his eyes up to heaven, and said: 'Lord, I thank You with all my heart. This is a great gift, and he is very welcome.'

Everyone there began talking happily and asking him what he was going to call the boy. But Giovanni kept on repeating: 'He is Welcome (Benvenuto).' So that was the name they decided on. I was baptized with it, and by the grace of God I carry it to this day.

When I was already about three years old my grandfather Andrea was still alive and over a hundred. One day they were changing a cistern pipe when a large scorpion which they had not noticed crawled out of it, slipped to the ground, and scuttled away under a bench. I caught sight of it, ran over, and picked the thing up. It was so big that when I had it in my little hand its tail hung out at one end and both its claws at the other. They say that laughing happily I ran up to my grandfather and said: 'Look, grandpapa, look at my lovely little crab.' He recognized what it was and almost dropped dead from shock and anxiety. Then he tried to coax me into giving it to him, but the more he did so the more I screamed tearfully, refusing to give it to anyone.

My father was also in the house and, hearing the noise, he ran in to see what it was all about. He was so terror-stricken that his mind refused to work and he could not think up any way of stopping the poisonous creature from killing me. Then his eyes fell on a pair of scissors and he managed to wheedle me into letting him snip off the scorpion's tail and claws. When the danger was past he regarded it as a good omen.

Another time, when I was about five, my father was sitting alone in one of our small rooms, singing and playing his viol. Some washing had just been done there and a good log fire was still burning. It was very cold, and he had drawn near the fire. Then, as he was looking at the flames, his eye fell on a little animal, like a lizard, that was running around merrily in the very hottest part of the fire. Suddenly realizing what it was, he called my sister and myself and showed it to us. And then he gave me such a violent box on the ears that I screamed and burst into tears. At this he calmed me as kindly as he could and said: 'My dear little boy, I didn't hit you because you had done wrong. I only did it so that you will never forget that the lizard you saw in the fire is a salamander, and as far as we know for certain no one has ever seen one before.'

Then he kissed me and gave me a little money.

THE AUTOBIOGRAPHY OF BENVENUTO CELLINI

On the Birth of His Son

Families, when a child is born
Want it to be intelligent.
I, through intelligence,
Having wrecked my whole life,
Only hope the baby will prove
Ignorant and stupid.
Then he will crown a tranquil life
By becoming a Cabinet Minister.

Su Tung-p'o (1036–1101)

Extracts from the Notebooks of Samuel Taylor Coleridge (1772–1834). His son Hartley was born in 1796.

1797–1798

– Hartley fell down & hurt himself – I caught him up crying & screaming – & ran out of doors with him. – The Moon caught his eye – he ceased crying immediately – & his eyes & the tears in them, how they glittered in the Moonlight!

Children in the wind – hair floating, tossing, a miniature of the agitated Trees, below which they play'd – the elder whirling for joy, the one in petticoats, a fat Baby, eddying half willingly, half by the force of the Gust – driven backward, struggling forward – both drunk with the pleasure, both shouting their hymn of Joy....

1799–1801

Sunday – Dec. 21, 1799, Hartley said – When I'm a man, I'll get a Ladder, & get up to the Sky, & pick out the Stars, & give them to Anny Sealy – I'll pick 'em out with a knife –

March 17, 1801. Tuesday – Hartley looking out of my study window fixed his eyes steadily & for some time on the opposite prospect, & then said – Will yon Mountains *always* be? – I shewed him the whole magnificent Prospect in a Looking Glass, and held it up, so that the whole was like a Canopy or Ceiling over his head, & he struggled to express himself concerning the Difference between the Thing & the Image almost with convulsive Effort. . . .

Sunday, November 1. 1801. Hartley breeched – dancing to the jingling of the money – but eager & solemn Joy, not his usual whirl-about gladness – but solemn to & fro eager looks, as befitted the importance of the aera.

To My Son

Three thinges there bee that prosper up apace
And flourish, whilest they growe a sunder farr,
But on a day, they meet all in one place,
And when they meet, they one an other marr;
And they bee theise, the wood, the weede, the wagg.
The wood is that, which makes the Gallow tree,
The weed is that, which stringes the Hangmans bagg,
The wagg my pritty knave betokeneth thee.
Harke well deare boy whilest theise assemble not,
Green springs the tree, hempe growes, the wagg is wilde,
But when they meet, it makes the timber rott,
It fretts the halter, and it choakes the childe.
    Then bless thee, and beware, and let us praye,
    Wee part not with thee at this meeting day.

Sir Walter Raleigh (?1552–1618)

Gosse's father was an eminent marine zoologist and also a fanatical fundamentalist Christian: an uneasy mixture in the era of Darwinism. Left an early widower, he brought up the young Edmund in the extraordinary atmosphere of the mid-nineteenth-century Plymouth Brethren.

I slept in a little bed in a corner of the room, and my Father in the ancestral four-poster nearer to the door. Very early one bright September morning at the close of my eleventh year, my Father called me over to him. I climbed up, and was snugly wrapped in the coverlid; and then we held a momentous conversation. It began abruptly by his asking me whether I should like to have a new mamma. I was never a sentimentalist, and I therefore answered, cannily, that that would depend on who she was. He parried this, and announced that, anyway, a new mamma was coming; I was sure to like her. Still in a non-committal mood, I asked: 'Will she go with me to the back of the lime-kiln?' This question caused my Father a great bewilderment. I had to explain that the ambition of my life was to go up behind the lime-kiln on the top of the hill that hung over Barton, a spot which was forbidden ground, being locally held one of extreme danger. 'Oh! I daresay she will,' my Father then said, 'but you must guess who she is.' I guessed one or two of the less comely of the female 'saints', and, this embarrassing my Father – since the second I mentioned was a married woman who kept a sweet-shop in the village – he cut my inquiries short by saying, 'It is Miss Brightwen.'

So far so good, and I was well pleased. But unfortunately I remembered that it was my duty to testify 'in season and out of season'. I therefore asked, with much earnestness, 'But, Papa, is she one of the Lord's children?' He replied, with gravity, that she was. 'Has she taken up her cross in baptism?' I went on, for this was my own strong point as a believer. My Father looked a little shame-faced, and replied: 'Well, she has not as yet seen the necessity of that, but we must pray that the Lord may make her way clear before her. You see, she has been brought up, hitherto, in the so-called Church of England.'

Our positions were now curiously changed. It seemed as if it were I who was the jealous monitor, and my Father the deprecating penitent. I sat up in the coverlid, and I shook a finger at him. 'Papa,' I said, 'don't tell me that she's a pedobaptist?' I had lately acquired that valuable word, and I seized this remarkable opportunity of using it. It affected my Father painfully, but he repeated his assurance that if we united our prayers, and set the Scripture plan plainly before Miss Brightwen, there could be no doubt that she would see her way to accepting the doctrine of adult baptism. And he said we must judge not, lest we ourselves be judged. I had just enough tact to let that pass, but I was quite aware that our whole system was one of judging, and that we had no intention whatever of being judged ourselves. Yet even at the age of eleven one sees that on certain occasions to press home the truth is not convenient.   FATHER AND SON *by Edmund Gosse*

Thomas wrote these poems in 1916 for his daughters Bronwen and her younger sister Baba, then aged five. The next year he was killed at the Battle of Arras.

> If I should ever by chance grow rich
> I'll buy Codham, Cockridden, and Childerditch,
> Roses, Pyrgo, and Lapwater,
> And let them all to my elder daughter.
> The rent I shall ask of her will be only
> Each year's first violets, white and lonely,
> The first primroses and orchises –
> She must find them before I do, that is.
> But if she finds a blossom on furze –
> Without rent they shall all for ever be hers,
> Codham, Cockridden, and Childerditch,
> Roses, Pyrgo and Lapwater, –
> I shall give them all to my elder daughter.

> What shall I give my daughter the younger
> More than will keep her from cold and hunger?
> I shall not give her anything.
> If she shared South Weald and Havering,
> Their acres, the two brooks running between,
> Paine's Brook and Weald Brook,
> With peewit, woodpecker, swan, and rook,
> She would be no richer than the queen
> Who once on a time sat in Havering Bower

Alone, with the shadows, pleasure and power.
She could do no more with Samarcand,
Or the mountains of a mountain land
And its far white house above cottages
Like Venus above the Pleiades.
Her small hands I would not cumber
With so many acres and their lumber,
But leave her Steep and her own world
And her spectacled self with hair uncurled,
Wanting a thousand little things
That time without contentment brings.

Edward Thomas (1878–1917)

So that we should get a taste for good books, my sister Eleanor
and I used to go every evening into my father's study to be read
aloud to. He was a practising architect, and it was full of such
voluptuous objects as creamy tracing-paper, coloured inks and
fine pens. The monotony of Scott or Dickens was relieved by each
of us being given a fat six-sided pencil, one red, one blue, and
paper to draw on, and my father used suddenly to interrupt his
reading and yell out, 'Change!' when red must be at once swapped
for blue. This odd sort of musical chairs and typically Victorian
compromise tended to blot out the book itself, and only now and
again did scenes from *Ivanhoe* or *Vanity Fair* float into consciousness, what followed being usually lost in the effort of illustrating them in red or blue. Sometimes my ear would be caught by
a love passage, which embarrassed me greatly. I didn't much mind
them myself, but I felt my father ought to.

MEMORIES *by Frances Partridge*

My father [Charles Darwin] was undoubtedly a slave though he
tried hard not to be, and now and again boasted in his letters of
having resolutely had a battle royal with me and won it. There is
something dreadfully pathetic in the picture given in these letters,
at which I try to look quite objectively, of the young father (he was
twenty-eight when my mother died) heartbroken by the blow,

from which in a sense I doubt if he ever recovered, picking up the pieces of his life again and clinging desperately to the child that was left to him. When I was about two and he was away working in a laboratory at Wurtzburg, he writes to Nain: 'My old German master is always giving me sentences to translate which makes my blood run cold, such as "When I came to my house, I found my son very ill." ' Another time he wrote, 'I think I should be helpless with fear if he was ill.' . . . He was a naturally amusing draughtsman as he was later a natural writer of amusing verse in any kind of poetry game. He could invent fascinating and terrific names for villains who lived in the passage. He was prepared to make sheaths for swords and to give endless rides on his shoulders up and down the passage, where the villains, especially one called Humpletog, were likely to spring out from round a shadowy corner. Here is a characteristic picture of him in a letter written when I was a little over three. 'B. was very pathetic about the old man of Aôsta in the Nonsense Book, "He had a fine cow but he lost her" and she is discovered up a tree. I entered into the grief of the old man too vividly, and I saw the tears come into his eyes; but he made me tell it again, and when I tried it in a cheerfuller manner, he said, "Say about when he cried." I could see he was nearly crying, so I said, "I don't think I had better tell you about it if it makes you cry" on which he burst into tears and said, "*Why* did she go up a tree?" I consoled him by the cow finding a most beautiful bird's nest.'

THE WORLD THAT FRED MADE *by Bernard Darwin (1876–1961)*

Darwin inherited his father's talent for light verse, and wrote the inimitable Tale of Mr Tootleoo. *Below is the rhyme by Edward Lear that he found so upsetting.*

There was an Old Man of Aôsta,
Who possessed a large Cow, but he lost her;
But they said, 'Don't you see, she has rushed up a tree?
You invidious Old Man of Aôsta!'

Baby Asleep After Pain

As a drenched, drowned bee
Hangs numb and heavy from a bending flower,
    So clings to me
My baby, her brown hair brushed with wet tears
    And laid against her cheek;
Her soft white legs hanging heavily over my arm
    Swing to my walking movement, weak
With after-pain. My sleeping baby hangs upon my life
    Like a burden she hangs on me;
She who had always seemed so light,
    Now wet with tears and pain hangs heavily,
    Even her floating hair sinks heavily
        Reaching downwards;
As the wings of a drenched, drowned bee
    Are a heaviness, and a weariness.

D. H. Lawrence (1885–1930)

'There's a snake!' I would cry.

'What, another?' my mother would shout.

And she would come running out to see what sort of a snake it was. If it was just a snake like any other snake – actually, they were all quite different! – she would beat it to death at once; and, like all the women of our country, she would work herself up into a frenzy, beating the snake to a pulp, whereas the men would content themselves with a single hard blow, neatly struck.

One day, however, I noticed a little black snake with a strikingly marked body that was proceeding leisurely in the direction of the workshop. I ran to warn my mother, as usual. But as soon as my mother saw the black snake she said to me gravely:

'My son, this one must not be killed: he is not as other snakes, and he will not harm you; you must never interfere with him.'

Everyone in our concession knew that this snake must not be killed; excepting myself, and, I suppose, my little playmates, who were still just ignorant children.

'This snake,' my mother added, 'is your father's guiding spirit.'

I gazed dumbfounded at the little snake. He was proceeding calmly towards the workshop; he was moving gracefully, very sure of himself, and almost as if conscious of his immunity; his body, black and brilliant, glittered in the harsh light of the sun. When he reached the workshop, I noticed for the first time, cut out level with the ground, a small hole in the wall. The snake disappeared through this hole.

'Look,' said my mother, 'the serpent is going to pay your father a visit.'

Although I was familiar with the supernatural, this sight filled me with such astonishment that I was struck dumb. What business would a snake have with my father? And why this particular snake? No one had to kill him, because he was my father's guiding spirit! At any rate, that was the explanation my mother had given me. But what exactly *was* a 'guiding spirit'? What were these guiding spirits that I encountered almost everywhere, forbidding one thing, commanding another to be done? I could not understand it at all, though their presences were around me as I grew to manhood. There were good spirits, and there were evil ones; and more evil than good ones, it seemed to me. And how was I to know that this snake was harmless? It looked the same as any other snake; it was, of course, a *black* snake, and certainly there was something unusual about it; but after all, it *was* only a snake! I was absolutely baffled, but I did not ask my mother about it: I felt I would have to ask my father himself about it, almost as if this mystery was something in which women could have no part; it was a mysterious affair that could only be discussed with men. I decided to wait until nightfall.

Immediately after the evening meal, when the palavers were over, my father bade his friends farewell and went to sit under the veranda of his hut; I went and sat near him. I began by questioning him in a roundabout manner, as all children do, and on every subject under the sun. Finally, unable to restrain myself any longer, I asked:

'My father, what is that little snake that comes to visit you?'

'What snake do you mean?'

'Why, the little black snake that my mother forbids us to kill.'

'Ah!' he said.

He gazed at me for a long while. He seemed to be considering whether to answer or not. Perhaps he was thinking about how old I was, perhaps he was wondering if it was not a little too soon to confide such a secret to a twelve-year-old boy. Then suddenly he made up his mind.

'That snake,' he said, 'is the guiding spirit of our race. Can you understand that?'

'Yes,' I answered, although I did not understand very well.

'That snake,' he went on, 'has always been with us; he has always made himself known to one of us. In our time, it is to me that he has made himself known.'

'That is true,' I said.

And I said it with all my heart, for it seemed obvious to me that the snake could have made himself known to no one but my father. Was not my father the head man in our concession? Was it not my father who had authority over all the blacksmiths in our district? Was he not the most skilled? Was he not, after all, my father? THE DARK CHILD *by Camara Laye*

Morning Glory

My father would begin each day
By standing in the backyard door
And giving one tremendous sneeze,
Mid-way between a gasp and roar:

Would clap a fist before hs eyes,
And give a kind of stamping dance,
As if his spirit wept and sang
To hear such goodly resonance.

And even now I can remember
His gaiters, and the scads of mire
He kicked before him, as this greeting
Sprang from his nostrils like a fire.

And cocks in every neighbouring yard
Would lift their heads, and strut and stir,
Sensing the challenge of some odd,
Irate and twanging chanticlere.

Michell Raper

Kenneth Grahame's (1859–1932) son Alistair refused to go to the seaside and miss hearing some of the adventures of Toad – his current bedtime stories – until his father promised to write him bulletins instead. Here are two such letters, later to be expanded into The Wind in the Willows.

10 May 1907

My Darling Mouse,

Have you heard about the Toad? He was never taken prisoner by brigands at all. It was all a horrid low trick of his. He wrote that letter himself – the letter saying that a hundred pounds must be put in the hollow tree. And he got out of the window early one morning, & went off to a town called Buggleton, & went to the Red Lion Hotel & there he found a party that had just motored down from London, & while they were having breakfast he went into the stable-yard & found their motor-car & went off in it without even saying Poop-poop! And now he has vanished & everyone is looking for him, including the police. I fear he is a bad low animal.

Goodbye, from
Your loving Daddy

23 May 1907

My Dearest Mouse,

No doubt you have met some of the animals & have heard about Toad's Adventures since he was dragged off to prison by the bobby & the constable. At first he lay full length on the floor, and shed bitter tears, and abandoned himself to dark despair. For he said 'How can I ever hope to be set free again, I who have been imprisoned – and justly – so often, for stealing so many – so many —— he could not utter the word, for his sobs choked him. Base

animal that I am (he said): O unhappy and ~~abandoned~~ [forsaken]
toad (he said); I must languish in this dungeon (he said) till people
have forgotten the very name of Mr Toad. With lamentations
such as these he passed his days & nights, refusing consolation,
refusing food or other light refreshments: till one day the gaoler's
daughter, who was a tender-hearted young woman, took pity on
him & said 'Cheer up toad! & try & eat a bit of dinner.' But the
toad lay on the floor & wailed & wouldn't eat his dinner. Then
the gaoler's daughter went & fetched a cup of hot tea & some very
hot buttered toast, cut thick, very brown on both sides, with the
butter running through the holes in it in great golden drops like
honey. When the toad smelt the buttered toast he sat up & dried
his eyes for he was exceedingly fond of buttered toast; & the
gaoler's daughter comforted him & he drank his tea & had
another plate of toast. Then they discussed plans for his escape
from the dungeon, & the gaoler's daughter said 'Tomorrow my
aunt, who is the washerwoman to the prison, will bring home
your week's washing, & I will dress you up in her clothes & you
will escape as the washerwoman.' So when the washerwoman
came with the linen, they dressed toad up in her clothes & put a
bonnet on his head & out he marched, past the gaolers, as bold as
you please. As he was passing one of them, the man said 'Hullo
mother washerwoman, why didn't you send home my Sunday
shirt last week, you lazy old pig?' & he took his stick & beat her
full sore. And the toad was mad with rage, because he wanted to
give him a punch in the eye, but he controlled himself & ran on
through the door, which banged behind him & he was *Free*. This
is as far as I have heard at present.

Your affectionate Daddy

The old and the new, the liberal touch and the patriarchal one,
fatal poverty and fatalistic wealth got fantastically interwoven in
that strange first decade of our century. Several times during a
summer it might happen that in the middle of luncheon, in the
bright, many-widowed, walnut-panelled dining-room on the first
floor of our Vyra manor, Aleksey, the butler, with an unhappy

expression on his face, would bend over and inform my father in a
low voice (especially low if we had company) that a group of
villagers wanted to see the *barin* outside. Briskly my father would
remove his napkin from his lap and ask my mother to excuse him.
One of the windows at the west end of the dining-room gave upon
a portion of the drive near the main entrance. One could see the
top of the honeysuckle bushes opposite the porch. From that
direction the courteous buzz of a peasant welcome would reach us
as the invisible group greeted my invisible father. The ensuing
parley, conducted in ordinary tones, would not be heard, as the
windows underneath which it took place were closed to keep out
the heat. It presumably had to do with a plea for his mediation in
some local feud, or with some special subsidy, or with the permission to harvest some bit of our land or cut down a coveted clump
of our trees. If, as usually happened, the request was at once
granted, there would be again that buzz, and then, in token of
gratitude, the good *barin* would be put through the national
ordeal of being rocked and tossed up and securely caught by a
score or so of strong arms.

In the dining-room, my brother and I would be told to go on
with our food. My mother, a tidbit between finger and thumb,
would glance under the table to see if her nervous and gruff
dachshund was there. '*Un jour ils vont le laisser tomber*,' would
come from Mlle Golay, a primly pessimistic old lady who had
been my mother's governess and still dwelt with us (on awful
terms with our own governesses). From my place at table I would
suddenly see through one of the west windows a marvellous case
of levitation. There, for an instant, the figure of my father in his
wind-rippled white summer suit would be displayed, gloriously
sprawling in mid-air, his limbs in a curiously casual attitude, his
handsome, imperturbable features turned to the sky. Thrice, to
the mighty heave-ho of his invisible tossers, he would fly up in this
fashion, and the second time he would go higher than the first and
then there he would be, on his last and loftiest flight, reclining, as
if for good, against the cobalt blue of the summer noon, like one of
those paradisiac personages who comfortably soar, with such a
wealth of folds in their garments, on the vaulted ceiling of a
church while below, one by one, the wax tapers in mortal hands

light up to make a swarm of minute flames in the mist of incense, and the priest chants of eternal repose, and funeral lilies conceal the face of whoever lies there, among the swimming lights, in the open coffin.

SPEAK, MEMORY by Vladimir Nabokov

As a child I was slow as my sister was quick of apprehension. And in each of us this was wrong. She should have been slow, being a girl – dedicated, as girls of her class then were, first to a life of Infanta-like seclusion and then to marriage. On the other hand my childish difficulty in pronouncing certain consonants was regarded as downright original sin.

The development of my character for which my father was looking was not the only trouble that existed between us. There was, for example, my misunderstanding of the nature of humour. ... We were in the middle of one of the great practical-joke epochs (it must have been about '97, when I was four years old). One morning I went with my father into the dining-room before luncheon. He was expecting as a guest at this forthcoming meal a supporter of his in politics, an alderman, mighty in stature, a very heavy man, and he now placed ready for him at the table a Chippendale chair, the seat of which collapsed when you sat down on it. As a matter of fact, over this particular incident my sense of humour at that time coincided entirely with my father's. I remember thinking it an extraordinarily funny joke. And so, after he had left the room, I changed this chair – with tremendous labour, for I was very small at that time – with his own, and then hid under the table to watch the effect. ... My father sat down, rather slowly, waiting for the alderman's collapse, and then fell through his own chair with an expression of intense amazement and consternation, while my merry laughter rang out from under the table. He was not in the least amused, but got up, very red in the face, remarking at the same time, 'I might have most seriously injured my back.' My laughter soon changed to tears and it was some time before I was forgiven. All the same, I had meant no harm.

LEFT HAND RIGHT HAND! by Osbert Sitwell

Children

My niece, who is six years old, is called 'Miss Tortoise';
My daughter of three, – little 'Summer Dress'.
One is beginning to learn to joke and talk;
The other can already recite poems and songs.
At morning they play clinging about my feet;
At night they sleep pillowed against my dress.
Why, children, did you reach the world so late,
Coming to me just when my years are spent?
Young things draw our feelings to them;
Old people easily give their hearts.
The sweetest vintage at last turns sour;
The full moon in the end begins to wane.
And so with men the bonds of love and affection
Soon may change to a load of sorrow and care.
But all the world is bound by love's ties;
Why did I think that I alone should escape?

Po Chü-i (772–846)

Pooh Bear – a mixed blessing.

I am often asked if I can remember when the stories were first read to me. Who read them? And where? And what did I think of them? Oddly, I can remember virtually nothing. One incident only survives.

My mother and I were in the drawing-room at Cotchford. The door opened and my father came in. 'Have you finished it?' 'I have.' 'May we hear it?' My father settled himself in his chair. 'Well', he said, 'we've had a story about the snow and one about the rain, and one about the mist. So I thought we ought to have one about the wind. And here it is.

'It's called:

'IN WHICH PIGLET DOES A VERY GRAND THING

'Half way between Pooh's house and Piglet's house was a Thoughtful Spot. . . .'

My mother and I, side by side on the sofa, settled ourselves comfortably, happily, excitedly to listen.

THE ENCHANTED PLACES *by Christopher Robin Milne (1920–   )*

The animals in the stories came for the most part from the nursery. My collaborator [his wife] had already given them individual voices, their owner [Christopher Robin] by constant affection had given them the twist in their features which denoted character, and Shepard drew them, as one might say, from the living model. They were what they are for anyone to see; I described rather than invented them. Only Rabbit and Owl were my own unaided work.

IT'S TOO LATE NOW *by A. A. Milne (1882–1956)*

If the Pooh books had been like most other books – published one year, forgotten the next – there would have been no problem. If I had been a different sort of person there might well have been no problem. Unfortunately the fictional Christopher Robin refused to die and he and his real-life namesake were not always on the best of terms. For the first misfortune (as it sometimes seemed) my father was to blame. The second was my fault. . . .

It was a problem caused by my shyness. I have already said that this was Grandfather Milne's responsibility rather than my father's: that I would have been plagued by shyness anyway, Christopher Robin or no. Nevertheless, Christopher Robin undoubtedly made things worse, though perhaps less so than might have been supposed. His appearances at school were few. Mostly we were occupied with other things, other anxieties, other delights. Fridays, for instance, were clouded by the thought of Latin, Latin, Maths, Soup, Fish, Biscuits, P.T., History, French. If I fussed over the Fish and dreaded the History this had nothing to do with a boy and his bear. Nevertheless, Christopher Robin was beginning to be what he was later to become, a sore place that looked as if it would never heal up. To begin with it was only sometimes sore; at other times it was quite the reverse. It would depend, of course, on the intentions of the person who raised the subject. If he intended to hurt, he could do so quite easily, for I was very vulnerable. I vividly recall how intensely painful it was to me to sit in my study at Stowe while my neighbours played the famous – and now cursed – gramophone record remorselessly over and over again. Eventually, the joke, if not the record, worn out, they handed it to me, and I took it and broke it into a hundred fragments and scattered them over a distant field. But mostly I had other things to think about and didn't bother about being Christopher Robin one way or the other. And because I spent so much time at school not bothering and the entire holidays not bothering, it never occurred to me that perhaps I ought to be blaming somebody for it all. In fact I blamed nobody. I felt no resentment. My relations with my father were quite unaffected.

THE ENCHANTED PLACES *by Christopher Milne*

In the context of Christopher Milne's somewhat ambivalent attitude to his alter ego, the tailpiece below reads more like a life sentence than an everlasting idyll.

So they went off together. But wherever they
go, and whatever happens to them on the way, in
that enchanted place on the top of the Forest a
little boy and his Bear will always be playing.

THE HOUSE AT POOH CORNER *by A. A. Milne*

20

TROUBLES

Peter Quennell, in The Marble Foot, *describes a moment of 'devastating gloom' experienced during a seaside holiday.*

I was not alone; it was caused, not by the absence of human companionship, but by the presence of my father. I was playing beside a pool at the edge of the sea, when he walked up and suggested that we should together build a fleet. In his pocket he carried some walnut-shells and a piece of sealing-wax, with which he began fixing match-sticks to the shells by way of masts. His kindness disturbed me. I became aware that there was something subtly, indefinably wrong about his well-meant zeal and patience; and that our respective attitudes — mine, trying to look more pleased than, alas, I really felt; his, exhibiting an enthusiasm that, I suspected, was probably half-assumed — put us both into a false position. I was embarrassed on his behalf. Why should a large grown-up person — his grown-upness emphasized by the slightly feral odour of a massive adult body — have troubled to join me in my lilliputian games? I feared, too, that he might notice my lack of interest; and with these fears, as I watched him hard at work, was presently mingled a secret sense of pity — for the colossus who had deliberately humbled himself in his futile efforts to amuse a child. The 'certain want and horror', of which Traherne speaks, gradually invaded my imagination, and drew a veil across the sky. Even the clear pool, where he was launching his nutshell craft, became a sad and slimy puddle.

Children suffer almost as much as adults from boredom, gloom and malaise; but they are particularly susceptible, I think, to the pangs of disappointment. With them 'looking forward' is still a favourite pursuit; they build up an imaginative picture of the experiences that lie ahead — how they will behave on such-and-such an occasion, and enjoy the treats they have been promised. Should reality fall short of the vision, even in the smallest detail,

305

romantic hopes may turn to grief and rage. Thus, again at the seaside, I observed the grown-ups shaping a heap of sand into something that I took to be a lion. My excitement grew; but, once they had modelled its paws and flanks, they proceeded to add a monstrous human head, flattened, lowering and repulsive. Here, they told me, was an ancient Egyptian sphinx. I had never seen a sphinx before; and I regarded it as merely the King of Beasts irremediably spoiled and degraded. I shed bitter tears; and, though I was afterwards persuaded to have my photograph taken glumly straddling the creature's spine, I was not sorry, next day, when I saw that the tide had obliterated it overnight.

Here is the Traherne passage referred to by Quennell, from Centuries of Meditations.

Another time, in a lowering and sad evening, being alone in the field, when all things were dead and quiet, a certain want and horror fell upon me, beyond imagination. The unprofitableness and silence of the place dissatisfied me; its wildness terrified me; from the utmost ends of the earth fears surrounded me. How did I know but dangers might suddenly arise from the East, and invade me from the unknown regions beyond the seas? I was a weak and little child and had forgotten there was a man alive in the earth.

My mother takes me, in the victoria, to somebody's birthday party at Cookham. (Why only me? But so it is.) On the sunny lawn are assembled about two dozen little girls and boys whom I have never seen before. We are lined up, given wooden spoons with plaster eggs in them. Ready, steady, GO! 'Run, run, don't drop, pick up your egg, run, steady now, well done Eric, Eric's won, who's next? Norah, well done Norah. ... Brenda third. ... Who comes in last, eggless, and in tears? 'Bad luck Rosie, never mind dear. ...' Where is my mother? Vanished indoors. What is this abomination of desolation called SPORTS?

The cruel children fly all over the lawn, casual and sharp as birds. They compete and compete, as if competing was the height of fun. They jump over obstacles and crawl under them and climb

up and down them; they tie their inside legs together with handkerchiefs and run in couples. I conceal myself appropriately
beneath a weeping willow and watch, despairing, from a distance.
A kind lady comes to coax me out: I will not come.

My state is such that when my mother comes at last with an
unpleased face to lead me to the tea-table she murmurs: 'Take no
notice of her'; and nobody does. Not one of those cheerful girls
and boys takes the slightest notice of the hiccuping sodden object
in their midst.

Now comes prize giving. Prizes, prizes, prizes, every sort and
kind, are displayed upon a trestle table on the lawn. At once my
eye is caught by a small round-bodied scent bottle, green glass
overlaid with silver fretwork, and with a lovely stopper like an
emerald jujube. It looks a bit lost among the other prizes, as if it
had been taken off somebody's dressing-table at the last moment,
just in case of a miscalculation. I covet it unspeakably. Every boy
or girl who has won a race is called up in turn to choose a prize.
Next, the also rans – not to choose, but to be given something.
Nobody will go home empty-handed. The table is getting barer.
The scent bottle remains.

'Oh, Rosie!' Our hostess looks at me dubiously, then at the
table, stripped of every single object except – 'You must have a
consolation prize. What about this little scent bottle?'

The joy is piercing. How can it be that this treasure has fallen
into no other hands but mine? How is it that, at the last moment, I
have become the luckiest girl at the party?

On the drive home, I remark happily:

'It's just exactly the one thing I wanted!'

'You didn't deserve it,' replied my mother, justly pointing to the
frightful abyss between my merits and my expectations. I clasp my
consolation prize, but it feels cold now, tarnished. No question of
it: I hold between my palms extravagant dishonour and reward.

THE SWAN IN THE EVENING *by Rosamond Lehmann*

Nov. 28. – Counting to the 19th, and not counting the day of
breaking up, it is now only three weeks to the holidays. I will give

you a history of getting home. From Lewes I shall look out for the castle and the Visitation church. Then I shall pass Ringmer, the Green Man Inn, Laughton, the Bat and Ball; then the Dicker, Horsebridge, the Workhouse, the turnpike, the turn to Carter's Corner, the turn to Magham Down, Woodham's Farm, the Deaf and Dumb House, the Rectory on the hill, the Mile Post – '15 miles to Lewes', Lime Wood, the gate (oh! when shall I be there!) – then turn in, the Flower Field, the Beaney Field, *the* gate – oh! the garden – two figures – John and Lea, perhaps you – perhaps even the kittens will come to welcome their master. Oh my Lime! in little more than three weeks I shall be there!

Hurrah for Dec. 1. – On Wednesday it will be, not counting breaking-up day, two weeks, and oh! the Wednesday after we shall say 'one week'. This month we break up! I dream of nothing, think of nothing, but coming home. Today we went with Mr Walker (the usher) to Chippenham, and saw where Lea and I used to go to sit on the wooden bridge. ... Not many more letters! not many more sums!

How vividly, how acutely, I recollect that – in my passionate devotion to my mother – I used, as the holidays approached, to conjure up the most vivid mental pictures of my return to her, and appease my longing with the thought of how she would rush out to meet me, of her ecstatic delight, etc.; and then how terrible was the bathos of the reality, when I drove up to the silent door of Lime, and nobody but Lea took any notice of my coming; and of the awful chill of going into the drawing-room and seeing my longed-for and pined-for mother sit still in her chair by the fire till I went up and kissed her. To her, who had been taught always to curtsey not only to her father, but even to her father's chair, it was only natural; but I often sobbed myself to sleep in a little-understood agony of anguish – an anguish that she could not really care for me.

THE STORY OF MY LIFE *by Augustus Hare*

Child of Delight! with sun-bright hair
And seablue seadeep eyes;
Spirit of Bliss, what brings thee here
Beneath these sullen skies?

Thou shouldest live in eternal spring
Where endless day is never dim;
Why, seraph, has thy erring wing
Borne thee down to weep with him?

'Ah! not from heaven am I descended
And I do not come to mingle tears,
But sweet is day though with shadows blended
And, though clouded, sweet are youthful years.

'I, the image of light and gladness,
Saw and pitied that mournful boy
And I swore to take his gloomy sadness
And give to him my beamy joy.

'Heavy and dark the night is closing
Heavy and dark may its biding be;
Better for all from grief reposing,
And better for all who watch like me.

'Guardian angel he lacks no longer;
Evil fortune he need not fear:
Fate is strong, but Love is stronger
And more unsleeping than angel's care.'

Emily Brontë

A fragment of autobiography from Roger Fry (1866–1934).

This garden . . . is still for me the imagined background for almost
any garden scene that I read of in books. The serpent still bends
down to Eve from the fork of a peculiarly withered and soot
begrimed old apple tree which stuck out of the lawn. And various
other scenes of seduction seem to me to have taken place within its
modest suburban precincts. But it was also the scene of two great
emotional experiences, my first passion and my first great disillu-
sion. My first passion was for a bushy plant of large red oriental

poppies which by some blessed chance was actually within the limits of the square yard of bed which had been allotted to me as my private and particular garden. The plants I bought and glued into the ground with mud, made with a watering pot and garden mould – the seeds which I sowed never came up to my expectations, generally in fact refused to grow at all but the poppies were always better than my wildest dreams. Their red was always redder than any thing I could imagine when I looked away from them. I had a general passion for red which when I also developed a romantic attachment for locomotives led me to believe that I had once seen a 'pure red engine'. Anyhow the poppy plant was the object of a much more sincere worship than I was at all able to give to 'gentle Jesus' and I almost think of a greater affection than I felt for anyone except my father. I remember on one occasion the plant was full of fat green flower buds with little pieces of crumpled scarlet silk showing through the cracks between the sepals. A few were already in flower. I conceived that nothing in the world could be more exciting than to see the flower suddenly burst its green case and unfold its immense cup of red. I supposed this happened suddenly and that it only required patience to be able to watch the event. One morning I stood watching a promising bud for what seemed hours but nothing happened and I got tired, so I ran indoors very hurriedly for fear of getting back too late and got a stool on which I proceeded to keep watch for what seemed an eternity and was I daresay half an hour. I was discovered ultimately by an elder sister and duly laughed at by her and when the story was known by all the grown-ups, for all passions even for red poppies leave one open to ridicule.

The other event was more tragic. It was in fact the horrible discovery that justice is not supreme, that innocence is no protection. It was again a summer morning and I was leaning against my mother's knee as she sat on a low wicker chair and instructed me in the rudiments of botany. In order to illustrate some point she told me to fetch her one of the buds of my *adored* poppy plant or at least that was what I understood her to say. I had already been drilled to implicit obedience and though it seemed to me an almost sacrilegious act I accomplished it.

Here his account ends. But in her life of Fry, Virginia Woolf completes the episode. There had been a misunderstanding; the child picked the poppy and was coldly rebuked by Lady Fry. His distress at having both sacrificed his treasure and being punished for so doing was remembered for the rest of his life.

A desperate plea from a child, writing in Greek on papyrus in the second or third century AD.

'Theon to his father Theon, greeting. Thank you for not taking me to town with you. If you won't take me with you to Alexandria I won't write you a letter or speak to you or say goodbye to you; and if you go to Alexandria I won't take your hand nor greet you again. That is what will happen if you won't take me. Mother said to Archelaus, "He drives me crazy: take him." Thank you for sending me presents. ... Send for me, *please*. If you don't I won't eat, I won't drink; there now!'

Disappointments over Queen Elizabeth's funeral recorded in the diary of the young Lady Anne Clifford (1590–1676).

1603
The 20th Mr Flocknall, my Aunt Warwick's man, brought us word from his Lady, that the Queen died about 2/3 o'clock in the morning.

This message was delivered to my Mother and me in the same chamber where afterwards I was married. (I was at Queen Elizabeth's death thirteen years and two months old.) ...

A little after this Queen Elizabeth's corpse came by night in a barge from Richmond to Whitehall, my Mother and a great company of ladies attending it, where it continued a great while standing in the Drawing Chamber, where it was watched all night by several lords and ladies, my Mother sitting up with it two or three nights, but my Lady would not give me leave to watch, by reason I was held too young. ... When the corpse of Queen Elizabeth had continued at Whitehall as the Council had thought fit, it was carried with great solemnity to Westminster, the lords and ladies going on foot to attend it, my mother and my Aunt of Warwick being mourners, but I was not allowed to be one, because I was not high enough, which did much trouble me then, but yet I stood in the church at Westminster to see the solemnities performed.

Nice mother! The first day when she had said goodbye she had put up her veil double to her nose to kiss him: and her nose and eyes were red. But he had pretended not to see that she was going to cry. She was a nice mother but she was not so nice when she cried. And his father had given him two five shilling pieces for pocket money. And his father had told him if he wanted anything to write home to him, and, whatever he did, never to peach on a fellow. They had cried to him from the car, waving their hands:

Goodbye, Stephen, goodbye!

Goodbye, Stephen, goodbye!

All the boys seemed to him very strange. They had all fathers and mothers and different clothes and voices. He longed to be at home and lay his head on his mother's lap. But he could not: and so he longed for the play and study and prayers to be over and to be in bed.

He drank another cup of hot tea and Fleming said:

What's up? Have you got a pain or what's up with you?

I don't know, Stephen said.

Sick in your breadbasket, Fleming said, because your face looks white. It will go away.

O yes, Stephen said.

But he was not sick there. He thought he was sick in his heart if you could be sick in that place. Fleming was very decent to ask him. He wanted to cry. He leaned his elbows on the table and shut and opened the flaps of his ears. Then he heard the noise of the refectory every time he opened the flaps of his ears. It made a roar like a train at night. And when he closed the flaps the roar was shut off like a train going into a tunnel.

The Christmas vacation was very far away: but one time it would come because the earth moved round always.

A PORTRAIT OF THE ARTIST AS A YOUNG MAN
by James Joyce (1882–1941)

Letter from a Westminster schoolboy in the early nineteenth century.

My dear Mother, if you don't let me come home, I die — I am all over ink and my fine clothes have been Spoilt. I have been tost in a blanket, and seen a ghost.

I remain, my dear, dear mother,

Your dutiful and most unhappy son,

Freddy

My room, which formed a corner of the house, seemed to me enormous, and my double bed was in keeping with its gigantic proportions. At night, alone in the dark, I felt as if I were drifting in an open boat, surrounded by a black and fathomless sea. The distant wall opposite, lit up by a seam of light above the door, was like a cliff, whose foot was lapped by the liquid carpet, and whose surface was pitted with the shadowy caves of alcoves and a great booming fireplace. Hanging above it was a pair of fairy pictures, whose wings were made from real butterflies, and in the half-dark they glittered like phosphorescent flying fish. All children experience these moments of nocturnal loneliness with a special and never-repeated intensity, but I believe only children, having no one to share them with, no one to call out to, experience them with extra horror. Certainly, I was too frightened to put a foot overboard for fear of sinking in the waves.

My bed was equipped with an old-fashioned, solid bolster, which ran the width of the bedhead and acted as a kind of gunwale, protecting me from the predatory swell. It failed me only once. I woke one night to find myself trapped beneath the blankets. I tunnelled towards the surface, but could not find an opening. I seemed to have been sewn into the bed, and like a kitten drowning in a bag, the harder I struggled the more I suffocated. In fact, my bolster had somehow blocked off my escape, but not knowing it, I turned round and began to thrash towards the bottom of the bed. Of course, I found my way out in the end, but to this day I cannot read of a death at sea without remembering the terror of my own dry drowning.

A WINTER'S TALE *by Fraser Harrison (1944–)*

Autobiography

In my childhood trees were green
And there was plenty to be seen.

Come back early or never come.

My father made the walls resound,
He wore his collar the wrong way round.

Come back early or never come.

My mother wore a yellow dress;
Gently, gently, gentleness.

Come back early or never come.

When I was five the black dreams came;
Nothing after was quite the same.

Come back early or never come.

The dark was talking to the dead;
The lamp was dark beside my bed.

Come back early or never come.

When I woke they did not care;
Nobody, nobody was there.

Come back early or never come.

When my silent terror cried,
Nobody, nobody replied.

Come back early or never come.

I got up; the chilly sun
Saw me walk away alone.

Come back early or never come.

September, 1940

Louis MacNeice (1907–63)

George MacBeth remembers anxious childhood episodes in Sheffield during the Blitz.

It was in the cold of October, and after the fall of darkness, that the German bombers began to patrol over England.

Sometimes I would hear them, or think I did, on the brink of going to sleep. Often, I was wrong. What I would really hear first, if there was to be a raid, or a warning, was the sound of the sirens.

I don't think any child who survived the Second World War could ever again hear that awesome rising and falling sound without experiencing a chill of fear. As with all wartime sources of terror, it was joked away as moaning Minnie, but moaning Minnie was a dark lady like the witch in *Snow White*, who dragged me half-awake out of a warm bed, and had me carried downstairs night after night to lie on a cold floor and listen to a remote, frightening droning interspersed with the dull, repeated thud of anti-aircraft guns.

In the morning, I would walk along Clarkhouse Road with my eyes glued to the pavement for shrapnel. It became the fashion to make a collection of this, and there were few days when I came home without a pocketful of jagged, rusting bits, like the unintelligible pieces from a scattered jigsaw of pain and violence.

Of course we didn't see them as this at the time. They were simply free toys from the sky, as available and as interesting as the horse chestnuts in the Botanical Gardens, or the nippled acorns in Melbourne Avenue....

On the Thursday night when the city was bombed we had had a warning from the sirens in good time, and my mother and father had wakened me and taken me down to the hall, which we regarded, rightly or wrongly, as the safest part of the house.

On this particular night we were wrapped up in clothes and blankets. I must have been very tired, because I dropped off to sleep almost immediately. The next thing I remember is waking up and thinking that my head was itchy. My hair seemed to be full of dust.

I was cold, and I could feel a wind blowing in through the front door, which had no glass in it. The glass lay all over the floor of the hall, a scatter of brightly coloured art nouveau panels. My father was on his feet, making a crunching sound on the glass, and my mother was lifting me up to make sure I was all right.

I hadn't heard the explosion, or felt the blast. The bomb was in fact a land-mine, of the sort that fell slowly in a parachute and exploded not on contact, but some minutes later, by a time device. It had landed at the end of our garden, and completely destroyed a large stone house about fifty yards away.

The blast had swept through some trees, across our garden, and hit the house at the rear, smashing all the windows, tearing doors off their hinges, and flinging shrubs and flowers into all the rooms. Then, by some curious trick of its own, it had turned and blown out all the windows at the front of the house.

When it was apparent that none of us was hurt, my father knelt down on the glass under the stairs. I was amazed to hear that he was saying a prayer of thanks for our safety.

Nothing else then or since has done more to convince me of how serious the explosion must have been. My father never presented hmself as a believer in God, and it was entirely out of character for him to show any public emotion, or make any form of ritual gesture.

After the prayer he stood up and made sure my mother and I were warmly wrapped up. Then he opened the door of the sitting-room – I suppose because the front door in the hall must have been blocked – and helped us over the wreckage of the furniture.

After the destruction of their home, the MacBeths move to a new house with an air raid shelter.

For myself, once I was awake, and not so grumpy, I rather enjoyed these nights in the Anderson shelter. I was made much of by the adults, and taught to play a form of solo whist. This was thought a very grown-up game at home, and would normally have been considered too old for me.

I liked the slippery, greasy feel of the old cards, the dim light as we peered for the suits, and the quiet, thoughtful concentration of the players. Hour after hour would go by huddled in blankets and listening to adult talk and adult jokes.

After the second raid, on the steel works, the Germans dropped no more bombs on Sheffield, but we were, of course, unaware of this at the time. Each night that took us down to the shelter brought an undertone of excitement and fear. There was the frequent sound of shells exploding, since the anti-aircraft gunners found it necessary to fire off plenty of rounds for practice, and to deter raiders on their way elsewhere.

There were searchlights, too, criss-crossing the sky like lighted scissors. But I would see these only when going down the garden, or returning to the house after the All Clear.

It still lifts the heart, the memory of that low, rising, sustained horn-blast, which told us the raiders had gone. Within those bracketing sirens, the rising and falling one for the warning, and the even, unvaried one for the All Clear, much of my night-life that winter was a history of interrupted slumber, broken dreams, and a legacy of subdued terror that haunted me for years, like a kind of shell-shock.

I began to have fears that I would die. I refused to sleep in my bedroom without a night-light, a form of low, safe candle in a paper wrapper that burned in a saucer and cast a dim, benevolent glow around an environment of sinister shadows.

Eventually I agreed to do without this, when I acquired my phosphorous dog with his mysterious aura, like the small round badges many people wore in their buttonholes to see by in the black-out....

Who I was, and what lay in store for me, were the troubled wonderings of a brain mostly caught up in its friendships, its violence and its play. But these questions barbed their arrows with the poison of uncertain sleep, and with the remembered sureness of windows emptied of all their glass, and rooms I had known and eaten in reduced to a rubble of tumbled chairs, and carpets messed with torn-up bushes, and massive doors ripped from their hinges and flung askew.

There is an echo of that one night of violence which rumbles down the years, detached in its precise cadence, and yet ultimately assignable to those moments of waking with stone dust in my hair and finding that the world had been shaken up like the coloured pieces inside a kaleidoscope.

It was one thing to go out and fight, and come back to a safe home for tea and treacle scones. It was another to have the very

core of safety torn out and thrown away, and shown to be
vulnerable like the skin of one's own body. Until that night in
December 1940, home had been synonymous with safety. It
would never be so again.

A CHILD OF THE WAR *by George MacBeth (1932–   )*

In the Shelter

In a shelter one night, when death was taking the air
Outside, I saw her, seated apart – a child
Nursing her doll, to one man's vision enisled
With radiance which might have shamed even death to its lair.

Then I thought of our Christmas roses at home – the dark
Lanterns comforting us a winter through
With the same dusky flush, the same bold spark
Of confidence, O sheltering child, as you.

Genius could never paint the maternal pose
More deftly than accident had roughed it there,
Setting amidst our terrors, against the glare
Of unshaded bulb and whitewashed brick, that rose.

Instinct was hers, and an earthquake hour revealed it
In flesh – the meek-laid lashes, the glint in the eye
Defying wrath and reason, the arms that shielded
A plaster doll from an erupting sky.

No argument for living could long sustain
These ills: it needs a faithful eye, to have seen all
Love in the droop of a lash and tell it eternal
By one pure bead of its dew-dissolving chain.

Dear sheltering child, if again misgivings grieve me
That love is only a respite, an opal bloom
Upon our snow-set fields, come back to revive me
Cradling your spark through blizzard; drift and tomb.

C. Day Lewis

During this, my first term, I became involved in a terrible row in which I was outlawed from school discipline.

What happened was this. At 11 a.m. each morning, during 'break', plates of bread, cut into pieces of a quarter of a slice each, were put out on tables. Each boy was allowed to eat one such quarter slice, and no more. Certain of the older boys who had bicycled up to the senior school for classes, arrived rather later than the rest of us for break and their bread. One day, five or six of the smaller boys were particularly hungry, and ate more than one of the quarter slices each. The result was that when the older boys returned from the upper school there was not enough bread to go round among them. They complained to the kitchen maids, who defended their mathematics, and it became obvious that some of us had taken more than one piece of bread.

The whole junior school was assembled, and the housemaster, Dr Wynne Wilson (related to many bishops, and an authority on divinity and bicycling), called upon the boys who had eaten more than one quarter slice to put up their hands. This a few of us did. Then addressing the rest of the school, Wynne Wilson said we were worse than Huns, we were Food Hogs. We were so wicked that he himself could not punish us. So he gave the other boys leave to do whatever they liked with us. We were outlawed for that afternoon.

I did not observe what happened to the others, because several boys set on me. They tied some rope, which they had found, round my hands and feet, and then pulled in different directions. After this I was flung down a hole at the back of the platform of the school dining-room, called the Kipper Hole, because heads of kippers were thrown there.

My chief preoccupation during all this time was whether I would get to my music lesson in time. The school had impressed on me strongly that salvation lay in obeying rules, conforming and being inconspicuous.

Finally, I tore myself away from my attackers and got on to my bicycle. I arrived in a sad state at the house of the music master, Mr Greatorex.

Mr Greatorex was one of those masters who attain at school an astonishing reputation. ... He had a manner perhaps more brusque than that of other masters, but less frightening. It had more of the warm great world than of the refrigerated school. While he conducted our singing, I used to stare at his domed bald head with the clusters of hair on each side and at the back, and pray that when I grew up I would be bald. For the child unquestioningly attributes beauty to whom he loves. Thus Greatorex seemed to me one of the most beautiful people I had ever seen.

So now, bending down over my handle bars, I bicycled, almost blinded by tears, to his house where he was to give me my piano lesson.

I sat at the keyboard and tried to begin to play. All I hoped was that somehow I would get through my lesson without disgracing myself. But without saying a word, Greatorex put his arm round my shoulders. Then he said: 'Tell me what is the matter.'

When he had heard my story he said quietly: 'Listen. You are unhappy now, and you may as well realize that you will be unhappy for a long time, perhaps throughout all your time at school. But I can assure you that a time will come, perhaps when you are about to go to University, when you will begin to be happy. You will be happier than most people.'

I never forgot Greatorex's remark, slipped like a banned letter into the concentration camp of my childhood; and when I was grown up, I wrote and thanked him for having made it, and confirmed that it was true.

WORLD WITHIN WORLD *by Stephen Spender (1909–)*

With Aunt Maggie gone, my mother could not earn enough to feed us and my stomach kept so consistently empty that my head ached most of the day. One afternoon hunger haunted me so acutely that I decided to try to sell my dog Betsy and buy some food. Betsy was a tiny, white, fluffy poodle and when I had washed, dried, and combed her, she looked like a toy. I tucked her under my arm and went for the first time alone into a white neighborhood where there were wide clean streets and big white houses. I went from door to door, ringing the bells. Some white people slammed the door in my face. Others told me to come to the rear of the house, but pride would never let me do that. Finally a young white woman came to the door and smiled.

'What do you want?' she asked.

'Do you want to buy a pretty dog?' I asked.

'Let me see it.'

She took the dog into her arms and fondled and kissed it.

'What's its name?'

'Betsy.'

'She is cute,' she said. 'What do you want for her?'

'A dollar,' I said.

'Wait a moment,' she said. 'Let me see if I have a dollar.'

She took Betsy into the house with her and I waited on the porch, marveling at the cleanliness, the quietness of the white world. How orderly everything was! Yet I felt out of place. I had no desire to live here. Then I remembered that these houses were the homes in which lived those white people who made Negroes leave their homes and flee into the night. I grew tense. Would someone say that I was a bad nigger and try to kill me here? What was keeping the woman so long? Would she tell other people that a nigger boy had said something wrong to her? Perhaps she was getting a mob? Maybe I ought to leave now and forget about Betsy? My mounting anxieties drowned out my hunger. I wanted to rush back to the safety of the black faces I knew.

The door opened and the woman came out, smiling, still hugging Betsy in her arms. But I could not see her smile now; my eyes were full of the fears I had conjured up.

'I just love this dog,' she said, 'and I'm going to buy her. I haven't got a dollar. All I have is ninety-seven cents.'

Though she did not know it, she was now giving me my opportunity to ask for my dog without saying that I did not want to sell her to white people.

'No, ma'am,' I said softly. 'I want a dollar.'

'But I haven't got a dollar in the house,' she said.

'Then I can't sell the dog,' I said.

'I'll give you the other three cents when my mother comes home tonight,' she said.

'No, ma'am,' I said, looking stonily at the floor.

'But, listen, you said you wanted a dollar . . .'

'Yes, ma'am. A dollar.'

'Then here is ninety-seven cents,' she said, extending a handful of change to me, still holding on to Betsy.

'No, ma'am,' I said, shaking my head. 'I want a dollar.'

'But I'll give you the other three cents!'

'My mamma told me to sell her for a dollar,' I said, feeling that I was being too aggressive and trying to switch the moral blame for my aggressiveness to my absent mother.

'You'll get a dollar. You'll get the three cents tonight.'

'No, ma'am.'

'Then leave the dog and come back tonight.'

'No, ma'am.'

'But what could you want with a dollar *now*?' she asked.

'I want to buy something to eat,' I said.

'Then ninety-seven cents will buy you a lot of food,' she said.

'No, ma'am. I want my dog.'

She stared at me for a moment and her face grew red.

'Here's your dog,' she snapped, thrusting Betsy into my arms. 'Now, get away from here! You're just about the craziest nigger boy I ever did see!'

I took Betsy and ran all the way home, glad that I had not sold her. But my hunger returned. Maybe I ought to have taken the ninety-seven cents? But it was too late now. I hugged Betsy in my arms and waited. When my mother came home that night, I told her what had happened.

'And you didn't take the money?' she asked.

'No, ma'am.'

'Why?'

'I don't know,' I said uneasily.

'Don't you know that ninety-seven cents is *almost* a dollar?' she asked.

'Yes, ma'am,' I said, counting on my fingers. 'Ninety-eight, ninety-nine, one hundred. But I didn't want to sell Betsy to white people.'

'Why?'

'Because they're white,' I said.

'You're foolish,' my mother said.

A week later Betsy was crushed to death beneath the wheels of a coal wagon. I cried and buried her in the back yard and drove a barrel staving into the ground at the head of her grave. My mother's sole comment was:

'You could have had a dollar. But you can't eat a dead dog, can you?'

BLACK BOY by Richard Wright (1908–60)

Oscar Wilde's trial and imprisonment in 1895 was the cause of much pain and bewilderment for his two little boys. The following account is by his younger son, Vyvyan.

On my return from school I remained in London for the time being, and my main recollection is of my mother, in tears, poring over masses of press-cuttings, mostly from Continental newspapers. I was of course not allowed to see them, though I could not help seeing the name OSCAR WILDE in large headlines; but I had no inkling of the true state of affairs.

The children were sent abroad to escape the subsequent hue and cry.

My mother remained behind, to be of what assistance she could to my father, until she too was driven from her home by the entrance of the bailiff's men, and the subsequent sale of all the contents of the house. . . .

For months afterwards, my brother and I kept asking for our soldiers, our trains and other toys, and we could not understand why it upset our mother, since of course we knew nothing about the sale. It was only when I saw the catalogue, many years later, that I realized why my mother had been upset. The sale consisted of 246 lots; number 237 was 'A large quantity of toys'; they realized thirty shillings.

Before being sent to a German boarding school, the boys were told that their name had been changed from Wilde to Holland.

My brother and I had fled from England with all our summer and winter clothing, but until this time we had had no occasion to wear our cricket flannels, which had been carefully wrapped up in brown paper and stowed away from moths. When the first half-holiday arrived and we went to our dormitory to change for cricket, we were aghast to find that, in the general Wilde–Holland change-over, these garments had apparently been overlooked and all bore the names Cyril Wilde and Vyvyan Wilde prominently displayed upon them. Luckily they were all written with marking-ink on tapes and sewn on to the garments, and I can see my brother now, in the comparative seclusion of the washing-place, frantically hacking away at the tapes with his pocket-knife. The most difficult name to remove was mine from my cricket-belt, as the stitching had gone deep into the webbing. Eventually, Cyril cut out the centre of the tape, leaving the edges adhering to the belt.

SON OF OSCAR WILDE *by Vyvyan Holland*

21

LOVE AND FRIENDSHIP

Two letters from Lewis Carroll (Charles Lutwidge Dodgson (1832–98)) to child friends. The first is to Agnes Hull, his favourite among a family of five lively children.

My dear Agnes,   *Nov.* 16, '78

I wrote that at 10 o'clock, and now it's half past 2. Just as I wrote it, there was a knock at the door, and in walked a baronet. That is a word you will have to explain to Jessie: no doubt she will think it means a 'barrow-net', that is, a net to catch wheel-barrows in. But I don't have to use a net for *that*: I could easily catch them with my hands, if I wished: but why should I catch wheel-barrows? I shouldn't know what to do with them when I *had* caught them. So it wasn't a *net* at all (tell her), but a live man who has 'Sir' before his name – 'Sir what-you-may-call-um Thing-um-bob' – (not that that is his *real* name, you know). Ever since 10, about, I've been lunching and lecturing (sometimes one, sometimes the other) till now –

As to your book, don't you know what a useful virtue *patience* is? You had better add it to the painfully small stock of virtues you have got at present – (your character, *at present*, being made up of two things only – deceit and sulkiness, with perhaps a *few* grains of greediness). The book is really so disfigured with dead beetles, I can't possibly send it till it has been to the laundress (and I haven't yet found one who can wash it: it wants a laundress who can 'get up' *book*-muslin) – Besides, I've only invented one new conundrum, 'Why is Agnes like a thermometer?' 'Because she won't rise when it's cold' – and perhaps you wouldn't like that put in.

Your loving friend
C. L. Dodgson

This letter in rhyme is to his neice, Violet Dodgson.

Dear Violet,   *May* 6. 1889.

    I'm glad to hear you children like the Magazine I ordered for you for a year: and if you happen to have seen the book about 'Lord Fauntlerroy', you'll find an interesting bit about the child that acts the Boy (now they have made a Play of it) in Number Six. She seems to be a child without one bit of pride: a pretty name too, hasn't she? the little 'Elsie Leslie Lyde'. I grieve to hear your bantam-hen is fond of rolling eggs away. You should remind it now and then, of 'Waste not, want not'. You should say 'a bantam-hen, that wastes an egg, is sure to get extremely poor, and to be forced at last to beg for hard-boiled eggs, from door to door. How would you like it, Bantam-hen,' you should go on, 'if all your brood were hard-boiled chickens? You would then be sorry you had been so rude!' Tell it all this, and don't forget! And now I think it's time for me to sign myself, dear Violet,

Your loving Uncle,
C.L.D.

First love in Melbourne, Australia, at the time of the First World War.

But, of course, words such as Anzac and Gallipoli and digger, dropping into my mind and vocabulary as into the minds and vocabularies of all Australians, are the seed-words of a new growth. As overtones and implications and prides swell and burst, my generation and the generation it breeds are inevitably showered with the pollen from these explosions of Australian nationalism.

    While huge banners are flapping and cracking ruddily over the horizon, and peppering down their dust of blood and glory and lies not to be disbelieved, while Mother and Father are planning to transplant me, I fall in love. The expression is absurd yet there seems no other. I am already involved in forms of love with Mother and Father, school, Angel and the Little Clowns in my weekly comic paper, with lightning and stars and the colour yellow, with the view from the front veranda, with my Teddy Bear, with an infinity of things. Any difference in the degree of love or its quality is imperceptible; there is merely difference in direction. How am I to tell, as much now as then, which of these emotions all called love, is of most value?

Now I am in love with a little girl.

Name?

Nameless.

Perhaps I never knew her name for it seems illogical to remember the names of people whose physical appearance is unrecallable – Mrs Easom, Elsie Easom, Dr Moss, Mrs Rule the pastry-cook who makes me a cake with crystallized violets on it for my fifth birthday, Mrs Richmond – and yet have no name for one whose appearance is far more vivid to me than that of someone I saw last week.

About my height, she can be presumed to be also about my age. She wears a grey velvet dress with a lace collar spreading over her shoulders. The collar contains an extra hole on the right shoulder that is larger than, and not, a lace-hole. This distresses me, on her behalf, as though it were a wound that can give her pain. From under a straw hat, four long cylindrical curls pour richly and blackly down over the school-bag on her back. Daisies with woolly yellow centres ring the crown of the hat. Her button boots and ribbed stockings are black. Together we walk down the sloping street from school. We walk with a slowness that is exquisite and treacherous for the more slowly we move the more my ecstasy increases, and increase will make my loss greater when Dr Moss's corner is reached, and we must part. What do we say? Or are we talking to ourselves in the crystal cages of our hearts as we walk downwards on the strip of unasphalted ground between the asphalted roadway and the drain. This strip is sprinkled with thousands of minute fragments of broken glass and china which catch the light and mysteriously sparkle. I shall never again see such a carven and tender face, never such a white skin, never such ink-blue polished eyes and sooty lashes, never such a circular mole as sits above her lips. It is like a spot from a moth's wing. We walk, and I watch us walk, with trance-like gravity, mildly on out of each other's lives, giving up, as we part, two facsimile wraiths that remain together and continue walking together.

THE WATCHER ON THE CAST-IRON BALCONY *by Hal Porter (1911–)*

The other amusements of my early childhood – games of patience, transfers, bricks – were all solitary. I had no playfellows . . . yes, though; I can recall one small friend, but alas, he was not a playfellow. When Marie took me to the Luxembourg Gardens, I used to meet a child there of about my own age, a delicate, gentle, quiet creature, whose pallid face was half hidden by a pair of big spectacles, the glasses of which were so dark that one could see nothing behind them. I cannot remember his name, perhaps I never knew it. We used to call him Mouton because of his little white woolly coat.

'Mouton, why do you wear spectacles?'

'I have bad eyes.'

'Let me see them.'

Then he had lifted the frightful glasses and the sight of his poor blinking, weak eyes had made my heart ache.

Not that we played together; I cannot remember that we did anything but walk about hand in hand without saying a word.

This first friendship of mine lasted only a short time. Mouton soon stopped coming. Oh, how lonely the Luxembourg seemed then! . . . But my real despair began when I realized that Mouton was going blind. Marie had met the little boy's nurse in the street and she told my mother what she had learnt; she spoke in a whisper so that I should not hear; but I caught these words: 'He can't find the way to his mouth!' An absurd remark, assuredly, for of course there is no need to see in order to find the way to one's mouth, as I immediately reflected, but nevertheless it filled me with dismay. I ran away to cry in my room and for several days I practised keeping my eyes shut and going about without opening them, so as to try and realize what Mouton must be feeling.

IF IT DIE . . . *by André Gide*

This is five-year-old Marjory Fleming's first letter, written to her sister Isa during a visit to Isabella Keith in Edinburgh.

My dear Isa,

I now sit down on my botom to answer all your kind and beloved letters which you was so so good as to write to me.

This is the first time I ever wrote a letter in my Life.

There are a great number of Girls in the Square and they cry just like a pig when we are under the painfull necessity of putting it to Death.

Miss Potune a lady of my acquaintance, praises me dreadfully. I repeated something out of Deen Swift and she said I was fit for the stage, and you may think I was primmed up with majestick Pride, but upon my word I felt myselfe turn a little birsay — birsay is a word which is a word that William composed which is as you may suppose a little enraged. This horid fat Simpliton says that my Aunt is beautifull which is intirely impossible for that is not her nature.

This letter is stitched on a piece of canvas: a real labour of love.

DEAR MOTHER, MY DUTY REMEMBER UNTO THE, AND MY DEAR LOVE UNTO MY SISTER. WHEN I SAW MY FATHER LAST HIS LOVE WAS TO THE, BUT I THOUGHT IT LONG BEFORE I SAW THE BUT I DID MY INDEAVOUR TO RITE UNTO THE NO MORE BUT THEY DUTYFULL DAFTER S F

FROM WANSTEAD 1693 THE 25 OF THE 5 MONTH.

In a little town of the Government of Tver lived a granddaughter of my father's eldest brother. Her name was Tatyana Kuchin. I had known her from childhood, but we seldom met: once a year, at Christmas or Shrovetide, she came to pay a visit to her aunt in Moscow. But we had become close friends. Though five years my senior, she was short for her age and looked no older than myself. My chief reason for getting to like her was that she was the first person to talk to me in a reasonable way: I mean, she did not constantly express surprise at my growth; she did not ask what lessons I did and whether I did them well; whether I intended to enter the Army, and, if so, what regiment; but she talked to me as most sensible people talk to one another, though she kept the little airs of superiority which all girls like to show to boys a little younger than themselves.

We corresponded, especially after the events of 1824; but letters mean paper and pen and recall the schoolroom table with its ink-stains and decorations carved with a penknife. I wanted to see her and to discuss our new ideas; and it may be imagined with what delight I heard that my cousin was to come in February (of 1826) and to spend several months with us. I scratched a calendar on my desk and struck off the days as they passed, sometimes abstaining for a day or two, just to have the satisfaction of striking out more at one time. In spite of this, the time seemed very long; and when it came to an end, her visit was postponed more than once; such is the way of things.

One evening I was sitting in the school-room with Protopopov [his tutor]. Over each item of instruction he took, as usual, a sip of sour broth; he was explaining the hexameter metre, ruthlessly hashing, with voice and hand, each verse of Gnedich's translation of the Iliad into its separate feet. Suddenly, a sound unlike that of town sledges came from the snow outside; I heard the faint tinkle of harness-bells and the sound of voices out-of-doors. I flushed up, lost all interest in the hashing process and the wrath of Achilles, and rushed headlong to the front hall. There was my cousin from Tver, wrapped up in furs, shawls, and comforters, and wearing a hood and white fur boots. Blushing red with frost and, perhaps, also with joy, she ran into my arms.

CHILDHOOD, YOUTH AND EXILE *by Alexander Herzen*

(Horsham)
Monday, July 18, 1803

Dear Kate,

We have proposed a day at the pond next Wednesday; and if you will come tomorrow morning I would be much obliged to you; and if you could any how bring Tom over to stay all night, I would thank you. We are to have a cold dinner over at the pond, and come home to eat a bit of roast chicken and peas at about nine o'clock. Mama depends upon your bringing Tom over tomorrow, and if you don't we shall be very much disappointed.

Tell the bearer not to forget to bring me a fairing – which

is some ginger-bread, sweetmeat, hunting-nuts, and a pocket book. Now I end.

> I am *not*,
> Your obedient servant,
>
> P. B. Shelley

A *letter from the eleven-year-old Percy Bysshe Shelley (1792–1822). Edmund Gosse's letter, below, was written at the age of nine.*

> June 3, 1858

My extremely precious Papa,

I am quite longing for the month to end (but still it is shorter than I thought it would be) and it is so lonely sometimes without you – Bolcera egis auratus has fatally burst. This morning a lerianthus Lyodii came (oh! such a monster) but I fear it is dead. I enjoyed myself very much at Miss Willses yesterday among the young ladies we played at Lotto, and Bell & Hammer and solitaire and I saw the gymtastics and held them too. We have not had such a brilliant day for a couple of months – how is it with you?

> I remain your
> afectionat Son
>
> E. Wm Gosse

Richard Meinertzhagen (1878–1967), who was to make his name as a big game hunter in Kenya, wrote this soon after his arrival at Harrow.

Henry VIII's Ode to Anne Boleyn

I loved Anne Boleyn for with love I was drunk
I cannot remember the thoughts which I thunk
But I winked at her once and she at me wunk.

You must kneel at my feet whispered Anne, and I knole.
I asked her to smile at me once and she smole
And then I felt happier than ever I fole. . . .

DIARY OF A BLACK SHEEP

Tolstoy recalls his old nurse – the key figure in his mother's household.

Ever since I can remember anything I remember Natalya Savishna and her love and tenderness; but only now have I learnt to appreciate their worth – it never occurred to me at the time to think what a rare and wonderful creature that old woman was. Not only did she never speak but it seems that she never even thought of herself: her whole life was compounded of love and self-sacrifice. I was so used to her disinterested tender affection for us that I could not imagine things otherwise. I was not in the least grateful to her and never asked myself whether she were happy and content.

Sometimes on the imperative plea of necessity I would escape from lessons to her room, to sit and dream aloud, not in the least embarrassed by her presence. She was always busy, either knitting a stocking or rummaging in the chests which filled her room, or making a list of the linen, while she listened to all the nonsense I uttered – about how when I became a general I would marry a great beauty and buy a chestnut horse, build myself a crystal house and send for Karl Ivanych's relations from Saxony; and so on. She would keep saying, 'Yes, my dear, yes.' Usually when I got up to go she would open a blue chest, inside the lid of which – I can see them now – were pasted a coloured sketch of a hussar, a picture off a pomade-box and one of Volodya's drawings, and take out an aromatic pastille, which she would light and wave about, observing:

'This, my dear, is still one of the Ochakov pastilles. When your sainted grandfather – may the Kingdom of Heaven be his! – went against the Turks he brought it back. This is the last bit,' she would add with a sigh.

The trunks which crowded her room contained absolutely everything. Whatever was wanted, the cry was always: 'Ask Natalya Savishna for it', and sure enough after a certain amount of searching she would produce the required article, saying, 'It's lucky I put it away.' In these trunks were thousands of objects about which nobody in the house but herself either knew or cared.

Once I lost my temper with her. This is how it happened. One day at dinner when I was pouring myself out some *kvass* I dropped the decanter and stained the tablecloth.

'Call Natalya Savishna to come and admire what her darling has done!' said mamma.

Natalya Savishna came in, saw the mess I had made and shook her head. Then mamma whispered something in her ear and she went out, shaking her finger at me.

After dinner I was on my way to the ball-room and skipping about in the highest of spirits when all at once Natalya Savishna sprang out from behind the door with the tablecloth in her hand, caught hold of me and despite desperate resistance on my part began rubbing my face with the wet cloth, repeating: 'Don't thee go dirtying tablecloths, don't thee go dirtying tablecloths!' I was so offended that I howled with rage.

'What!' I said to myself, pacing up and down the room and choking with tears, 'To think that Natalya Savishna – no, plain *Natalya* says *thee* to *me*, and hits me in the face with a wet tablecloth as if I were a serf-boy. It's abominable!'

When Natalya Savishna saw that I was gasping with fury she immediately ran off, while I continued to walk to and fro considering how I could pay out the impudent *Natalya* for the way she had insulted me.

A few minutes later Natalya Savishna returned, came up to me timidly and started trying to pacify me.

'Hush now, dearie, don't cry . . . Forgive an old fool . . . it was all my fault . . . Pray forgive me, my pet . . . Here's something for you.'

From under her shawl she took a screw of red paper in which there were two caramels and a grape, and offered it to me with a trembling hand. I could not look the kind old woman in the face; with averted eyes I accepted her present, my tears flowing faster than ever, but from love and shame now, and no longer from anger.

CHILDHOOD *by Leo Tolstoy*

In this extract from 'Frost at Midnight', Coleridge addresses his sleeping child, Hartley.

> . . . Dear Babe, that sleepest cradled by my side,
> Whose gentle breathings, heard in this deep calm,
> Fill up the interspersed vacancies
> And momentary pauses of the thought!
> My babe so beautiful! it thrills my heart
> With tender gladness, thus to look at thee,
> And think that thou shalt learn far other lore
> And in far other scenes! For I was reared
> In the great city, pent 'mid cloisters dim,
> And saw naught lovely but the sky and stars.
>
> But thou, my babe! shalt wander like a breeze
> By lakes and sandy shores, beneath the crags
> Of ancient mountain, and beneath the clouds,
> Which image in their bulk both lakes and shores
> And mountain crags: so shalt thou see and hear
> The lovely shapes and sounds intelligible
> Of that eternal language, which thy God
> Utters, who from eternity doth teach
> Himself in all, and all things in himself.
> Great universal Teacher! he shall mould
> Thy spirit, and by giving make it ask.
>
> Therefore all seasons shall be sweet to thee,
> Whether the summer clothe the general earth
> With greenness, or the redbreast sit and sing
> Betwixt the tufts of snow on the bare branch
> Of mossy apple-tree, while the nigh thatch
> Smokes in the sun-thaw; whether the eve-drops fall
> Heard only in the trances of the blast,
> Or if the secret ministry of frost
> Shall hang them up in silent icicles,
> Quietly shining to the quiet Moon.

From the diaries of Francis Kilvert:

Monday, 19 October [1874]

In Harden Ewyas Park the stately elms that stood towering about the gentle slopes were gorgeous in their bright autumn livery of gold and green and at the quaint old cottage on the crest of the hill opposite the old turnpike house I witnessed a pretty loving meeting between a young mother and a child in a red cloak under the boughs of an apple tree in the cottage garden. It reminded me, I know not why, of that sweet passage in Virgil so true to nature that surely he must have drawn it from early recollections, 'You were little when I first saw you. You were with your Mother, gathering fruit in our orchard and I was your guide. I was entering my thirteenth year and just able to reach the boughs from the ground.'

The following is an affectionately teasing letter written five hundred years ago. When Katherine had eaten up enough meat to become a grown woman, she married Betson, author of the letter and her father's partner in the wool trade. She is here about twelve years old.

Thomas Betson to his Kinswoman Katherine Ryche, 1 June 1476

Mine own heartily beloved Cousin Katherine, I recommend me to you with all the inwardness of my heart. And now lately you shall understand that I received a token from you, the which was and is to me right heartily welcome, and with glad will I received it; and over that I had a letter from Holake, your gentle Squire, by the which I understand right well that you be in good health of body, and merry at heart. And I pray God heartily to his pleasure to continue the same: for it is to me very great comfort that you so be, so help me Jesus. And if you would be a good eater of your meat allways, that you might wax and grow fast to be a woman, you should make me the gladdest man of the world, by my troth: for when I remember your favour and your serious loving dealing towards me, forsooth you make me even very glad and joyous in my heart: and on the other side again when I remember your young youth, and see well that you are not an eater of your meat, the which should help you greatly in waxing, forsooth then you make me very heavy again. And therefore I pray you, mine own sweet Cousin, even as you love me to be merry and to eat your meat like a woman. . . . I pray you greet my horse, and pray him to give you three of his years to help you withal: and I will at my coming home give him four of my years and four horseshoes as amends. Tell him that I prayed him so . . . I pray you, gentle Cousin, command me to the Clock, and pray him to amend his unthrift manners: for he strikes ever in undue time, and he will be ever afore, and that is a shrewd condition. . . . And I trust you will pray for me: for I shall pray for you, and, so it may be, none so well. And Almighty Jesu make you a good woman, and send you many good years and long to live in health and virtue to his pleasure. At great Calais on this side of the sea, the first day of June, when every man was gone to his Dinner, and the Clock smote nine, and all our household cried after me and bade me come down; come down to dinner at once! and what answer I gave them you know it of old.

By your faithful Cousin and lover
Thomas Betson

I send you this ring for a token.

To my faithful and heartily beloved Cousin Katherine Ryche at Stonor this letter be delivered in haste.

Maggie Tulliver's love for her brother Tom in The Mill on the Floss *is thought to be closely modelled on George Eliot's childhood feelings for her own brother. Here are two sonnets about their relationship.*

Brother and Sister

I

I cannot choose but think upon the time
When our two lives grew like two buds that kiss
At lightest thrill from the bee's swinging chime,
Because the one so near the other is.

He was the elder, and a little man
Of forty inches, bound to show no dread,
And I the girl that, puppy-like, now ran,
Now lagged behind my brother's larger tread.
I held him wise, and when he talked to me
Of snakes and birds, and which God loved the best,
I thought his knowledge marked the boundary
Where men grow blind, though angels knew the rest.
If he said 'Hush!' I tried to hold my breath;
Whenever he said 'Come!' I stepped in faith.

II

School parted us; we never found again
That childish world where our two spirits mingled
Like scents from varying roses that remain
One sweetness, nor can evermore be singled;
Yet the twin habit of that early time
Lingered for long about the heart and tongue:
We had been natives of one happy clime
And its dear accent to our utterance clung:
Till the dire years whose awful name is Change
Had grasped our souls still yearning in divorce.
And, pitiless, shaped them into two forms that range,
Two elements which sever their life's course.
But were another childhood world my share,
I would be born a little sister there.

George Eliot (1819–80)

. . . at some earlier period my small soul had suffered a more
piercing injury which left an ineluctable scar. It was a dreadful
experience, for which nobody was to blame. What fell upon me,
out of the blue, was nothing less than bereavement, in its sharpest,
most widowing form. Our parents had been invited to spend a
fortnight with some French acquaintances in a country house near
Sedan, and had decided to take my elder brother with them. He
and I had never, so far as I can remember, spent a night apart, but
in my ignorance of the working of the human heart, I had no

forebodings about the coming separation. The day of departure came, and I stood on the gravel and cheerfully waved them away. I then turned back into the house, and in the familiar Entrance Hall, a few minutes ago all happy bustle and excitement, loneliness, a strange and unknown horror, overwhelmed me like a tidal wave. I crawled upstairs to the Blue Dressing-Room, where for some reason I was then sharing with my brother a huge canopied Victorian double bed. On his side of the bed lay his felt land-and-water hat and his leather belt. The sight of these familiar belongings of the Lost One tore me to pieces. I lay on the bed and sobbed, clasping the belt. I had nobody to turn to. I was desolate, bereft, and widowed, without a philosophy and without a comforter. For days I wandered about the gardens and farm, reminded by every sight and scent of lost happiness and of my empty, forlorn situation. There lay his hoe; here was an unaccustomed silence; and in the warm angle of the walls where the hutches stood I dropped slow tears into the rabbits' bran. . . .

My brother returned from France with a present for me – a slender black walking-stick with an ivory greyhound's head for a handle – and an enlarged mind. It was a pleasure to possess a walking-stick with a greyhound's head for a handle, and I never mentioned my sufferings to him or to my mother.

A VICTORIAN BOYHOOD *by L. E. Jones*

The second stanza of the following poem does not appear in any Edith Sitwell collection. It was included by Walter de la Mare in his anthology Come Hither *and it is possible that Dame Edith wrote it especially for him.*

> The King of China's daughter,
> She never would love me,
> Though I hung my cap and bells upon
> Her nutmeg tree.
> For oranges and lemons,
> The stars in bright blue air
> (I stole them long ago, my dear)
> Were dangling there.

The Moon did give me silver pence,
The Sun did give me gold,
And both together softly blew
And made my porridge cold;
But the King of China's daughter
Pretended not to see
When I hung my cap and bells upon
The nutmeg tree.

The King of China's daughter
So beautiful to see
With her face like yellow water, left
Her nutmeg tree.
Her little rope for skipping
She kissed and gave it me –
Made of painted notes of singing-birds
Among the fields of tea.
I skipped across the nutmeg grove, –
I skipped across the sea;
But neither sun nor moon, my dear,
Has yet caught me.

Edith Sitwell (1887–1964)

22

FOOD

... the most remarkable accident during our stay was caused by a small juvenile Caristò, who, during the mid-day meal, climbed abruptly on to the table, and before he could be rescued, performed a series of struggles among the dishes, which ended by the little pickle's losing his balance and collapsing suddenly in a sitting posture into the very middle of the maccaroni dish, from which P—— and I rejoiced to think we had been previously helped. One sees in valentines Cupids on beds of roses, or on birds' nests; but a slightly clothed Calabrese infant sitting in the midst of a hot dish of maccaroni appears to me a perfectly novel idea.

Journals of a Landscape Painter in
Southern Calabria *by Edward Lear*

The infant Charles James Fox (1749–1806) is also permitted to indulge himself.

... on one occasion at Holland House, when the children entered the dining-room towards the end of the meal at a grand dinner party, he expressed an urgent desire to climb into the cream bowl. At his father's request it was placed on the carpet so that he could paddle about it in his petticoats to his heart's content. At a subsequent dinner party at Holland House a pig roasted at the kitchen fire was served with the traditional apple in its mouth and a note in verse from the chef: 'While at the fire I foam'd and hiss'd, A fox's cub upon me piss'd.' The guests greeted this intelligence with applause.

Besides going to Coombe we went at the end of the summer to Devonshire, to Membland, near the villages of Noss Mayo, and Newton, and not far from the river Yealm, an arm of the sea. It was when getting ready for the first of these journeys that I remember, while I was being dressed in the nursery, my father's servant, Mr Deacon, came up to the nursery and asked me whether I would like a ticket. He then gave me a beautiful green ticket with a round hole in it. I asked him what one could do with it, and he said, 'In return for that ticket you can get Bath buns, Banbury cakes, jam-rolls, crackers, and pork sausages.' In the bustle of departure I lost it. Paddington Station resounded with the desperate cries of the bereaved ticket-holder. In vain I was given half a white first-class ticket. In vain Mr Bullock, the guard, offered every other kind of ticket. It was not the same thing. That ticket, with the round hole, had conjured up visions of wonderful possibilities and fantastic exchanges. Sausages and Banbury cakes and Bath buns (all of them magic things), I knew, would be forthcoming to no other ticket. The loss was irreparable. I remember thinking the grown-up people so utterly wanting in understanding when they said: 'A ticket? Of course, he can have a ticket. Here's a ticket for the dear little boy.' As if that white ticket was anything like the unique passport to gifts new and unheard of, anything like that real green ticket with the round hole in it. At the end of one of these journeys, at Kingsbridge Road, the train ran off the line. We were in a saloon carriage, and I remember the accident being attributed to that fact by my mother's maid, who said saloon carriages were always unsafe. It turned out to be an enjoyable accident, and we all got out and I was given an orange.

THE PUPPET SHOW OF MEMORY *by Maurice Baring*

Henry King

Who chewed bits of String, and was early cut off in
Dreadful Agonies.

The Chief Defect of Henry King
Was chewing little bits of String.
At last he swallowed some which tied
Itself in ugly Knots inside.
Physicians of the Utmost Fame
Were called at once; but when they came

They answered, as they took their Fees,
'There is no Cure for this Disease.
Henry will very soon be dead.'
His Parents stood about his Bed
Lamenting his Untimely Death,
When Henry, with his Latest Breath,
Cried – 'Oh, my Friends, be warned by me,
That Breakfast, Dinner, Lunch, and Tea
Are all the Human Frame requires . . .'
With that, the Wretched Child expires.

Hilaire Belloc

The grown-ups with whom I came in contact had a remarkable incapacity for understanding the intensity of childish emotions. When, at the age of four, I was taken to be photographed in Richmond, the photographer had difficulty in getting me to sit still, and at last promised me a sponge cake if I would remain motionless. I had, until that moment, only had one sponge cake in all my life and it had remained as a high point of ecstasy. I therefore stayed as quiet as a mouse and the photograph was wholly successful. But I never got the sponge cake.

THE AUTOBIOGRAPHY OF BERTRAND RUSSELL

Our nursery breakfast was ordered, without reference to any but Houghton customs, to be dry bread and cold milk the year round, with the exception of three winter months, when in honour of our Scotch blood we were favoured with porridge; the meal came from Scotland with the kegs of butter and barrels of eggs and bags of cheese, etc., but it was boiled by the English maids in any but north country fashion. Had we been strong children this style of food might have suited us, many large healthy families have thriven on the like; but though seldom ailing, we inherited from my father a delicacy of constitution demanding great care during our infancy.

. . . Another serious grief we had connected with our food. We could refuse nothing that was prepared for us; if we did we not only got nothing else, but the dish declined was put by to appear again at the next meal, and be disposed of before we were permitted to have what else there was. Jane greatly disliked green vegetables, spinach or cabbage in particular; it was nature speaking (poor nature! so unheeded in those times), for these plants disagreed with her, yet she must eat them. I have known a plate of spinach kept for her from dinner one day to supper the next, offered at each meal and refused, and not even a bit of bread substituted all those long hours, till sheer hunger got the better of her dislike, and she gave herself a night of sickness by swallowing the mess. Fancy a young child kept thirty hours without food and then given poison! the dungeons of feudal times were in their degree not more iniquitous than these proceedings.

Of course under this régime the rhubarb bottle became a necessity in the nursery. I had my French beans antipathy, and it was to be overcome in the same way, followed by the same cure for its effects. In addition to the dose of rhubarb, nauseous enough in itself, our breakfast on medicine mornings was water gruel – I can see it now, unstrained, thick, black, and seasoned with salt; this frightful bowl gave me an obstinate fit in Jane's style, from which I suffered in the same way; breakfast, dinner, and supper passed, and the cold gruel remained untouched; faint from hunger I lay down in the evening on the floor of the closet where I had passed the summer's day, and sobbed out that I wished to die! One of the housemaids on her tour of window-shutting, a Hertfordshire girl named Sally Withan, whom I remember with gratitude to this hour, unturned the key which kept me prisoner, and threw beside me some red-streaked apples. I have loved apples ever since. Good-humoured, rosy-cheeked Sally Withan! She said if she could find that nasty gruel, it should not plague her sweet young lady no more, she'd answer for it! I was not slow to give the hint, and certainly on being called to bed, whither I went without a kiss or a good-night or even appearing downstairs, fresh gruel, better it seemed to me, warm at any rate, and a slice of bread, were thankfully received after the miserable day of fasting.

MEMOIRS OF A HIGHLAND LADY
by Elizabeth Grant of Rothiemurchus (1797–1830)

Lines to be Embroidered on a Bib
Or, The Child is Father of the Man, but Not
for Quite a While

So Thomas Edison
Never drank his medicine;
So Blackstone and Hoyle
Refused cod-liver oil;
So Sir Thomas Malory
Never heard of a calory;
So the Earl of Lennox
Murdered Rizzio without the aid of vitamins or
    calisthenox;
So Socrates and Plato
Ate dessert without finishing their potato;
So spinach was too spinachy
For Leonardo da Vinaci;
Well, it's all immaterial,
So eat your nice cereal,
And if you want to name your own ration,
First go get a reputation.

Ogden Nash

E. M. Forster's great-aunt, Marianne Thornton, remembers childhood holidays at Barley Wood in Somerset, the home of Hannah More, celebrated member of the Blue Stocking Society, and her four sisters.

Surely there never was such a house, so full of intellect and piety and active benevolence. They lived in such uninterrupted harmony with each other, were so full of their separate pursuits, enjoyed with such interest and vivacity all the pleasures of their beautiful home, or wholly laid aside all the forms of society that were irksome, that young or old one felt oneself in a brighter and happier world, alloyed indeed by the most fearful attacks of illness occasionally, but even when these occurred the patience and cheerfulness of both patient and nurses never failed. I can now imagine our arrival at the door covered with roses, and 'the ladies' as they were always called, rushing out to cover us with kisses, and then take us into the kitchen to exhibit us to Mary and Charles, the housemaid and coachman, then running themselves to fetch the tea things, Mrs Patty allowing no one but herself to fry the eggs for 'the darling', the brown loaf brought out, the colour of a mahogany table, baked only once a week, of enormous size but excellent taste. Then the 2 cats called 'Non-resistance' and 'Passive obedience' who were fed by us all day long, and then the next day crowns of flowers were made for ourselves, garlands for the sheep; the peas we were set to pick, and then shell, perched upon the kitchen dresser, while Sally made the room resound with some of her merry stories of the cottagers round, and then we were sent off by ourselves or with some village child to buy chickens at the next farm, and when we returned dragging along our purchases, how we were fed with strawberries and cream, and told to lie down in the hay whilst Charles the coachman, gardener bailiff and carpenter, made us a syllabub under the cow.

MARIANNE THORNTON *by E. M. Forster*

Enter Satan, in the form of Mr Trent the baker, in Julian Fane's Morning. *Though written as fiction,* Morning *is essentially an account of the author's own childhood in the late 1930s.*

Ten minutes to luncheon: nothing to do: no time for anything. A delivery-van is bumping along the back-drive. He runs out of the house and over the paving and gazes through the gate in the garden wall. The van sways round the dovecote and pulls up in a perfect position, hidden by a circular yew-tree from the nursery windows. It is Mr Trent the baker from Long Cretton.

Vere lifts the latch of the gate and saunters towards the van. 'Oh, good morning, Mr Trent,' he says. 'How are you?'

'Why, Master Vere, good morning. I'm nicely, thanks, and how's yourself? Come to see what I've brought along, have you? Let's take a look.'

'I was on my way in actually,' Vere protests, following the baker to the rear of the van.

The doors are unlocked and opened. The sweet smell of fresh-baked bread assails his nostrils. . . .

The baker says, 'What, Master Vere, I do declare, you haven't seen your favourites today,' and the fatal tray full of cream-buns is held out for inspection.

The buns are brown and soft and slit in the middle, and the scent of the cream with the indescribable flavour which rests in the slits is wafted upwards.

'I can't afford one,' Vere says faintly.

Mr Trent seems not to hear him. In a voice as creamy and tantalizing as his buns he continues, 'Isn't that a pretty sight? Shall I tell you what we'll do? You keep your tuppence. Now you choose a little favourite. How's that? – But eat it up quick, before Nurse catches you. Oh listen, there's the bell!'

Vere feels liquid with desire and apprehension. The luncheon bell is ringing from the nursery window, the forbidden bun is proffered temptingly, the pennies are already in his pocket, time is passing. If only Mr Trent had come earlier. The lack of appetite at luncheon will be suspect for certain.

'Thank you very much, Mr Trent. Good morning.'

Vere takes the bun. His hand is trembling though his voice is controlled. He walks with faltering steps towards the stable archway, sits on the stone mounting-block, bolts the bun in four mouthfuls, unable to indulge the ecstasy of the cream-filling, runs into the yard and across it, and starts to climb the fire-escape to the nursery window.

Mr Trent calls up to him, 'See you tomorrow, Master Vere!' and puts his finger to his lips as he enters the house.

Vere hiccups, squeezes through the window, drops onto the floor, then goes into the day-nursery. Flora the nursery-maid is trying to decide if she has laid correctly for luncheon. Her eyes when she looks at him are wide and abstracted.

'Flora, I've got you a present,' he says, giving her a Milky Way.

'Oh Vere, you shouldn't have.' Her voice is caressing, rather broken, sometimes throaty, sometimes clear. 'You haven't been with Mr Trent?'

'Don't tell Nanny, Flora.'

She jerks her head in a manner denoting trouble in store, the eyebrows raised and the tongue clicking, and sends him to wash his hands.

When he returns luncheon is on the table. There is a dish with a domed silver cover: two vegetable dishes stand beside it. He hopes they contain something fresh and tasty: roast beef, for instance, dark sharp gravy, flowery boiled potatoes and those French beans, succulent and steaming, scraped to a tender green and with the strings removed. – That is what he could eat today, that is what he would prefer above everything. Nanny enters, the baby is strapped into the high chair, grace is said. Vere closes his eyes, praying fervently for French beans. The lids are lifted.

Under the silver dome is a fricassée of chicken, drops of melted butter gilding its rich surface. Mashed potato and stalky spring greens have been squashed flat by the covers of the other dishes.

'Not too much for me, please, Nanny,' Vere says, and to hide his despair turns to the baby. 'Hullo, Faith. Hullo, Faithie.'

The baby, gazing greedily at the food and kicking her chair, seizes his finger in a vice-like grip.

'Where's your appetite, Vere?' Nanny asks.

'Let go of my finger, Faith. I'm just not hungry, I'm afraid.'

'You'll never grow up to be big and strong if you don't eat.'

I will, he thinks with dull resentment. A plate is laid before him and he starts to pick half-heartedly at the white concoction. Everything tastes of Mr Trent's bun.

Nanny says, 'Now Vere, eat up this minute.'

The rebuke injures him. He assumes a reproachful expression, but a chasm of sharp indigestion suddenly yawns beneath him. Faith's excited cries between each mouthful, the click of cutlery, the twittering flutter of the budgerigars – all are unpleasant, threatening. He cannot move – he must not even try: the weight of his fork disturbs his balance: the sunlight is too bright and too hot: he feels sick.

'Come along, sweetheart, eat a bit for me.'

'No, thank you, Flora.'

The care with which he speaks makes the words sound cold. He attempts to smile at Flora, but manages only a pained grimace.

'And it's no good making up to Flora,' Nanny says. 'Just get on with your lunch.'...

'Please, sweetheart, please, you must eat up, you know.'

He does not answer. He cannot. Flora's soft voice, the whole idea of Flora and her kindness and love, is insupportable, the blow for which he is not prepared. His eyes prick and he is unable to control the quivering of his lower lip. The outline of the mustard-pot blurs, the lump in his throat prevents him from swallowing. A tear trickles down his cheek, quick and damp, and falls onto his leather shorts.

. . . Nanny asks Flora, 'Have you any idea why he can't eat?'

Flora pauses. 'He's never much appetite, has he?'

'But he must eat something. A growing boy.'

'Shall I make you a castle, Vere, and you can eat it up?'

'All right, Flora,' he agrees, forgetting his notions of revenge and suddenly feeling hungry.

'You've not been eating sweets, Vere?'

'No,' he replies in a shocked voice, taking an active interest in the lay-out of the castle, the moat of sauce, the walls of mashed potato and the wood of greens in the castle grounds. 'What about a draw-bridge? Oughtn't it to have a drawbridge?' He makes the query general, but Nanny supplies no answer. She is not to be diverted. He feared as much. He might as well try to divert the sea. He looks at Flora hopelessly. 'It ought to have a drawbridge,' he says.

'Has Mr Trent been up today?' Nanny asks.

'Mr Trent? I think he has,' says Vere.

'I see.'

'Shall I eat some of the moat, Flora?'

'What did Mr Trent give you, Vere?'

'Thank you, Flora – look, the moat is leaking now!'

'Those buns, I suppose, Vere?'

'Wait a minute, Nanny!'

'Has Vere been eating buns, Flora?'

'Oh, oh, the moat is running away——'

'Please answer me, Flora. Has Vere been eating Mr Trent's buns?'

'Yes,' he interrupts, 'I have been eating buns.'

Everyone is surprised, even the baby. Nanny is the first to collect herself.

'Well Vere, in that case you're a very naughty boy,' she says.

MORNING *by Julian Fane*

After my father's desertion, my mother's ardently religious disposition dominated the household and I was often taken to Sunday school where I met God's representative in the guise of a tall, black preacher. One Sunday my mother invited the tall, black preacher to a dinner of fried chicken. I was happy, not because the preacher was coming but because of the chicken. One or two neighbors also were invited. But no sooner had the preacher arrived than I began to resent him, for I learned at once that he, like my father, was used to having his own way. The hour for dinner came and I was wedged at the table between talking and laughing adults. In the center of the table was a huge platter of golden-brown fried chicken. I compared the bowl of soup that sat before me with the crispy chicken and decided in favor of the chicken. The others began to eat their soup, but I could not touch mine.

'Eat your soup,' my mother said.

'I don't want any,' I said.

'You won't get anything else until you've eaten your soup,' she said.

The preacher had finished his soup and had asked that the platter of chicken be passed to him. It galled me. He smiled, cocked his head this way and that, picking out choice pieces. I forced a spoonful of soup down my throat and looked to see if my speed matched that of the preacher. It did not. There were already bare chicken bones on his plate, and he was reaching for more. I tried eating my soup faster, but it was no use; the other people were now serving themselves chicken and the platter was more than half empty. I gave up and sat staring in despair at the vanishing pieces of fried chicken.

'Eat your soup or you won't get anything,' my mother warned.

I looked at her appealingly and could not answer. As piece after piece of chicken was eaten, I was unable to eat my soup at all. I grew hot with anger. The preacher was laughing and joking and the grownups were hanging on his words. My growing hate of the preacher finally became more important than God or religion and I could no longer contain myself. I leaped up from the table, knowing that I should be ashamed of what I was doing, but unable to stop, and screamed, running blindly from the room.

'That preacher's going to eat *all* the chicken!' I bawled.

The preacher tossed back his head and roared with laughter, but my mother was angry and told me that I was to have no dinner because of my bad manners.

BLACK BOY *by Richard Wright*

There was a particular kind of wheaten biscuit with a very pale pure unsweetened flavour – I am reminded now of the Host – which only my mother had the right to eat. They were kept in a special biscuit-tin in her bedroom and sometimes as a favour I was given one to eat dipped in milk. I associate my mother with a remoteness, which I did not at all resent, and with a smell of eau-de-cologne. If I could have tasted her I am sure she would have tasted of wheaten biscuits. She paid occasional state visits to the nursery in the School House, a large confused room which looked out on the flint church and the old cemetery, with toy cupboards and bookshelves and a big wooden rocking-horse with wicked eyes and one large comfortable wicker-chair for the nurse beside the steel fireguard, and my mother gained in my eyes great dignity from her superintendence of the linen-cupboard, where a frightening witch lurked, but of that later. The wheaten biscuit remains for me a symbol of her cool puritan beauty – she seemed to eliminate all confusion, to recognize the good from the bad and choose the good, though where her family was concerned in later years she noticed only the good. If one of us had committed murder she would, I am sure, have blamed the victim.

A SORT OF LIFE *by Graham Greene*

I suppose it must have been during a lean year, when we were devoid even of servants, that my father would inaugurate some lark. One afternoon he came home early and suggested that it was just the sort of day for making toffee. The boys sprang to the idea, but mother hesitated, as she didn't know quite how to make it. But when my father said that he knew all about it because they had made it at school once, we all followed him in a glad rush to the kitchen. Barnholt was sent to the grocer close by for 'a pound of his worst butter'. All grins, Barnholt flew forth on his errand. The grocer was annoyed at such a request, but, as Barnholt pointed out to him, if he had a best butter he must have a worst. Not seeing the obvious retort to this, he grumblingly served out a pound of something which my father declared to exceed his worst expectations. Meanwhile mother had brought out sugar, and, after much searching of cupboards, some treacle. All was put in a saucepan and Dym was placed to stir it over the fire, while Charles measured out a tablespoonful of vinegar. My part was to get in everyone's way and ask why each thing was done. My father's explanation of the vinegar was peculiar, having some strange reference to the Franco-Prussian War. When mother had greased some flat tins the mixture was poured into them, and we had to wait a bit till it was set. I can't remember what it tasted like, but I know we were all in a glorious mess.

Another time it was a Welsh rabbit that my father had a mind for, and a syndicate was again formed for its creation. In this case the Franco-Prussian ingredient was a little beer. My father did the careful stirring this time, and two of the boys got round his legs making toast. Mother hovered around, shaking her head, prophesying indigestion and the doctor. But she ate her share and wished it had been bigger.

The best of these impromptu feasts was a positive shoal of sprats that my father came home with one evening. 'They're practically alive,' said he, 'and they were almost giving them away in Farringdon Market. Now, Mary, bring out your biggest frying-pan and some dripping, make up the fire, and you boys put the plates to warm. You shall have some fish on them before you know where you are.' And lo, it was so. There was a sizzling and a tossing, and soon the crisp little fish were tumbling on to our outstretched plates, while mother was cutting bread and butter as fast as she could. I have had elegantly dressed sole at a grand dinner, salmon straight from the Dart, trout fresh from a Welsh stream, and perch that I caught myself in a Canadian river, but no fish has ever had the magic quality of those sprats 'given away' in London and cooked by my father.

A LONDON CHILD OF THE 1870S *by M. V. Hughes*

23

FAITH

The first religious experience that I can remember is getting under the nursery table to pray that the dancing mistress might be dead before we got to the Dancing Class. I was about half-way through the exasperating business which dancing class entailed: being changed right down to my skin, and washed and brushed, and having the comfortable dirt taken out of my fingernails. Margaret was sitting on the table, while Nana made her hair into long sausage-curls, with a wet brush round her finger. We thought the sausages very ugly, but Nana admired them, and we all loved Nana so much that we would do anything she liked. So Margaret bore it as well as she could, and only gave a little snarl when a drop of cold water fell on her bare neck. Charles was carefully washing his hands without any soap, the usual expression of philosophic calm on his round face. I think that he sometimes washed without any water either, for I well remember the smooth and permanent pale grey texture of his fingers.

When I was about half-dressed, as I said, in my white flannel petticoat to be exact, I considered my costume suitable, and I got under the table for religious seclusion, and took up an attitude modelled on Sir Joshua Reynolds' 'Infant Samuel kneeling in Prayer', as the correct position for divine transactions. We knew the Infant Samuel very well, from the picture-card game of National Gallery, which we often played.

It was not that I had any particular grudge against that particular dancing mistress, who was called, I think, Miss Ratcliffe. Of course, all dancing mistresses were affected jades. Hamlet's words perfectly described them, when I read them later on: '*You jig, you amble, you lisp and nickname God's creatures and make your wantonness your ignorance.*' But that would not have mattered to me if only they had kept their jigging and ambling to themselves and left me in peace. But as it was, we were forced to go, and I really could think of no other weapon of self-defence except prayer. Not that I believed in that much; still, perhaps it was worth trying.   PERIOD PIECE *by Gwen Raverat*

My school days began when I was four years and a half old. . . . Mrs Horr was a New England lady of middle age with New England ways and principles and she always opened school with prayer and a chapter from the New Testament; also she explained the chapter with a brief talk. In one of these talks she dwelt upon the text 'Ask and ye shall receive', and said that whosoever prayed for a thing with earnestness and strong desire need not doubt that his prayer would be answered.

I was so forcibly struck by this information and so gratified by the opportunities which it offered that this was probably the first time I had heard of it. I thought I would give it a trial. I believed in Mrs Horr thoroughly and I had no doubts as to the result. I prayed for gingerbread. Margaret Kooneman, who was the baker's daughter, brought a slab of gingerbread to school every morning; she had always kept it out of sight before but when I finished my prayer and glanced up, there it was in easy reach and she was looking the other way. In all my life I believe I never enjoyed an answer to prayer more than I enjoyed that one; and I was a convert, too. I had no end of wants and they had always remained unsatisfied up to that time, but I meant to supply them and extend them now that I had found out how to do it.

But this dream was like almost all the other dreams we indulge in in life, there was nothing in it. I did as much praying during the next two or three days as anyone in that town, I suppose, and I was very sincere and earnest about it too, but nothing came of it. I found that not even the most powerful prayer was competent to lift that gingerbread again, and I came to the conclusion that if a person remains faithful to his gingerbread and keeps his eye on it he need not trouble himself about your prayers.

THE AUTOBIOGRAPHY OF MARK TWAIN

Our Bog is Dood

Our Bog is dood, our Bog is dood,
They lisped in accents mild,
But when I asked them to explain
They grew a little wild.
How do you know your Bog is dood
My darling little child?

We know because we wish it so
That is enough, they cried,
And straight within each infant eye
Stood up the flame of pride,
And if you do not think it so
You shall be crucified.

Then tell me, darling little ones,
What's dood, suppose Bog is?
Just what we think, the answer came,
Just what we think it is.
They bowed their heads. Our Bog is ours
And we are wholly his.

But when they raised them up again
They had forgotten me
Each one upon each other glared
In pride and misery
For what was dood, and what their Bog
They never could agree.

Oh sweet it was to leave them then,
And sweeter not to see,
And sweetest of all to walk alone
Beside the encroaching sea,
The sea that soon should drown them all,
That never yet drowned me.

Stevie Smith

Of living on the Chelsea Embankment I have not one smallest
recollection. Perhaps it was at this time that Dorelia called with a
troop of us at Helen's lodging. Helen was out; on her return the
landlady said there had been a lady asking for her – 'foreign, if
anything'. The house in Church Street I remember well enough. It
had a cupboard in the bathroom with no bottom to it, leading
down to the place where all wicked children went. So my aunt
Edie told me. Ideas of heaven and hell must be inherent in the
human mind: I had had no instruction whatever on the subject,
yet as I looked down into those depths of fathomless darkness I
could hear a hissing that never ceased. My imagination easily
supplied the cause of it – black flames, springing from row upon
row of round gas rings. Not that I was morbid about this terrible
hole; I merely accepted its presence in our midst as one of the
unpleasant things about life, and was careful to avoid it as much
as possible. Good behaviour, according to my youthful creed, led
to a place where policemen constructed entirely out of gold
walked streets of the same material: bad behaviour, to the cupboard in the bathroom.

THE SEVENTH CHILD *by Romilly John*

*A Kikuyu child, cured of a long illness through Karen Blixen's
intervention, becomes her houseboy.*

Kamante when I first met him looked as if he were six years old,
but he had a brother who looked about eight, and both brothers
agreed that Kamante was the eldest of them, so I suppose he must
have been set back in growth by his long illness; he was probably
then nine years old. . . . His legs remained forever as thin as sticks.
A fantastic figure he always was, half of fun and half of diabolism;
with a very slight alteration, he might have sat and stared down,
on the top of the cathedral of Notre Dame in Paris. He had in him
something bright and live; in a painting he would have made a
spot of unusually intense colouring; with this he gave a stroke of
picturesqueness to my household. He was never quite right in the
head, or at least he was always what, in a white person, you would
have called highly eccentric.

One night, after midnight, he suddenly walked into my bed-room with a hurricane-lamp in his hand, silent, as if on duty. It must have been only a short time after he first came into my house, for he was very small; he stood by my bedside like a dark bat that had strayed into the room, with very big spreading ears, or like a small African Will-o'-the-wisp, with his lamp in his hand. He spoke to me very solemnly. 'Msabu,' he said, 'I think you had better get up.' I sat up in bed bewildered; I thought that if anything serious had happened, it would have been Farah who would have come to fetch me, but when I told Kamante to go away again, he did not move. 'Msabu,' he said again, 'I think that you had better get up. I think that God is coming.' When I heard this, I did get up, and asked him why he thought so. He gravely led me into the dining-room which looked west, towards the hills. From the door-windows I now saw a strange phenomenon. There was a big grass-fire going on, out in the hills, and the grass was burning all the way from the hill top to the plain; when seen from the house it was a nearly vertical line. It did indeed look as if some gigantic figure was moving and coming towards us. I stood for some time and looked at it, with Kamante watching by my side; then I began to explain the thing to him. I meant to quiet him, for I thought that he had been terribly frightened. But the explanation did not seem to make much impression on him one way or the other; he clearly took his mission to have been fulfilled when he had called me. 'Well, yes,' he said, 'it may be so. But I thought that you had better get up in case it was God coming.'

OUT OF AFRICA *by Karen Blixen*

On Peckham Rye (by Dulwich Hill) it was, as he in after years related, that while quite a child, of eight or ten perhaps, he had his first vision. Sauntering along, the boy looked up and saw a tree filled with angels, bright angelic wings bespangling every bough like stars. Returned home he related the incident, and only through his mother's intercession escaped a thrashing from his honest father, for telling a lie. Another time, one summer morn, he saw the haymakers at work, and amid them angelic figures walking.

LIFE OF WILLIAM BLAKE *by Alexander Gilchrist*

I was lying in a wide bed, with a thick blanket folded four times around me, listening to grandmother, who was saying her prayers. She was on her knees; and pressing one hand against her breast, she reverently crossed herself from time to time with the other. Out in the yard a hard frost reigned; a greenish moonlight peeped through the ice patterns on the window-panes, falling flatteringly on her kindly face and large nose, and kindling a phosphorescent light in her dark eyes. Her silky, luxuriant tresses were lit up as if by a furnace; her dark dress rustled, falling in ripples from her shoulders and spreading about her on the floor.

When she had finished her prayers grandmother undressed in silence, carefully folding up her clothes and placing them on the trunk in the corner. Then she came to bed. I pretended to be fast asleep.

'You are not asleep, you rogue, you are only making believe,' she said softly. 'Come, my duck, let's have some bedclothes!'

Foreseeing what would happen, I could not repress a smile, upon seeing which she cried: 'So this is how you trick your old grandmother?' And taking hold of the blanket she drew it towards her with so much force and skill that I bounced up in the air, and turning over and over fell back with a squash into the soft feather bed, while she said with a chuckle: 'What is it, little Hop o' my Thumb? Have you been bitten by a mosquito?'

But sometimes she prayed for such a long time that I really did fall asleep, and did not hear her come to bed.

The longer prayers were generally the conclusion of a day of trouble, or a day of quarrelling and fighting; and it was very interesting to listen to them. Grandmother gave to God a circumstantial account of all that had happened in the house. Bowed down, looking like a great mound, she knelt, at first whispering rapidly and indistinctly, then hoarsely muttering:

'O Lord, Thou knowest that all of us wish to do better. Michael, the elder, ought to have been set up in the town – it will do him harm to be on the river; and the other is a new neighbourhood and not overdone. I don't know what will come of it all! There's Father now. Jaakov is his favourite. Can it be right to love one child more than the others? He is an obstinate old man; do Thou, O Lord, teach him!'

Gazing at the dark-featured ikon, with her large, brilliant eyes, she thus counselled God:

'Send him a good dream, O Lord, to make him understand how he ought to treat his children!'

After prostrating herself and striking her broad forehead on the floor, she again straightened herself, and said coaxingly:

'And send Varvara some happiness! How has she displeased Thee? Is she more sinful than the others? Why should a healthy young woman be so afflicted? And remember Gregory, O Lord! His eyes are getting worse and worse. If he goes blind he will be sent adrift. That will be terrible! He has used up all his strength for grandfather, but do you think it likely that grandfather will help him? O Lord! Lord!'

She remained silent for a long time, with her head bowed meekly, and her hands hanging by her sides, as still as if she had fallen asleep, or had been suddenly frozen.

'What else is there?' she asked herself aloud, wrinkling her brows.

'O Lord, save all the faithful! Pardon me – accursed fool as I am! – Thou knowest that I do not sin out of malice but out of stupidity.' And drawing a deep breath she would say lovingly and contentedly: 'Son of God, Thou knowest all! Father, Thou seest all things.'

I was very fond of grandmother's God Who seemed so near to her, and I often said:

'Tell me something about God.'

She used to speak about Him in a peculiar manner – very quietly, strangely drawing out her words, closing her eyes; and she made a point of always sitting down and arranging her head-handkerchief very deliberately before she began.

'God's seat is on the hills, amidst the meadows of Paradise; it is an altar of sapphires under silver linden trees which flower all the year round, for in Paradise there is no winter, nor even autumn, and the flowers never wither, for joy is the divine favour. And round about God many angels fly like flakes of snow; and it may be even that bees hum there, and white doves fly between Heaven and earth, telling God all about us and everybody. And here on earth you and I and grandfather each has been given an angel.

God treats us all equally. For instance, your angel will go and tell God: "Lexei put his tongue out at grandfather." And God says: "All right, let the old man whip him." And so it is with all of us; God gives to all what they deserve – to some grief, to others joy. And so all is right that He does, and the angels rejoice, and spread their wings and sing to Him without ceasing: "Glory be unto Thee, O God; Glory be unto Thee." And He just smiles on them, and it is enough for them – and more.' And she would smile herself, shaking her head from side to side.

'Have you seen that?'

'No, I have not seen it, but I know.'

When she spoke about God, or Heaven, or the angels, she seemed to shrink in size; her face grew younger, and her liquid eyes emitted a curious warm radiance. I used to take her heavy, satiny plait in my hands, and wind it round my neck as I sat quite still and listened to the endless but never tedious story.

MY CHILDHOOD *by Maxim Gorky*

Mirth

If you are merry sing away,
    And touch the organs sweet;
This is the Lord's triumphant day,
Ye children in the galleries gay,
    Shout from each goodly seat.

It shall be May tomorrow's morn,
    A-field then let us run,
And deck us in the blooming thorn,
Soon as the cock begins to warn,
    And long before the sun.

I give the praise to Christ alone,
    My pinks already show;
And my streaked roses fully blown,
The sweetness of the Lord make known,
    And to his glory grow. . . .

With white and crimson laughs the sky,
  With birds the hedgerows ring;
To give the praise to God most high,
And all the sulky fiends defy,
  Is a most joyful thing.

Christopher Smart (1722–71)

Until I was ten years old or thereabouts my life was a consistent, undeviating search for God, pure, simple and undefined. I was fortunately too young to read for myself the Old Testament, which unexpurgated is far more disturbing to adolescents than *Fanny Hill*. Instead I had to rely upon a selection of stories in a little book with a cover by Caldecott called, if I recollect rightly, *The Peep of Day*.

This book made the deepest impression upon me. I made my reluctant mother, who far preferred Hans Andersen, read it over and over again. No wonder she considered me a bit of a prig as I brushed aside every endeavour to listen for a change to *The Brave Tin Soldier*, or *The Beetle who went on his Travels*. No, it had to be the story of the infant Samuel, the angel who miraculously shielded those egregious bores Shadrach, Meshach and Abednego in the fiery furnace, Daniel in the lions' den, or Joseph through every phase of his goody-goody career. Freud may advance some complex reason why I identified myself with the hero in every case. I will offer my perfectly simple explanation. I craved the unattainable – notoriety. I longed to be admired by my father. Instead I was quite rightly ignored by him because I never showed a vestige of bravery on any possible occasion. And bravery was the chief virtue which could make a boy conspicuous in the sort of nursery from which the likes of myself sprang. . . .

While the *Peep of Day* influence lasted I made myself very tiresome by adopting the role of the various Old Testament heroes whose exploits my mother read to me. As the infant Samuel I would 'minister unto the Lord', which consisted in delivering myself of pious little dissertations in the servants' hall, and once accosting the Vicar as Eli the High Priest, and foretelling the total destruction of his house on account of the iniquity of his children (who incidentally were my own age and of spotless innocence). God had disclosed to me, I solemnly averred, that the manner of their destruction 'will make the ears of everyone that heareth it, tingle'. Such too was my ability to assume the role of a super-natural being that once as the fourth man, 'in form like the Son of God', I had to be forcibly prevented from walking into the nursery fire by the nursemaid and two other servants who, to my chagrin, declined to impersonate Shadrach, Meshach and Abednego. On another occasion during my Daniel-in-the-Lions'-Den role, I was found by the groom nestling in a loose-box between the legs of a particularly savage hunter. These were not acts of courage, but presumption, because I was absolutely convinced the Lord would not allow me to come to harm. Again my Joseph impersonation led to some awkward misunderstandings. I followed the example of Pharaoh's steward who put money and a silver cup into his brethren's sacks of corn, by surreptitiously opening the packed luggage of departing guests while they were at breakfast down-stairs on Monday mornings, and throwing handfuls of coins – my mother always left money lying about – on top of their folded nightdresses. I even managed to jam into a full Gladstone bag the prized Hunt Cup won by my father at Cheltenham Races. Not until the owner of the luggage reached home and unpacked was this precious, but dented, object revealed. His embarrassment must have been acute, and how he managed to explain it away in his bread-and-butter letter I never learned.

ANOTHER SELF *by James Lees-Milne*

Matthew Prior (1664–1721) writes, only a year before his death, to a five-year-old friend.

A Letter to the Child
Lady Margaret Cavendish Holles-Harley

My noble, lovely, little Peggy,
Let this my First Epistle beg ye,
At dawn of morn and close of even,
To lift your heart and hands to Heaven.

In double beauty say your prayer:
'Our Father' first, then 'Notre Père'.
And, dearest child, along the day,
In every thing you do and say,
Obey and please my lord and lady,
So God shall love, and angels aid ye.

If to these precepts you attend,
No second letter need I send,
And so I rest your constant friend.

The Irish novelist Kathleen Coyle (1886–1942), who had been crippled from early childhood, describes a pilgrimage of thanksgiving for her cure.

On an early morning Mary O'Connell and I set forth upon our pilgrimage. We arrived at a very desolate place at nightfall. An old woman was bent over a turf fire, stirring a mixture in a hanging pot. I had to sleep in the same bed as Mary O'Connell. I was prevented from going to sleep for she was picking her corns. I was compelled to listen. We arose at dawn and said our prayers, kneeling on the earthen hearth with the old woman. Everything was clean but poor and bare, a table and a stool and the little unadorned window with a flower in a jam pot. The earth outside consisted of low stretching fields, full of mists. Larks rose and little shy things twittered and broke in flight over the grassy pattern. We had to walk to the Well in our bare feet. The sky was very low. It was coming in like a tide, breaking into ripples that were edged with gold. It was not pleasant having to walk in bare feet but Mary led and I was obliged to follow. There was no sign of the shrine. We came upon it suddenly, blossoming like a white rosebush at the end of the fields. The roses turned out to be pilgrim rags and when we got there we found that the bushes were hung with old shoes and sticks and crutches. Mary had brought my crutches. She laid them down solemnly upon a path of stones. We prayed together. Then she dipped into the Well and gave me the water to sip. It tasted of salt and soda and I wanted to spit it out but did not dare. Mary prayed loudly in ups and downs like the priest who performed miracles. I did not pray. I was in that state of grace when the peace of a place falls upon you like a mantle. We were alone at the shrine. We were alone in the sharp misty morning – in our bare feet. I could smell the heather. I could smell the dark moist earth. I was abroad in the country space, untroubled by any demand for favours. It was sufficient to be there – and to get rid of my crutches. . . .

We came back to the old peasant woman across the fields. She was standing on her threshold, shading her eyes with her hand. It was strangely peaceful in the little kitchen – the fire blazing and the crooked hand-patterned bowls on the table, with iron spoons. There was the smell of the night-washed earth, drying out from its dews; the smell of *distance* – of untraversed space. I was too young then to analyse it, but I had a distinct feeling of holiness, of one-ness, of what was unbroken. I was content – a child with two old women in the wilderness.

THE MAGICAL REALM

The gardeners, of whom Mr Basham was third, brought in to family prayers a faint, and the stable-men a stronger, whiff of manure, and sat on slender benches behind the maids. A marble angel, restraining a child from treading upon a serpent, presided, very white, over the shadowy space where the household sat. Our own little wicker chairs, that creaked if we fidgeted, faced the servants; and at the words 'Let us pray' we all rose, turned round, and aimed our rumps at one another, family against domestics, like the children defying the wolves in *Peter Pan*. This manoeuvre seemed to us to be entirely proper, natural, and religious. I do not think it could have occurred to any of the Christians kneeling in the Inner Hall that it would be possible to pray to God standing up, as the Presbyterians do. Made in His Image, as we were (except Mrs Pleasance, the laundrywoman, who was made in the image of a cottage-loaf), we did not, it must be admitted, make the best of our divine shapes when praying. It was the fault, no doubt, of the benches, and of our small chairs, for being so low; but to One looking down from Above through the sky-light, the spectacle must have been, even if endearingly, ridiculous. . . .

We children could be reverent and subdued; we were sensitive to the suggestions of posture, of clasped hands and shut eyes; but although we ended our evening prayer with

> Keep me, oh keep me, King of Kings,
> Beneath Thine own almighty wings,

I do not remember having any comfort from those wings when frightened in the night. A call to Nanny was more effective, and she alone could dispel the horror of a recurring nightmare of enormous red-faced fishmongers, in blue striped aprons, thronging and hanging over my bed. Our belief in God was implicit, but He bored us rather than interested us, and although we elder ones were genuinely shocked when a younger brother, invited to come and hear some 'Sunday reading', said 'If it's anything about Jethuth, I'd rather not come', we were shocked by his temerity in saying it, not by his point of view, which was secretly our own. We were taken to Church at an early age, but sat with our mother in the galilee, so as to avoid disturbing the congregation when we clattered out before the sermon. Even so, the schoolchildren looked round at us, and, had we been consulted, we should have rather borne with the sermon than with this publicity. But our attendance must have been irregular, because one Rector preached 'at' my mother, taking as his text the story of the Infant Samuel. 'Did Samuel's mother stay at home, and read to him from a Child's Bible? No, *she* took him *with* her to the Temple.'. . .

A VICTORIAN BOYHOOD *by* L. E. Jones

The Bible, during my early years, failed to inspire me with the proper sentiments of reverence and affection. Indeed, I regret to say I even felt an active antipathy for the Holy Book, an attitude which was largely, if not entirely, the fault of my grandmother, Lady Bourchier.

The Bible occupied so prominent a position in her scheme of life that I grew to associate it with her own austere personality and the grim little study at Stackwell. I feared that, were I to allow it to become an obsession (as it had become in her case), my own character might end by assuming that same forbidding Calvinistic tinge. I was not sufficiently cultured to be able to appreciate the beauties of biblical language, and the numerous copies of the Bible that my grandmother had thrust into my reluctant hands had been, all of them, cheap, ill-bound editions. The ugly, common bindings, the villainous print and the double columns were not calculated to arouse aesthetic interest, while the rigid numbering of the verses seemed to impart an unpleasantly didactic tone to the contents. Having been told that the book had been written by God himself, I often wondered why One who had shown himself, in most respects, lavish to the point of extravagance should have been so economical in the presentation of his literary efforts to the public.

On Sundays, 'early school' was always taken by Mr Gambril himself. One Sunday morning towards the end of the Summer Term, whilst we were all assembled awaiting his arrival, I entered into a theological discussion with the sanctimonious Creeling, in the course of which he asserted that anyone speaking irreverently of the Bible or maltreating it in any way would inevitably be punished by God.

'What form,' I asked, 'do you suppose the punishment would take?'

'Well, you'd probably be struck by lightning, or else lose all your money.'

'What absolute rot!'

'Well, at any rate,' Creeling demurred, 'it would bring frightful bad luck.'

'Supposing,' I suggested, 'I were to get up now and throw my Bible across the room?'

'Just you try it and see!'

He was reckoning on my cowardice, a kind of assumption that arouses the meanest spirit. I at once stood up and hurled my Bible across the room.

At that very moment the door opened and Mr Gambril appeared. The book missed him by a few inches and fell with a thud at his feet. I was paralysed with horror, and he was obliged to ask twice over 'Who threw that book?' before I was able to get my voice into working order.

'Oh, it was you,' he said, in that ominously suave voice which one knew from experience was like the lull preceding the storm. He bent down and examined the book. Then the storm broke.

'The Bible!' he shouted. 'The Bible, sir! You have thrown the Bible – and on Sunday too! Stand up on the form!'

I climbed up on to the form. My knees were trembling with such violence that I had difficulty in keeping my balance. Somebody laughed.

'Silence!' said Mr Gambril. 'This is no laughing matter!

'Now, sir,' he turned to me, 'may I ask for what reason you threw your Bible?'

I hesitated. I could think of no valid reason.

'What did you throw your Bible for? Answer me at once!'

'I threw it for a bet.'

As the words left my lips I realized their infelicity. I suppose 'bravado' was the word I had meant to use, but panic confused my thought.

'For a bet? Indeed! This makes your offence even worse than I had imagined. You have the effrontery to tell me, sir, that, for a bet, which is in itself reprehensible, you actually threw God's Sacred Book across the room! Are you aware that this constitutes an act of sacrilege, liable in ordinary circumstances to be punished by a long term of imprisonment?'

I was not aware; but it seemed, at that moment, to be quite probable. I was too frightened to recognize it as merely one of those over-statements with which the Head was wont to emphasize his speech.

He turned to the assembled school. 'Never,' he proclaimed, 'in all my long experience of school life have I come across so flagrant a case of wilful blasphemy and godlessness. Boys, I am sure you are all disgusted. You will now express your condemnation of such behaviour by hissing the culprit.'

This was an entirely new form of punishment. To me, as I stood on the form with bowed head, surrounded, as it were, by a roomful of infuriated vipers, it seemed to be the most terrible thing that had ever happened to anyone, and the suggestion of mass-hatred in a peculiarly venomous shape intensified my sense of guilt. I felt as though I were branded for ever with the mark of Cain.

When the hissing had died down the Headmaster said to me in the tones of a judge delivering a death-sentence, 'You will remain standing on the form during the lesson and afterwards you will come to my study.'

This, of course, implied that a birching was in store for me. How I got through the remainder of the lesson would be too painful to relate. There were moments when I would have welcomed annihilation. The horror of seeing what I believed to be a comparatively innocent action transformed in the twinkling of an eye into an appalling crime, followed by public shame, the experience of the pillory and finally the condemned cell. I was also smarting under a sense of injustice, complicated by the horrible doubt as to whether perhaps after all Creeling had not been right in saying that the Bible possessed magic powers of self-protection. In this case, at any rate, the insult offered to it had been followed by swift retribution.

The lesson came to an end at last. I got down from the form and followed the Headmaster out of the room in the midst of a silence that I knew to be fraught with a gloating expectancy.

As I entered the study, Mr Gambril took up one of his birches and laid it on the table. He then proceeded to deliver a forcible homily on sacrilege and wickedness in general, in the course of which he expressed grave misgivings about my future career. But although he fingered the birch and, from time to time, shook it at me menacingly, he finally dismissed me without having used it. The implication was that my offence had been far too serious for mere corporal punishment and that I was lucky to have escaped expulsion. I only thought that I was lucky to have escaped the birch. FIRST CHILDHOOD *by Lord Berners*

24

CHRISTMAS

One of the greatest enigmas of my earliest years, aside from the riddle of birth, was the means by which the Christmas toys got down the chimney. I evolved a Byzantine rationale to account for how the larger toys could logically get down the chimney if Father Christmas dropped them from above. Apropos of a large model sailboat (which, as I learned later, was a present from one of my older brother's friends) I solved the problem by accepting the following hypothesis: since God is omnipotent, he creates the toys just where I find them, without their having to pass through the chimney. My amazement at the sight of the enormous boat at the bottom of the narrow shaft was something like that which the sight of a ship inside a narrow-necked bottle in a nearby shop-window caused me each time I passed it.

When I learned that children were created in the womb, and when the mystery of Christmas was explained to me, I felt I had acceded to a kind of majority; this was connected in my mind with the concept of the Age of Reason, a period when – in principle – the first degree of initiation is passed. Once I knew what pregnancy was, the problem of childbirth became analogous to that of how the toys got down the chimney: How did the baby get out?

MANHOOD *by Michel Leiris (1901–   )*

I remained the only child of my parents and I was entirely satisfied with this arrangement. . . .

Only once in every year did I ardently wish to have brothers and sisters – on Christmas Eve. For all I would have cared they could have packed up and flown away again on Christmas Day after the roast goose and dumplings, the red cabbage and the celery salad. I would gladly have given up my own helping of goose and eaten giblets instead if only I did not have to be alone on the evening of the twenty-fourth of December. They could have had half my presents. And what truly glorious presents they were!

Why did I not wish to be alone and not to be an only child on this, the most beautiful evening of a child's year? Because I was afraid. I dreaded the presentation of the gifts. I dreaded it, and I dared not show that I did. It is not surprising if you do not understand this right away. I have been pondering for a long time past whether I should speak of it or not. But since I am going to speak of it, I had better explain it to you.

Their love of me made my parents jealous of each other. They tried to hide it, and they often succeeded. But on the most beautiful day of the year they did not succeed. At all other times they were so careful to get on well together for my sake, but on Christmas Eve they simply could not manage it. It was beyond their power. I knew all about it, but for the sake of all three of us I had to behave as if I did not know it.

For weeks beforehand my father had sat down in the cellar half the night making, for instance, a wonderful toy stable for me. He had carved and nailed, glued and painted, done miniature writing, cut and sewn miniature harness, plaited through the horses' manes with ribbons, filled the mangers with hay and, down there by the smoky paraffin lamp, had thought again and again of something else to add – another joint, another band or clasp, another hook, another broom for the stable, another box for the oats, until at last, grinning contentedly, he was able to say to himself, 'It takes me to do a job like that!'

Another time he made a dray complete with beer barrels, a drop ladder, wheels with hub-covers and iron rims – a solid vehicle with wheel axles, and interchangeable shafts according to whether I wished to yoke one horse to it or two; with leather cushions for letting the beer barrels down on and whips and brakes at the driver's seat. And this toy, too, was a faultless masterpiece, a work of art.

These were gifts at the sight of which even little princes would have clapped their hands with joy. But my father would not have given them to princes.

For weeks on end my mother spent half the day roaming through the town searching the shops. Every year she bought so many gifts that her hiding-place, the chest of drawers, bulged. She bought roller-skates, building-bricks, coloured pencils, tubes of paints, painting-books, dumb-bells and clubs for the gym class, a football for playing in the yard, ice-skates, musical tops, hiking-boots, a Norwegian sledge, a little box of precision instruments on blue velvet, a little printing-press with a set of compositor's letters and, under the guidance of Paul Schurig and the Teachers' Guild of Saxony, a great many good children's books. And of course quantities of handkerchiefs, stockings, gym shorts, knitted caps, woollen gloves, sweaters, sailor blouses, swimsuits, shirts and similar useful things.

It was a rivalry in their love for me and it was a bitter one. It was a drama with three characters, and the last act took place every year on Christmas Eve. A little boy played the principal part. Whether the piece turned out a tragedy or a comedy depended on his talent in improvisation. Even now when I think of it, my heart is in my mouth.

I sat in the kitchen and waited to be called into the best room, under the Christmas tree, for the presentation. I had my own presents ready – a little box of ten or perhaps twenty-five cigars for Papa; for Mamma a scarf, a watercolour drawing painted by myself or – as happened once when I possessed only sixty-five pfennigs – the 'seven articles' beautifully packed in a cardboard box from Kuhne's drapery. What are 'the seven articles'? A reel of white and a reel of black sewing-silk, a packet of pins and a packet of needles, a spool of white thread, a spool of black thread, and a dozen medium-sized black press-studs – seven different articles for sixty-five pfennigs! That, I thought, was a record achievement. And I would have been proud of it if I had not been so afraid at the time.

I stood at the kitchen window and looked at the windows opposite. Here and there they were already lighting the Christmas candles. The snow on the street shone in the light of the street-lamps. I could hear Christmas carols. The fire was crackling in the heating-stove, yet I was freezing cold. The kitchen smelt of raisin buns, vanilla sugar and candied peel, yet I felt utterly miserable. But at any moment now I should have to smile, though I felt much more like crying.

And then I heard my mother call, 'Now you can come!' I grabbed the prettily wrapped presents for the two of them and went into the passage. The door of the best room stood open. The Christmas tree was lit up. Father and Mother had taken up their positions to right and left of the table, each beside their own gifts as if the room and the festival, had been divided in half. 'Oh, how beautiful!' I exclaimed, meaning both halves. I still kept near the door so that my efforts to smile happily would be taken as referring unmistakably to both. Papa, with the cigar gone out in his mouth, beamed at the brightly varnished stable. Mamma looked triumphantly down at the mountain of gifts on her right. We all three smiled in an effort to smile down our triple uneasiness. But I could not go on standing at the door.

I walked hesitantly up to the glorious but, alas, divided table, and with every step my feeling of responsibility, my fear and my determination to get over the next quarter of an hour successfully grew stronger. Ah, if I could only be alone, alone with the presents and with the heavenly feeling of being doubly loaded with gifts – gifts from a united love! How lucky I should have been, and what a happy child! But I had to play my role so that the Christmas drama should end happily. I was a diplomat, more grown-up than my parents, and it was up to me to see that our solemn Three-Power Conference under the Christmas tree should pass off without discord. Already at five or six, and still more so later on, I was the master of ceremonies of Christmas Eve, and I performed the heavy task with considerable aptitude, but with a trembling heart.

I stood at the table and expressed my joy in a shuttle movement. I showed joy towards the right, to the delight of my mother. Then I showed joy towards the left of the table, over the toy stable, in a general way. Then I showed joy to the right again, this time over the toboggan; and then to the left once more, taking particular notice of the leather harness. And once more to the right, and once more to the left, never too lengthily, never too hurriedly. I rejoiced sincerely, but I had to divide up and dissemble my joy. Then I gave each of them a kiss on the cheek. My mother first. I presented my gifts, beginning with the cigars. In this way, while Papa was opening the box with his penknife and sniffing the cigars, I was able to stand a little longer beside my mother than beside him. She admired my gift and I gave her a little secret hug, as secret as if it were a sin. Had he noticed it? Was it making him sad?

Next door in the Grüttners' flat they were singing 'O Come, All Ye Faithful'. My father took out of his pocket a purse he had made down in the cellar and held it out to my mother, saying, 'I had almost forgotten this.' She pointed to her half of the table, on which were socks, long woollen underpants and a tie for him. Sometimes we were already eating our sausage and potato salad before they realized that they had forgotten to give each other their gifts. And Mother would say, 'It's time enough after supper.'

WHEN I WAS A LITTLE BOY *by Erich Kästner*

Of our dealings with the 'Saints', a fresh assortment of whom met us on our arrival in Devonshire, I shall speak presently. My Father's austerity of behaviour was, I think, perpetually accentuated by his fear of doing anything to offend the consciences of these persons, whom he supposed, no doubt, to be more sensitive than they really were. He was fond of saying that 'a very little stain upon the conscience makes a wide breach in our communion with God', and he counted possible errors of conduct by hundreds and by thousands. It was in this winter that his attention was particularly drawn to the festival of Christmas, which, apparently, he had scarcely noticed in London.

On the subject of all feasts of the Church he held views of an almost grotesque peculiarity. He looked upon each of them as nugatory and worthless, but the keeping of Christmas appeared to him by far the most hateful, and nothing less than an act of idolatry. 'The very word is Popish', he used to exclaim, 'Christ's Mass!' pursing up his lips with the gesture of one who tastes assafoetida by accident. Then he would adduce the antiquity of the so-called feast, adapted from horrible heathen rites, and itself a soiled relic of the abominable Yule-Tide. He would denounce the horrors of Christmas until it almost made me blush to look at a holly-berry.

On Christmas Day of this year 1857 our villa saw a very unusual sight. My Father had given strictest charge that no difference whatever was to be made in our meals on that day; the dinner was to be neither more copious than usual nor less so. He was obeyed, but the servants, secretly rebellious, made a small plum-pudding for themselves. (I discovered afterwards, with pain, that Miss Marks received a slice of it in her boudoir.) Early in the afternoon, the maids, – of whom we were now advanced to keeping two, – kindly remarked that 'the poor dear child ought to have a bit, anyhow', and wheedled me into the kitchen, where I ate a slice of plum-pudding. Shortly I began to feel that pain inside which in my frail state was inevitable, and my conscience smote me violently. At length I could bear my spiritual anguish no longer, and bursting into the study I called out: 'Oh! Papa, Papa, I have eaten of flesh offered to idols!' It took some time, between my sobs, to explain what had happened. Then my Father sternly said: 'Where is the accursed thing?' I explained that as much as was left of it was still on the kitchen table. He took me by the hand, and ran with me into the midst of the startled servants, seized what remained of the pudding, and with the plate in one hand and me still tight in the other, ran till we reached the dust-heap, when he flung the idolatrous confectionery on to the middle of the ashes, and then raked it deep down into the mass. The suddenness, the violence, the velocity of this extraordinary act made an impression on my memory which nothing will ever efface.

FATHER AND SON *by Edmund Gosse*

The Oxen

Christmas Eve, and twelve of the clock.
  'Now they are all on their knees,'
An elder said as we sat in a flock
  By the embers in hearthside ease.

We pictured the meek mild creatures where
  They dwelt in their strawy pen,
Nor did it occur to one of us there
  To doubt they were kneeling then.

So fair a fancy few would weave
    In these years! Yet, I feel,
If someone said on Christmas Eve,
    'Come, see the oxen kneel

'In the lonely barton by yonder coomb
    Our childhood used to know,'
I should go with him in the gloom,
    Hoping it might be so.

                              Thomas Hardy

A *Miserable Merry Christmas*

What interested me in our new neighborhood was not the school, nor the room I was to have in the house all to myself, but the stable which was built back of the house. My father let me direct the making of a stall, a little smaller than the other stalls, for my pony, and I prayed and hoped and my sister Lou believed that that meant I would get the pony, perhaps for Christmas. I pointed out to her that there were three other stalls and no horses at all. This I said in order that she should answer it. She could not. My father, sounded, said that some day we might have horses and a cow; meanwhile the stable added to the value of a house. 'Some day' is a pain to a boy who lives in and knows only 'now'. My good little sisters, to comfort me, remarked that Christmas was coming, but Christmas was always coming and grown-ups were always talking about it, asking you what you wanted and then giving you what they wanted you to have. Though everybody knew what I wanted, I told them all again. My mother knew that I told God, too, every night. I wanted a pony, and to make sure that they understood, I declared that I wanted nothing else.

'Nothing but a pony?' my father asked.

'Nothing,' I said.

'Not even a pair of high boots?'

That was hard. I did want boots, but I stuck to the pony. 'No, not even boots.'

'Nor candy? There ought to be something to fill your stocking with, and Santa Claus can't put a pony into a stocking.'

That was true, and he couldn't lead a pony down the chimney either. But no. 'All I want is a pony,' I said. 'If I can't have a pony, give me nothing, nothing.'

Now I had been looking myself for the pony I wanted, going to sales stables, inquiring of horsemen, and I had seen several that would do. My father let me 'try' them. I tried so many ponies that I was learning fast to sit a horse. I chose several, but my father always found some fault with them. I was in despair. When Christmas was at hand I had given up all hope of a pony, and on Christmas Eve I hung up my stocking along with my sisters, of whom, by the way, I now had three. . . . They were so happy that Christmas Eve that I caught some of their merriment. I speculated on what I'd get; I hung up the biggest stocking I had, and we all went reluctantly to bed to wait till morning. Not to sleep; not right away. We were told that we must not only go to sleep promptly; we must not wake up till seven-thirty the next morning – or if we did, we must not go to the fireplace for our Christmas. Impossible.

We did sleep that night, but we woke up at 6 a.m. We lay in our beds and debated through the open doors whether to obey till, say, half-past six. Then we bolted. I don't know who started it, but there was a rush. We all disobeyed; we raced to disobey and get first to the fireplace in the front room downstairs. And there they were, the gifts, all sorts of wonderful things, mixed-up piles of presents; only, as I disentangled the mess, I saw that my stocking was empty; it hung limp; not a thing in it; and under and around it – nothing. My sisters had knelt down each by her pile of gifts; they were squealing with delight, till they looked up and saw me standing there in my nightgown with nothing. They left their piles to come to me and look with me at my empty place. Nothing. They felt my stocking: nothing.

I don't remember whether I cried at that moment, but my sisters did. They ran with me back to my bed, and there we all cried till I became indignant. That helped some. I got up, dressed, and driving my sisters away, I went alone out into the yard, down to the stable, and there, all by myself, I wept. My mother came out to me by and by; she found me in my pony stall, sobbing on the floor, and she tried to comfort me. But I heard my father outside; he had come part way with her, and she was having some sort of angry quarrel with him. She tried to comfort me; besought me to come to breakfast. She left me and went on into the house with sharp words for my father.

I don't know what kind of breakfast the family had. My sisters said it was 'awful'. They were ashamed to enjoy their own toys. They came to me, and I was rude; I ran away from them. I went around to the front of the house, sat down on the steps, and, the crying over, I ached. I was wronged, I was hurt — I can feel now what I felt then, and I am sure that if one could see the wounds upon our hearts, there would be found still upon mine a scar from that terrible Christmas morning. And my father, the practical joker, he must have been hurt, too, a little. I saw him looking out of the window. He was watching me or something for an hour or two, drawing back the curtain ever so little lest I catch him, but I saw his face, and I think I can see now the anxiety upon it, the worried impatience.

After — I don't know how long — surely an hour or two — I was brought to the climax of my agony by the sight of a man riding a pony down the street, a pony and a brand-new saddle; the most beautiful saddle I ever saw, and it was a boy's saddle; the man's feet were not in the stirrups; his legs were too long. The outfit was perfect; it was the realization of all my dreams, the answer to all my prayers. A fine new bridle, with a light curb bit. And the pony! As he drew near, I saw that the pony was really a small horse, what we called an Indian pony, a bay, with black mane and tail, and one white foot and a white star on his forehead. For such a horse as that I would have given, I could have forgiven, anything.

But the man, a disheveled fellow with a blackened eye and a fresh-cut face, came along, reading the numbers on the houses, and as my hopes — my impossible hopes — rose, he looked at our door and passed by, he and the pony, and the saddle and the bridle. Too much. I fell upon the steps, and having wept before, I broke now into such a flood of tears that I was a floating wreck when I heard a voice.

'Say, kid,' it said, 'do you know a boy named Lennie Steffens?'

I looked up. It was the man on the pony, back again, at our horse block.

'Yes,' I spluttered through my tears. 'That's me.'

'Well,' he said, 'then this is your horse. I've been looking all over for you and your house. Why don't you put your number where it can be seen?'

'Get down,' I said, running out to him.

He went on saying something about 'ought to have got here at seven o'clock; he told me to bring the nag here and tie him to your post and leave him for you. . . .'

'Get down,' I said.

He got down, and he boosted me up to the saddle. He offered to fit the stirrups to me, but I didn't want him to. I wanted to ride.

'What's the matter with you?' he said angrily. 'What are you crying for? Don't you like the horse? He's a dandy, this horse. I know him of old. He's fine at cattle; he'll drive 'em alone.'

I hardly heard, I could scarcely wait, but he persisted. He adjusted the stirrups, and then, finally, off I rode, slowly, at a walk, so happy, so thrilled, that I did not know what I was doing. I did not look back at the house or the man; I rode off up the street, taking note of everything – of the reins, of the pony's long mane, of the carved leather saddle. I had never seen anything as beautiful. And mine! I was going to ride up past Miss Kay's house. But I noticed on the horn of the saddle some stains like raindrops, so I turned and trotted home, not to the house but to the stable. There was the family, father, mother, sisters, all working for me, all happy. They had been putting in place the tools of my new business: blankets, currycomb, brush, pitchfork – everything, and there was hay in the loft.

'What did you come back so soon for?' somebody asked. 'Why didn't you go on riding?'

I pointed to the stains. 'I wasn't going to get my new saddle rained on,' I said. And my father laughed. 'It isn't raining,' he said. 'Those are not raindrops.'

'They are tears,' my mother gasped, and she gave my father a look which sent him off to the house. Worse still, my mother offered to wipe away the tears still running out of my eyes. I gave her such a look as she had given him, and she went off after my father, drying her own tears.

My sisters remained and we all unsaddled the pony, put on his halter, led him to his stall, tied and fed him. It really began to rain; so all the rest of that memorable day we curried and combed that pony. The girls plaited his mane, forelock, and tail, while I pitchforked hay to him and curried and brushed, curried and brushed. For a change we brought him out to drink; we led him up and down, blanketed like a racehorse; we took turns at that. But the best, the most inexhaustible fun, was to clean him.

When we went reluctantly to our midday Christmas dinner, we smelt of horse, and my sisters had to wash their faces and hands. I was asked to, but I wouldn't, till my mother bade me look in the mirror. Then I washed up – quick. My face was caked with muddy lines of tears that had coursed over my cheeks to my mouth. Having washed away that shame, I ate my dinner, and as I ate I grew hungrier and hungrier. It was my first meal that day, and as I filled up on the turkey and stuffing, the cranberries and the pies, the fruit and the nuts – as I swelled, I could laugh. My mother said I still choked and sobbed now and then, but I laughed, too; I saw and enjoyed my sisters' presents till – I had to go out and attend to my pony, who was there, really and truly there, the promise, the beginning of a happy double life. And – I went and looked to make sure – there was the saddle, too, and the bridle.

But that Christmas, which my father had planned so carefully, was it the best or the worst I ever knew? He often asked me that; I never could answer as a boy. I think now that it was both. It covered the whole distance from broken-hearted misery to bursting happiness – too fast. A grown-up could hardly have stood it.

THE AUTOBIOGRAPHY OF LINCOLN STEFFENS *(1866–1936)*

My mother knew well how hurtful a broken illusion could be. The most trifling disappointment took on for her the dimensions of a major disaster. One Christmas Eve, in Vyra, not long before her fourth baby was to be born, she happened to be laid up with a slight ailment and made my brother and me (aged, respectively, five and six) promise not to look into the Christmas stockings that we would find hanging from our bedposts on the following morning but to bring them over to her room and investigate them there, so that she could watch and enjoy our pleasure. Upon awakening, I held a furtive conference with my brother, after which, with eager hands, each felt his delightfully crackling stocking, stuffed with small presents; these we cautiously fished out one by one, undid the ribbons, loosened the tissue paper, inspected everything by the weak light that came through a chink in the shutters, wrapped up the little things again, and crammed them back where they had been. I next recall our sitting on our mother's bed, holding those lumpy stockings and doing our best to give the performance she had wanted to see; but we had so messed up the wrappings, so amateurish were our renderings of enthusiastic surprise (I can see my brother casting his eyes upward and exclaiming, in imitation of our new French governess, 'Ah, que c'est beau!'), that, after observing us for a moment, our audience burst into tears.

SPEAK, MEMORY *by Vladimir Nabokov*

From 'A Child's Christmas in Wales'

There are always Uncles at Christmas.
The same Uncles. And on Christmas mornings,
with dog-disturbing whistle and sugar fags,
I would scour the swatched town for the news of
the little world, and find always a dead bird
by the white Post Office or by the deserted swings;
perhaps a robin, all but one of his fires out.
Men and women wading or scooping back from chapel,
with tap-room noses and wind-bussed cheeks,
all albinos, huddled their stiff black jarring
feathers against the irreligious snow.
Mistletoe hung from the gas brackets in all
the front parlours; there was sherry and walnuts
and bottled beer and crackers by the dessertspoons;
and cats in their fur-abouts watched the fires;
and the high-heaped fire spat, all ready for
the chestnuts and the mulling pokers. . . .

. . . Then I would be
slap-dashing home, the gravy smell of the dinners
of others, the bird smell, the brandy, the
pudding and mince, coiling up to my nostrils, when
out of a snow-clogged side lane would come a boy
the spit of myself, with a pink-tipped cigarette
and the violet past of a black eye, cocky
as a bullfinch, leering all to himself.

I hated him on sight and sound, and would be
about to put my dog whistle to my lips
and blow him off the face of Christmas when
suddenly he, with a violet wink, put *his* whistle
to *his* lips and blew so stridently, so high,
so exquisitely loud, that gobbling faces,
their cheeks bulged with goose, would press
against their tinselled windows, the whole length
of the white echoing street. For dinner
we had turkey and blazing pudding, and after
dinner the Uncles sat in front of the fire,
loosened all buttons, put their large moist
hands over their watch chains, groaned a little
and slept. Mothers, aunts and sisters scuttled
to and fro, bearing tureens. Auntie Bessie, who
had already been frightened, twice, by a
clock-work mouse, whimpered at the sideboard
and had some elderberry wine. The dog was sick.
Auntie Dosie had to have three aspirins,
but Auntie Hannah, who liked port, stood in
the middle of the snowbound back yard, singing
like a big-bosomed thrush. I would blow up
balloons to see how big they would blow up to;
and, when they burst, which they all did,
the Uncles jumped and rumbled. In the rich
and heavy afternoon, the Uncles breathing
like dolphins and the snow descending,
I would sit among festoons and Chinese lanterns
and nibble dates and try to make a model man-o'-war,

following the Instructions for Little Engineers,
and produce what might be mistaken for
a sea-going tramcar.

Always on Christmas night there was music.
An uncle played the fiddle, a cousin sang
'Cherry Ripe', and another uncle sang 'Drake's Drum'.
It was very warm in the little house.
Auntie Hannah, who had got on to the parsnip
wine, sang a song about Bleeding Hearts and Death,
and then another in which she said her heart
was like a Bird's Nest; and then everybody
laughed again; and then I went to bed.
Looking through my bedroom window, out into
the moonlight and the unending smoke-coloured snow,
I could see the lights in the windows
of all the other houses on our hill and hear
the music rising from them up the long, steadily
falling night. I turned the gas down, I got
into bed. I said some words to the close and
holy darkness, and then I slept.

Dylan Thomas

A longer version of this traditional Mummers' Play was still being performed at Christmas in Hampshire villages in the 1930s with Father Christmas introduced as an extra character.

[*Enter the Presenter*]

Presenter. I open the door, I enter in;
    I hope your favour we shall win.
    Stir up the fire and strike a light,
    And see my merry boys act tonight.
    Whether we stand or whether we fall,
    We'll do our best to please you all.

[Enter the actors, and stand in a clump]

Presenter. Room, room, brave gallants all,
    Pray give us room to rhyme;
    We're come to show activity,
      This merry Christmas time;
    Activity of youth,
    Activity of age,
    The like was never seen
      Upon a common stage.
    And if you don't believe what I say,
    Step in St George – and clear the way.

[Enter St George]

St George. In come I, Saint George,
    The man of courage bold;
    With my broad axe and sword
    I won a crown of gold.
    I fought the fiery dragon,
      And drove him to the slaughter,
    And by these means I won
      The King of Egypt's daughter.
    Show me the man that bids me stand;
    I'll cut him down with my courageous hand.

Presenter. Step in, Bold Slasher.

[Enter Bold Slasher]

Slasher. In come I, the Turkish Knight,
    Come from the Turkish land to fight.
    I come to fight St George,
      The man of courage bold;
    And if his blood be hot,
      I soon will make it cold.

St George. Stand off, stand off, Bold Slasher,
    And let no more be said,
    For if I draw my sword,
      I'm sure to break thy head.

Thou speakest very bold,
   To such a man as I;
I'll cut thee into eyelet holes,
   And make thy buttons fly.

Slasher. My head is made of iron,
   My body is made of steel,
My arms and legs of beaten brass;
   No man can make me feel.

St George. Then draw thy sword and fight,
   Or draw thy purse and pay;
For satisfaction I must have,
   Before I go away.

Slasher. No satisfaction shalt thou have,
   But I will bring thee to thy grave.

St George. Battle to battle with thee I call,
   To see who on this ground shall fall.

Slasher. Battle to battle with thee I pray,
   To see who on this ground shall lay.

St George. Then guard thy body and mind thy head,
   Or else my sword shall strike thee dead.

Slasher. One shall die and the other shall live;
   This is the challenge that I do give.

       [*They fight. Slasher falls*]

                        Anon

25

WORK

The want of affection in the English is strongly manifested towards their children; for after having kept them at home till they arrive at the age of 7 or 9 years at the utmost, they put them out, both males and females, to hard service in the houses of other people, binding them generally for another 7 or 9 years. And these are called apprentices, and during that time they perform all the most menial offices; and few are born who are exempted from this fate, for every one, however rich he may be, sends away his children into the houses of others, whilst he, in return, receives those of strangers into his own. And on inquiring their reason for this severity, they answered that they did it in order that their children might learn better manners. But I, for my part, believe that they do it because they like to enjoy all their comforts themselves, and that they are better served by strangers than they would be by their own children.

The above adverse comments on the farming-out of English children, written in 1497, come from a Venetian diplomat at the court of Henry VII. Below is a verse of practical advice to such a child.

The Boy Serving at Table

My dear child, first thyself enable
With all thine heart to virtuous discipline;
Afore thy sovereign, standing at the table,
Dispose thou thee after my doctrine
To all nurture thy courage to incline.
First, when thou speakest be not reckless,
Keep feet and fingers still in peace.
Be simple of cheer, cast not thine eye aside,

Gaze not about, turning thy sight over all.
Against the post let not thy back abide,
Neither make thy mirror of the wall.
Pick not thy nose, and, most especial,
Be well ware, and set hereon thy thought,
Before thy sovereign scratch nor rub thee nought.

John Lydgate (?1370–1450)

At Ten Years old, I was taken home to assist my Father in his Business, which was that of a Tallow Chandler and Sope-Boiler. A Business he was not bred to, but had assumed on his Arrival in New England and on finding his Dying Trade would not maintain his Family, being in little Request. Accordingly I was employed in cutting Wick for the Candles, filling the Dipping Mold, and the Molds for cast Candles, attending the Shop, going of Errands, &c. I dislik'd the Trade and had a strong Inclination for the Sea; but my Father declar'd against it; however, living near the Water, I was much in and about it, learnt early to swim well, and to manage Boats, and when in a Boat or Canoe with other Boys I was commonly allow'd to govern, especially in any case of Difficulty; and upon other Occasions I was generally a Leader among the Boys, and sometimes led them into Scrapes, of which I will mention one Instance, as it shows an early projecting public Spirit, tho' not then justly conducted. There was a Salt Marsh that bounded part of the Mill Pond, on the Edge of which at Highwater, we us'd to stand to fish for Minews. By much Trampling, we had made it a mere Quagmire. My Proposal was to build a Wharf there fit for us to stand upon, and I show'd my Comrades a large Heap of Stones which were intended for a new House near the Marsh, and which would very well suit our Purpose. Accordingly in the Evening when the Workmen were gone, I assembled a Number of my Playfellows, and working with them diligently like so many Emmets, sometimes two or three to a Stone, we brought them all away and built our little Wharff. The next Morning the Workmen were surpriz'd at Missing the Stones; which were found in our Wharff; Enquiry was made after the Removers; we

were discovered and complain'd of; several of us were corrected
by our Fathers; and tho' I pleaded the Usefulness of the Work,
mine convinc'd me that nothing was useful which was not honest.

THE AUTOBIOGRAPHY OF BENJAMIN FRANKLIN *(1706–90)*

A large party are invited to dinner – a great display is to be made –
and about half an hour before dinner there is an alarm that the
kitchen chimney is on fire! It is impossible to put off the distinguished personages who are expected. It gets very late for the soup
and fish, the cook is frantic -- all eyes are turned upon the sable
consolation of the master chimney-sweeper – and up into the
midst of the burning chimney is sent one of the miserable little
infants of the brush! There is a positive prohibition of this practice; and an enactment of penalties in one of the Acts of Parliament which respects chimney-sweepers. But what matter Acts of
Parliament, when the pleasures of genteel people are concerned?
Or what is a toasted child, compared to the agonies of the mistress
of the house with a deranged dinner?

Sydney Smith (1771–1845)

The Chimney Sweeper

When my mother died I was very young,
And my father sold me while yet my tongue
Could scarcely cry ''weep! 'weep! 'weep! 'weep!'
So your chimneys I sweep, & in soot I sleep.

There's little Tom Dacre, who cried when his head,
That curl'd like a lamb's back, was shav'd: so I said
'Hush, Tom! never mind it, for when your head's bare
'You know that the soot cannot spoil your white hair.'

And so he was quiet, & that very night,
As Tom was a-sleeping, he had such a sight!
That thousands of sweepers, Dick, Joe, Ned, & Jack,
Were all of them lock'd up in coffins of black.

And by came an Angel who had a bright key,
And he open'd the coffins & set them all free;
Then down a green plain leaping, laughing, they run,
And wash in a river, and shine in the Sun.

Then naked & white, all their bags left behind,
They rise upon clouds and sport in the wind;
And the Angel told Tom, if he'd be a good boy,
He'd have God for his father, & never want joy.

And so Tom awoke; and we rose in the dark,
And got with our bags & our brushes to work.
Tho' the morning was cold, Tom was happy & warm;
So if all do their duty they need not fear harm.

William Blake

Once upon a time there was a little chimney-sweep, and his name was Tom. That is a short name, and you have heard it before, so you will not have much trouble in remembering it. He lived in a great town in the North country, where there were plenty of chimneys to sweep, and plenty of money for Tom to earn and his master to spend. He could not read nor write, and did not care to do either; and he never washed himself, for there was no water up the court where he lived. He had never been taught to say his prayers. He never had heard of God, or of Christ, except in words which you never have heard, and which it would have been well if he had never heard. He cried half his time, and laughed the other half. He cried when he had to climb the dark flues, rubbing his poor knees and elbows raw; and when the soot got into his eyes, which it did every day in the week; and when his master beat him, which he did every day in the week; and when he had not enough to eat, which happened every day in the week likewise. And he laughed the other half of the day, when he was tossing halfpennies with the other boys, or playing leapfrog over the posts, or bowling stones at the horses' legs as they trotted by, which last was excellent fun, when there was a wall at hand behind which to hide. As for chimney-sweeping, and being hungry, and being beaten, he took all that for the way of the world, like the rain and snow and thunder, and stood manfully with his back to it till it was over, as his old donkey did to a hail-storm; and then shook his ears and was as jolly as ever; and thought of the fine times coming, when he would be a man, and a master sweep, and sit in the public-house with a quart of beer and a long pipe, and play cards for silver money, and wear velveteens and ankle-jacks, and keep a white bull-dog with one grey ear, and carry her puppies in his pocket, just like a man. And he would have apprentices, one, two, three, if he could. How he would bully them, and knock them about, just as his master did to him; and make them carry home the soot sacks, while he rode before them on his donkey, with a pipe in his mouth and a flower in his button-hole, like a king at the head of his army. Yes, there were good times coming; and, when his master let him have a pull at the leavings of his beer, Tom was the jolliest boy in the whole town.

THE WATER BABIES *by Charles Kingsley (1819–75)*

The following testimony was given by the master sweep Ruff of Nottingham to the Children's Employment Commission of 1863.

No one knows the cruelty which a boy has to undergo in learning. The flesh must be hardened. This is done by rubbing it, chiefly on the elbows and knees with the strongest brine, as that got from a pork-shop, close by a hot fire. You must stand over them with a cane, or coax them by a promise of a halfpenny, etc. if they will stand a few more rubs.

At first they will come back from their work with their arms and knees streaming with blood, and the knees looking as if the caps had been pulled off. Then they must be rubbed with brine again, and perhaps go off at once to another chimney. In some boys I have found that the skin does not harden for years.

The best age for teaching boys is about six. That is thought a nice trainable age. But I have known two at least of my neighbours' children begin at the age of five. I once saw a child only $4\frac{1}{2}$ years in the market-place in his sooty clothes and with his scraper in his hand ... he began when he was four.

William Hutton was only seven when he was sent away to work.

My days of play were now drawing to an end. The Silk-mill was proposed. One of the clerks remarked to the person who took me there, that the offer was needless, I was too young. However, the offer was made; and, as hands were wanted, in the infant state of this work, I was accepted. It was found, upon trial, that nature had not given me length sufficient to reach the engine, for, out of three hundred persons employed in the mill, I was by far the least and the youngest.

It is happy for man that invention supplies the place of want. The superintendents wisely thought, if they could lengthen one end it would affect both. A pair of high pattens were therefore fabricated, and tied fast about my feet, to make them steady companions. They were clumsy companions, which I dragged about one year, and with pleasure delivered up.

I had now to rise at five every morning during seven years; submit to the cane whenever convenient to the master; be the constant companion of the most rude and vulgar of the human race, never taught by nature, nor ever wishing to be taught. A lad, let his mind be in what state it would, must be as impudent as they, or be hunted down. I could not consider this place in any other light than that of a complete bear-garden....

Entering the gates of the mill, at noon, a strong wind blew off my hat, which rolled before me into the Derwent. I could have gone swifter than the hat, but knew I should acquire a velocity that would have run me into the river, which, being deep, I had lost my life. In distress, I travelled by its side, the whole length of the building, but it continued just out of my reach. I mourned its loss the whole afternoon, as well as dreaded the consequence.

My master informed the chief Governor, who ordered him to take me to a hatter, and purchase another. I was asked whether I would have a plain band, or one with a silver tassel? What child refuses finery? I chose the latter, and became the envy of the mill.

Christmas holidays were attended with snow, followed by a sharp frost. A thaw came on, in the afternoon of the 27th, but in the night the ground was again caught by a frost, which glazed the streets. I did not awake, the next morning, till daylight seemed to appear. I rose in tears, for fear of punishment, and went to my father's bed-side, to ask what was o'clock? 'He believed six;' I darted out in agonies, and from the bottom of Full street, to the top of Silkmill lane, not 200 yards, I fell nine times! Observing no lights in the mill, I knew it was an early hour, and that the reflection of the snow had deceived me. Returning, it struck two. As I now went with care, I fell but twice. . . .

In pouring some bobbins out of one box into another, the cogs of an engine caught the box in my hand. The works in all the five rooms began to thunder, crack and break to pieces; a universal cry of 'Stop mills' ensued; all the violent powers of nature operated within me. With the strength of a madman I wrenched the box from the wheel; but, alas, the mischief was done. I durst not shew my face, nor retreat to dinner till every soul was gone. Pity in distress was not found within those walls.

THE LIFE OF WILLIAM HUTTON *by Himself*

The 'Water Boy' in this Negro folksong was the boy who brought water to the convicts working on the roads.

Water Boy where are you hiding;
If you don't-a come
Gwine tell-a yoh Mammy.

There ain't no hammer
That's on-a this mountain
That ring-a like mine, boys,
That ring-a like mine.

Done bus' this rock, boys,
From hyeh to Macon
All th' way to th' jail, boys,
Yes back to th' jail.

You Jack-o-Di'monds,
Yo Jack-o-Di'monds
Ah know yeh of old, boys,
Yes, know yeh of ol'.

You robbed my pocket,
Yes robba my pocket
Done a-robba my pocket,
Of silver an gol'.

... I recollect that soon after I was able to walk I was employed in
the cotton manufacture. My mother used to bat the cotton wool
on a wire griddle. It was then put into a deep brown mug with a
strong ley of soap suds. My mother then tucked up my petticoats
about my waist, and put me in the tub to tread upon the cotton at
the bottom. When a second riddleful was batted I was lifted out
and it was placed in the mug, and I again trod it down. The
process was continued until the mug became so full that I could no
longer safely stand in it, when a chair was placed beside it, and I
held on by the back.

THE LIFE AND TIMES OF SAMUEL CROMPTON
(1753–1827) by Gilbert French

The blacking warehouse was the last house on the left-hand side
of the way, at old Hungerford-stairs. It was a crazy, tumble-down
old house, abutting of course on the river, and literally overrun
with rats. Its wainscoted rooms, and its rotten floors and staircase, and the old grey rats swarming down in the cellars, and the
sound of their squeaking and scuffling coming up the stairs at all
times, and the dirt and decay of the place, rise up visibly before
me, as if I were there again. The counting-house was on the first
floor, looking over the coal-barges and the river. There was a
recess in it, in which I was to sit and work. My work was to cover
the pots of paste-blacking; first with a piece of oil-paper, and then
with a piece of blue paper; to tie them round with a string; and
then to clip the paper close and neat, all round, until it looked as
smart as a pot of ointment from an apothecary's shop. When a
certain number of grosses of pots had attained this pitch of
perfection, I was to paste on each a printed label; and then go on
again with more pots. Two or three other boys were kept at

similar duty down stairs on similar wages. One of them came up, in a ragged apron and a paper cap, on the first Monday morning, to show me the trick of using the string and tying the knot. His name was Bob Fagin; and I took the liberty of using his name, long afterwards, in *Oliver Twist....*

No words can express the secret agony of my soul as I sunk into this companionship; compared these every day associates with those of my happier childhood; and felt my early hopes of growing up to be a learned and distinguished man, crushed in my breast. The deep remembrance of the sense I had of being utterly neglected and hopeless; of the shame I felt in my position; of the misery it was to my young heart to believe that, day by day, what I had learned, and thought, and delighted in, and raised my fancy and my emulation up by, was passing away from me, never to be brought back any more; cannot be written....

I was such a little fellow, with my poor white hat, little jacket, and corduroy trowsers, that frequently, when I went into the bar of a strange public-house for a glass of ale or porter to wash down the saveloy and the loaf I had eaten in the street, they didn't like to give it me. I remember, one evening (I had been somewhere for my father, and was going back to the borough over Westminster-bridge), that I went into a public-house in Parliament-street, which is still there though altered, at the corner of the short street leading into Cannon-row, and said to the landlord behind the bar, 'What is your very best – the VERY *best* – ale, a glass?' For, the occasion was a festive one, for some reason: I forget why. It may have been my birthday, or somebody else's. 'Two-pence,' says he. 'Then,' says I, 'just draw me a glass of that, if you please, with a good head to it.' The landlord looked at me, in return, over the bar, from head to foot, with a strange smile on his face; and instead of drawing the beer, looked round the screen and said something to his wife, who came out from behind it, with her work in her hand, and joined him in surveying me. Here we stand, all three, before me now, in my study in Devonshire-terrace. The landlord, in his shirt sleeves, leaning against the bar window-frame; his wife, looking over the little half-door; and I, in some confusion, looking up at them from outside the partition. They asked me a good many questions, as what my name was, how old I was, where I lived, how I was employed, etc. etc. To all of which, that I might commit nobody, I invented appropriate answers. They served me with the ale, though I suspect it was not the strongest on the premises; and the landlord's wife, opening the little half-door and bending down, gave me a kiss that was half-admiring and half-compassionate, but all womanly and good, I am sure.   THE LIFE OF CHARLES DICKENS *by John Forster*

An interview for domestic service:

Laura once accompanied a schoolfellow to interview a mistress who was said to require a maid. At ordinary times a mother took her daughter to such interviews; but Mrs Beamish was near her time, and it was not thought safe for her to venture so far from home. So Martha and Laura set out, accompanied by a younger brother of Martha's, aged about ten. Martha in her mother's best coat with the sleeves turned back to the elbows and with her hair, done up for the first time that morning, plaited into an inverted saucer at the back of her head and bristling with black hairpins. Laura in a chimney-pot hat, a short brown cape, and buttoned boots reaching nearly to her knees. The little brother wore a pale grey astrakan coat, many sizes too small, a huge red knitted scarf, and carried no pocket-handkerchief.

It was a mild, grey November day with wisps of mist floating over the ploughed fields and water drops hanging on every twig and thorn of the hedgerows. The lonely country house they were bound for was said to be four miles from the hamlet; but, long before they reached it, the distance seemed to them more like forty. It was all cross-country going; over field-paths and stiles, through spinneys and past villages. They asked the way of every-body they met or saw working in the fields and were always directed to some short cut or other, which seemed to bring them out at the same place as before. Then there were delays. Martha's newly done-up hair kept tumbling down and Laura had to take out all the hairpins and adjust it. The little brother got stones in his shoes, and all their feet felt tired from the rough travelling and the stiff mud which caked their insteps....

In response to their timid knock, the door was opened by a

youngish woman. She was like no one Laura had ever seen. Very slight – she would have been called 'scraggy' in the hamlet – with a dead white face, dark, arched brows, and black hair brushed straight back from her forehead, and with all this black and whiteness set off by a little scarlet jacket that, when Laura described it to her mother later, was identified as a garibaldi. She seemed glad to see the children, though she looked doubtful when she heard their errand and saw Martha's size.

'So you want a place?' she asked as she conducted them into a kitchen as large as a church and not unlike one with its stone-paved floor and central pillar. Yes, she wanted a maid, and she thought Martha might do. How old was she? Twelve? And what could she do? Anything she was told? Well, that was right. It was not a hard place, for, although there were sixteen rooms, only three or four of them were in use. Could she get up at six without being called? There would be the kitchen range to light and the flues to be swept once a week, and the dining-room to be swept and dusted and the fire lighted before breakfast. She herself would be down in time to cook breakfast. No cooking was required, beyond preparing vegetables. After breakfast Martha would help her with the beds, turning out the rooms, paring the potatoes and so on; and after dinner there was plenty to do – washing up, cleaning knives and boots and polishing silver. And so she went on, mapping out Martha's day, until at nine o'clock she would be free to go to bed, after placing hot water in her mistress's bed-room.

Laura could see that Martha was bewildered. She stood, twisting her scarf, curtseying, and saying 'Yes, mum' to everything.

'Then, as wages, I can offer you two pounds ten a year. It is not a great wage, but you are very small, and you'll have an easy place and a comfortable home. How do you like your kitchen?'

Martha's gaze wandered round the huge place, and once more she said, 'Yes, mum.'

'You'll find it nice and cosy here, eating your meals by the fire. You won't feel lonely, will you?'

This time Martha said, 'No, mum.'

'Tell your mother I shall expect her to fit you out well. You will want caps and aprons. I like my maids to look neat. And tell her to let you bring plenty of changes, for we only wash once in six weeks. I have a woman in to do it all up,' and although Martha knew her mother had not a penny to spend on her outfit, and that she had been told the last thing before she left home that morning to ask her prospective employer to send her mother her first month's wages in advance to buy necessaries, once again she said, 'Yes, mum.'

'Well, I shall expect you next Monday, then. And, now, are you hungry?' and for the first time there was feeling in Martha's tone as she answered, 'Yes, mum.'

Soon a huge sirloin of cold beef was placed on the table and liberal helpings were being carved for the three children. It was such a joint of beef as one only sees in old pictures with an abbot carving; immense, and so rich in flavour and so tender that it seemed to melt in the mouth. The three plates were clean in a twinkling.

'Would any of you like another helping?'

Laura, conscious that she was no principal in the affair, and only invited to partake out of courtesy, declined wistfully but firmly; Martha said she would like a little more if 'mum' pleased, and the little brother merely pushed his plate forward. Martha, mindful of her manners, refused a third helping. But the little brother had no such scruples; he was famishing, and accepted a third and a fourth plateful, the mistress of the house standing by with an amused smile on her face. She must have remembered him for the rest of her life as the little boy with the large appetite.

It was dark before they reached home, and Laura got into trouble, not only for spoiling her best boots, but still more for telling a lie, for she had led her mother to believe they were going into the market town shopping. But even when she lay in bed supperless she felt the experience was worth the punishment, for she had been where she had never been before and seen the old house and the lady in the scarlet jacket and tasted the beef and seen Tommy Beamish eat four large helpings.

LARK RISE by Flora Thompson (1876–1947)

A Suffolk farmer's memories of the mid-nineteenth century:

If you lived in the country as I do, you would sometimes see a sight which would make your blood run cold, and yet it is so common a sight that we country people grow accustomed to it. You would see a great lumbering tumbril, weighing a ton or two with two wheels nearly six feet high, loaded with manure, drawn by a great Suffolk cart horse as big as an elephant; and conducted by a tiny thing of a boy who can hardly reach the horse's nose to take hold of the rein; and, even if he can, has neither the strength nor weight to make such a huge monster feel, much less obey. Some of these urchins are employed upon the highroad which is comparatively safe for them. It is when they come into the fields with deep wheel-tracks, as deep nearly as half their little legs, it is turning into gate spaces where the children are obliged to cling to the horse's bridle and stumble along tip-toes, that the danger is.

ASK THE FELLOWS WHO CUT THE HAY *by George Ewart Evans*

Lavender's blue, dilly, dilly,
  Lavender's green;
When I am king, dilly, dilly,
  You shall be queen.
Call up your men, dilly, dilly,
  Set them to work,
Some to the plough, dilly, dilly,
  Some to the cart.
Some to make hay, dilly, dilly,
  Some to cut corn,
While you and I, dilly, dilly,
  Keep ourselves warm.

Anon

Our neighbour's son was employed then in a clothing factory, where he earned a small weekly wage; I on the other hand loafed, as they said, and did nothing, so my mother decided that I too should go to the factory: 'It's not for the sake of what he earns,' she said, 'but it's so that I shall know where he is.' My old grandmother took me there and deeply grieved she was; she had never thought to see me going together with all the poor youths, she told me. A number of Germans worked there; they sang and talked gaily; there were many coarse jokes which aroused great mirth, I listened to them and learned thereby that a child can hear such things with innocent ears, for it did not reach my heart.

At that time I had a curiously high and pretty soprano voice which I kept until I was fifteen. I knew that people liked to hear me sing, and when I was asked at the factory if I knew any songs, I started to sing at once and received great applause. The other boys were given my work to do. When I had sung, I told them that I could also act comedies: I remembered whole scenes of Holberg and Shakespeare and recited these. The men and women there gave me friendly nods, laughed and clapped their hands. In this way I found my first few days in the factory most amusing; but then one day when I was standing there singing and they were saying how clear and remarkably high my voice was, one of the men exclaimed: 'I'm sure he's not a boy, but a little girl!' He laid hold of me, I shrieked and wailed, the other men found the coarse joke amusing, they held my arms and legs, I bawled at the top of my voice and, bashful as any girl, rushed out of the building and home to my mother who at once promised that I need never go there again.

THE MERMAID MAN: *Autobiography of Hans Christian Andersen (1805–75)*

26

DRAMAS

As an autobiographer I am unlucky for there was nothing remarkable in my childhood, which began in a garrison town. I was born on the border between the second and third Victorian eras, the heyday of the squires, when a man could still be passing rich on a few thousand a year. Nothing but mess and manoeuvres happened, save when my parents hired for a large party a French *chef* who, having secretly consumed all the liqueurs, sent in, as a first course, to their first entertainment, two cheeses adorned by a hatchet and followed by dead silence. He then hid behind the kitchen door and threw Father, sent out to investigate, out of the window. I thought this funny, though nobody else did; indeed the hatchet increased distrust of foreigners in general and 'frogs' in particular. ... So these *hors d'oeuvres* were no laughing matter, and I mention this episode in the annals of a quiet neighbourhood because, having never since been sure what is laughable and what is not, I have felt foredoomed to error.

THE MIST PROCESSION *by Lord Vansittart (1881–1957)*

At Uxbridge, when we are naked after a bath in front of the fire, I snatch my glass slate from my brother and sit on it so that he cannot see what I have drawn. The slate smashes and cuts two large slices in my bottom. Mother rushes screaming with me to the surgery, is saved from wheeling me into the canal in the pitch dark by a policeman. At the surgery I am given a sniff of chloroform and, coming to, see the doctor walking upside down on the ceiling. 'Another inch,' says the doctor, 'and he would have had them off.' What? I get a fort, soldiers, a fire in my bedroom for this. It is worth it.

A CAB AT THE DOOR *by V. S. Pritchett*

At the age of five or six, I was the victim of an assault. I mean that I endured an operation on my throat to remove certain growths; the operation took place in a very brutal manner, without my being anaesthetized. My parents had first made the mistake of taking me to the surgeon without telling me where we were going. If my recollections are correct, I believed we were on the way to the circus; I was therefore far from anticipating the nasty trick about to be played on me by our old family doctor, who assisted the surgeon, as well as by the latter himself. The occasion went off, point for point, like a play that had been rehearsed, and I had the feeling that I had been lured into a hideous ambush. Matters proceeded as follows: leaving my parents in the waiting room, the old doctor led me into another room where the surgeon was waiting for me, wearing a huge black beard and a white gown (such, at least, is the image I have kept of the ogre); I saw various sharp instruments and must have looked frightened, for the old doctor took me on his lap and said to reassure me: 'Come here, *mon petit coco*! Now we're going to play kitchen.' From this moment on I can remember nothing except the sudden assault of the surgeon, who plunged some kind of sharp instrument into my throat, the pain that I felt, and the scream – like that of a slaughtered animal – that I uttered. My mother, who heard me from the next room, was terrified.

On the way home in the carriage, I did not speak a word; the shock had been so violent that for twenty-four hours it was impossible to get a word out of me; my mother, completely disoriented, wondered if I had become a mute. All I can remember about the period immediately following the operation is the carriage ride, my parents' vain attempts to make me speak and then, back at the house, my mother holding me in her arms in front of the living-room fireplace, the sherbets she had me swallow, the blood I spat up at each mouthful and which mingled with the raspberry colour of the sherbets.

This recollection is, I believe, the most painful of all my childhood memories. Not only did I not understand why I had been hurt, but I had the notion of a deception, a trap, a terrible perfidy on the part of the adults who had been kind to me only to be able to make a fierce assault upon my person.

MANHOOD *by Michel Leiris*

Ann, Ann!
    Come! quick as you can!
There's a fish that *talks*
    In the frying-pan.
Out of the fat,
    As clear as glass,
He put up his mouth
    And moaned 'Alas!'
Oh, most mournful,
    'Alas, alack!'
Then turned to his sizzling,
    And sank him back.

                              Walter de la Mare

Some days ago Isabella had a terrable fit of the toothake and she
walked with a long nightshift at dead of night like a gost and I
thought she was one She prayed for tired natures sweet restorer
bamy sleep but did not get it a ghostly figure she was indeed
enought to make a saint tremble it made me quever & sheke from
top to toe but I soon got the better of it & and next morning I quite
forgot it Superstition is a very mean thing & should be dispised &
shuned

                  From the Third Journal of Marjory Fleming (aged seven)

A week or two later in that June [1887] I had an adventure. Nanny
had brought us to Kensington Gardens, and I was looking at the
flower-beds in front of Kensington Palace with the absorption I
always gave to flowers, when on turning round I saw to my alarm
that Nanny and the perambulator had vanished. I can feel now the
beating of my heart when I found myself alone. I ran to the Broad
Walk. There was no sign of the perambulator. I ran back to the
front of the Palace. I was still alone. There was only one thing to
be done; I must appeal to the police. With thudding heart I ran as
fast as I could go to the gate leading out of the Gardens into High
Street and then I ran along the narrow pavement, still narrow
today, toward Church Street. As I look at myself running I do not
see complete people in my mind's eye but only many pairs of legs

round which I hurry, panting. At last I reach the dangerous crossing of Church Street and see the blue lamp over the door of the police station on the opposite side. A blue omnibus coming from Earl's Court Road stops to take on a third horse so that the omnibus will not have to be walked up Campden Hill, at the top of which the extra horse will be released to walk back to St Mary Abbot's. That third horse, called the cock-horse, was always ridden by a boy, and how one envied him! On this morning, however, I was too much overwhelmed by the problem of being lost to think about that lucky boy. As I stood there waiting for the traffic to be clear of the crossing I considered what I should say when I entered the police-station. Then I crossed, went into it and announced:

'My name is Edward Montague Compton Mackenzie. I live at 54 Avonmore Road, and I'm lost. Will you take me home, please.'

One of the policemen picked me up and seated me on the charge counter, and as I looked round I saw to my surprise that the policemen were all without their tunics; it had not occurred to me before that policemen ever undressed.

Those Kensington policemen, the youngest of whom if he be still alive would be ninety-six today, were most kind and friendly, and finally that youngest policeman was told to take me back to Avonmore Road. He was tall with fair, curly hair, and riding on his shoulder down the shopping side of High Street, Kensington, I felt pleased that I had been lost. As we went along he kept pointing out the Jubilee decorations in the houses of those dignified terraces in Upper Phillimore Gardens, Lower Phillimore Gardens and the rest which today have vanished under the megahyaline concrete ant-hills and bee-hives of the swarming present. I see the V.R.s and profiles of the Queen in multitudinous gas-jets which would be lighted after dusk to celebrate her Golden Jubilee.

The main thought that preoccupied me, however, was the importance of giving the policeman who had brought me home half a crown. This coin represented for me the zenith of human wealth as the tip one was given by old friends of the family and uncles. I am glad to remember that half a crown was produced by Nanny and accepted with a grin.

My Life and Times *by Compton Mackenzie*

Written by John Ruskin at the age of seven:

Harry knew very well what it was and went on with his drawing but Lucy soon called him away and bid him observe a great black cloud from the north which seemed rather electrical. Harry ran for an electrical apparatus which his father had given him and the cloud electrified his apparatus positively after that another cloud came which electrified his apparatus negatively and then a long train of smaller ones but before this cloud came a great cloud of dust rose from the ground and followed the positive cloud and at length seemed to come in contact with it and when the other cloud came a flash of lightning was seen to dart through the cloud of dust upon which the negative cloud spread very much and dissolved in rain which presently cleared the sky. After this phenomenon was over and also the surprise Harry began to wonder how electricity could get where there was so much water but he soon observed a rainbow and a rising mist under it which his fancy soon transformed into a female form. He then remembered the witch of the waters of the Alps who was raised from them by takeing some water in the hand and throwing it into the air pronouncing some unintelligable words. And though it was a tale it affected Harry now when he saw in the clouds something like it.   PRAETERITA

A Criminal's Lament

O unkind fate! I am so frail,
For twenty years I've been in gaol.
The court would not allow me bail –
     So here I am.

One day, 'bout twenty years ago,
I 'lowed I'd lay Tom Jones right low,
And to his house I then did go –
     So here I am.

For after leaving my abode
I bought a knife in Union Road,

And then some murderous thoughts I showed –
So here I am.

Then, late that night, Tom Jones lay dead,
His head all bloody on the bed,
And to the prison I was led –
So here I am.

Contributed to a school magazine by L.W.Y.

Biddy's house looks as though it has not been cleaned in genera-
tions. It is a place of darkness, smoke, mutterings and impreca-
tions. Biddy herself is more often than not lurking at the half-open
door, her eyes rolling terribly in her grimy face, her hair starting
from her head in matted, whitish locks. As we go past she slams
the door. 'She can reeve a door the best I ever knowed,' Francey
MacAllister says, quite unfazed.

The MacAllisters are more courageous than we are (except
perhaps for Eiram and Morgan, who have a wild courage mixed
with great timidity), and Biddy to them is an old mad woman,
whereas we are put about to live so near someone who tallies with
our idea – engendered by illustrations in books – of a witch. She
makes manifest our threatening world of fantasy, and this is
profoundly scaring; for if she exists, what does not? The idea of
Biddy becomes another supernatural terror to add to the ever-
increasing hoard and horde of terrors and devils in our minds. On
an ordinary, natural level, too, we are frightened of her because
she seems to simmer with hate. 'She would put the evil eye on you
as soon as look at you,' Ellen warns us, and we scuttle past,
avoiding looking at her lest one dreadful cyclopic eye cleave to us
like a shiny, dreadful wart.

She is a widow, and her children became deranged or came to
some sort of sorry end. Her only surviving daughter, Lena, regularly tries to drown herself in a shallow spring well which lies
down the Brae Hill, along the loaning that leads to our low-lying
meadows. . . .

John-Joe's loaning was a living paradise for a child, a deep
green alleyway made narrow by the lushness of vegetation, overgrown by trees and hedges and lined with high banks of wild herbs

and wild flowers. Under this sweet cover grew wild strawberries which some of us threaded on to a long stalk of sedge grass the better to savour them all at once. The more prodigal ate them one by one. I always threaded mine, grading them carefully, making a marvellous mouth-watering necklace – and then generally dropped it, lost it, fell into a cowpat with it, or engaged in some other early form of self-inflicted deprivation.

When I was an infant, perhaps five years old, I set off on the small tricycle which was the communal toy and, having puffed my way up the loaning, climbed off and set about searching for the strawberries. When I had picked a stalkful I went back to the tricycle well enough pleased with myself and found Lena standing beside it. I sensed her strangeness and tried to back away, but she reached for me and took the strawberries from my hand and, tilting her throat, put the full stalk deep into her mouth. Silent and frightened I climbed on to the tricycle and tried to pedal away, but she was beside me on all fours, feral as Dally's dog, her mouth red with the juices of the strawberries, and she sank her teeth into my hand so that they met through my flesh.

ALL OF US HERE *by Polly Devlin (1941–   )*

The Sweet-Shop Round the Corner

The child dreaming along a crowded street
Lost hold of his mother, who had turned to greet
Some neighbour, and mistakenly matched his tread
With a strange woman's. 'Buy me sweets,' he said,
Waving his hand, which he found warmly pressed;
So dragged her on, boisterous and self-possessed:
'The sweet-shop's round the corner!' Both went in,
And not for a long while did the child begin
To feel a dread that something had gone wrong:
Were Mother's legs so lean, or her shoes so long,
Or her skirt so patched, or her hair tousled and grey?
Why did she twitter in such a ghostly way?
'*O Mother, are you dead?*'

What else could a child say?

Robert Graves

Black childhood in Memphis.

One winter morning in the long-ago, four-year-old days of my life I found myself standing before a fireplace, warming my hands over a mound of glowing coals, listening to the wind whistle past the house outside. All morning my mother had been scolding me, telling me to keep still, warning me that I must make no noise. And I was angry, fretful, and impatient. In the next room Granny lay ill and under the day and night care of a doctor and I knew that I would be punished if I did not obey. I crossed restlessly to the window and pushed back the long fluffy white curtains – which I had been forbidden to touch – and looked yearningly out into the empty street. I was dreaming of running and playing and shouting, but the vivid image of Granny's old, white, wrinkled, grim face, framed by a halo of tumbling black hair, lying upon a huge feather pillow, made me afraid.

The house was quiet. Behind me my brother – a year younger than I – was playing placidly upon the floor with a toy. A bird wheeled past the window and I greeted it with a glad shout.

'You better hush,' my brother said.

'You shut up,' I said.

My mother stepped briskly into the room and closed the door behind her. She came to me and shook her finger in my face.

'You stop that yelling, you hear?' she whispered. 'You know Granny's sick and you better keep quiet!'

I hung my head and sulked. She left and I ached with boredom.

'I told you so,' my brother gloated.

'You shut up,' I told him again.

I wandered listlessly about the room, trying to think of something to do, dreading the return of my mother, resentful of being neglected. The room held nothing of interest except the fire and finally I stood before the shimmering embers, fascinated by the quivering coals. An idea of a new kind of game grew and took root in my mind. Why not throw something into the fire and watch it burn? I looked about. There was only my picture book and my mother would beat me if I burned that. Then what? I hunted around until I saw the broom leaning in a closet. That's it.... Who would bother about a few straws if I burned them? I pulled out the broom and tore out a batch of straws and tossed them into the fire and watched them smoke, turn black, blaze, and finally become white wisps of ghosts that vanished. Burning straws was a teasing kind of fun and I took more of them from the broom and cast them into the fire. My brother came to my side, his eyes drawn by the blazing straws.

'Don't do that,' he said.

'How come?' I asked.

'You'll burn the whole broom,' he said.

'You hush,' I said.

'I'll tell,' he said.

'And I'll hit you,' I said.

My idea was growing, blooming. Now I was wondering just how the long fluffy white curtains would look if I lit a bunch of straws and held it under them. Would I try it? Sure. I pulled several straws from the broom and held them to the fire until they blazed; I rushed to the window and brought the flame in touch with the hems of the curtains. My brother shook his head.

'Naw,' he said.

He spoke too late. Red circles were eating into the white cloth; then a flare of flames shot out. Startled, I backed away. The fire soared to the ceiling and I trembled with fright. Soon a sheet of yellow lit the room. I was terrified; I wanted to scream but was afraid. I looked around for my brother; he was gone. One half of the room was now ablaze. Smoke was choking me and the fire was licking at my face, making me gasp.

I made for the kitchen; smoke was surging there too. Soon my mother would smell that smoke and see the fire and come and beat me. I had done something wrong, something which I could not hide or deny. Yes, I would run away and never come back. I ran out of the kitchen and into the back yard. Where could I go? Yes, under the house! Nobody would find me there. I crawled under the house and crept into a dark hollow of a brick chimney and balled myself into a tight knot. My mother must not find me and whip me for what I had done. Anyway, it was all an accident; I had not really intended to set the house afire. I had just wanted to see how the curtains would look when they burned. And neither did it occur to me that I was hiding under a burning house.

Presently footsteps pounded on the floor above me. Then I heard screams. Later the gongs of fire wagons and the clopping hoofs of horses came from the direction of the street. Yes, there was really a fire, a fire like the one I had seen one day burn a house down to the ground, leaving only a chimney standing black. I was stiff with terror. The thunder of sound above me shook the chimney to which I clung. The screams came louder. I saw the image of my grandmother lying helplessly upon her bed and there were yellow flames in her black hair. Was my mother afire? Would my brother burn? Perhaps everybody in the house would burn! Why had I not thought of those things before I fired the curtains? I yearned to become invisible, to stop living. The commotion above me increased and I began to cry. It seemed that I had been hiding for ages, and when the stomping and screaming died down I felt lonely, cast forever out of life. Voices sounded near-by and I shivered.

'Richard!' my mother was calling frantically.

I saw her legs and the hem of her dress moving swiftly about the back yard. Her wails were full of an agony whose intensity told me that my punishment would be measured by its depth. Then I saw her taut face peering under the edge of the house. She had found me! I held my breath and waited to hear her command me to come to her. Her face went away; no, she had not seen me huddled in the dark nook of the chimney. I tucked my head into my arms and my teeth chattered.

'Richard!'

The distress I sensed in her voice was as sharp and painful as the lash of a whip on my flesh.

'Richard! The house is on fire. Oh, find my child!'

Yes, the house was afire, but I was determined not to leave my place of safety. Finally I saw another face peering under the edge of the house; it was my father's. His eyes must have become accustomed to the shadows, for he was now pointing at me.

'There he is!'

'Naw!' I screamed.

'Come here, boy!'

'Naw!'

'The house is on fire!'

'Leave me 'lone!'

He crawled to me and caught hold of one of my legs. I hugged the edge of the brick chimney with all of my strength. My father yanked my leg and I clawed at the chimney harder.

'Come outta there, you little fool!'

'Turn me loose!'

I could not withstand the tugging at my leg and my fingers relaxed. It was over. I would be beaten. I did not care any more. I knew what was coming. He dragged me into the back yard and the instant his hand left me I jumped to my feet and broke into a wild run, trying to elude the people who surrounded me, heading for the street. I was caught before I had gone ten paces.

From that moment on things became tangled for me. Out of the weeping and the shouting and the wild talk, I learned that no one had died in the fire. My brother, it seemed, had finally overcome enough of his panic to warn my mother, but not before more than half the house had been destroyed. Using the mattress as a stretcher, Grandpa and an uncle had lifted Granny from her bed and had rushed her to the safety of a neighbor's house. My long absence and silence had made everyone think, for a while, that I had perished in the blaze.

'You almost scared us to death,' my mother muttered as she stripped the leaves from a tree limb to prepare it for my back.

BLACK BOY *by Richard Wright*

The following scenario was written by Evelyn Waugh at the age of six:

The Curse of the Horse Race

Chapter I

BETTING

I bet you 500 pounds I'll win. The speaker was Rupert a man of about 25 he had a dark bushy mistarsh and flashing eyes.

I shouldnot trust to much on your horse said Tom for indeed he had not the sum to spear.

The race was to take pleace at ten the folowing morning.

Chapter II

THE RACE

The next moring Tom took his seat in the gront stand while Rupert mounted Sally (which was his horse) with the others to wate for the pistol shot which would anounse the start.

The race was soon over and Rupet had lost. What was he to do could he do the deed? Yes I'll *kill* him in the night, he though

Chapter III

THE FIRE

Rupert crept stedfustly along with out a sound but as he drew his sword it squeeked a little this awoke Tom seasing a candle he lit it just at that moment Rupert struck and sent the candle flying

The candle lit the cuntain Rupert trying to get away tumbled over the bed Tom maid a dash for the door and cleided with a perlisman who had come to see what was the matter and a panic took place.

Chapter IIII

EXPLAIND

While Tom and the peliesman were escaping through the door Rupert was adoping quite a diffrat methard of escape he puld the matris of the bed and hurled the it out of the window then jumed out he landed safe and sound on the matris then began to run for all he was worth.

Now let us leave Rupert and turn to Tom and the peliesman as soon as they got out Tom told the peliesman what had hapend.

Chapter V

HOT ON THE TRAIL

'See there he is' said Tom 'We must folow him and take him to prizen' said the peliesman.

Theres no time to spere said Tom letts get horses said the peliesman so they bort horses and and galerpin in the direcion thet had seen him go.

On they went until they were face to face with each other. the peliesman lept from his horse only to be stabed to the hart by Rupert then Tom jumped down and got Rupert a smart blow on the cheak.

Chapter VI

A DEADLY FIGHT

This enraged Rupert that that he shouted and made a plung but Tom was too quick for him artfully dogeing the sword he brout his sword round on Rupert's other cheak.

Just at that moment Ruper slashed killed the peliesmans horse then lept on Toms horse and golapt off.

Chapter VII

THE MYSTERIOUS MAN

Of cause ther was no chance of catching him on foot so Tom walked to the nearest inn to stay the night but it was ful up he had to share with another man.

Thou Tom was yery tired he could not sleep, their was something about the man he was he did not like he reminded him of some one he didnot know who.

Sudnly he felt something moveing on the bed looking up he saw the man fully dressed just gettimg off the bed

Chapter VIII

RUN TO ERTH

Now Ton could see that the mysteraous man was Rupert. Has he come to do a merder? Or has he only cometostay the night? thees were the thoughts that rushed throu Toms head.

he lay still to what Rupert would do first he opend a cuberd and took out a small letter bag from this he too some thing wich made Toms blud turn cold it was a bistol Tom lept forward and seesed Rupert by the throught and flung him to the ground.

then snaching a bit of robe from the ground he bound Rupert hand and foot.

Chapter IX

HUNG

then Tom drest hinself then Ton took Rupert to the puliese cort Rupert was hung for killing the pulies man. I hope the story will be a leson to you never to bet.

A boy called Ramsden, who never said much in class, put a tin chamberpot on his head and no one could get it off. To avoid public derision Ramsden was moved from the dormitory to the sanatorium. The doctor was sent for and the school carpenter, but no solution was found. In order to subdue public disquiet Noah [the headmaster] would issue a bulletin at almost every meal about the progress of the crisis.

'Ramsden may think he has done something extremely clever,' Noah boomed sadly. 'He may think he has drawn attention to himself in some unusual and original manner Oh ye of little judgement, would you laugh at Ramsden? What he has done is just very silly and dangerous. He is missing lessons, which will put him well behind for the School Cert. He is causing the unhappy couple who gave birth to him needless anxiety. So I say unto you, go about your daily business, work hard and do your best in the class-room and at school sports. Do not pay Ramsden the compliment of whispering about him in corridors. His exploits are best forgotten.'

In fact Ramsden, when we peered at him through a crack in the sanatorium door, presented an unforgettable spectacle. He was sitting bolt upright in bed, wearing striped flannel pyjamas, his ears flattened by a huge chamber-pot of chipped enamel, his face decorated by a grin that was at once sheepish and proud. At a subsequent meal Noah reassured us. 'A man has been sent for,' he announced. 'Expert in these matters. It is to be hoped that in due course Ramsden will be released. Every boy to remember, this is no subject for laughter!' That afternoon a man in dungarees with a bag of tools drove up in a van, and later on an uncrowned Ramsden rejoined the class and resumed his habitual 'low profile'.

CLINGING TO THE WRECKAGE *by John Mortimer*

There is no doubt but youth is a fine thing though my own is not over yet and wisdom comes with age.

I am a boy who was born and bred in the Great Blasket, a small truly Gaelic island which lies northwest of the coast of Kerry, where the storms of the sky and the wild sea beat without ceasing from end to end of the year and from generation to generation against the wrinkled rocks which stand above the waves that wash in and out of the coves where the seals make their homes. . . .

One Tuesday in the month of May I washed and cleaned myself with a heavy heart for school. Then I wandered out and sat down at the end of the lane to wait for my comrade, Tomás Owen Vaun.

Before long I saw the master coming down the glen. I was smitten with the weariness of the world. How envious I felt of the old men who were driving up their cattle into the hill, even of the bird that would float above my head, with nothing to trouble it but it singing to itself when it wished, and flying off when it wished, and going asleep when it wished. When shall I be a man? When shall I be free from the oppression of the master I see coming down the glen?

Tomás came up. 'We'll be late,' said he. He was smiling.

'Do you not feel at all lazy before school, Tomás?'

'Ah, musha,' said he with a frown, 'if anyone is as bad as I, I don't know what to say.'

'As bad as you! Oh, Tomás, if you are as bad as I am, I am content, for I thought there was no one in the world so wretched as myself.'

We went inside and sat down on the bench. The master took up a book. 'Now,' said he, 'we will do some dictation.'

'Oh Lord!' said Tomás, giving me a prod in the thigh.

'Long, long ago,' dictated the master, 'there was a man living in the village of Ballyboy.'

But he had only read so far when we heard a clamour outside. I looked out of the window and saw the Púncán and the King going down the Causeway with thole-pins and ropes, three or four hurrying after them, all with the same gear. 'Your soul to the devil, Tomás, more wreckage!'

The master went out to the door. He stayed there a while and then walked up to the mistress.

'Something wonderful is after happening,' said he; 'go out and see what it is.'

'The devil take you,' I whispered to Tomás, 'the dictation is over.'

The mistress came back, looking pale.

'What has happened?' said the master.

We were all listening.

'A big ship has gone down in the Sorrowful Cliff.'

He opened his eyes in astonishment. 'Look after the school till I come back,' said he.

'Look now,' said Tomás, 'we'll have the day under the hedge.'

We were all in the hurry of our lives for twelve o'clock, making the noise of the world without any thought of the dictation, for we had no fear of the mistress. She herself was in and out the door all the time, ever and ever, till twelve o'clock came. Away we ran joyfully as fast as our heels would carry us.

Great King of Virtues, it was a marvellous sight – tins, barrels of flour, big black boxes, big white boxes, big boxes of bacon, not a living being to be seen nor a curragh on the stays.

'The devil, Tomás, come west to the Spit of Seals' Cove. It's there the whole village is gathered!'

Away we ran leaping for delight. As we approached the Great Glen we met Maura Andrew with three cardboard boxes. 'Oh, my heart, a big ship is gone down on the Lóchar Rock and the sea is full of all sorts of riches,' said she.

We ran off wildly and darted like birds along the lane to the west till we went down on to Shingle Strand. Everything was in confusion, – boxes and chests of every shape and colour, not an inch of the sand but was covered in wreckage.

'Oh, Lord,' cried Tomás, throwing his cap into the air, 'we are rich for ever!'

As soon as I set foot on the shingle, I saw Mickil Shamus on my left with his head in a barrel, Dermod O'Shea beside him and his mouth stained with drink.

'What is in the barrel, Dermod?'

Mickil Shamus drew out his head. There was the same stain on his mouth.

'Now is the time for you to blow out your waists,' said Dermod.
'What is it?'
'Cod-liver oil.'
I put my head over the barrel.
'Ah, don't be sniffing it, crow, but swallow it down. It will put marrow into your bones, a thing they lack now.'
I took a mouthful, but if I had got a thousand pounds I couldn't have taken more. I spat it out.
At that moment I heard a shout from Tomás: 'Oh, the devil, Maurice, look east at the King with all the chocolates!'
He had opened a big chest which had a number of small boxes inside it, and he was laying them out on the shingle. 'Now, my lads,' he called out, 'if you have good teeth!'
He gave each of us a box. Thanking him, we ran east among the rocks and sat down without a word of talk till at last we were sick of the taste of them, for they were very strong.
'Your soul to the devil, Tomás, isn't it well we came!'
'Your soul to the devil, it is true for you.'

TWENTY YEARS A-GROWING *by Maurice O'Sullivan (1904–50)*

In The Ledge Between the Streams *Ved Mehta continues the account of his childhood begun in* Vedi. *Here he is eight years old and home in Lahore from his school for the blind.*

In the course of a day, if the weather was right, one or another of my boy cousins – 'cousin-brothers', they are called – was sure to climb to the terraced roof of his house and send up a kite. As soon as the kite was spotted, my other cousin-brothers and boys living near Mehta Gulli would race up to the terraced roofs of their houses and send up their own kites. In no time, kites would be tangling in the air, and the kite fliers would be trying to cut one another's kite strings.

One morning, I found myself alone with Cousin Yog on the roof. 'I'm going to fly this big *patang*,' he told me. A *patang* was a heavy, many-cornered kite, and had the status of royalty among *guddis*, which were lighter, square kites. He continued, almost to himself, 'If I am lucky, maybe my *patang* can bring the tangle right down onto this roof. But you can never tell. Some measly little *guddi* can appear at the last minute, from nowhere, and make the booty fall into the *gulli*.' He walked this way and that way, muttering about wanting a stringwallah. He suddenly asked me, 'Do you know how to be a stringwallah?'

'Of course I know,' I said.

From being around kite fliers, I knew that the ball of string rolled about on the roof as the kite flier ran around, letting in and hauling out the kite. The string had a tendency to get tangled, especially if the kite was hauled in quickly, or if the resin was fresh, or if the ball had not been wound symmetrically. .... I was very excited at being Cousin Yog's stringwallah.

Cousin Yog was moving from parapet to parapet in search of some breeze to launch his kite. It was summer, and although it was the early morning the air seemed close and it was already getting hot. I felt a stirring of the wind to my right, and I called to Cousin Yog. He ran over. I heard the rustle of the *patang* as he threw it over the parapet.

'There she goes!' he exclaimed. 'She's caught the wind. She's climbing. Quick, more string!'

I crawled all over the roof with the ball, ducking under Cousin Yog's hands and arms as they almost bicycled in the air. One minute, I was yanking string off the ball as Cousin Yog needed more string; the next minute, I was winding string back onto the ball as it became heaped in bunches around his feet. I had never worked with the string in that way before, and it was so highly resined that it felt alive, fresh, and dangerous. ...

Up and down Mehta Gulli and beyond, on Temple Road, boys were shouting '*Bo-kata! ... Bo-kata!*' and I could hear them running toward the spot where they thought the kites were going to fall. The best way of acquiring a cache of good kites was to capture a booty of fallen ones, because a good ready-made kite from the bazaar was expensive, and a homemade kite, no matter how carefully it was put together, fell apart in battle. We small boys, when we had nothing else to do, would try to serve as scouts for falling kites. I had good hearing, and I had trained myself to tell the direction of the cries of '*Bo-kata!*'

'At the Mehta Gulli gate, Cousin Yog!' I now shouted.

Cousins Yog and Surinder started running in that direction.

Ordinarily, Ravi and Usha would be at my side and I would alternately propel and lead them toward the sounds of the chase. It used to be that as we were running from roof to roof and from house to house they would call out to me, 'Take a long step. ... Climb down. ... Jump. ... Not that side – there's a table in the way,' but after a while they noticed that I could somehow tell by myself what to do, and for the most part they left off warning and helping me. At the time, I could not have explained any more than Ravi and Usha could how I knew by myself when to take a long step or how to avoid crashing into a table, but I later learned that the explanation had to do not only with memory but also with what is called 'facial vision' – an ability that the blind develop to sense objects and terrain by the feel of the air and by differences in sound. The air at the edge of a roof feels lighter than the air near a table, and sounds echo differently in different rooms, depending on the size of the room, the number of its open and shut windows, and so on. Those who lose their sight in childhood develop this ability naturally and fearlessly, and therefore to a higher degree than those who lose their sight in later life.

Now here I was on the roof without Ravi and Usha, and Cousins Yog and Surinder were running to be the first to get to the fallen kites. I heard them leap over the parapet and jump down onto the eaves of the next house. I followed; I leaped over the parapet, but I missed my foothold on the eaves. My heart skipped a beat. I was so terrified that I could scarcely breathe. I thought I was going to fall straight down to the *gulli* two stories below, like a deadweight. I frantically reached for something to hold on to that would break my fall. I hit my chin on the edge of the eaves, caught hold of it even though it seemed to have been sloped expressly to precipitate a fall, and pulled myself up with such force that it seemed that I hit my knees on the bottom of the eaves and my forehead on the top at the same time. Without stopping to take stock of my injuries, I balanced myself on the eaves and listened. Cousins Yog and Surinder were clambering down the drainpipe ahead. I inched along the eaves sidewise, clutching the parapet above, found the drainpipe, and slipped down it. Cousins

Yog and Surinder had already jumped from the drainpipe into an open window opposite and were thundering down a staircase inside the house. I tried to reach out and find the open window but discovered that my arms were too short. I threw myself across, almost flying through the air, like a football. I took the stairs two or three at a time, heedless of the turns where the steps narrowed to points.

At the Mehta Gulli gate, so many boys were shouting and threatening that I could scarcely tell the voices of Cousins Yog and Surinder from the others. I slipped through the knot of legs, caught hold of two small kites fluttering under a big one that was being dragged through the mud, got them free, and started running away. Suddenly, I myself was the object of a chase. Someone with a long arm reached over my shoulder and made a grab for the kites. As I was about to resist, I heard Cousin Yog's voice behind me and realized that it was his arm. I immediately let the booty go. He was the tallest among us and had the longest legs, and he ran with the kites into Mehta Gulli.

. . . When Mamaji came to hear about the incident, she forbade me to have anything more to do with kite flying. 'You are to stay with your big sisters and let them watch you,' she said.

I complained to Daddyji, but he wouldn't listen.

For many days, Mamaji and my big sisters did not let me out of their sight. But then, one day, they began letting me do what I liked. Years later, Daddyji explained, 'You grew irritable and sullen. You would throw a tantrum at the smallest thing, like not getting your meal on time. I noticed the change and decided that yours was one case where an ounce of prevention was not beter than a pound of cure. I told everyone to let you do whatever you wished.'

I remember that after Daddyji's decision I ran around with my cousin-brothers from morning to night, and even flew my own kites. There was hardly a day when I didn't get bumps or bruises, but my cousins began treating me as if I were really one of them – with, as Cousin Yog once put it, 'two good eyes'.

*Jack, Richard Church's elder brother, has just been granted his
heart's desire.*

It was my brother who broke the spell. His taciturnity for once
gave way under pressure of this long-nurtured passion. His dark,
full eyes flashed, the long lashes flickered, and he spoke.

'It's an aquarium,' he whispered. And he repeated it; teaching
me something.

'Is it any use to you?' asked Mrs Langton. Her question had the
intended rhetorical effect, for my brother put on his cap, and I
dragged on my tasselled tam-o'-shanter, while Mrs Langton
opened the door. 'Now go steady,' she said, and gave me a final
hug as I followed my brother, who had seized the aquarium in his
bare hands, and was groping his way up the area steps, stubbing
his toes on the risers because his attention was wholly concentrated upon the precious burden, the almost holy burden.

Once he stumbled and might have fallen backwards to disaster,
but was saved by his own powerful infatuation, which gave him a
sixth sense, and a superhuman authority over the laws of nature,
especially that of gravity.

I was also there to steady him from beneath. Thus, an uneasy
tandem, we reached street level, and did not even turn to wave
good-bye to Mrs Langton, who had cried out in alarm at the
near-disaster on the steps. We did not realize that we had failed to
thank her, an omission that haunted us later when we got home,
and Mother inquired, 'And what did Mrs Langton say when you
thanked her?' It was always her habit to want to know what
people said, and to be given verbatim the whole of a conversation
in which she had not taken part because of her absence from that
particular drama.

Now began the balanced pursuit of the journey home. I have
described how we ordered it, with Jack leading the way, like a
priest of one of the more austere brotherhoods carrying the Host,
or a casket of reliquary bones; I, a nervous acolyte, grasping his
coat-tails.

Tite Street and Chelsea Embankment were empty, and the day
was dying under a shroud of frost. Through this fawn-grey world
we made our way, moving with spasmodic slowness, the spasms

due to bursts of eager excitement, our desire to get home safely with the aquarium, tempered by fear of dropping it.

At the back of my mind lurked a greater fear. I knew that, once across the bridge, we were likely to encounter schoolfellows, bands of marauding freebooters of the Battersea gutters, ripe for any action, so long as it was destructive. I knew that the sight of a large glass aquarium in the arms of a boy somewhat more warmly dressed than themselves would rouse their hunting gusto. . . .

To see Jack's hands clasping the cold metal and glass, and growing stiff in nervous tension and clay-like under the insidious caress of the falling night-frost, filled me with foreboding. I could have shed a few tears; but I dared not. It was as much as I could do to keep up with his wolf-like flight. For he too was apprehensive of a thousand dangers. The air was full of swords, and treachery waited at every street corner. I watched those hands, studied the signs of numbness, the dead-white of the knuckles, the earthy pallor of the finger-nails as the blood fled from the combined attack of frost without and morbid concentration within. . . .

We were now in our home country, or at least on its outskirts, and my small-radius instincts came to life again: with that life, alas, the certainty of trouble ahead. For our local streets, thickly populated by lower middle class, artisan, and labouring folk, were prolific in children who ignored these three social barriers, and swarmed together like wild bees, buzzing about the neigh-bourhood in search of the honey of adventure. And by a miracle of ingenuity and ruthlessness, they found it. . . .

A boy hailed us; a big boy whom I did not know. My brother tried to quicken his steps, but by this time he was near exhaustion. The aquarium had become a monster. I could see Jack's arms trembling, and I could feel how the pain had made him set his lips more grimly than usual.

Again the boy hailed us, his voice brawny and powerful with that general-public indifference which in the end is more penetra-ting than true curiosity. 'What-yer got there?' he yelled. The shadows deepened, and the menace gathered. We again tried to hurry, and I struggled to come alongside my brother, to bring a flanking protection to the aquarium.

Our furtiveness was noticed, however. It was obvious that we had something to hide, and therefore it must be valuable. This Francis Drake of the back streets thereupon gave a brain-piercing whistle, to summon other buccaneers, who must have been lurking in Surrey Lane and the streets that turned off at regular intervals, each the length of two houses and two backyards.

In twos and threes they gathered, with an eleventh-hour reluctance more dreadful than the most eager blood-lust. They came from yards and doorways where they had dispersed, about to go under cover for the night. Darkness had not completely come down over the streets, their 'steep Atlantick', and there was enough twilight for a last adventure. My brother and I, vaguely known to them, never wholly of their brotherhood, were fair game. And at that moment, with our precious cargo exposed in such brittleness, we might have been likened to a fat Spanish galleon sneaking up the Trade Winds, heavy with ingots.

The familiar sinking feeling in my stomach assailed me. Nausea soured my mouth and I wanted to be sick; but an antidote of dull anger kept me going. Jack was now gliding along under the power of a self-hypnosis, the aquarium still safe, still borne aloft with religious awe.

Cries of excitement approached, and the pursuers began to run after us.

We had only two more streets to pass before reaching our own; and our home lay half-way along that. Not many yards, but we were handicapped by terror, and for all the progress we appeared to make, we might have been running backwards, or working a treadmill.

'Come on!' breathed my brother, without a glance to right or left. 'Take no notice!'

It was a command, not advice. I braced myself, and released my hold of his coat, thus intending to throw myself to the wolves, in the hope of giving him a momentary advantage.

This act of heroism, however, came to nothing, for as we passed the top of the first of the two remaining streets, the hunted and the pursuers were divided by another drama. I saw my brother look swiftly down the street at a second gang of urchins. It was following a navvy, a hatless figure with features flaming and eyes distorted by drink and fear. He was running, and gasping as he ran,

One trouser-leg was gartered below the knee, the other had burst the garter, and this gave his flight a clumsy lopsided character that added to the effect of panic.

He turned the corner as we reached it, almost knocking us down. Jack fortunately was a yard ahead, and I spurted to avoid the crash. I heard the man whimpering for breath; and I smelled sweat and beer. I heard too the chorus of jeers and yells from the juvenile furies that followed. But between him and them was the real cause of his flight. It was a woman, ragged and shameful, her hair torn down, her blouse gaping, and one eye laid open and bleeding on her cheek. She was mad with fury and screaming with pain, plunging blindly to right and left, but striving by sheer power of rage to follow her man who had thus ill-treated her. The mob was at her skirts, urging her on, making an Elizabethan sport of this horror.

It was a lucky intervention. Our own pursuers at once joined this larger hunt, and in a moment we were alone, with the uproar dying away along Surrey Lane, in the direction from which we had fled. We did not pause or look back....

The worry of it, and the horror at the sight of blood coming after the mixed excitements which had stormed round me so extravagantly since Jack and I left home after the midday meal, now sent me running ahead, crying with hysteria. Jack followed, still master of himself, and still responsible for me. But he was concerned, at the same time, to bring the treasure home safely, and he hardly altered his pace. Our mother, who had grown anxious as darkness began to fall, was at the gate, and I collapsed, shouting incoherently, into her arms, and was instantly sick over the front step.

OVER THE BRIDGE *by Richard Church*

27

ON THE THRESHOLD

There Was a Child Went Forth

There was a child went forth every day,
And the first object he look'd upon, that object he became,
And that object became part of him for the day or a certain part of
   the day,
Or for many years or stretching cycles of years.

The early lilacs became part of this child,
And grass and white and red morning-glories, and white and red
   clover, and the song of the phoebe-bird,
And the Third-month lambs and the sow's pink-faint litter, and
   the mare's foal and the cow's calf,
And the noisy brood of the barnyard or by the mire of the
   pondside,
And the fish suspending themselves so curiously below there, and
   the beautiful curious liquid,
And the water-plants with their graceful flat heads, all became
   part of him.

The field-sprouts of Fourth-month and Fifth-month became part
   of him,
Winter-grain sprouts and those of the light-yellow corn, and the
   esculent roots of the garden,
And the apple-trees cover'd with blossoms and the fruit afterward, and wood-berries, and the commonest weeds by the
   road,
And the old drunkard staggering home from the outhouse of the
   tavern whence he had lately risen,
And the schoolmistress that pass'd on her way to the school,
And the friendly boys that pass'd, and the quarrelsome boys,

And the tidy and fresh-cheek'd girls, and the barefoot negro boy
and girl,
And all the changes of city and country wherever he went.

His own parents, he that had father'd him and she that had
conceiv'd him in her womb and birth'd him,
They gave this child more of themselves than that,
They gave him afterward every day, they became part of him.

The mother at home quietly placing the dishes on the supper-
table,
The mother with mild words, clean her cap and gown, a whole-
some odour falling off her person and clothes as she walks by,
The father, strong, self-sufficient, manly, mean, anger'd, unjust,
The blow, the quick loud word, the tight bargain, the crafty lure,
The family usages, the language, the company, the furniture, the
yearning and swelling heart,
Affection that will not be gainsay'd, the sense of what is real, the
thought if after all it should prove unreal,
The doubts of day-time and the doubts of night-time, the curious
whether and how,
Whether that which appears so is so, or is it all flashes and specks?
Men and women crowding fast in the streets, if they are not
flashes and specks what are they?
The streets themselves and the façades of houses, and goods in the
windows,
Vehicles, teams, the heavy-plank'd wharves, the huge crossing at
the ferries,
The village on the highland seen from afar at sunset, the river
between,
Shadows, aureola and mist, the light falling on roofs and gables of
white or brown two miles off,
The schooner near by sleepily dropping down the tide, the little
boat slack-tow'd astern,
The hurrying tumbling waves, quick-broken crests, slapping,
The strata of colour'd clouds, the long bar of maroon-tint away
solitary by itself, the spread of purity it lies motionless in,
The horizon's edge, the flying sea-crow, the fragrance of salt
marsh and shore mud,

These become part of that child who went forth every day, and who now goes, and will always go forth every day.

Walt Whitman (1819–92)

On March 11th, 1830, after Mr Davys had gone home, Princess Victoria opened *Howlett's Tables* of the Kings and Queens of England, to begin her history lesson with Lehzen. She found to her surprise that an extra page had been slipped into the book. 'I never saw that before,' she exclaimed. 'No, Princess,' said Lehzen. 'It was not thought necessary that you should.' Victoria studied the genealogical table. So many possible heirs to the throne but each one with the date of death written after the name, until she came to the names of her two uncles, George and William, and then her own. She drew the deduction. 'I am nearer to the throne than I thought.' Then she burst into tears. After the 'little storm' had subsided she pointed out to her dear Lehzen that whereas many children might boast of the splendour they would not realize the difficulties. Lifting up the forefinger of her right hand she spoke the famous words: 'I will be good.'

VICTORIA R.I. *by Elizabeth Longford (1906–   )*

When I was eight I stole a look in the mirror;
Already could paint my long eyebrows.
At ten, I went out for the Spring Festival
And made myself a skirt of water lilies.
At twelve, I learned to play the lute;
The silver claws never left my fingers.

At fourteen, I hid away from strangers,
Guessing that I was still to marry.
At fifteen, I weep in the spring wind,
And turn away my face behind the garden swing.

from 'Seven Love Poems' by Li Shang-yin (?812–58)

Satyr and nymphs: Augustus John watches some members of his ramified family at play.

In the summer we spent whole days bathing in the Avon. Near Fordingbridge, at Bickton, the river foamed over a weir into a deep exciting whirlpool. And here we plunged in and tumbled over the waterfall at the weir and swished downstream on the strong current. This became such a passion with us, that when we were staying at Fryern we left our warm beds at dawn, and still in our nightgowns, rode bareback down to the river. The morning air cooled the skin, while the blood pulsed from the exercise warmed us inside. Tying the horses to a clump of bushes, we discarded our nightgowns and plunged naked into the water. The current dragged us over the foaming weir and below the surface of the whirlpool. I loved the soft stroking of the long green weeds, and swam under water to find a dim yellow-ochre world barred with shafts of light; down in this water world I felt protected from the worries of the world above. We swam on until we were washed up like wreckage in the still shallows. Our nightgowns clinging to our wet bodies, we mounted the horses for the gallop home. With our wet legs sticking to the fur, we felt like Amazons. Footprints marked our return to bed, where we slept, as only the young can sleep, to wake in time for another bathe before lunch.

Augustus followed us, not to bathe, but to watch, his dominating eyes following the movements of our limbs as we struggled up the muddy, reedy bank. And the old cry went up, 'Oh damn, there's Daddy again.' TWO FLAMBOYANT FATHERS *by Nicolette Devas*

Snatches of this poem were recited during the famous 'boeuf en daube' dinner party in Virginia Woolf's To The Lighthouse. *It remained unpublished in its entirety, however, until Harold Nicolson and Vita Sackville-West included it in their anthology* Another World Than This . . . *(1945).*

> Come out and climb the garden path
>   Luriana, Lurilee.
> The China rose is all abloom

And buzzing with the yellow bee.
We'll swing you on the cedar bough,
    Luriana, Lurilee.

I wonder if it seems to you,
    Luriana, Lurilee,
That all the lives we ever lived
And all the lives to be,
Are full of trees and changing leaves,
    Luriana, Lurilee.

How long it seems since you and I,
    Luriana, Lurilee,
Roamed in the forest where our kind
Had just begun to be,
And laughed and chattered in the flowers,
    Luriana, Lurilee.

How long since you and I went out,
    Luriana, Lurilee,
To see the Kings go riding by
Over lawn and daisy lea,
With their palm leaves and cedar sheaves,
    Luriana, Lurilee.

Swing, swing, swing on a bough,
    Luriana, Lurilee,
Till you sleep in a humble heap
Or under a gloomy churchyard tree,
And then fly back to swing on a bough,
    Luriana, Lurilee.

Charles Elton (1839–1900)

The Mitford clan begin to revolt against the rigours of life with Farve.

[Farve's] fury was redoubled when Nancy announced her intention to move to London and study art at the Slade School. As usual, we got only the echoes of the titanic rows going on down-stairs. We came down for meals that were eaten in dead silence, and returned to the schoolroom to hear the occasional tantaliz-ingly muffled thunder of my father's voice. Muv must have inter-ceded, for Nancy finally won her point and went to live in a furnished bed-sitting-room in Kensington. I watched her action with immense interest, and was terribly disappointed when she came home after about a month.

'How *could* you! If I ever got away to a bed-sitter I'd never come back.'. . .

Dimly, through the eyes of childhood, I glimpsed another world; a world of London bed-sitters, art students, writers . . . a world of new and different ideas . . . a world from which Swin-brook would seem as antiquated as a feudal stronghold. A mar-vellous idea flashed into my mind – one of those ideas to be cherished, polished, perfected until it can become a reality. I decided to run away from home. Not yet – I knew a twelve-year-old would hardly have a chance to survive for long without being discovered and returned to the family – but one day, when I had worked out a thoroughly satisfactory plan, and had saved enough money to support myself for a while. I wrote immediately to Drummond's Bank; in a couple of days I had their answer:

'Dear Madam, – We respectfully beg leave to acknowledge receipt of ten shillings as initial deposit in your Running Away Account. Passbook Number —— enclosed. We remain, dear Madam, your obedient servants . . .'.

HONS AND REBELS *by Jessica Mitford (1917–)*

It is September 1939, a month of hard departures, as Vere's father receives his call-up papers and Vere himself prepares to leave the world of the nursery and set off for boarding school.

For the last week he has worn only sandals, shorts and open-necked shirts, and the long black trousers he now climbs into, the socks and lacing shoes he puts on, and the stiff shirt that fastens with a stud – these unnatural clothes oppress him. But he has so much to say to Nanny that he scarcely notices what he is doing until the time comes for him to fix his starched Eton collar.

'Have I got to wear that?' he exclaims.

'Of course, Vere,' Nanny answers.

Together they tug and pull, bruising their fingertips, and eventually manage to attach the collar to the studs. Nanny slips on his black waistcoat and short jacket, and he goes to the mirror to brush his hair. And his heart sinks with new and horrible violence. His shield seems to bend beneath the blow. He cannot believe it will withstand this sickening onslaught, yet out of a curious perversity he continues to stare at his dreadful reflection, to look out of the window at the waiting car, and to strengthen the very forces he is trying to overcome. But his valiant shield holds. His horror and his fear retreat.

Nanny, who has been fetching his toothbrush, re-enters his room and regards him oddly. He is not surprised. He feels pale and ill, and wonders what would happen if his heart should sink again in such a way. For his interior armour now seems to disintegrate. In its place – in place of his protective shield – is something large and battered, raw, swollen and extremely sensitive. . . .

For a little longer they talk in polite strained tones. Then Nanny looks at the clock on the high mantelshelf and says, 'Well, Vere, you've a good drive ahead of you. I suppose you'd better be going.' And she stares at him solemnly through her spectacles.

He wishes he could instantly depart, but Nanny has risen and begun to unfold a black overcoat which has lain across the back of the sofa.

'Whose is that?' he asks, knowing quite well but wanting to say something light and possibly funny.

'It's yours, Vere. I'll help you on with it,' Nanny replies seriously.

'I won't need it,' he says.

'Yes, you will – it's sharp out.'

'But I was in my pyjamas! . . .' The memory of that happy time in his pyjamas hurts him. He adds savagely, 'And look at all I've got on now!'

Flora says, 'But sweetheart, the front of the car's open and Albert's wearing a heavy coat.'

He turns and sticks out his arms behind him. While Nanny

helps him into the coat he studies a corner of the ceiling. Then he says, 'I'm absolutely boiling as it is!' and looks round with a smile that trembles, still trying to make light of his impossible situation. But both Nanny and Flora now regard him solemnly and remain silent, so he returns to his study of the beamed ceiling and says in a deep jerky voice, 'The coat goes under my collar, Nanny.'

'Vere, I don't think it does,' Nanny answers.

He waits a second before saying, 'I've seen Leo with it under his collar a hundred times.'

'Are you sure, sweetheart?'

'Yes!'

'Well, we'll try it, Vere.'

He knows he is not believed. The insupportability of this further disagreement causes the sensitive lump inside him to swell. As Nanny struggles with the collar which already covers his waistcoat and jacket, and the tightness round his neck increases, the cruel pressure seems to bear directly on that lump, enlarging it moment by moment and paining him more and more. Yet he does not protest. He is certain he is right. And to give way over the collar would be to give way completely, to everything.

'There you are, Vere,' Nanny says finally.

He turns. Suddenly, because the collar is too tight, because he realizes he has been wrong, because of the fond earnest glances that he meets, and the expectant hush, and all that has gone before, he is overpowered by violent anger, antagonism and resentment. He starts to say something. Burning damaging words rise to his lips. He makes a single unintelligible sound, then everything changes. His rage and hatred leave him. The whole edifice of conflict, control, containment of his grief, topples to the ground.

'I can't breathe,' he says.

'It's all right, child, it's all right now,' Nanny says quickly, removing the coat from beneath his collar.

'I can't go,' he says.

'You must, Vere.'

'I can't!' he cries.

'Please, Vere . . . Sweetheart . . . Child . . .'

'No, Nanny . . . No, no, Flora!'

Albert helps him into the car. Nanny and Flora stand by the gate in the wire fence.

'I'm so sorry,' he tries to say.

'Be a good boy, Vere . . . Be good, won't you?' Nanny repeats.

He nods. Everything becomes blurred: Nanny, Flora, Chinky chasing the car, Little Lodge, a curtain blowing through an open window, the trees in the lane, the bright morning sunlight. He lowers his head and abandons himself to his sobs.

Very slowly, after a stretch of time which he cannot estimate, Vere pulls his handkerchief out of its new pocket. He wipes his eyes that are damp and sandy, and his face, hands and overcoat that are wet. Then he lays his hands with the fingers splayed on his knees to dry, and attempts to concentrate on the spasmodic movements of the needles of the black dials set into the dashboard. But he believes that he feels too miserable, too lethargic: therefore he sits hunched, blows out his hot swollen lips, allows his vision to become fixed and obscured. And again time passes.

'Sixty-five miles an hour!' states Albert unexpectedly.

'Really?' says Vere, looking out of the window.

Albert says no more, yet his single comment and the start of latent interest it has aroused force Vere to admit to himself that for some little while he has felt neither miserable nor lethargic, but strangely tense and excited.

He tries not to think of his strange excitement and continues to look about him. Birds swerve out of the thickset hedges, horses canter in a misty field. The car halts and a flock of sheep scuttles by. Vere returns the salute of the grave shepherd, watches his active dog, savours the warm smell of the animals, observes their yellow eyes.

And suddenly it seems to him that the world is not as it was. He cannot postpone realization any longer: each object of the once more moving scene deepens his ache of wonder and of joy. For everything is changed. He thinks of Nanny and of Flora, then of sheep, shepherd, trees and pale blue sky, of all he sees, all he has known and may ever know – and he is not afraid.

'All right now?' Albert asks.

'All right,' Vere answers.

MORNING *by Julian Fane*

Camara Laye reaches the milestone of the Malinke circumcision ritual.

Three times that day we appeared in the main square to dance the 'coba'; and three times again during the night, by torchlight; and each time the men enclosed us in a living hedge. We did not get any sleep; no one went to bed: the whole town stayed awake and danced all through the night. As we left our hut for the sixth time, dawn was breaking.

'*Coba! Aye coba, lama!*'

Our bonnets still moved in time to the rhythm, our boubous were still stretched over our straddling legs; but we were beginning to flag, our eyes were burning feverishly and our anxiety was mounting. If we had not been urged on, carried away by the tom-tom beat . . . But it urged us on, carried us away! And we danced on obediently, our heads curiously light from lack of sleep, curiously heavy, too, with thoughts of the fate that was to be ours.

'*Coba! Aye coba, lama!*'

As we came to the end of the dance, dawn began to lighten the main square. This time, we did not go back to our hut; we went immediately into the bush; we went a long way, to where there was no risk of our being disturbed. In the main square the dancing had stopped: the people had all gone home. Nevertheless, a few men followed us out. The rest awaited, in their huts, the ceremonial shots that would announce to all that one more man, one more Malinke, had been born.

We had reached a circular clearing, the ground completely bare. All round, grasses grew high, higher than the men's heads; it was the most secluded spot one could have wished to find. We were lined up, each of us in front of a stone. At the other end of the clearing the men stood facing us. And we took off our clothes.

I was afraid, terribly afraid, and I needed all my will-power not to show it. All those men standing in front of us and watching us must see nothing of my fear. My companions showed themselves no less brave, and it was absolutely necessary that it should be so; among those men standing in front of us was perhaps our future father-in-law, or a future relative; we dared not let ourselves down now!

Suddenly the operator appeared. We had caught a glimpse of him the night before, when he had performed his dance in the main square. And now, also, I only caught a brief glimpse of him. I had hardly realized he was there, before I saw him standing in front of me.

Was I afraid? I mean, was I even more afraid, had I at that particular moment a fresh access of fear – for I had been beset by fears ever since I had entered the clearing? I did not have time to be afraid. I felt something like a burn, and I closed my eyes for a fraction of a second. I do not think I cried out. No, I cannot have cried out; I certainly did not have time to do that either. When I opened my eyes, the operator was bent over my neighbour. In a few seconds the dozen or so boys there were that year became men: the operator made me pass from one state to the other, with an indescribable rapidity. . . .

Finally the time came when the healer considered us completely recovered and handed us over to our parents again. But I was still at school and I could no longer join in the excursions which my companions were going on among the neighbouring towns and villages. Nor could I take part in their labours in our healer's fields, work which they undertook to repay the care he had taken of us. My parents arranged with him for me to be exempted from it.

When I finally got back to my concession, the whole family was waiting for me. My parents held me tightly in their arms, particularly my mother, as if she was wanting secretly to proclaim that I was still her son, that my second birth had done nothing to alter the fact that I was still her son. My father watched us for a moment, then he said to me, almost regretfully:

'From now on, this is your hut, my son.'

The hut stood opposite my mother's.

'Yes,' said my mother, 'you will sleep there now. But as you can see, I am still within earshot.'

I opened the door of the hut; my clothes were laid out on the bed. I went up to it and took them in my hands one by one, then put them carefully back; they were men's clothes. Yes, the hut was opposite my mother's, I was still within earshot of her voice, but the clothes on the bed were men's clothes. I was a man!

'Are you pleased with your new clothes?' asked my mother.

Pleased? Yes, I was pleased; naturally I was pleased. At least I think I was pleased. They were fine clothes, they were . . . I turned towards my mother: she was smiling sadly at me. . . .

THE DARK CHILD *by Camara Laye*

Spring and Fall

Margaret, are you grieving
Over Goldengrove unleaving?
Leaves, like the things of man, you
With your fresh thoughts care for, can you?
Ah! as the heart grows older
It will come to such sights colder
By and by, nor spare a sigh
Though worlds of wanwood leafmeal lie;
And yet you will weep and know why.
Now no matter, child, the name:
Sorrow's springs are the same.
Nor mouth had, no nor mind, expressed
What heart heard of, ghost guessed:
It is the blight man was born for,
It is Margaret you mourn for.

Gerard Manley Hopkins (1844–89)

A farewell to Egypt and childhood:

Somewhere in the air the thought of school in England hung, obtruding itself between the bright days and the evenings beside the crisp log fire. Part of me wanted it; needed the harder lessons, the faster runners, a world of bigger and better Joneses with whom to keep up. Part of me wanted very much to come to grips with the larger, tougher, grown-up world of England. Part of me wanted complete independence. A very small part of me knew that an added stringency was necessary, that I had grown out of

this Eden and indeed was all set to become its serpent. And a
larger part longed, like the man with the load of sugar cane on his
back, to remain for ever the irresponsible child of loving parents,
doing as I liked and receiving the forgiveness and acceptance that
came to me as their child; living out my life in this idyllic sun-
spattered land, seeing the Nile rise and fall, seeing the Pyramids
stand in the glow of morning, feeding silkworms and canaries and
rabbits, playing easy imaginary games with Alethea, watching
the growth of my forest. A kind of enchanted sadness hung
over everything, aggravated no doubt by post-whooping-cough
depression. . . .

My father sat at breakfast in the dining-room. I had come down to
ask him some necessary question about the ring round Saturn,
was it solid or not? He could be trusted to know. He was eating
yoghourt out of a small earthenware bowl, not for health reasons
which had not then been thought of, but because it was a local
dish and he liked it. . . . [He] was reading the *Egyptian Gazette*
and did not look up. I came and swung, tiresomely, with one wrist
on the table and one on the arm of his chair.

He put the paper down and began on his letters and I began on
Saturn. His fingers were blunt-edged and stained with nicotine. I
noticed suddenly that he was having difficulty in opening the
envelope, and this gripped me without warning in a spasm of
astonished pain. I underwent that strange unbearable wrench by
which one's soul seems to be corkscrewed out of one's being and
into someone else's, there to suffer for them a quantity of things
which they are not even thinking of suffering for themselves. It
was the very slight opening of a door which would never again
shut quite so tightly, a door into a world where other people had
existences of their own; where other people loved, felt, endured;
were lonely, exultant, or bloody-minded, without reference to
me. For one whose quickened imagination could focus only upon
itself, this was a sharp blow in the solar plexus, an unprecedented
heaving of the solid ground beneath the feet. Hitherto my father
had existed only in this function, never as a person in his own
right. That he could grow old, or diminish, or fail in any way had
never entered into my conception of him. For the first time I saw

him as a man like other men; subject to old age, feebleness, disaster, even death. An experience that was in the main sentimental, it was also briefly, revealing, even appalling; like a sudden fall which drained one of blood as one rushed through unfamiliar air. I sat down abruptly on a Chippendale chair and forgot the ring of Saturn. From the hall came the sound of the cuckoo clock striking half-past eight, and I remembered that I had failed to complete my homework, which was papering a room twenty feet by twelve, and the principal events of the reign of Louis Quatorze.

The last morning arrived, and was as heartlessly beautiful as ever. I dressed with an unforgetting, photographing eye fixed upon the pyramid of Cheops. My footfalls sounded sadly round the garden, even the squeak of the last swing had a melancholy fall. The leaves of the apricot grove glittered in the brilliance of the morning, datura flowers hung richly in their green gloom. Mohammed smiled as ever, the kindness of his pock-marked face was an ache against the heart.

The birds still sang as my new luggage was loaded at the gate. 'If you can manage not to cry,' my mother had said, 'it will make things easier for your father.' But would it be possible? In theory I was coming back, perhaps for some distant Christmas holidays, in spite of the ten days' journey from England. In theory I was coming back, grown-up, to enjoy the sweets and splendours of adult Cairo life. In theory this was no goodbye. But children, like dogs, sometimes know things in their bones, and what my bones were saying this bright morning was goodbye for ever.

It was impossible to look back at the green-shuttered house, at the stone steps leading up to the front door with their pots of freesias and cinerarias and pelargoniums, at the stone gate posts on whose broad top Alethea and I had so often sat, two non-matching heraldic beasts. The road was spattered with bright sunlight and deep shadow, with the lozenge-shaped leaves of the leboc trees spreading out into the sun. The timeless Nile rolled under, the horses' hooves rang out again across the iron of the Boulac Bridge. As the train drew out of Cairo station, leaving my father's grey-flannelled figure on the platform, leaving the comprehending faces of Mohammed and Suliman, I reached the end of this particular tether, and the fields of the Delta dissolved before my eyes. 'Well done,' my mother said, 'you lasted out.' I was pleased that she was pleased, but otherwise this victory seemed of little worth. From her corner Rose Hunt sniffed sympathetically; Alethea, glancing up from *Little Folks*, seemed to look faintly diverted. By Tanta I was deep in *The Viper of Milan*, and half-way through a box of Turkish Delight, and for once no one seemed concerned about my spoiling my lunch.

As we sat that evening on the dimly lit upper deck of the ship, my mother unaccountably decided that the moment had come for a sex talk. Perhaps, what with her social life, and the Authorized Version, and the continued presence of Alethea in the night nursery, she had never before had an opportunity. I was twelve and a half; it seems strange that living in uninhibited Egypt, I had not got around to knowing the facts of life before. Her discourse, which in any case was halting, less from embarrassment than from a determination (unrealized) to make it all entirely clear, was interrupted by the arrival of the late train from Cairo, and by the consequent irruption on to the deck of a number of friends. Sent by their wives in search of bookable deck chairs, they advanced smilingly, Colonel this and Sir Mortimer that; approaching from time to time with kindly expressions of pleasure at finding that our journey was to be made in company. In the intervals my mother pressed on with her task. The coming and going of all these stately fellows seemed to make the whole thing even more improbable than it sounded. Could they have engaged in these droll and surprising gymnastics? Yet all, except Sir Ronald Storrs, were known to be fathers. I looked at them with goggle eyes.

In the background, across the dark waters of the harbour, the lights of Alexandria winked and flickered a sardonic accompaniment.

A LATE BEGINNER *by Priscilla Napier*

Nothing Gold Can Stay

Nature's first green is gold,
Her hardest hue to hold.
Her earliest leaf's a flower;
But only so an hour.
Then leaf subsides to leaf.
So Eden sank to grief,
So dawn goes down today.
Nothing gold can stay.

Robert Frost (1874–1963)

SOURCES AND ACKNOWLEDGEMENTS

Henry Adams, *The Education of Henry Adams*, first published by the Massachusetts Historical Society, 1918. Copyright renewed Charles Francis Adams, 1946.

Sergei Aksakov, *Years of Childhood*, published in Russian 1858; in this translation by J. D. Duff with an introduction by David Cecil, Oxford, 1983. Reprinted by permission of Oxford University Press.

Louisa Alcott, *Little Women*, New York, 1868–9.

Mulk Raj Anand, *Seven Summers: The Story of an Indian Childhood*, London, 1951. Reprinted by permission of Century Hutchinson.

Hans Andersen, *The Mermaid Man: the Autobiography of Hans Christian Andersen*, a new abridged version, translated by Maurice Richard, London, 1955.

Anonymous essay, 'The Owl' from *Plain Words: A Guide to the use of English*, by Sir Ernest Gowers, London, 1948. Crown copyright. Reprinted by permission of the Controller of Her Majesty's Stationery Office.

Anonymous, c. 1480, 'Manners at Table when Away from Home' from the *The Oxford Book of Children's Verse*, chosen and edited with notes by Iona and Peter Opie, Oxford, 1973.

Anonymous Venetian diplomat from *Italian Relations of England*, translated by Charlotte Sneyd, Camden Society, 1847.

Anonymous: 'The Mummers' Play' and 'Water boy where are you hiding?', Negro folksong from *The Poet's Tongue: An Anthology*: edited by W. H. Auden and J. Garrett, London, 1948. Reprinted by permission of Unwin Hyman Ltd.

Daisy Ashford, *The Young Visiters*, London, 1919. Reprinted by permission of the estate of the author and Chatto & Windus.

St Augustine, *Confessions*, translated with an introduction by R. S. Pine-Coffin (Penguin Classics, 1961). Copyright © R. S. Pine-Coffin, 1965. Reprinted by permission of Penguin Books Ltd.

Jane Austen, 'The History of England from the Reign of Henry the 4th to the Death of Charles the 1st by a Partial, Prejudiced, and Ignorant Historian' (1791) from *Minor Works*, edited by R. W. Chapman, Oxford, 1954.

Maurice Baring, *The Puppet Show of Memory*, London, 1922. Reprinted by permission of A. P. Watt Ltd on behalf of the Maurice Baring Will Trust. *Lost Diaries*, London, 1913. Reprinted by permission of Gerald Duckworth.

Max Beerbohm, *A Peep into the Past and other prose pieces*, collected and introduced by Rupert Hart-Davis, London, 1972. Reprinted by permission of Mrs Eva Reichmann.

Hilaire Belloc, 'Franklin Hyde' and 'Henry King, who chewed bits of string...' from *Cautionary Tales for Children: Designed for the Admonition of Children between the ages of eight and fourteen years*, London, 1918. Reprinted by permission of Gerald Duckworth. 'The Yak' from *The Bad Child's Book of Beasts*, Oxford, 1896.

Arnold Bennett, *The Truth about an Author*, London, 1903.

Lord Berners (Gerald Tyrwhitt-Wilson), *First Childhood*, London, 1934. Reprinted by permission of the literary executors of the Berners estate.

John Betjeman, *Summoned by Bells*, London, 1960. Reprinted by permission of John Murray (publishers) Ltd.

Thomas Betson, letter to Katherine Ryche, *Stonor Letters and Papers 1290–1482*, Part II, edited by Charles Lethbridge Kingsford, Camden Society, 1919.

Thomas Bewick, *Memoir: by himself*, first published by his daughter Jane, Newcastle-upon-Tyne, 1862. This edition with an introduction by Montague Weekley, London, 1961.

Laurence Binyon, 'The Little Dancers' from *London Visions*, London, 1898. Reprinted by permission of Mrs Nicolete Gray and The Society of Authors on behalf of the Laurence Binyon estate.

438

William Blake, 'Infant Sorrow' and 'The Schoolboy' from *Songs of Experience*, London, 1794. 'The Chimney Sweep' from *Songs of Innocence*, London, 1789.

Karen Blixen, *Out of Africa*, London, 1937. Reprinted by permission of the estate of the author and The Bodley Head.

Georges Bompas, *Life of Frank Buckland (1826–1885)*, by his brother-in-law, London, 1885.

Elizabeth Bowen, *Seven Winters*, London, 1942. Reprinted by permission of Virago Press.

Paul Bowles, *Without Stopping: an autobiography*, London, 1972. Reprinted by permission of Peter Owen, London.

Maurice Bowra, *Memories 1898–1939*, London, 1966. Reprinted by permission of George Weidenfeld & Nicolson Ltd.

Emily Brontë, 'Song to A.A.', 'Tell me, tell me, smiling child' and 'Child of Delight' from *Poems* by Currer, Ellis & Acton Bell, London, 1846.

Christy Brown, *My Left Foot*, London, 1954. Reprinted by permission of Martin Secker & Warburg Ltd.

John Buchan, *Memory Hold-the-Door*, London, 1940. Reprinted by permission of A. P. Watt Ltd on behalf of the Rt Hon. Lord Tweedsmuir of Elsfield, CBE.

Samuel Butler, *The Way of All Flesh*, London, 1903.

Lewis Carroll, from *A Selection from the Letters of Lewis Carroll*, edited with an introduction and notes by Evelyn M. Hatch, London, 1933.

Charles Causley, 'Timothy Winters' from *Union Street*, London, 1957. Reprinted by permission of Grafton Books, a Division of Collins Publishers.

Benvenuto Cellini, *The Autobiography of Benvenuto Cellini*, written 1558–66; translated by George Bull (Penguin Classics, 1956). Copyright © George Bull, 1956. Reprinted by permission of Penguin Books Ltd.

Charles Chaplin, *My Autobiography*, London, 1964. Reprinted by permission of the estate of Charles Chaplin and The Bodley Head.

The Child's Spelling-Book: Calculated to Render Reading Completely Easy to Little Children, Hartford, USA, 1798.

Chin Shengt'an; translated by Lin Yutang, *The Importance of Living*, London, 1938. Copyright Lin Yutang, 1938. Reprinted by permission of Curtis Brown Ltd.

Agatha Christie, *An Autobiography*, London, 1977. © Agatha Christie Ltd, 1977.

Richard Church, *Over the Bridge: an Essay in autobiography*, London, 1955. Reprinted by permission of the estate of Richard Church.

Thomas Clarke, testimony quoted in *Climbing Boys; A Study of Sweeps' Apprentices, 1773–1875*, edited by K. H. Strange, London, 1982. Reprinted by permission of W. H. Allen.

Lady Anne Clifford, *The Diary of Lady Anne Clifford*, with an introductory note by V. Sackville-West, London, 1923.

Richard Cobb, *Still Life: Sketches from a Tunbridge Wells Childhood*, London, 1984. Reprinted by permission of the author and Chatto & Windus.

Samuel Taylor Coleridge, from *The Notebooks of Samuel Taylor Coleridge*, Vol. I, 1794–1804, edited by Kathleen Coburn, London, 1957. 'Frost at Midnight', 1798 from *Poetical Works*, London, 1828.

George Colman the Younger, *Random Records*, London, 1830.

Cyril Connolly, *Enemies of Promise*, London, 1938. © 1973 Cyril Connolly. Published by André Deutsch Ltd. Used by permission.

Benjamin Constant, *The Red Note-Book*, with an introduction by Harold Nicolson, translated by Norman Cameron, London, 1948. Reprinted by permission of Hamish Hamilton Ltd.

Abraham Cowley, 'Of Myself' from *The Works of Abraham Cowley*, 1668.

William Cowper, 'On Receipt of my Mother's Picture out of Norfolk' from *Poems*, London, 1798.

Kathleen Coyle, *The Magical Realm: autobiography*, New York 1942. Copyright 1943 by E. P. Dutton, renewed 1971 by Kestrel Allen O'Maher. Reprinted by permission of E. P. Dutton, a division of NAL Penguin Inc.

Vincent Cronin, *Louis XIV*, London, 1964. Reprinted by permission of the author and Collins Publishers.

e. e. cummings, 'in Just' from *Tulips and Chimneys*, edited by George James Firmage, New York, 1923. Copyright © 1923, 1925, and renewed 1951, 1953 by e. e. cummings. Copyright © 1973, 1976 by the trustees for the e. e. cummings Trust. Copyright © 1973, 1976 by George James Firmage. Reprinted by permission of Liveright Publishing Corporation.

Bernard Darwin, *The World that Fred Made: An Autobiography*, London, 1955. Reprinted by permission of A. P. Watt Ltd on behalf of Lady Darwin, Ursula Mommens and the N. M. E. Fenn Will Trust.

W. H. Davies, *The Autobiography of a Super-Tramp*, London, 1908. Reprinted by permission of the executors of the W. H. Davies estate and Jonathan Cape Ltd.

C. Day Lewis, 'O Dreams O Destinations' and 'In the Shelter' from *Collected Poems*, London, 1954. Reprinted by permission of the executors of the estate of C. Day Lewis, Jonathan Cape Ltd and The Hogarth Press. *The Buried Day*, London, 1960. Reprinted by permission of the executors of the estate of C. Day Lewis and Chatto & Windus.

Walter de la Mare, 'The Bards' from *Collected Rhymes and Verses*, London, 1970. 'If I were Lord of Tartary' from *Songs of Childhood*, London, 1902. 'Ann, Ann' from *Peacock Pie: A Book of Rhymes*, London, 1913. Reprinted by permission of the Literary Trustees of Walter de la Mare and The Society of Authors as their representative.

Daniel Defoe, *The Life of Colonel Jack*, London, 1722.

Nicolette Devas, *Two Flamboyant Fathers*, London, 1966. Reprinted by permission of A. D. Peters & Co. Ltd.

Polly Devlin, *All of Us Here*, London, 1983. Reprinted by permission of Polly Devlin and George Weidenfeld & Nicolson Ltd.

Alastair Dunnett, 'My Mother' from *Among Friends*, London, 1984. Reprinted by permission of Century Hutchinson.

John Earle, 'A Child' from *Microcosmographie*, London, 1628.

George Eliot (Mary Ann Evans), 'Brother and Sister' from *The Legend of Jubal and Other Poems*, 1879.

T. S. Eliot, 'Animula', an Ariel Poem: Faber & Faber Christmas card for 1929. 'Landscapes': I. 'New Hampshire' from *Collected Poems 1909–62*, London, 1963. Reprinted by permission of Faber & Faber Ltd.

Charles Elton, 'Luriana Lurilee', first published in *Another World Than This: an anthology*, compiled by V. Sackville-West and Harold Nicolson, London, 1945.

George Ewart Evans, *Ask the Fellows who Cut the Hay*, London, 1956. Reprinted by permission of Faber & Faber Ltd.

Julian Fane, *Morning*, London, 1956. Copyright © Julian Fane. Published by Hamish Hamilton Ltd, St George's Press Ltd 1986 and by Sceptre 1988.

Marjory Fleming, letters and journal entries from *The Story of Pet Marjorie (Marjory Fleming)*, by L. McBean, London, 1904. 'Three Turkeys' from *The Complete Marjory Fleming: her journals, letters and verses*, transcribed and edited by Frank Sidgwick, London, 1934.

E. M. Forster, *Marianne Thornton 1797–1887: A Domestic Biography*, London, 1956. Reprinted by permission of Edward Arnold.

John Forster, *The Life of Charles Dickens*, London, 1872–4.

C. J. Fox, anecdote referring to him, quoted in *The English*, by Christopher Hibbert, London, 1987. Reprinted by permission of Grafton Books, a Division of the Collins Publishing Group.

Benjamin Franklin, *The Autobiography of Benjamin Franklin*, written 1771–90, published posthumously, 1817. This edition edited by Leonard W. Labaree, Ralph L. Ketcham, Helen C. Boatfield and Helen H. Fineham, Yale, 1964. Reprinted by permission of The Huntington Library, San Marino.

Antonia Fraser, *Mary Queen of Scots*, London, 1969. Reprinted by permission of George Weidenfeld & Nicolson Ltd.

G. J. French, *The Life and Times of Samuel Crompton*, London, 1860.

Robert Frost, 'Nothing Gold can Stay' from *The Poetry of Robert Frost* edited by Edward Connery Lathem, London, 1971. Reprinted by permission of the estate of Robert Frost, the editor and Jonathan Cape Ltd. Copyright © 1923 by Holt, Rinehart & Winston Inc., and renewed 1951 by Robert Frost. Reprinted by permission of Henry Holt and Company Inc.

Angelica Garnett, *Deceived with Kindness: A Bloomsbury Childhood*, London, 1984. Reprinted by permission of the author and Chatto & Windus.

Elizabeth Gaskell, *The Life of Charlotte Brontë*, 1857.

Bob Geldof with Paul Vallely, *Is That It?*, London, 1986. Reprinted by permission of Sidgwick & Jackson.

André Gide, *If it Die . . .*, published as *Si le grain ne meurt . . .*, France, 1924; this translation by Dorothy Bussy, London, 1951. Reprinted by permission of Martin Secker & Warburg Ltd and Random House Inc.

Alexander Gilchrist, *Life of William Blake*, 1863, this edition edited by Ruthven Todd, London and New York, 1942.

Maxim Gorky (Alexei Maximovich Peshkov), *My Childhood*, translated by Gertrude M. Foakes, London, 1915.

Reprinted by permission of The Bodley Head.

Edmund Gosse, *Father and Son: A Study of Two Temperaments*, London, 1907.

Stephen Graham, *Peter the Great*, London, 1929.

Kenneth Grahame, letters taken from *First Whisper of 'The Wind in the Willows'*, edited with an introduction by Elspeth Grahame, London, 1944.

Elizabeth Grant of Rothiemurchus, afterwards Mrs E. Smith of Battiboys, *Memoirs of a Highland Lady*, edited by Lady Strachey (E.M.), London, 1898.

Robert Graves, *Goodbye to All That*, London, 1929. 'Henry and Mary', 'The Beach' and 'The Sweet Shop Round the Corner' from *Collected Poems*, London, 1975. Reprinted by permission of A. P. Watt Ltd on behalf of the executors of the estate of Robert Graves.

Henry Green, *Pack My Bag: A Self-Portrait*, London, 1979. Reprinted by permission of the estate of the author and Chatto & Windus.

Graham Greene, *A Sort of Life*, London, 1971. Reprinted by permission of the author and Laurence Pollinger Ltd.

Thomas Hardy, 'Childhood Among the Ferns', 'The Self-Unseeing', 'Midnight on the Great Western' and 'The Oxen', first published in *Moments of Vision*, 1917. From *The Complete Poems of Thomas Hardy*, London, 1976.

Florence Hardy, *The Life of Thomas Hardy 1840–1928*: compiled largely from contemporary notes, letters, diaries and biographical memoranda, as well as from old information in conversations extending over many years by Florence Emily Hardy, first published in one volume, later in two, 1928, 1930. London, 1962.

Augustus Hare, *The Story of My Life*, London, 1896.

Fraser Harrison, *A Winter's Tale*, London, 1987. Reprinted by permission of the author and Collins Publishers.

Seamus Heaney, 'Mosbawn' from *Preoccupations: Selected Prose 1968–1978*, London, 1980. Reprinted by permission of Faber & Faber Ltd.

Alexander Herzen, *Childhood, Youth and Exile*, Parts I and II of *My Past and Thoughts*, 1885, in this translation from the Russian by J. A. Duff, with an introduction by Isaiah Berlin, Oxford, 1980. Reprinted by permission of Oxford University Press.

Heinrich Hoffmann, *The English Struwwelpeter; or, Pretty Stories and Funny Pictures*, London, 1909.

James Hogg, 'A Boy's Song', published posthumously in *Poetical Works*, Vol. V, 1840.

Vyvyan Holland, *Son of Oscar Wilde*, London, 1954. Reprinted by permission of Merlin Holland.

Michael Holroyd, *Lytton Strachey: A Critical Biography*, Vol. I: *The Unknown Years (1880–1932)*, London, 1967. Reprinted by permission of the author and William Heinemann Ltd.

Gerard Manley Hopkins, 'Spring and Fall' from *Poems*, published posthumously, London, 1918.

W. H. Hudson, *Far Away and Long Ago: A Childhood in Argentina*, London, 1918.

M. V. Hughes, *A London Child of the 1870's*, Oxford, 1934. Reprinted by permission of Oxford University Press.

William Hutton, *The Life of William Hutton including a particular account of The Riots at Birmingham in 1791, to which is subjoined The History of His Family, written by Himself*, and published by his daughter, Catherine Hutton (written in 1798), London, 1816.

Henry James, 'A Small Boy and Others', London, 1913, published with an introduction by Frederick W. Dupee as part of *Henry James: Autobiography*, London, 1956. Reprinted by permission of W. H. Allen.

Romilly John, *The Seventh Child: A Retrospect*, London, 1975. Reprinted by permission of the author and Jonathan Cape Ltd.

L. E. Jones, *A Victorian Boyhood*, London, 1955. Reprinted by permission of Macmillan London Ltd.

James Joyce, *A Portrait of the Artist as a Young Man*, first published in *The Egoist*, 1914–15. Reprinted by permission of the executors of the James Joyce estate and Jonathan Cape Ltd.

Tamara Karsavina, *Theatre Street: The Reminiscences of Tamara Karsavina*, London, 1930. Reprinted by permission of David Higham Associates Ltd and William Heineman Ltd.

Erich Kästner, *When I was a Little Boy*, Zürich, 1957, translated from the German by Isabel and Florence McHugh, London, 1959. Reprinted by permission of Atrium Verlag, Zürich and Jonathan Cape Ltd.

John Keats, letter to his sister Fanny, 1818, taken from *Letters of John Keats to his Family & Friends*, edited by Sidney Colvin, London, 1891.

Frank Kendon, *The Small Years*, Cambridge,

1930. Reprinted by permission of the author and Cambridge University Press.

James Kenward, *The Suburban Child*, Cambridge, 1955. Reprinted by permission of the author and Cambridge University Press.

Francis Kilvert, *Selections from the Diary of the Rev. Francis Kilvert*, chosen, edited and introduced by William Plomer, London, 1938. Reprinted by permission of Mrs Sheila Hooper and Jonathan Cape Ltd.

Magdalen King-Hall, *The Story of the Nursery*, London, 1958: 'Conversation Manual' by Peter Erondell, 1605 and 'Master Boscawen'.

Charles Kingsley, *The Water Babies: A Fairy Tale for a Land-Baby*, London, 1863.

Rudyard Kipling, *Something of Myself For My Friends Known and Unknown*, London, 1936.

James Kirkup, *The Only Child: an Autobiography of Infancy*, London, 1957. Copyright James Kirkup, 1957. Reprinted by permission of Curtis Brown Ltd.

Giuseppe di Lampedusa, *Two Stories and a Memoir*, first published in Milan as *Raconte*, 1961; in this translation by Archibald Colquhoun with an introduction by E. M. Forster, London, 1962. Copyright © 1962 by William Collins & Co. Ltd and Pantheon Books Inc. Reprinted by permission of Collins Harvill and Pantheon Books, a Division of Random House Inc.

Osbert Lancaster, *All Done from Memory*, London, 1963. Reprinted by permission of John Murray (Publishers) Ltd.

D. H. Lawrence, 'Baby asleep after pain' from *Rhyming Poems*, London, 1928.

Camara Laye, *The Dark Child*, translated from the French by James Kirkup with an introduction by William Plomer. First published in French as *L'Enfant Noir*, Librairie Plon, 1954. This edition, London, 1955. Reprinted by permission of Collins Publishers.

Edward Lear, 'The New Vestments' and 'There was an Old Man of Aosta' from *Laughable Lyrics: a Fourth Book of Nonsense Poems, Songs, Botany, Music, etc, by Edward Lear*, London, 1877; incorporated in *The Complete Nonsense of Edward Lear*, edited and introduced by Holbrook Jackson, London, 1947. 'In Calabria' from *The Journals of a Landscape Painter in Southern Calabria*, London, 1852.

Laurie Lee, *Cider with Rosie*, London, 1959.

Reprinted by permission of the author and The Hogarth Press.

James Lees-Milne, *Another Self*, London, 1970. Reprinted by permission of the author and David Higham Associates Ltd.

Rosamond Lehmann, *The Swan in the Evening: Fragments of an Inner Life*, London, 1967. Reprinted by permission of The Society of Authors and Miss Rosamond Lehmann.

Michel Leiris, *Manhood: Preceded by The Autobiographer as Torero*, first published as *L'Age d'Homme*, Paris, 1946; this edition translated from the French by Richard Howard, London, 1968. Copyright © 1963, 1984 by Michael Leiris. Reprinted by permission of North Point Press.

Norman Lewis, *Jackdaw Cake*, London 1985. Copyright © Norman Lewis. Reprinted by permission of Hamish Hamilton Ltd.

Li Shang-Yin, 'Seven Love Poems', translated by A. C. Graham, from *Anthology of Chinese Literature from Earliest Times to the Fourteenth Century*, compiled and edited by Cyril Birch, London, 1967.

Frederick Locker (Locker-Lampson), 'A Terrible Infant' from *Poems*, London, 1884.

Elizabeth Longford, *Victoria R.I.*, London, 1964. Reprinted by permission of George Weidenfeld & Nicolson Ltd.

Amy Lowell, 'Chacago' from *First Lines: Poems written in youth, from Herbert to Heaney*, edited and introduced by Jon Stallworthy, Manchester, 1987.

Percy Lubbock, *Percy Earlham*, London, 1922. Reprinted by permission of the estate of Percy Lubbock and Jonathan Cape Ltd.

John Lydgate, 'The Boy Serving at Table', (*Stans puer ad Mensam*), transcribed by F. J. Furnival, Early English Text Society, no. 32, 1868.

George MacBeth, *A Child of the War*, London, 1987. Reprinted by permission of Anthony Shiel Associates on behalf of George MacBeth.

Compton Mackenzie, *My Life and Times: Octave One 1883–1891*, London, 1963. Reprinted by permission of The Society of Authors as the literary representative of the estate of Compton Mackenzie.

Louis MacNeice, 'Autobiography' from *Collected Poems 1925–48*, London, 1949. Reprinted by permission of Faber & Faber Ltd.

Piero de' Medici, letters to his father,

Lorenzo the Magnificent, translated by Iris Origo, in *The Vagabond Path: An Anthology*, London, 1972. Reprinted by permission of Iris Origo and Chatto & Windus.

Ved Mehta, *Vedi*, Oxford, 1982. Reprinted by permission of A. P. Watt Ltd on behalf of Ved Mehta. *The Ledge between the Streams*, London, 1984. Reprinted by permission of the author and Collins Harvill.

Richard Meinerzhagen, *Diary of a Black Sheep*, Edinburgh, 1964.

Colin Middleton Murry, *One Hand Clapping: A Memoir of Childhood*, London, 1975. Reprinted by permission of the author.

John Stuart Mill, *Autobiography*, London, 1874.

A. A. Milne, *It's Too Late Now: the Autobiography of a Writer*, London, 1939. Copyright © A. A. Milne 1939, reprinted by permission of Curtis Brown Ltd. *The House at Pooh Corner*, London, 1928. Reprinted by permission of Methuen Children's Books.

Christopher Milne, *The Enchanted Places*, London, 1974. Copyright © 1974 by Christopher Milne. Reprinted by permission of Methuen and Curtis Brown Ltd.

Julian Mitchell, 'Holiday' from *Here Today: Modern Poems*, edited by Ted Hughes, London, 1963. Reprinted by permission of A. D. Peters & Co. Ltd.

Jessica Mitford, *Hons and Rebels*, London, 1960. Reprinted by permission of Victor Gollancz Ltd.

C. E. Montague, *Disenchantment*, London, 1922.

Sir Thomas More, 'To His Children' from the *Latin Epigrams*, collected posthumously, 1535. This extract probably written in 1517.

John Mortimer, *Clinging to the Wreckage*, London, 1982. Reprinted by permission of George Weidenfeld & Nicolson Ltd.

J. B. Morton, 'The Marseillaise', taken from *Little Innocents: Childhood Reminiscences*, edited by Alan Pryce-Jones, Oxford, 1986. Reprinted by permission of A. D. Peters & Co. Ltd.

Wolfgang Amadeus Mozart, *Letters*, translated and edited by Emily Anderson, London, 1966. Reprinted by permission of Macmillan London Ltd.

Vladimir Nabokov, *Speak Memory: an Autobiography Revisited*, London, 1967. Reprinted by permission of George Weidenfeld & Nicolson Ltd.

Priscilla Napier, *A Late Beginner*, London, 1966. Reprinted Hamish Hamilton, 1986.

Ogden Nash, 'Reflections on Babies' and 'Lines to be embroidered on a Bib' or 'The Child is Father of the Man, but Not for Quite a While' from *Family Reunion*, London, 1951. Reprinted by permission of André Deutsch Ltd.

J. E. Neale, *Queen Elizabeth*, London, 1934. Reprinted by permission of the estate of J. E. Neale and Jonathan Cape Ltd.

E. Nesbit, *Long Ago When I Was Young*, London, 1966.

Roger North, *The Lives of the Rt Hon. Francis North, Baron Guildford, the Hon. Sir Dudley North, and the Hon. & Rev. Dr John North*, vol. 3, edited by Augustus Jessop, London, 1890.

Maurice O'Sullivan, *Twenty Years A-Growing*, taken from the original Irish by Moya Llewelyn Davies and George Thomson, with an introductory note by E. M. Forster, London, 1936. Reprinted by permission of the estate of the author and Chatto & Windus.

William Owens, *This Stubborn Soil*, New York, 1966, London, 1967. Reprinted by permission of the author.

Frances Partridge, *Memories*, London, 1981. Reprinted by permission of Victor Gollancz Ltd.

Coventry Patmore, 'The Toys' from *The Unknown Eros*, London, 1877.

Konstantin Pavstovsky, *Story of a Life: Childhood and Schooldays*, translated by Manya Harari and Michael Duncan, London, 1964. Reprinted by Permission of Collins Harvill.

Victor Perera, *Rites: A Guatemalan Boyhood*, London, 1986. Reprinted by permission of André Deutsch Ltd.

Plato, 'Lysis' from *Political and Social Life in the Great Age of Athens* edited by John Ferguson and Kitty Chisholm, translated by John Ferguson, Milton Keynes, 1978.

Po Chü-i, 'Children', translated by Arthur Waley in *170 Chinese Poems*, London, 1918. Reprinted by permission of Constable Publishers.

Hal Porter, *The Watcher on the Cast-Iron Balcony: An Australian Autobiography*, London, 1963. Reprinted by permission of Faber & Faber Ltd.

Stephen Potter, *Steps to Immaturity*, London, 1959. Reprinted by permission of the trustees of the Stephen Potter estate.

Brian Power, *The Puppet Emperor*, London, 1986 and *The Ford of Heaven*, London, 1984. Reprinted by permission of Peter

Owen, London.

Matthew Prior, 'A Letter to the Child, Lady Margaret Cavendish Holles-Harley' from *The Oxford Book of Children's Verse*, chosen and edited with notes by Iona and Peter Opie, Oxford, 1973.

V. S. Pritchett, *A Cab at the Door*, London, 1968. Reprinted by permission of the author, Chatto & Windus and A. D. Peters Ltd.

Marcel Proust, *Swann's Way*, first volume of *Remembrance of Things Past*, translated by C. K. Scott Moncrieff, London, 1922. First published as *Du Coté de Chez Swann*, first volume of *A la Recherche du Temps Perdu*, 1913.

Peter Quennell, *The Marble Foot: An Autobiography 1905–38*, London, 1976. Reprinted by permission of the author and Collins Publishers.

Sir Arthur Quiller-Couch, *Memories and Opinions: An Unfinished Autobiography*, by Q, edited with an introduction by S. C. Roberts, Cambridge, 1944. Reprinted by permission of Cambridge University Press.

Kathleen Raine, *Farewell Happy Fields: Memories of Childhood*, London, 1973. Reprinted by permission of the author.

Sir Walter Raleigh, 'To My Son', from *A Choice of Sir Walter Raleigh's Verse*, selected with an introduction by Robert Nye, London, 1972.

Michell Raper, 'Morning Glory' from *Here Today: Modern Poems*, edited by Ted Hughes, London, 1963.

Gwen Raverat, *Period Piece: A Cambridge Childhood*, London, 1952. Reprinted by permission of Faber & Faber Ltd.

Freddy Reynolds, letter written in the 1770s. Reprinted by permission of Westminster School Archives.

Ralph Richardson, 'The Age of Innocence', from *Vogue*, March 1979. Reprinted by permission of Lady Richardson.

Rainer Maria Rilke, 'The Merry-go-Round', Jardin du Luxembourg ('Das Karussell') and 'The Boy' ('Der Knabe') from *Selected Works of Rainer Maria Rilke*, translated by J. B. Leishman, London, 1960. Reprinted by permission of St John's College, Oxford and The Hogarth Press.

Jean-Jacques Rousseau, *The Confessions*, 1770, translated by J. M. Cohen (Penguin Classics 1954), copyright © J. M. Cohen, 1954. Reprinted by permission of Penguin Books Ltd.

Ruff of Nottingham reporting to the Children's Employment Commission, from *Climbing Boys: A Study of Sweeps' Apprentices*, edited by K. H. Strange,

London, 1982. Reprinted by permission of W. H. Allen.

John Ruskin, *Praeterita*, London, 1885–99.

Bertrand Russell, *The Autobiography of Bertrand Russell*, London, 1967. Reprinted by permission of Unwin Hyman Ltd.

V. Sackville-West, 'Full Moon' from *Orchard and Vineyard*, London, 1921. Reprinted by permission of Curtis Brown Ltd on behalf of the author's estate.

'Lady Sarashina' from *As I Crossed a Bridge of Dreams: Recollections of a Woman in Eleventh-Century Japan*, translated with an introduction by Ivan Morris, London and New York, 1971. © 1971 Ivan Morris.

Vernon Scannell, 'Autobiographical Note' from *A Sense of Danger*, London, 1962.

Albert Schweitzer, *Memoirs of Childhood and Youth*, Translation by C. T. Campion, London, 1925. Reprinted by permission of Mr G. Wyott.

Sir Walter Scott, *Autobiography*, published in *The Life of Sir Walter Scott* by J. G. Lockhart, his son-in-law, in seven volumes, Edinburgh, 1837–38.

Sei Shonagon, *The Pillow Book of*, translated by Ivan Morris, Oxford, 1967. Reprinted by permission of Oxford University Press.

William Shakespeare, *King John*.

Osbert Sitwell, *Left Hand Right Hand!*, London, 1945. Reprinted by permission of David Higham Associates Ltd.

Edith Sitwell, 'The King of China's Daughter' taken from *Come Hither: A Collection of Rhymes and Poems for the Young of all Ages*, by Walter de la Mare, London, 1936. Reprinted by permission of David Higham Associates Ltd.

Christopher Smart, 'Mirth' from *Hymns for the Amusement of Children*, London, 1771.

Stevie Smith, 'Childhood and interruption' from *Me Again: the Uncollected Writings of Stevie Smith*, edited by Jack Barbera and William McBrien with a Preface by James MacGibbon, London, 1981. Reprinted by permission of Virago Press. 'Archie and Tina' and 'Our Bog is Dood' from *The Collected Poems of Stevie Smith*, London, 1975. Reprinted by permission of James MacGibbon.

Sydney Smith, from *Climbing Boys: A Study of Sweeps' Apprentices*, edited by K. H. Strange, London, 1982. Reprinted by permission of W. H. Allen.

Stephen Spender, 'Rough' from *Collected Poems 1928–85*, London, 1985. Reprinted by permission of Faber & Faber Ltd.

World within World, London, 1951. Reprinted by permission of A. D. Peters & Co. Ltd.

Lady Hester Stanhope, anecdote from her memoirs, quoted in *The English* by Christopher Hibbert, London, 1987 Reprinted by permission of Grafton Books, a Division of the Collins Publishing Group.

Enid Starkie, *A Lady's Child*, London, 1941. Reprinted by permission of Faber & Faber Ltd.

Amy Steedman, 'Frederick the Great' from *When they were Children: Stories of the Childhood of Famous Men and Women*, (1913).

Lincoln Steffens, *The Autobiography of Lincoln Steffens*, New York, 1931.

Stendhal (Henri Beyle), *The Life of Henri Brulard* by Stendhal, first published as *La Vie de Henri Brulard*, 1890, translated by Jean Stewart and B. C. J. G. Knight, Manchester, 1958. Reprinted by permission of The Merlin Press.

Robert Louis Stevenson, 'The Sick Child' from *Underwoods*, London, 1887; and 'I should like to rise and go' from *A Child's Garden of Verses*, London, 1885.

Julia Strachey and Frances Partridge, *Julia: A Portrait by Herself and Frances Partridge*, London, 1983. Reprinted by permission of Victor Gollancz Ltd.

Richard Strachey, *A Strachey Child*, Oxford, 1979.

Igor Stravinsky, *An Autobiography*, translated from *Chroniques de ma Vie*, London, 1936. Reproduced by permission of Alfred Knopf Inc.

Su Tung-po, 'On the Birth of His Son', translated by Arthur Waley in *170 Chinese Poems*, London, 1918. Reprinted by permission of Constable Publishers.

Jeremy Taylor, *XXV Sermons*, 1653.

TH, Letter from an eighteenth-century Eton schoolboy. Transcribed from an exhibition in the Drawing School at Eton College, July 1943. Reprinted by permission of the Provost and Fellows of Eton College.

Thérèse of Lisieux, *Autobiography of a Saint: Thérèse of Lisieux*, first published posthumously as *L'Histoire d'une Ame*, France, 1898; published in this translation by Ronald Knox, London, 1958. Reprinted by permission of Collins Harvill.

R. S. Thomas, 'Children's Song' from *Song at the Year's Turning: Poems 1942–54*, with an introduction by John Betjeman, London, 1956. Reprinted by permission of Grafton Books, a Division of the Collins

Publishing Group.

Dylan Thomas, 'Fern Hill', 'The Song of the Mischievous Dog' and 'A Child's Christmas in Wales' from *Collected Poems 1934–52*, London, 1968. Reprinted by permission of J. M. Dent and David Higham Associates Ltd.

Edward Thomas, two poems to his daughter from *Poems*, London, 1917.

Flora Thompson, *Lark Rise to Candleford*, Oxford, 1939. Reprinted by permission of Oxford University Press.

Leo Tolstoy, *Childhood*, first published 1852. Taken here from *Childhood, Boyhood, Youth*, translated by Rosemary Edmonds (Penguin Classics, 1964), copyright © Rosemary Edmonds. Reprinted by permission of Penguin Books Ltd.

Thomas Traherne, 'Centuries of Meditations' from *The Political Works of Thomas Traherne*, edited by Bertrand Dobell and published by him, London, 1903.

W. J. Turner, 'The Hunter', 1916, in *Selected Poems*, Oxford, 1939.

Mark Twain (Samuel Clemens), *The Autobiography of Mark Twain*, first published 1924, edited by A. B. Paine; this edition edited by Charles Neider, London, 1960.

Lord Vansittart, *The Mist Procession: the Autobiography of Lord Vansittart*, London, 1958.

Giorgio Vasari, *The Lives of the Artists*, first published 1550; this edition translated by George Bull (Penguin Classics, 1956), copyright © George Bull, 1956. Reprinted by permission of Penguin Books Ltd.

Henry Vaughan, *Silex Scintillans* from 'The Retreat', London, 1650.

Edmund Verney to his son Edmund, 1682, from *Memoirs of the Verney Family during the Seventeenth Century*, edited by Margaret Verney, London, 1904.

'Memoirs of Queen Victoria's Early Years', written by the Queen in 1872, and taken from *The Letters of Queen Victoria: a Selection from Her Majesty's Correspondence*, First Series 1837–61 edited by A. C. Benson and Viscount Esher, London, 1907.

Evelyn Waugh, *A Little Learning: Fragments of an Inner Life*, London, 1967. 'The Curse of the Horse Race', taken from *Little Innocents: Childhood Reminiscences*, edited by Alan Pryce-Jones, Oxford, 1986. Reprinted by permission of A. D. Peters & Co. Ltd.

Edith Wharton, *A Backward Glance*, New York, 1934. Copyright © 1933, 1934 William R. Tyler; copyright renewed 1961, 1962. Reprinted by permission of the estate of Edith Wharton and Charles Scribner's Sons, an imprint of Macmillan Publishing Co.

Walt Whitman, 'There was a Child Went Forth' from *Leaves of Grass*, New York, 1855. Nine subsequent editions in the poet's lifetime with alterations and additions; issued as part of his *Complete Works*, 1902, edited by his executors.

Kyffin Williams, *Across the Straits: an Autobiography*, London, 1973. Reprinted by permission of Gerald Duckworth.

Diana Witherby, 'Child's Evening' from *Collected Poems*, 1973. Reprinted by permission of A. F. and G. Witherby.

Leonard Woolf, *Sowing: an Autobiography of the Years 1880–1904*, London, 1960. Reprinted by permission of the estate of the author and The Hogarth Press.

Virginia Woolf, 'A Sketch of the Past' from *Virginia Woolf: Moments of Being*, unpublished autobiographical writings, edited by Jeanne Schulkind, 1976. *Roger Fry: a Biography*, London, 1940. Reprinted by permission of the estate of

the author and The Hogarth Press.

William Wordsworth, *The Prelude*, completed 1805 but published posthumously in London, 1850 in its final version. *The Excursion*, London, 1814.

Lady Mary Wortley Montagu, *The Letters of Lady Mary Wortley Montagu*, edited by Lord Wharncliffe, London, 1837.

Richard Wright, *Black Boy: A Record of Childhood and Youth*, New York, 1945, London, 1946. Reprinted by permission of Mrs Ellen Wright and Jonathan Cape Ltd. Copyright © 1937, 1942, 1944, 1945 by Richard Wright. Reprinted by permission of Harper & Row Publishers Inc.

W. B. Yeats, 'To a Child Dancing in the Wind' from *Responsibilities* (1914), subsequently in *Collected Poems*, London, 1933. Reprinted by permission of A. P. Watt Ltd on behalf of Michael B. Yeats and Macmillan London Ltd.

INDEX

NOTE: Page numbers in roman refer to authors and sources; those in *italic* refer to the subjects of comment